Bridging the Gap Between Conversation Analysis and Poetics

This collection extends the conversation beginning with Gail Jefferson's seminal 1996 article, "On the Poetics of Ordinary Talk," linking the poetics of ordinary talk with the work of poets to bring together critical perspectives on new data from talk-in-interaction and applications of Jefferson's poetics to literary discourse.

Bringing together contributions from Conversation Analysis and literary scholars, the book begins by analyzing the conference presentation which served as the genesis for Jefferson's article to highlight the occurrence of poetics in institutional talk. The first section then provides an in-depth examination of case studies from Conversation Analysis which draw on new data from naturally occurring discourse. The second half explores literary poetics as a form of institutional talk emerging from the poetics of ordinary talk, offering new possibilities for interpreting work in classics, biblical studies, folklore studies, and contemporary literature. Each chapter engages in a discussion of Jefferson's article toward reinforcing the relationships between the two disciplines and indicating a way forward for interdisciplinary scholarship.

The collection highlights the enduring influence of Jefferson's poetics to our understanding of language, both talk-in interaction and literary discourse, making this book of particular interest to students and researchers in Conversation Analysis, literary studies, stylistics, and pragmatics.

Raymond F. Person, Jr. is Professor of Religion at Ohio Northern University, USA. Although his primary area of expertise is the study of the Hebrew Bible, he has published three monographs and various journal articles applying insights from conversation analysis (CA) not only to the Bible, but also to Homer, Shakespeare, and other literature, the most recent being *From Conversation to Oral Tradition: A Simplest Systematics for Oral Traditions* (Routledge, 2016).

Robin Wooffitt is Professor of Sociology at the University of York, UK. He is interested in language, interaction, everyday poetics, and ostensibly anomalous experiences. He is the author or co-author of eight books, including *Conversation Analysis* (with Ian Hutchby; Polity, 2008), *Looking in and Speaking Out: Introspection, Communication, Consciousness* (with Nicola Holt; Imprint Academic, 2011), and *Telling Tales of the Unexpected: The Organisation of Factual Discourse* (Harvester Wheatsheaf, 1992).

John P. Rae is Reader in Psychology, University of Roehampton, UK. His research focuses on talk and body movement in social interaction in both informal and service-related settings, including psychotherapy. He is interested in human diversity, particularly in interactions involving participants with autism spectrum disorder. He recently co-edited *Atypical Interaction: The Impact of Communicative Impairments within Everyday Interaction* (with Ray Wilkinson and Gitte Rasmussen, Palgrave Macmillan, 2020).

Routledge Research in Language and Communication

The Pragmatics of Text Messaging
Making Meaning in Messages
Michelle A. McSweeney

Multiliteracies, Emerging Media, and College Writing Instruction
Santosh Khadka

Emoticons, Kaomoji, and Emoji
The Transformation of Communication in the Digital Age
Edited by Elena Giannoulis and Lukas R.A. Wilde

Interpersonal Positioning in English as a Lingua Franca Interactions
Svitlana Klötzl and Birgit Swoboda

The Discourse of Food Blogs
Multidisciplinary Perspectives
Daniela Cesiri

Discourses of Perfection
Representing Cosmetic Procedures and Beauty Products in UK
Lifestyle Magazines
Anne-Mette Hermans

The Dialects of British English in Fictional Texts
Edited by Donatella Montini and Irene Ranzato

Discursive Approaches to Socio-political Polarization and Conflict
Edited by Laura Filardo-Llamas; Esperanza Morales-López and Alan Floyd

Bridging the Gap Between Conversation Analysis and Poetics
Studies in Talk-In-Interaction and Literature Twenty-Five Years after Jefferson
Edited by Raymond F. Person, Jr., Robin Wooffitt, and John P. Rae

For more information about this series, please visit: www.routledge.com/
Routledge-Research-in-Language-and-Communication/book-series/RRLC

Bridging the Gap Between Conversation Analysis and Poetics

Studies in Talk-In-Interaction and Literature Twenty-Five Years after Jefferson

Edited by Raymond F. Person, Jr., Robin Wooffitt, and John P. Rae

NEW YORK AND LONDON

First published 2022
by Routledge
605 Third Avenue, New York, NY 10158

and by Routledge
2 Park Square, Milton Park, Abingdon, Oxon, OX14 4RN

Routledge is an imprint of the Taylor & Francis Group, an informa business

© 2022 selection and editorial matter, Raymond F. Person, Jr., Robin Wooffitt and John P. Rae; individual chapters, the contributors

The right of Raymond F. Person, Jr., Robin Wooffitt and John P. Rae to be identified as the authors of the editorial material, and of the authors for their individual chapters, has been asserted in accordance with sections 77 and 78 of the Copyright, Designs and Patents Act 1988.

All rights reserved. No part of this book may be reprinted or reproduced or utilised in any form or by any electronic, mechanical, or other means, now known or hereafter invented, including photocopying and recording, or in any information storage or retrieval system, without permission in writing from the publishers.

Trademark notice: Product or corporate names may be trademarks or registered trademarks, and are used only for identification and explanation without intent to infringe.

Library of Congress Cataloging-in-Publication Data
A catalog record for this book has been requested

ISBN: 978-0-367-34950-9 (hbk)
ISBN: 978-1-032-19788-3 (pbk)
ISBN: 978-0-429-32893-0 (ebk)

DOI: 10.4324/9780429328930

Typeset in Times New Roman
by Apex CoVantage, LLC

Throughout this volume, the contributors quote significantly from Jefferson's article on poetics. As a whole, this volume pays tribute to this ground-breaking work. The editors thank Taylor & Francis for the permission to quote from the following:

Gail Jefferson (1996) On the poetics of ordinary talk, *Text and Performance Quarterly*, 16:1, 1–61.

DOI: 10.1080/10462939609366132

Copyright © National Communication Association

Reprinted by permission of Taylor & Francis Ltd, http://www.tandfonline.com on behalf of National Communication Association.

Contents

List of Contributors	vii
Notes on Transcription Conventions	ix

**Introduction: Bridging the Gap: Conversation Analysis
and Poetics From Jefferson to Now**   1
JOHN P. RAE, ROBIN WOOFFITT, AND RAYMOND F. PERSON, JR.

PART 1
Studies in Poetics: Talk-In-Interaction   29

**1 Poetics and Performativity in the Management of Delicacy
and Affiliation**   31
IAN HUTCHBY

**2 A Walk on the Wild Side: Exploring Associations Across
Topic Transition in Interaction**   52
ELIZABETH HOLT

**3 On Doing Things Through Topical Puns and Near-Synonyms
in Conversation**   79
JOHN P. RAE

4 The Poetics in Jefferson's Poetics Lecture   97
ROBIN WOOFFITT, DARREN REED, JESSICA A. YOUNG,
AND CLARE JACKSON

vi *Contents*

PART 2
Studies in Poetics: Literature 117

5 The Poetics of Mrs Gamp's Conversation—Are They
Dickens's 'Slips of the Pen'? 119
HUGO BOWLES

6 Dialogic Syntax in Ancient Greek Conversation 140
ANNA BONIFAZI

7 Repetition, Parallelism, and Non-Repetition:
From Ordinary Talk to Ritual Poetry and Back
Again 180
FROG

8 Poetics and List-Construction: A Study of Text-Critical
Variants in Lists Found in the New Testament, Homer,
and the Hebrew Bible 218
RAYMOND F. PERSON, JR.

Author Index 247
Subject Index 251

Contributors

Anna Bonifazi is Professor in the Linguistics department of the University of Cologne, Germany. She is interested in pragmatic, cognitive, and semiotic aspects of literary as well as non-literary discourse beyond the sentence level. She has been working on various linguistic phenomena in different genres of ancient Greek literature (lyric, epic, historiography), in Serbo-Croatian epic songs, and is now expanding her research to corpora in modern languages.

Hugo Bowles is Professor of English at the University of Foggia, Italy. His research interests cover many areas of applied linguistics, particularly the relationship between spoken English and literary and non-literary texts. He co-edited (with Paul Seedhouse) the collection *Conversation Analysis and Language for Specific Purposes* (Peter Lang, 2007) and has written two monographs: *Storytelling and Drama: Exploring Narrative Episodes in Plays* (John Benjamins, 2010) and *Dickens and the Stenographic Mind* (Oxford University Press, 2019).

Frog is a researcher in folklore at the University of Helsinki, responsible for the Academy of Finland project 'Mythology, Verbal Art and Authority in Social Impact' (2016–2022) and leader of the Kone Foundation project 'Materiality, Verbal Art, Mythic Knowledge and the Lived Environment (ASME)' (2021–2025). Although he has broad comparative interests, his specialization concerns Scandinavian and Finnic traditions, and he has begun working with Rotenese and Tetun traditions in Indonesia. He has published over a hundred articles and edited numerous collections, including, with William Lamb, *Weathered Words: Formulaic Language and Verbal Art* (Harvard University Press, 2021).

Elizabeth Holt is Subject Leader of Linguistics and Modern Languages at the University of Huddersfield, UK. She uses conversation analysis (CA) to study interaction, with particular interest in figurative expressions, reported speech, and laughter. She has co-edited two volumes, one on reported speech and one on laughter, and has published numerous journal articles on these and other aspects of interaction, including death announcements and joking in call-center interactions.

Ian Hutchby is Honorary Professor of Sociology at the University of York, UK. His research is in the field of CA applied to a range of areas, including media

viii *Contributors*

talk, psychotherapy, and political communication. He has published ten books, including *Confrontation Talk* (Erlbaum, 1996), *Conversation and Technology* (Polity, 2001), *Conversation Analysis* (with Robin Wooffitt; Polity, 2008) and *The Political Interview: Broadcast Talk in the Interactional Combat Zone* (Rowman and Littlefield, 2021).

Clare Jackson is a Senior Lecturer in the Sociology Department at the University of York. In her research, she uses CA to explore topics such as gender and sexuality, person reference, turn-design, and decision-making in clinical settings, especially with respect to childbirth.

Raymond F. Person, Jr. is Professor of Religion at Ohio Northern University, USA. Although his primary area of expertise is the study of the Hebrew Bible, he has published three monographs and various journal articles applying insights from CA not only to the Bible, but also to Homer, Shakespeare, and other literature, the most recent being *From Conversation to Oral Tradition: A Simplest Systematics for Oral Traditions* (Routledge, 2016).

John P. Rae is Reader in Psychology, University of Roehampton, UK. His research focuses on talk and body movement in social interactions in both informal and service-related settings, particularly psychotherapy. He is interested in interactions involving neurodiverse individuals and recently co-edited *Atypical Interaction: The Impact of Communicative Impairments within Everyday Interaction* (with Ray Wilkinson and Gitte Rasmussen, Palgrave Macmillan, 2020).

Darren Reed is a Social Scientist and Senior Lecturer in the Sociology Department, University of York. His research encompasses the study of performance and musical instruction, and he has a history in the study of technological interaction and Human-Computer Interaction. He is a member of the Science and Technology Studies Unit (SATSU), York University. He employs an ethnomethodological approach through the use of Embodied CA to verbal and embodied behaviors.

Robin Wooffitt is Professor of Sociology at the University of York, UK. He is interested in language, interaction, everyday poetics, and ostensibly anomalous experiences. He is the author or co-author of eight books, including *Conversation Analysis* (with Ian Hutchby; Polity, 2008), *Looking in and Speaking Out: Introspection, Communication, Consciousness* (with Nicola Holt; Imprint Academic, 2011), and *Telling Tales of the Unexpected: The Organisation of Factual Discourse* (Harvester Wheatsheaf, 1992).

Jessica A. Young is a PhD candidate at Flinders University, Australia, and Western University, Canada. Her work explores issues of human rights for persons living with dementia, with a focus on power dynamics, 'voice', and decision-making. She has a keen interest in various qualitative research methods and methodologies, including CA, narrative inquiry, and critical theory.

Notes on Transcription Conventions

The early practitioners of Conversation Analysis (CA), especially Gail Jefferson, developed a transcription system with conventions to represent the sequential aspects of the audible elements of conversation. For those readers unfamiliar with CA transcription and interested in learning more about the transcription system(s) used in CA, we highly recommend Schegloff's transcription module on his website: www.sscnet.ucla.edu/soc/faculty/schegloff/TranscriptionProject/index.html. There you will find examples of transcription symbols with the audio excerpts illustrating each symbol.

The following transcription conventions are used in this volume:

CAPS	indicates loud speech
underline	indicates higher pitch
:	indicates that the previous sound is lengthened
[ ]	indicates that the items bracketed is overlapped by other speech; the first bracket of the second speaker's utterance will be indented as well
(1.2)	numerals within parentheses indicates the length of pauses in seconds, in this case a pause of 1.2 seconds
,	a comma usually indicates falling then rising intonation
=	an equal sign indicates no gap between the end of one speaker's utterance and the beginning of the next speaker's utterance
.	a period indicates falling intonation at the end of a word or phrase
?	a question mark indicates rising intonation at the end of a word or phrase
-	a hyphen indicates an abrupt ending
wo(h)rd	laughter within a word
↓	a downward arrow indicates that the following syllable has falling intonation
↑	an upward arrow indicates that the following syllable has rising intonation
(( ))	double parentheses are used to bracket comments made by the analysts within the examples

x   *Notes on Transcription Conventions*

A few other transcription conventions are used that are specific to some of the examples discussed concerning a particular issue; in these cases, they will be explained just prior to those specific examples in each chapter.

Introduction

Bridging the Gap: Conversation Analysis and Poetics From Jefferson to Now[1]

John P. Rae, Robin Wooffitt, and Raymond F. Person, Jr.

Jefferson's Poetics

Jefferson's 'On the Poetics of Ordinary Talk' (1996, 2018) is a lightly edited transcript of a presentation originally delivered in 1977 to the Boston University Conference on Ethnomethodology and Conversation Analysis. Fortunately, a video-recording of Jefferson's talk is available and has been transcribed (Nevile, 2015, see also Wooffitt et al., this volume). In her talk and in the subsequent published version, she outlined how she came to poetics through a request from Harvey Sacks, which arose from his preliminary thoughts on ostensibly poetic features he was finding in his data. She then reviewed a range of conversational poetics, bringing together the disparate threads of ideas and observations into a catalogue. This catalogue, we suggest, was a step towards the formalization of work on poetics in Conversation Analysis (CA), in that it was the first attempt to identify in a systematic way the phenomena or provide a sustained analysis of conversational poetics. Despite the systematic description of relevant phenomena, Jefferson presented this work as an example of what she called the 'wild side' of CA. In this introduction, we explore how Jefferson's walk on the wild side developed from Sacks' early observations, consider the scope and nature of Jefferson's paper, and sketch some of the impacts of her ideas and findings in subsequent research in CA and in literary studies.

It is important to emphasize two points about the character of Jefferson's paper at the outset. First, its scope is limited to certain aspects of poetics, principally word-selection. Second, rather than offering a detailed analysis, it aims to present a range of empirical phenomena, a 'guided tour of the data' (Jefferson, 1996, p. 2). Such an exposition was a departure from Sacks' observations on poetics that are available from his published lectures.

As he was beginning to study interactional data, Sacks was finding a range of poetic phenomena in his recordings of everyday interaction, such as clustering of sounds, curiously playful turn-designs, conspicuously well-fitted word-selections, and so on. He observed that poetic forms seem to occur more systematically than one might expect. He recognized the possibility that they were no more than a pleasing but wholly random happenstance and did not exhibit interactionally

DOI: 10.4324/9780429328930-1

2 John P. Rae et al.

relevant and ordered properties. He was, however, willing to suspend any scepticism about the orderliness of poetic phenomena so as to be open to the possibility of finding systematic properties.

Sacks made a case for the robustness of poetically informed turn-design, usually through close inspection of single cases. For example, Sacks argued that there was strong evidence that one of the word-selection procedures in poetics revolved around categorical relationships: simply the way that categories of events or things seem to be invoked in conspicuous ways. In one of his lectures, he considered the following utterance from a conversation in which the speaker is describing a disappointing visit to a bar. She said, 'God there wasn't a soul in, we were the only ones at the bar' (Sacks, 1992, vol. 2, p. 291). Sacks observed that 'God' and 'soul' have a categorical relationship. They both can be heard as coming from the category of 'religion'. He argued that it was at least reasonable to suggest that this speaker's utterance, particularly the use of the phrase 'wasn't a soul', was triggered in some way by the categorical tone or expectation set by the first word, 'God'.

There is also a very nice pun here. The speaker's utterance described the emptiness of the venue, and that sense was conveyed by the phrase 'wasn't a soul'. This is a common phrase. But 'soul' is also a homonym of 'sole'. In that sense, the word 'soul' was delicately designed to relate to the category established by the word 'God' *and* to invoke the 'solitary' meaning of 'sole'.

In one of his lectures, Sacks explored the broadly inferential concerns that might be mediated via poetic forms. He discussed an exchange from a New York talk radio programme, in which members of the public call in to the station to talk to the host about topics of the day. A caller, who had a sight problem and used a cane, called in and began to complain about the conduct of New Yorkers. Her complaint was that they did not make allowances for her disability, despite the fact that her use of a cane made it clear that she was visually impaired. She said, 'they don't see it', referring either to the cane or her impairment. But this is also a pun on her disability: 'they don't see it' captured her condition as well as the behaviour of New Yorkers. Her complaint about their inconsiderate behaviour was emphasized in the poetic, pun-like quality of her description. In this case, the host tried to mitigate New Yorkers' behaviour by offering a reason for their apparent indifference to the caller's impairment. Sacks noted that the host made the point that New Yorkers were so focused on their own concerns that they become unaware of the circumstances of other people. This did not excuse their behaviour, but it softened the nature of the perceived offence. It is not that they did not care about others, but that they did not notice them. In building this mitigation, the host claimed that New Yorkers were 'preoccupied'. Sacks noted the relationship between the words 'preoccupied' and 'ocular', relating to matters of the eyes. Sacks argued that, in using the word '*preoc*cupied', the host established a problem common to the caller and New Yorkers about whom she has called to complain: neither have clear vision (Sacks, 1992, vol. 2, pp. 266–267).

Introduction 3

A note from Sacks to Jefferson led to her exploration of conversational poetics. Early in the paper (and in somewhat more detail in the 1977 talk), Jefferson mentioned finding a handwritten note he had left on her desk:

> With regard to the issue of word selections by reference to sound patterns, the question is, where to begin?
> One possibility is with rephrased repetitions: the second variants might exhibit such patterns in a way that would allow attribution to the pattern to be made.
>
> 's breaking my folks
> My insanity's breaking their bankbook
>
> B-K form perhaps relevant to 'bankbook' usage
>
> *Have Gail check this out*
> (Jefferson, 1996, p. 2; emphasis in original)

The data in question is from the Group Therapy Session (GTS), involving a group of young people whose behaviour had been found to be problematic, which Sacks drew on extensively in his lectures. The speaker, who was responding to a criticism of their footwear, was making a characteristically cynical comment about their predicament in therapy and its implications for his parents. A number of observations can be made. First, words 'selected by reference to a sound-row' (Jefferson, 1996, p. 13) succinctly captured one set of phenomena that Jefferson examined in the paper. In this case, we have the 'B-K form' (as in 'breaking') 'perhaps relevant to "bankbook" usage'. Second—and this is a key point—Sacks raised the issue of how to get an analytic handle on this phenomenon. He suggested that there could be an organization feature that might be relevant in rephrased repetitions.

We might note too that the speaker seemed to be producing a variation on the idiom 'to break the bank' (to be too expensive, or to cost a lot of money), and was perhaps undertaking a refocusing from the impersonal 'bank' and more directly onto the speaker's parents' 'bankbook'. We may further observe that this note appeared to involve a pun: rather than, for example, 'have Gail *look* into this' we have the banking-related word 'check'. This is a pun on the US English 'check' as a written instruction for payment, and a homonym of the British English version 'cheque'.

Jefferson set the scene for the1977 talk in the Abstract to the 1996 paper:

> This article is based on a talk presented in 1977. Harvey Sacks, the founder of Conversation Analysis, had been killed in a traffic accident in 1975. Without his extraordinary presence the field seemed to be becoming defined by a paper published in 1974, 'A simplest systematics for the organization of turn-taking in conversation'. The 1977 talk was specifically directed to loosening up people's sense of the sort of work done in the field of Conversation Analysis.

4   *John P. Rae et al.*

Among his abundant and wide-ranging interests Harvey Sacks had been exploring (and eventually discussing in his lectures) various aspects of a phenomenon which somewhere along the line came to called 'poetics'—most roughly, that occasionally, talk appears to be produced at least in part by reference to, e.g. sounds and associations. Many of Sacks' students found the phenomenon appealing and began to contribute not only further instances of things he had considered, but new possibilities as well. The result was a mountain of roughly-sorted materials. The 1977 talk was a rather casual guided tour of a selected sample of those materials. This article is a more considered and elaborated version of that talk.

(Jefferson, 1996, p. 1)

And in the Foreword:

The talk was given at the Boston University Conference on Ethnomethodology and Conversation Analysis in June, 1977. It was then a year and a half since Harvey Sacks' death, and the field of Conversation Analysis was coming to be identified almost exclusively by reference to the Sacks et al. paper 'A simplest systematics for the organization of turntaking for conversation' published in 1974. As an antidote to that drastically constricted version of the field, I decided to present the wild side; stuff which we'd pretty much kept to ourselves and played with as a hobby. The stuff was wild, not only in its content, but in its lack of organization or development. It was, and still is, a big heap divided into not terribly descriptive or generative sub-heaps. In the years since that Boston conference I've gotten nowhere with it. It's remained a hobby, I'm still picking up cases, but that's as far as it goes. I present it now in the spirit I presented it back in 1977; an expression of the wild side of Conversation Analysis.

(Jefferson, 1996, p. 2)

Notwithstanding her characterization of her treatment as 'casual', Jefferson's presentation was clear and circumspect. Nevertheless, the paper retains its informal style; for example, Jefferson wrote:

I developed an enormous affection for one guy, W.L. Woods, MD. In his studies of psychotic talk he seems to have a sense for what he called 'the living language.' That is, you don't run *tests* on people to see how they talk and how they make words, you *talk* to them and you listen to them and you pull it out of the talk. And you get a kick out of it.

(Jefferson, 1996, p. 3)

This quotation captures two features of Gail Jefferson's métier and a specific feature of the paper. First, there is the focus on conversation and 'living language' (actually 'living speech' in Woods, 1938, p. 296, also p. 309) rather

Introduction 5

than, for example, speech samples generated in experimental settings. Second, there is the intellectual excitement of analyzing phenomena found in the talk. Third, although Jefferson mentioned Freud on speech errors, her primary reference was Woods' rather obscure 1938 study of the talk of schizophrenic patients, rather than, for example, any of the psychological literature on speech production.

As previously mentioned, Jefferson's poetics paper does not consider the full range of phenomena of poetics. Rather, the term 'poetics' was used as a way of referring to how word-selections could be apparently touched off by reference to sound-patterns or by semantic connections. Broadening upon Jefferson's poetics, Person (2016) demonstrated how CA research into a number of key organizations in talk-in-interaction (for example, story-telling in interaction, opening and closing conversations, and repair in interaction) can also contribute to the analysis of oral traditions. One aspect of poetics, prosody, has been extensively examined in talk-in-interaction (e.g., Couper-Kuhlen and Selting, 1996).

The Phenomena Examined

Jefferson organized her 'guided tour of the data' (Jefferson, 1996, p. 1) in terms of four sections and a number of subsections. Although she urged us not to take the labels that she used too seriously, they are nevertheless useful in getting an overview of the phenomena she explored. Table 0.1a and Table 0.1b list the categories of phenomena that Jefferson presented, with one or two examples that we have selected. Here, Table 0.1a shows groups 1–3; these are all phenomena that occur within a single speaker's talk. Table 0.1b shows the fourth category, which (largely) consists of cases where the phenomenon of interest involves two (or more) elements produced by different speakers. (This summary is not, however, a substitute for reading the paper and viewing the video of the 1977 talk.)

1. *Errors*

Jefferson began her treatment with errors. In sound-formed errors, a feature acquires momentum and leads to an error, so in extract (1.a.1.), a speaker who produces a number of words containing /k/ apparently starts to say 'countries' rather than 'areas'. In category-formed errors, a speaker produces one member of an intended category, but the wrong one, for example in (1.b.1.) 'sister' for 'brother'.

2. *Correct Sound- and Category-Formed Components*

The second category again concerns sound-formed and category-formed components, though here this is no error. In sound-formed components we get

6   *John P. Rae et al.*

a sound-row, for example, a series of productions of 'b' (2.a.1.). Category-selected components involve two kinds of pun. In co-class puns, we first get terms from different spheres that, through puns, meet in a shared class—for example, 'Fall' (the season) and 'stand' (as in 'I can't stand [up]') meeting in the class 'stand-fall' (as in 'success'-'failure') (2.b.1.4.). Second, in topical puns, we get a word that is a pun on a topic in the utterance—for example, on the topic of 'agricultural college', we get 'steered' as in 'directed', which puns on 'steer' as in 'bullock'.

3.   *Sub-Collections*

Although this grouping lacks a descriptive label, there is a family resemblance between the phenomena collected here. In names in sound-rows, there is a sound-connection between a proper noun and a subsequent word-choice—for example, the name of an American football quarterback, 'Stabler', and his impact, that he 'stabilized the club' (3.a.2.). In numbers, there is a similar connection, this time between a numerical expression—for example, 'ninety'—and a subsequent word, 'asinine' (3.b.1.). With respect to colours, the relationship between two expressions is semantic, rather than acoustic—for example, reference to an American footballer, surname 'Lavender', and what he saw as a 'golden opportunity' (3.c.l.). Categorically related assessments identify a potential connection between an entity and a subsequent categorization such that an assessment is visible. For example, a white speaker in the late 1960s describes The Harlem Clowns, an African-American basketball team, using an expression that refers to violent protest: 'They're a riot' (3.d.1.). Finally, in fractured idioms, a speaker uses an expression that can heard as a version of an off-stage idiom, as in when speaker says 'the bill kid', closely resembling the moniker of the gunfighter Billy the Kid, the protagonist of a movie of that time (3.e.1.).

Table 0.1a Categories of Poetic Phenomena: Single Speaker[i]

1. Errors

1.a. Sound-Formed Errors

```
        (1.a.1) [Crandall Show] (p.5)
        B.C.:  The arti[c]le thetchu [q]uote here refers to
               Roman [C]atholicism in what [kuh] - in what areas?
```

1.b. Category-Formed Errors

```
        (1.b.1) [GJ:FN] (p.10)
        Larry:  Hi. I'm Carol's sister- uh brother
```

Introduction 7

2. Correct Sound- and Category-Formed Components

2.a. Sound-Formed Components

```
(2.a.1)  [Lamb Interviews](p.13)
Mrs.R:   [B]ut at the time it really,(0.3)[b]ugged
         us,[b]ecause we were in[B]ermuda.
```

2.b. Category-Selected Components

(2.b.1.)
Co-Class
Puns
```
(2.b.1.4) [Lamb Interviews](p.16; emphasis added)
Mr.N.:    I voted for Cranston in the [Fall]
          mainly because I couldn't [stand]Rafferty.
```

(2.b.2.)
Topical
Puns
```
(2.b.2.1) [Lamb Interviews](p.17)
Mrs.A.:   I wanted to go to an [agricultural]college
          but my mother[steered]me away from that.
```

3. Sub-Collections

3.a. Names in Sound-Rows

```
(3.a.2)  [Football Broadcasts](p.19)
 (a) Bill [Knox][knocked] the ball loose . . .
 (b) Kenny[Stabler] has really [stabilized] the club.
```

3.b. Numbers

```
(3.b.1)  [GTS:11:2:65](p.20)
Roger:   We mebe g(h)o [nine]dy miles o(h)n a Friday night.
         Going nowhere. An' my dad thinks it's asi[nine].
```

3.c. Colours

```
(3.c.1)  [Football Broadcast](p.22)
Announcer: Joe [Lavender] ... saw a [golden] opportunity.
```

3.d. Categorically Related Assessments

```
(3.d.1)  [GTS:V:9](p.25)
The Harlem Clowns is an African-American team
Ken:     Have you ever seen the [Harlem Clowns] before?
         (1 sec)
(Jim):   [Pro ball?
Ken:     [The basketball team?
Dan:     Oh yes, Mm hm,
Ken:     I saw 'em last night [at our school.
Jim:                          [They're a [riot].
```

3.e. Fractured Idioms

```
(3.e.1)  [Jack Green Data] Unit:Billy the Kid (p.26)
Jack:    As long as your parents are footing [the bill kid],
         you just go right ahead.
```

---

[i] Page references are to Jefferson (1996). When Jefferson identifies the target elements in her extracts, she does so by enclosing them in square brackets. In this table, we have additionally shown them in bold. In cases where Jefferson did not identify the target elements, we have shown them in bold without square brackets and indicated in the page reference that emphasis has been added.

8   *John P. Rae et al.*

4.   *Cross-Speaker Poetics*

Whilst most of the previous cases involve relationships within a single speaker's talk (an exception being category-related assessments), the final category relates to phenomena that occur across speakers (though a number of the examples show the proposed relationship within a single speaker's talk). In cross-speaker sound-selection, the sound of a previous speaker's talk re-surfaces in the words of a subsequent speaker—for example, 'Or do' and 'ordinarily' (4.a.3.). Two phenomena are presented under flurries. Sound flurries involve the repetition of related sounds, as in the example mentioned in the note that Sacks left with which Jefferson began her paper, where the utterance of 'bankbook' resonated with the previously produced 'breaking' (4.b.1.). In categorial flurries, a pun-like relationship can be seen across two expressions—for example, where a body-part connection occurs between 'footing' and 'ahead' (4.b.2.).

The phenomena so far included in the category of cross-speaker poetics relate to word-choice: a previously uttered word appears to touch off the selection of a subsequent word, or, conversely, a subsequent word appears to show a connection with the previous one. In the final two phenomena, however, the proposed connection goes beyond mere word-choice. In Triggered Topics, an utterance apparently triggers a new topic in the talk by another speaker. For example, in the context of talking about health and avoiding preservative-laden food, one speaker reported 'We don't eat a lot of crap', whereupon another launched a new topic about a TV horror show in which a character had to 'eat the sins' (4.c.6.). In Triggered Termination, one speaker's talk triggered another speaker's moving to close the conversation. For example, one speaker's use of reported speech depicting the closing of another interaction, '. . . an' you say y'know guhbye love y'know because when y'get back I'll see you when yuh get back' triggered the recipient's citing a constraint that presages a move to close the conversation: 'Talking about getting back I've gotta take my mother home' (4.d.l.). It is not merely that an allusion to the closing of a conversation that triggered moving to close the present conversation, but rather the terms of that allusion 'when y'get back' recurred in the way in which moving to close the conversation is formulated by the subsequent speaker: 'Talking about getting back'.

In order to grasp the character of Jefferson's paper, it is necessary to appreciate the particular sense in which Jefferson referred to the 'wild side' of CA. To do this, we need to consider the non-wild side, the broken-in, controlled, domesticated side, or the side that takes a 'cautious, reasonable, sensible position' (Jefferson, 1996, p. 9). We will take the classic paper on turn-taking (Sacks, Schegloff, and Jefferson, 1974) as an example of non-wild CA, the same paper that Jefferson contrasted with her lecture.

Early in the paper, Sacks et al. (1974) offered several observations on what they term grossly apparent facts of interaction. The paper then provides an

Introduction 9

Table 0.1b Categories of Poetic Phenomena: Cross-Speaker[ii]

---

4. Cross-Speaker Poetics

4.a. Cross-Speaker Sound-Selection

```
(4.a.3) [SPC Calls](p.29)
Caller:  I wasn't aware of the fact at that time that you do
         have certain people that you send out
Caller   when necessary.
Desk:    Well wait a minute.
Caller:  [Or d]o you.
Desk:    [Ord]inarily we don't.
```

4.b. Flurries[1]

(4.b.1.)
Sound
Flurries

```
(0.1) [GTS:1:2:1] (pp. 2-3; emphasis added)
Rogers   's breaking mah folks.
         (2 sec)
Ken:     a(hh)h!
Roger    My insanity's breaking their bankb'k.
```

(4.b.2.)
Categorial
Flurries

```
(3.e.1) [Jack Green Data] Unit:Billy the Kid (p.26;
emphasis added)
Jack:    As long as your parents are footing the bill kid
         you just go right ahead.
```

4.c. Triggered Topics

```
(4.c.6) [Theodore: Alt](p.42; simplified)
"Night Gallery" is a TV horror show
Milly:   I don't eat things that give me headaches
         (0.3)
Tina:    [We don't [eat] a lot of [cra:p]. =tht's
         [got preservatives ]'n stuff=
Brenda:  [uhh hmh-hmh-m-hmh, ]
Jason:   =En spea:[king o::f,         ]
Brenda:           [She az a pinch]ed nerve
Jason:   Speaking of [wei:rd ex] perience.        ]
Tina:                [B't thazz] nah w't causes] the
         hea:dache. That's sep['rate [(really)]
Jason:                         [Did- [e Did] ]anybuddy see
         that Ni:ght Ga:llery where the guy hastuh [ea:t]
         (.) the [si::ns].
```

4.d. Triggered Terminations

```
(4.d.1) [Goldberg Data](p.43; emphasis added)
Maggie:  . . .an' you say y'know [guhbye love] y'know
         because when y'get back I'll see you when yuh
         get back. °hh [hh a:n-
Lynnie                 [Talking about getting back
         I've gotta take my mother home.
         (0.6)
Lynnie   Uh: she was over here t'day an' I've gotta drive
         her back t'Beverly Hills. - - When c'n I come over
         . . .
```

[ii] Despite most of Jefferson's examples in these sections being **cross-speaker**, the examples selected in this table are **within-speaker** cases for purposes of brevity.

10 *John P. Rae et al.*

account of a turn-taking mechanism that can account for these facts, and then demonstrates how the proposed mechanism accounts for the facts via examination of some properties of the proposed system. There are two key features of the turn-taking paper. First, it is concerned with general properties of any conversation. As such, the treatment has an abstract quality. It is not, however, abstraction for its own sake; rather, the abstraction emerges because the turn-taking system under analysis is inherently generalizable. It is context-free, but at the same time capable of 'context-sensitivity'—that is, the system is observable in the particulars of any actual conversational interaction. Second, the paper proposes a formal analysis of the social system that it seeks to account for. The turn-taking paper presents a constricted view of CA, because people do not engage in conversation merely to take turns at talk. Moreover, in the early days of CA, Sacks and his colleagues did not set out to explain turn-taking. Rather, in the course of examining conversational materials, it is readily apparent that whatever participants in talk are doing, turn-taking is fundamental to the social actions produced in the turn-by-turn unfolding of interaction. Consequently, if conversation is to be examined in detail, then an account of turn-taking is necessary. Our view is that when Jefferson referred to the constricted view of CA, she was referring to the first key feature of the paper: the attempt to provide a formal account of turn-taking norms and procedures that is both context-free and context-sensitive.

It is useful also to consider Sacks' paper 'On Some Puns, with Some Intimations' (1972), which was mentioned by Jefferson in her poetics paper. Sacks' paper, though published in conference proceedings, illustrates his formal analytic approach in relation to puns, one of the phenomena Jefferson examined in her talk and paper.

In his paper, Sacks remarked that prior to a serious analysis, we might say of puns that 'they occur here, there, and anywhere in conversation and that there is no formal relation between the positioning of pun and punned on' (Sacks, 1972, p. 137). Sacks' aim, of course, was to advance on this, and to seek to establish whether a formal relationship can be identified and described systematically. He went on to present two observations. The first related to the composition of turns containing puns, and the second to their sequential position.

A first such observation is: (Sometimes) puns occur in 'proverbial' expressions.
(Sacks, 1972, p. 137)

Our second observation is then: (Sometimes) proverbials occur on story completions. When done there by a story recipient they are at least partially occupied interactionally with exhibiting understanding of the story they succeed.
(Sacks, 1972, p. 138)

Introduction 11

In a later section, Sacks proceeded to show that the previous observations are not mere possibilities, but that 'there is a systematic basis for the occurrence of proverbials as the utterance of a story recipient upon story completions', and that, furthermore, 'because there is a systematic basis for puns occurring in proverbials, there is, therefore, a systematic basis for puns occurring in that slot' (Sacks, 1972, p. 140). Sacks then proposed a rule that applies to (1) responding to the completion of a story, (2) using a proverbial expression that contains a pun, and (3) the relationship between the pun and the nub of the story. We can paraphrase the rule as follows: *When a recipient of a story responds to the completion of the story by producing a proverbial expression which contains a pun, the pun will be on the issue in the story that the recipient understands. This issue is also relevant for understanding the proverbial expression.*

Note then, as Sacks asked us to, that we have gone beyond saying that the pun occurs somewhere in the vicinity of the punned-upon component of the talk. We now have a *formal* account of the relationship between the pun and the issue that it is a pun on. This is perhaps what Jefferson had in mind when she wrote, 'This is not a paper. I don't know if there ever will be a paper' (Jefferson, 1996, p. 2). In this sense, it is not just that the phenomena were 'wild' in the sense that they were unexpected and unpredictable, but rather that they had not been subjected to a disciplined examination that identified regularities in their distribution and function in interaction. That is, Jefferson was acknowledging that there remained much work to do on poetics before that work would no longer be 'wild', but approaching the 'cautious, reasonable, sensible' work of CA.

Mechanisms

In the course of Jefferson's exposition of the different kinds of poetic phenomena in talk, she suggested a number of mechanisms that might account for them. In her oral lecture, she simply referred to 'mechanisms' (Jefferson, 1977, lines 1385, 1386, 1407, 1427); however, in her article, she used phrases that suggest a little more development: 'sound-productional mechanisms' (1996, p. 8), 'gross selection-mechanism' (1996, p. 9), and 'triggering mechanisms' (1996, p. 39). It is important to note that, even in the published version, her descriptions of these mechanisms remain significantly provisional. One of Jefferson's numerous caveats was that 'all of what I'll be saying, please do treat as nothing more than a glimpse of phenomena which are yet to be systematically collected and described' (1996, p. 5). She made clear that her treatment did not accomplish systematic collection and description, let alone explanation. Nevertheless, a number of her suggestions may briefly be highlighted.

Jefferson conveyed an overall sense of the processes involving the use of poetic phenomena throughout a spectrum of those with different levels of

12   *John P. Rae et al.*

sociolinguistic competence, from the most proficient—that is, poets whose job concerns '[t]he *arrangement* of sounds and categories' (Jefferson, 1996, p. 4)—to the majority of us who engage in 'ordinary talk' to those who lack some competency (e.g., Woods' patients with schizophrenia). She quoted Woods' observation that '[t]he patient progresses from one . . . word to another by associations determined by similarities in sound, category or phrase' (Woods p. 295 in Jefferson, p. 4). She then picked up on Woods' comment that such associations are common to everyone, and that poets are especially proficient in the use of these mechanisms.

First, in connection with her exposition of 1.a. Sound-Formed Errors, Jefferson's term 'sound row' suggests an arrangement of sounds. In this section, she referred to a potential 'process, *sound-selection*,' which she informally defined as the following: 'A tendency for sounds-in-progress to locate particular next words' (1996, p. 6). At the end of this same section, she referred to 'sound-productional mechanisms' (1996, p. 8), presumably simply another term for sound-selection. A special case of this occurs in what she dubbed consonant-vowel/consonant-consonant-vowel alternation (CV/CCV alternation), which she introduced as part of her critical account of Freudian slips.

```
(1) [Crandall Show]  (Jefferson, 1996, p. 6)
1   B.C   [B]ig [b]eautiful savings from America's [l]argest c[l]othier.
2         [Bl]oh- Bond's. Blondes, my goodness.
3         Wuh that's a Freudian Slip.
```

Of Extract (1), Jefferson wrote, 'In this instance there's a double sound-row underway, [b] and [l]. And now there's a projected two word [b]-row, the first word of which is [b]+vowel (Bond's), the second of which is [b] + [l] + vowel (Blue). Call it a CV/CCV alternation. In classic tongue-twister fashion, the projected double consonant occurs first, yielding instead of "Bond's Blue", something moving towards blondes boo' (1996, p. 6).

Second, also in her discussion of 1.a. Sound-Formed Errors, and despite her critical comments concerning Freudian slips, Jefferson pointed out that psychological and sociological matters can surface in talk (a number of the examples that she considered relate to racial prejudice). In discussing these, she referred to '*suppression-release*', which she described as 'You're being very careful not to say something, and you succeed in not saying it, and it sneaks out in the next utterance' (1996, p. 8).

```
(2) [Football broadcast]  (Jefferson, 1996, p. 8)
1   Announcer Jones was not open on the [pay]-[play], both [backs] in
2              their [block]ing.
```

Jefferson noted that the two backs in question are both African-American and she proposed that the speaker was working to avoid saying 'both blacks' (something that the upcoming 'blocking' might engender). She suggested that as consequence of working to avoid 'blacks' for 'back', we get 'pay' rather than

Introduction   13

'play'. She further noted that in the next turn the announcer commented on the player's Oakland Raiders black uniforms and suggested that this an instance of suppression-release. It is notable in this example that the proposed concern of the speaker (the race of the players) did not reside in the talk, but was a visible feature of the setting.

Third, Jefferson perhaps came closest to talking in terms of a psychological mechanism in her discussion of 1.b. Category-Formed Errors.

> This is a series of errors in which you have objects that very strongly belong together; sometimes as contrasts, sometimes as co-members, very often as pairs. Up-down, right-left, young-old, husband-wife. What seems to happen is that a gross selection-mechanism delivers up a category, but not the specific *member* of that category, and it's sort of a matter of pot luck whether the correct one gets said. It's like the whole package gets dropped down and it's up to . . . who knows what? your tastebuds? to decide which word is going to come out.
>
> (1996, pp. 9–10)

As we saw previously in her discussion of sound-formed errors, category-formed errors suggest an analogous category-selection, and can also illustrate suppression-release. Several of the groups of cases in Jefferson's catalogue involve category-related associations. For example, in Extract (3), when Norm continued to speak (line 4) following an interjection by another speaker (line 3), Norm chose the expression 'Barring', which has a complex relationship to the setting. In Gail's question, 'his name' (line 3) was in the same category as 'Bart' (line 4), since these were person references to the same third-party individual. However, Norm qualified his earlier utterances (lines 1–2 'after one' and 'now') with 'Barring any unforeseen trouble', an utterance that began with a word with a sound-association with the name 'Bart', which he was delaying producing in his answer.

```
(3) [GJ:FN]  (Jefferson, 1996, p. 20; emphasis added)
1   Norm:      He'll be here a little after one. He's
2              [at my house now.
3   Gail:      [What's his name.
4   Norm:      Barring any unforeseen trouble. His name's Bart.
```

Jefferson added, 'This could be another case of *"suppression-release,"* . . . something being avoided . . . slips out. Here, building a display of imperturbably going on with one's own talk, not deigning to answer an "interruptive" question the moment it is asked, something wonderfully close to that answer pops out'. (1996, p. 20).

A specific kind of association occurs with colours. Jefferson tentatively identified a phenomenon whereby by 'Color begets color' (1996, p. 24). The speaker (in a group therapy session) had previously not mentioned the ethnicity of the police

14   *John P. Rae et al.*

officer with whom he had an encounter—until he mentioned a colour (white). Jefferson also noted that suppression-release might be relevant here.

```
(4) [GTS:3:47-8] (Jefferson, 1996, p. 23)
   Ken:      Looks at it really carefully and says I'm not
             eighteen. He says well you know, you went
             two foot over that stop sign. Now uh, I'm
             very sorry but I'm gonna have to writechu
             out a ti-citation on this.... He says
             's against the law to go over that [white]
             line. And he gives me a big long lecture
             he's a [colored] guy.
```

Although Jefferson made the limitations of her analysis clear, she nevertheless indicated some mechanisms that might be at work. Rejecting the uncritical application of the idea of Freudian slips, she nevertheless outlined what might be described as putative psycholinguistic processes that can intersect with important sociological matters, such as the speaker's stance with respect to ethnicity.

Reception of Jefferson's 'On the Poetics of Ordinary Talk'

Jefferson's (1996) poetics paper is well known within the field, yet it has enjoyed a somewhat marginal status. It is not included in many well-known textbooks on CA (Markee, 2000; ten Have, 2007; Hutchby and Wooffitt, 2008; Sidnell, 2010; Clift, 2016) nor in Sidnell and Stivers' (2013) *The Handbook of Conversation Analysis*. An exception is Stokoe's recent book (2018). In term of bibliometrics, the paper has been well cited: according to Google Scholar, it has received 128 citations (as of 15 June 2021), but it ranks low in the list of Jefferson's cited publications. Nevertheless, interest in the paper has grown with an average of around seven citations per year over the last decade (see Figure 0.1).

Whilst it is not possible to review all the works that have cited Jefferson's poetics, a number of rough groupings can be delineated with some representative examples.

Robert Hopper, editor of a special edition which had planned to include a transcript of Jefferson's poetics, drew on the number of publications concerning poetics with respect to word-selection (Stringer and Hopper, 1998). Hopper himself wrote an elegant paper on poetics and speech errors, noting how a speech error may poetically encapsulate a substantive topic of talk and can be a resource for the development of a playfully flirtatious series of turns (Hopper, 1992).

A more sustained analysis of the interpersonal work of poetics in conversation comes from Beach's study of talk between a bride-to-be and her grandmother. The grandmother was concerned that the young woman may have been

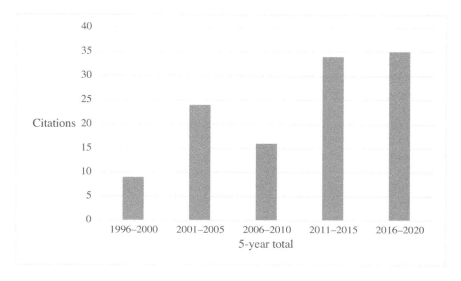

Figure 0.1 Number of Citations of Jefferson (1996) in Google Scholar

developing an eating disorder as she tried to lose weight to get into her wedding dress. There is, then, a tension between them, which manifested as a predicament for the soon-to-be-bride. Beach argued that a remark by the bride-to-be poetically captured her predicament and ongoing concerns about the wedding (Beach, 1993). The woman's predicament was that a close relative was attributing a negative trait to her: that she was deliberately inducing vomiting to make sure she lost weight. This is a form of identity work. The grandmother was making relevant the social identity 'anorexic', which could have been the basis for inferences of mental health issues, physical self-abuse, and so on. At one point the grandmother made an observation about blood on her granddaughter's toothbrush (which could indicate gum problems caused by the acid in excessive vomiting). The woman responded, 'Grandma I thought you said we were gonna change the subject'. This clearly demonstrates the young woman recognized the grandmother's concerns, though she rejected them, and clearly did not want to talk about her eating.

Later in the conversation the woman was talking about attendance at the forthcoming wedding and she said, 'God, it's hard fitting everyone in my wedding. Grandma, there's so many people different sizes'. This poetically expressed the grandmother's concerns about unhealthy eating to fit into a small-sized wedding dress, but it was framed in terms of physically accommodating people in a church. In this poetic turn, therefore, the woman appropriated the grandmother's concern *but made it her own*. Moreover, the way the remark was designed ensured that

16 *John P. Rae et al.*

it will be treated sympathetically. The grandmother was thus being presented with a remark that she would agree with, but which was designed to validate the granddaughter's concerns about fitting into the dress. In this way, the poetic turn embodied the woman's predicament and her concerns in such a way that was likely to ensure the grandmother's affiliation.

Several studies relating to psychological phenomena in action have drawn on Jefferson's paper, for example, the analysis of surprise in interaction (Wilkinson and Kitzinger, 2006), the surfacing of suppressed thoughts (Schegloff, 2003), the representation of mental state descriptions in interaction (Edwards and Potter, 2005; te Molder and Potter, 2005). In addition, poetic phenomena have been examined in the contexts of reports of introspective experience (Wooffitt and Holt, 2011a; 2011b), and in reports of 'enigmatic' communication (Wooffitt, Fuentes-Calle, and Campbell, 2020). Finally, the paper has been cited in several studies of children's language—for example, in studies of conversation between children (Cekaite, Blum-Kulka, Grøver, and Teubal, 2014), on school playgrounds (Butler, 2016), in family settings (Goodwin and Cekaite, 2018), and in mealtime interaction (Pontecorvo and Fasulo, 1999). Poetic phenomena have also been identified as a particular resource in the study of language play (Cekaite and Aronsson, 2004; Cekaite and Aronsson, 2005).

Despite these studies that make some use of Jefferson's poetics, we assert that the highly suggestive character of her work continues to be undervalued, especially in the lack of others providing a more domesticated analysis of the many types of poetic phenomena she identified in her 'wild' catalogue. Of course, Jefferson herself voiced scepticism in her doing such work herself, which may have adversely affected how much subsequent scholars have generally avoided discussions of poetics.

Reception of Jefferson's Poetics in Literary Studies

With its emphasis on naturally occurring data, scholars in CA have generally avoided discussion of written texts, especially literature.[2] Nevertheless, the theoretical basis for CA studies including written texts as a form of naturally occurring data was expressed well in 1983 by J. Maxwell Atkinson: 'an adequate understanding of how texts are produced and responded to may remain elusive so long as the issue is pursued without making close comparative reference to how talk works' (1983, p. 230). That is, following a basic assumption in CA, written texts can only be fully understood when approached as institutional talk adapted from everyday conversational practices. In this same work, Atkinson analysed newspaper accounts of political speeches, and had a reference to Shakespeare. Other early work in CA using texts was Michael Mulkay's study of the exchange of letters between scholars (1985; 1986). Due to the increasing influence of electronic media on communication, more recent studies have included an analysis of written texts in various social interactions—for example, studies

Introduction 17

concerning texting (e.g., Rendle-Short, 2015) and Facebook chat (e.g., Meredith and Stokoe, 2014).

Beginning in the 1980s, some scholars of literature began using insights in CA in their literary analyses, especially a group of scholars in the United Kingdom who applied speech act theory and discourse analysis to the study of literature, including Ronald Carter, Mick Short, Paul Simpson, Roger Fowler, and Michael Toolan.[3] These early literary studies generally made observations about the turn-taking system and preference organization as they applied to literature, primarily concerned with how plot and characterization are developed through the representation of the characters' dialogue (e.g., Toolan, 1985; Short, 1995; Fludernik, 1996; Person, 1996). In these and other studies, CA was also used to correct a common assumption in literary studies that ordinary talk is random and messy and, by implication, a comparison of ordinary talk and literary discourse would result in little insight (e.g., Toolan, 1990; Person, 1999). These early studies showed promise in the use of CA in discussions of literature, but none of them referred to Jefferson's poetics, probably because of its 'wildness' within the field of CA. That is, these early studies emphasized observations in CA that were then and remain now central to the field—that is, the turn-taking system and preference organization. To a large degree, this emphasis continues in the use of CA for the analysis of literature (e.g., Norrick, 2000a; Bowles, 2010). In fact, despite their knowledge of CA, both Neal Norrick in his article 'Poetics and Conversation' (2000b/2001) and Hugo Bowles in his discussion of 'poeticity' as 'a phenomenon of natural talk' (2011) did not refer to Jefferson's poetics.

An exception to this trend is in Raymond Person's monograph *From Conversation to Oral Tradition: A Simplest Systematics for Oral Traditions* (2016). Drawing from both CA (including Jefferson's poetics) and the comparative study of oral traditions, Person challenged the critique made by many critics of the comparative study of oral traditions that the 'literary' character of great works of literature, such as Homer, *Beowulf*, and the Bible, could not possibly be orally composed. Scholars of oral traditions and orally derived literature have intuitively countered their critics, based on fieldwork with living oral performers. They have concluded that what Albert Lord called the 'special grammar' of an oral tradition (1960, pp. 35–36) and what John Miles Foley called the 'oral traditional register' used by oral performers (1995, Chapter 2) must be an adaptation of practices that the oral poets used in their everyday conversation. Drawing significantly from CA, Person demonstrated that these intuitions of Lord, Foley, and others have the support of observations made in CA. For example, the poetic lines which are often understood as the smallest units of meaning have analogies to TCUs, and word-selection within poetic lines provide excellent examples of both sound-triggering and category-triggering. For example, Foley noted that Old English verse depends on stress-based meter (an adaptation of prosody) and alliteration (a form of sound-triggering) as illustrated in the following line from *Beowulf* (Foley, 1990, pp. 108, 111). Each half-line has two stressed syllables, and the whole line contains one stressed

18   *John P. Rae et al.*

syllable from each half-line with alliterating elements. The remaining stressed syllable in each half-line is a grammatically significant word.

/   x   /   x | /   /   x x
dryhten Geata | dracan sceawian
Lord of the Geats | to examine the dragon

The alliteration of *dr* between the two half-lines is stressed, and the other stresses occur on the stressed syllables of those words most significant to the action described—that is, the actor, the Lord of the *Geats*, and his actions, *examining* the dragon. Furthermore, some poetic lines have a formulaic character to them that allows for the substitution of elements within the line, depending on its narrative context. In the following lines from *Beowulf,* the second half-line is formulaic (Foley, 1990, p. 213):

paet hie ne moste, pa Metod nolde
That he might now [draw] him, if the Ruler did not wish it

Ic hine ne mihte, pa Metod nolde
I might not [hinder] him, if the Ruler did not wish it.

Both first half-lines have a striking similarity—both contain verbs that require completion by an infinitive from the following line (denoted by the brackets in the translation) located in the same position (that is, *moste/mihte* taking the second stressed position in the half-line). The second half-lines are exactly the same. Although these are the only two occurrences of the formula *pa/paet* [X] *nolde* in *Beowulf,* another Old English poem, *The Battle of Maldon,* has two other instances—*paet se eorl nolde* ('if the Earl did not wish it') and *paet se cniht nolde* ('if the youth did not wish it'). Thus, this half-line formula allows for the substitution of a noun for person reference within its narrative context, what seems to be a formulaic system that functions on the basis of something at least approaching category-triggering. Thus, word-selection within poetic lines within oral traditions and literature with roots in oral tradition seems to be influenced by sound-triggering and/or category-triggering (Person, 2016, pp. 74–87). Furthermore, just as TCUs occur within sequences, Person demonstrated an analogous relationship between poetic lines and thematic structures, so that even 'complex' 'literary' structures such as ring composition (ABCBA) can be understood as aesthetic adaptations/exaggerations of practices in everyday conversation (sequence organization). Such exaggerations can occur in the adaptations found in literary discourse, because what Foley (drawing from the work of Richard Bauman, Dell Hymes, and Dennis Tedlock) described as the 'communicative economy' of the 'performance arena' (Foley, 1995). That is, according to Person's extension of Foley, the communicative economy has changed, especially in that oral performers do not have to compete within a turn-taking system, so that they can draw from an oral traditional register that has been developed by generations of poets for the purpose of traditional aesthetics (Person, 2016, pp. 81–87). Building upon Person's earlier

Introduction   19

work, the last four chapters in this volume provide further evidence of how rich Jefferson's poetics can be in the study of literature.

Summary of Chapters

Following this introduction, the volume is divided into two parts, one containing four chapters written by scholars whose primary area of research is CA, and one containing four chapters written by scholars whose primary area of research is literature. What all eight chapters have in common is some discussion of the validity of Jefferson's poetics as a basis for further research into the poetics of language in general. Jefferson herself understood the relationship between the 'ordinary' and literature:

> It's pretty much figured out that all these wonderful mixtures of sounds and meanings are the provenance of poets who make it their business to work out, to seek, to really endeavor to find just the right word. . . . Ordinary people neither reject the task nor make it their life work. They just get it done.
>
> (Jefferson, 1996, p. 4)

Thus, this volume includes studies that explore the work of 'ordinary' talkers as well as 'professional' poets.

In the first chapter in Part 1: 'Studies in Poetics: Talk-In-Interaction', Ian Hutchby develops the idea of poetics in interaction to include more than just word-selections, sound-runs, and categorical associations and puns. He extends the term to include two additional types of phenomena. First, there is a form of exaggerated prosody: the way that words are uttered. Second, he also includes para-verbal phenomena, such as facial expression and other movements of the body. In his analysis of data from ordinary conversation, radio talk programmes, and a television talk show, he examines how this broader range of poetics is a resource in the production of sensitive social actions: complaints, apologies, and delicate personal revelations of a potentially upsetting nature. In these analyses, Hutchby demonstrates how this expanded range of poetics is performative in interaction, in subtle ways, to manage sensitivities associated with the topic of the talk. For example, in an analysis of a televised talk show, he examines the role of facial expression as the female guest, in the presence of her husband and new female lover, describes how she came out to her husband about her sexuality and her new romantic partner. Hutchby shows how the interplay of talk, head movement, and facial expression work to establish a parodic telling, thereby mitigating the degree of seriousness merited by the events being reported, and by the speaker's own earlier framing of the import of her account. In his conclusion, Hutchby ties together the focus on the performativity of poetics in with Jefferson's analytic skill in not only identifying the structural aspects of the organization of talk without overlooking the people's lived, contingent, interpersonal projects.

Holt's paper is an analysis of poetic phenomena in conversational interaction. She begins by describing the cognitive and linguistic view, in which talk is viewed

20   *John P. Rae et al.*

merely as a medium in which information, pre-formed in the brain of one person, is made public and transmitted to the brain of another. In opposition to this view, she emphasizes the CA perspective, in which talk is designed and produced for the interaction of which it is constitutive component. From this focus on the interactional rather than the cognitive, she analyzes conversational data to explore the ways in which poetic phenomena are implicated in a series of interactional moments. She takes the position from Sacks and Jefferson that word-choice in turn-design is 'historically sensitive', and that prior sounds and word-selections may influence subsequent turn-design, both by the speaker and co-participants. She treats poetics as forms of tying phenomena by which associations within turns and associations between turns are developed and which are central to the social actions for which those turns are designed. She illustrates these important tying properties by examining, for example, how sound-runs form associations across turns, and how more pun-like categorical word-selections may establish associations between speakers at moments of disjunctive topic change. Through these analyses, Holt demonstrates that poetic phenomena are not merely a curiosity of a pleasing happenstance of interaction, but are implicated in core interactional business of conversation.

In her lecture and in the subsequent paper, Jefferson observes that a starting point for analysis might be an oddity: for example, the choice of a word that seems conspicuous or out of place. These conspicuous features of turn-design may lead to the discovery of systematic interactional processes. In his chapter, John P. Rae exemplifies the kind of CA work that might be prompted by word-selections that seem a little odd. He focuses on near-synonyms: cases in which a word is selected which is not quite a perfect synonym to the (inferably) targeted word, but which is close. His argument is that these near-synonyms can be occasioned by and oriented to aspects of the ongoing talk and may work to support or further the kind of conversational action in which the near-synonym has occurred. An example from his paper is the case of a complaint about rail service information. The speaker's complaint in part rests on the fact that his line of work means that he does not have a fixed schedule and that the availability of accurate rail service information is crucial. Instead of using 'schedule' to refer to his work commitments, he uses the word 'timetable'. Of course, this is a near-synonym of 'schedule', but it is entirely fitted to the object of his complaint: rail service information, to which the word 'timetable' has clear relevance. Rae's argument is that near-synonym constructions support the action undertaken in the utterance and, moreover, that they display to co-participants the nature of the speakers' concerns, thereby making publicly available what from other more psychological perspectives can be considered as private concerns. This psychological relevance is explored in his discussion of Jefferson's use of Woods' work on the talk of people with severe mental health issues. This provides the foundation for an interdisciplinary rapprochement between more psychological perspectives and the approach of CA.

The chapter by Wooffitt, Reed, Young, and Jackson examines poetic phenomena in a public academic lecture, and illustrates some of the kinds of phenomena that Jefferson identified in conversational interaction and institutional settings and

Introduction 21

which she catalogues in her paper. They take the unusual step of using the recording and transcript of Jefferson's 1977 lecture on poetics as their data, showing how the phenomena she describes formally in her paper also inform her largely unscripted lecture. They analyse the Jefferson talk to support Hopper's (1992) argument that poetic phenomena may be more deeply implicated in our talk than previously recognized, and may even exhibit properties similar to formal poetic structures. They begin by examining a prominent sound-run in an early part of the Jefferson talk and argue that, while this sound-run is in progress, there is evidence that it may inform word-selection, ensuring that the run is maintained. They also identify two other kinds of poetic organization. They argue that the talk contains examples of what they call short form poetics, in which turn-design exhibits recognizable poetic structures in embryonic form. Finally, they identify a poetic structure that occurs in Jefferson's response to a question from the audience following her talk. Here, they argue that there is a segment in her response that closely resembles a poetic form known as a clerihew, eponymously named after the English poet Edmund Clerihew Bentley.

In the first chapter in Part 2: 'Studies in Poetics: Literature', Hugo Bowles notes that Jefferson's description of the poetics of ordinary talk challenges the common view in literary studies that literary discourse proceeds from authors' conscious manipulation in the writing process. Rather, sometimes literary authors may be accessing the poetics of their own conversational abilities and unconsciously reproducing them in their fictional characters' dialogues. He argues that (1) literary authors' practice of inner speech—that is, rehearsing the characters' conversations in sub-vocalization or actual vocalization—may activate sound-triggering as a means of generating poetic effects naturally and, (2) once such poetic features have entered the characters' dialogue, spreading activation will intensify the diffusion of poetic features in the echo chamber. That is, using Jefferson's terminology, category-triggering and sound-triggering give rise to the poetics of the characters' speech (sometimes unconsciously) and, once something poetic has occurred, the poetic feature may continue to influence new poetics (not unlike flurries in ordinary talk). He illustrates his argument well by drawing from the work of Charles Dickens, especially the speech of the colourful character Mrs Gamp in the novel *Martin Chuzzlewit*. He also notes that Dickens was trained to transcribe speech in his youth, and often vocalized his characters' talk as part of his writing process. Dickens himself noted that, like some of his characters, he himself had a predilection of speaking sometimes in blank verse, suggesting a connection between his own conversational practices and that of his literary characters.

Anna Bonifazi makes a similar argument concerning the relationship between conversation and literary dialogue: that is, the aesthetics and function of literary dialogue is based on the poetics of natural conversation. Drawing significantly from the work of the linguist John Du Bois on 'dialogic syntax', she shows how Du Bois' diagraphs—his way of charting linguistic structures—are an extension of Jefferson's poetics, especially in terms of category-selection at the morphological, semantic, syntactic, and pragmatic levels. Despite this emphasis on category,

22   *John P. Rae et al.*

she demonstrates that sound-triggering and category-triggering are interwoven in ways that permit listeners and readers to integrate the meanings at different levels. Her illustrations come from narrated discourse in six varieties of ancient Greek literature and provide excellent examples of the artfulness of the texts based on conversational poetics.

Frog also draws from the work of Du Bois's idea of 'dialogic syntax', which points to the role of parallelism in poetics. Focusing on synonymous parallelism, he notes that in the secondary literature, repetition is emphasized with little attention to non-repetition—that is, the repetition of ideas expressed in synonyms depends on the non-repetition of lexical terms. He concludes in poetic traditions with canonical parallelism that non-repetition of lexical terms creates a constraint that eliminates possible lexemes in performance, so that category-triggering becomes necessary to select synonymous lexemes. He also demonstrates well how sound-triggering functions at times in canonical parallelism, including how sound-triggering may cause some inference in shifting to non-ideal forms of repetition. He illustrates his arguments with examples from a variety of traditions: Rotenese ritual discourse, Finno-Karelian kalevalaic poetry, Old Norse eddic poetry, Khany poetry, Arandic song-poetry, and K'iche' Mayan ritual discourse.

Whereas the previous chapters focus on poetics in composition, Raymond Person's chapter shifts the focus to transmission of literary texts. Earlier work on scribal performance and scribal memory suggests that ancient scribes seem to allow some creative flexibility in how they copy existing manuscripts before them as they create new manuscripts of the same literary texts; therefore, based on collective memory, scribes are somewhat analogous to oral performers, in that they allow a certain degree of variation in the transmission of literary texts. He then suggests how Jefferson's poetics helps us understand list-construction better—that is, when adequate representivity is achieved in a list, the list represents a category of co-class members in ways that allows for the addition, omission, or substitution of co-class members, whether in conversation or textual transmission. Thus, text-critical 'variants' in literary lists can be understood as analogous to collaborative list-construction in conversation in ways that the 'same'-yet-'different' list does not change the literary function of the list. That is, the 'different' lists provide adequate representivity to the 'same' category, so that in one sense, nothing has changed. He illustrates his arguments with examples from ancient Hebrew and ancient Greek literature, specifically the Bible and Homeric epic.

Poetics: Looking Back, Thinking Ahead

As Jefferson's work suggests, poetic forms are everywhere in our discourse, written and spoken. They sneak up on us and insert themselves into our language, uninvited. For example, there is a body part-related pun in the subtitle previous to this sentence, innocently produced by one of the editors of this volume as he began to draft this final section of the introductory chapter. Poetic forms are seemingly irresistible, and yet have not received the kind of sustained analytic attention in studies of-talk-in interaction given to other practices in conversational and

Introduction 23

institutional interaction. In fact, in some CA data sessions, conversational poetics have been described as the 'monster in the room' that is best avoided. One of the objectives of this book is to argue for the importance of poetic phenomena and show how we might develop more formal approaches to their analysis in interactional materials and in literary texts. The chapters by Hutchby, Holt, and Rae each identify how various kinds of poetic phenomena are implicated in, and resources for, the production of mutually intelligible social actions. That is, poetic phenomena are not merely moments of pleasing artifice that are overlayed on the lived actions of people that do not exhibit robust features. They have systematic properties, which yield to formal analysis. Poetics may mitigate the serious nature of reporting a sensitive story publicly when those involved in the past social conflict are co-present (Hutchby). Pun-like categorical word-selections in disjunctive topic change may establish associations between speakers (Holt). Near-synonyms may display the speakers' private concerns (Rae). We strongly suspect that these are just a few of the ways that poetics play a more important role in interactional moments than previously acknowledged, and may even exhibit structures that can be described as poetic. For example, Wooffitt et al. identify a sequence in Jefferson's own talk in an answer to a question as the conversational prototype for the poetic form of a clerihew, a poetic form that whimsically reveals something unknown about a famous person that mitigates the aura that comes with their reputation. In Jefferson's answer, her poetic form performs the social action of mitigating her initially forceful response by playfully using poetics to undercut to some degree her own authority. Together, these chapters clearly illustrate how future studies should consider conversational poetics more seriously in how they function within social actions in talk-in-interaction.

There has, of course, been much greater attention to the poetic forms in literary works. Jefferson's article was published in *Text and Performance Quarterly* (founded as *Literature in Performance*), where there is explicit interest in the work done by rhetorical figures; however, despite this, there have been few attempts to link conversational poetics as understood in CA with the poetics in oral traditions and literature (e.g., Person, 2016). Chapters in this volume provide evidence that such unconscious application of conversational poetics may occur in the composition of both oral traditions and literature with examples taken from a variety of oral traditions (e.g., Rotenese ritual discourse and K'iche' Mayan ritual discourse in Frog's chapter), ancient literature (e.g., the Greek classics in Bonifazi's chapter and Old Norse eddic poetry in Frog's chapter), and modern literature (e.g., Charles Dickens' *Martin Chuzzlewit* in Bowles' chapter). Person's chapter demonstrates that the influence of conversational poetics is not limited to the composition of literature, but extends even to its transmission by later scribes who are 'copying' earlier manuscripts of the same piece of literature. These chapters lay the groundwork for a more sustained analysis of the way that poetic forms in literature may be advanced through a familiarization with, or framed in terms of, conversional poetics. Interestingly, two of the chapters by conversation analysts also reference literature: malapropisms in Sheridan's play *The Rivals* and word-selection in Herman Melville's *Moby Dick* (Rae) and a discussion of

24 *John P. Rae et al.*

the poetic form of a clerihew, which was 'invented' by the novelist Edmund Clerihew Bentley (Wooffitt et al.). We hope all of the chapters in this volume are not only stand-alone intellectually satisfying analyses of poetic phenomena, but cumulatively suggest trajectories and topics for future analytic work in talk-in-interaction and literature.

The starting point for this volume is Jefferson's 1977 talk and her 1996 published version of that talk. But why Jefferson, and not Sacks? He had been discussing poetic phenomena in his lectures prior to Jefferson's presentation, and by her own account, her interest in the phenomenon was piqued by a note from Sacks. Moreover, in the paper on puns we discussed earlier, he had started to formalize an approach to poetic phenomena that anticipated the standard procedure of most subsequent CA work—that is, to identify the structural and sequential properties of puns in interaction. But there are several reasons we have focused on Jefferson's work as a platform for a volume on poetic phenomena.

Poetics was not a central concern of Sacks' published work; Sacks' observations—limited mostly to his lectures—were fragmented. His most focused contribution concerned puns and, while they are clearly a poetic form, there are so many other kinds of poetic phenomena. One of Jefferson's key contributions was to focus on conversational poetics in her lecture and published article. Her paper was a catalogue of the kind of poetic phenomena that Sacks and his colleagues had been noticing and collecting. Her paper was not an analysis of the inferential import of these phenomena (as had been, for example, Sacks' observations on the call to the New York talk radio show) nor was it an attempt to locate these phenomena in relation to sequential organizations (as Sacks did in the puns paper). It was simply a clarification of what she meant by the term 'poetics', and an indication of some of the word-selection processes suggested by those poetic phenomena.

Jefferson's paper (and the presentation on which it was based) was a substantial taxonomic overview of the range of poetic phenomena that we might study. It cleared the ground for any further study by presenting scholars across all communication disciplines a range of possible starting points for empirical research. That so few have taken up that opportunity is a pity and correcting that is one of the motivations for this volume. Her paper is a treasure trove of analytic leads, and it deserves to be plundered.

There was something else in her paper that appeared to us as editors and as scholars with discrete yet complementary interests in conversational poetic phenomena that is easily overlooked when first encountering Jefferson's work—that is, although Jefferson's catalogue of phenomena is extensive, it is clearly not exhaustive. We may be dazzled by the conversational poetics she presents to us, but it should also motivate us to look for other kinds of poetic phenomena. Her work is, then, doubly generous: first, it gives us plenty to go on, but secondly, it suggests that there is more beyond, so that her work encourages us to be exploratory and open-minded about the possible systematicities of poetics and their reach in social life.

Introduction   25

Finally, Jefferson died in 2008. This means that there is an increasing number of conversation analysts, scholars of communication more widely, and literary scholars who will only know Jefferson through her publications. Those of us old and lucky enough to have met her, hear her talk, or take part in one of her data sessions (including Rae and Wooffitt) can attest that she was a charismatic and intellectually energizing individual. It is a rare fortune that we have a video recording of one of her lectures; that it was her lecture on poetics is especially auspicious, given our interests in conversational poetics. In fact, one of us editors (Person) is old enough but not lucky enough to have experienced Jefferson in face-to-face interaction, so that he has depended on her publications, stories told by her CA colleagues, and the video-recording of her poetics lecture. Nevertheless, by giving prominence to this recording in this volume, the three of us hope more people will glimpse what a compelling scholar and person she was as we recognize her continuing influence in our own work, in this volume and into future projects, and we hope that others will join us and other contributors to this volume in our attempt to domesticate the 'wild side' of CA as a continuation of Jefferson's work.

Notes

1. The genesis of this volume was the panel 'Poetics, the "Wild" Side of CA: Twenty Years after Jefferson' at the 2017 biennial meeting of the International Pragmatics Association held in Belfast organized by Raymond Person. After the panel, over drinks in an Irish pub, the three editors began their planning for the volume, and we are really pleased that the other contributors joined us in this project.
2. In contrast, linguists have often shown interest in literature and its relationship to everyday language. For example, Deborah Tannen produced a series of studies emphasizing the close connections between ordinary discourse and literature (1982; 1984; 1985; 1986; 1987; 1990a; 1990b; 1992; 1998). As such, when scholars of literature have referred to secondary literature on the relationship between literature and conversation, Tannen's work is most often cited.
3. Each of these scholars has served as chair of the Poetics and Linguistics Association. Their work and related work is found in the monograph series INTERFACE, which was edited by Ronald Carter and published by Routledge, in the association's journal *Language and Literature*, as well as many other places.

Works Cited

Atkinson, J.M. (1983), Two devices for generating audience approval: a comparative study of public discourse and texts. In K. Ehlich, H.C. van Riemsdijk, (Eds.) *Connectedness in Sentence, Discourse and Text* pp. 199–236. Tilburg, Netherlands, Katholieke Hogeschool Tilburg.

Atkinson, J.M. (1984). Public speaking and audience responses: some techniques for inviting applause. In J.M. Atkinson and J. Heritage (Eds.), *Structures of Social Action: Studies in Conversation Analysis*. Cambridge: Cambridge University Press, pp. 370–409.

Beach, W.A. (1993). The delicacy of preoccupation. *Text and Performance Quarterly*, 13, 299–312.

Bowles, H. (2010). *Storytelling and Drama: Exploring Narrative Episodes in Plays*. Amsterdam: John Benjamins.

26   *John P. Rae et al.*

Bowles, H. (2011). The contribution of CA to the study of literary dialogue. *Research on Youth and Language*, 5, 161–168.

Butler, C.W. (2016). *Talk and Social Interaction in the Playground*. London: Routledge.

Cekaite, A., and Aronsson, K. (2004). Repetition and joking in children's second language conversations: playful recyclings in an immersion classroom. *Discourse Studies*, 6, 373–392.

Cekaite, A., and Aronsson, K. (2005). Language play, a collaborative resource in children's L2 learning. *Applied Linguistics*, 26, 169–191.

Cekaite, A., Blum-Kulka, S., Grøver, V., and Teubal, E. (Eds.) (2014). *Children's Peer Talk: Learning from Each Other*. Cambridge: Cambridge University Press.

Clift, R. (2016). *Conversation Analysis*. Cambridge: Cambridge University Press. https://doi.org/10.1017/9781139022767

Couper-Kuhlen, E., and Selting, M. (Eds.) (1996). *Prosody in Conversation: Interactional Studies*. Cambridge: Cambridge University Press. https://doi.org/10.1017/CBO9780511597862

Edwards, D., and Potter, J. (2005). Discursive psychology, mental states and descriptions. In H. te Molder and J. Potter (Eds.), *Talk and Cognition: Discourse, Mind and Social Interaction*. Cambridge: Cambridge University Press, pp. 241–259.

Fludernik, M. (1996). *Towards a 'Natural' Narratology*. London: Routledge.

Foley, J.M. (1990). *Traditional Oral Epic: The Odyssey, Beowulf, and the Serbo-Croatian Return Song*. Berkeley: University of California Press.

Foley, J.M. (1995). *The Singer of Tales in Performance*. Bloomington: Indiana University Press.

Goodwin, M.H., and Cekaite, A. (2018). *Embodied Family Choreography: Practices of Control, Care, and Mundane Creativity*. London: Routledge.

Hopper, R. (1992). Speech errors and the poetics of conversation. *Text and Performance Quarterly*, 12(2), 113–124.

Hutchby, I., and Wooffitt, R. (2008). *Conversation Analysis: Principles, Practices and Applications* (Second edition). Oxford: Polity Press.

Jefferson, G. (1977). *Boston University Conference on Ethnomethodology and Conversation Analysis* [video recording]. Retrieved from: https://ca.talkbank.org/browser/index.php?url=Jefferson/Poetics/Poetics.cha

Jefferson, G. (1996). On the poetics of ordinary talk. *Text and Performance Quarterly*, 16, 11–61.

Jefferson, G. (2018). On the poetics of ordinary talk. In P. Drew and J. Bergmann (Eds.), *Repairing the Broken Surface of Talk: Managing Problems in Speaking, Hearing, and Understanding in Conversation*. Oxford: Oxford University Press, pp. 127–206.

Lord, A.B. (1960). *The Singer of Tales*. Cambridge, MA: Harvard University Press.

Markee, N. (2000). *Conversation Analysis*. Mahwah, NJ: Lawrence Erlbaum.

Meredith, J., and Stokoe, E. (2014). Repair: comparing Facebook 'chat' with spoken interaction. *Discourse & Communication*, 8, 181–207.

Mulkay, M. (1985). Agreement and disagreement in conversation and letters. *Text*, 5, 201–227.

Mulkay, M. (1986). Conversations and texts. *Human Studies*, 9, 303–321.

Nevile, M. (2015). *Transcription of Gail Jefferson*. Boston University Conference on Ethnomethodology and Conversation Analysis, 9 June 1977.

Norrick, N.R. (2000a). *Conversational Narrative: Storytelling in Everyday Talk*. Amsterdam: John Benjamins.

Norrick, N.R. (2000b/2001) Poetics and conversation. Connotations, 10, 243–226.

Introduction 27

Person, R.F., Jr. (1996). *In Conversation with Jonah: Conversation Analysis, Literary Criticism, and the Book of Jonah*. Sheffield: Sheffield Academic Press.

Person, R.F., Jr. (1999). *Structure and Meaning in Conversation and Literature*. Lanham: University Press of America.

Person, R.F., Jr. (2016). *From Conversation to Oral Tradition: A Simplest Systematics for Oral Traditions*. London: Routledge.

Pontecorvo, C., and Fasulo, A. (1999). Planning a typical Italian meal: a family reflection on culture. *Culture & Psychology*, 5, 313–335.

Rendle-Short, J. (2015). Dispreferred response when texting: delaying that 'no' response. *Discourse & Communication*, 9, 643–661.

Sacks, H. (1972). On some puns with some intimations. In R.W. Shuy (Ed.), *Report of the Twenty-Third Annual Round Table Meeting on Linguistics and Language Studies*. Washington: Georgetown University Press, pp. 135–144.

Sacks, H. (1992). *Lectures on Conversation* (2 volumes). G. Jefferson and E.A. Schegloff (Eds.). Oxford and Cambridge, MA: Basil Blackwell.

Sacks, H., Schegloff, E.A., and Jefferson, G. (1974). A simplest systematics for the organization of turn-taking for conversation. *Language*, 50, 696–735.

Schegloff, E.A. (2003). The surfacing of the suppressed. In P.J. Glenn, C.D. LeBaron, and J. Mandelbaum (Eds.), *Studies in Language and Social Interaction: In Honor of Robert Hopper*. Mahwah, NJ: Lawrence Erlbaum, pp. 241–262.

Short, M. (1995). Understanding conversation undercurrents in 'The Ebony Tower' by John Folwes. In P. Verdonk and J.J. Webers (Eds.), *Twentieth-Century Fiction: From Text to Context*. London: Routledge, pp. 45–62.

Sidnell, J. (2010). *Conversation Analysis: An Introduction*. Malden, MA: Wiley-Blackwell.

Sidnell, J., and Stivers, T. (Eds.) (2013). *The Handbook of Conversation Analysis*. Chichester: Wiley Blackwell, 191–209.

Stokoe, E. (2018). *Talk: The Science of Conversation*. London: Little, Brown.

Stringer, J.L., and Hopper, R. (1998). Generic 'he' in conversation? *Quarterly Journal of Speech*, 84, 209–221.

Tannen, D. (1982). Oral and written strategies in spoken and written narratives. *Language*, 58, 1–21.

Tannen, D. (1984). Spoken and written narrative in English and Greek. In D. Tannen (Ed.), *Coherence in Spoken and Written Discourse*. Norwood: ABLEX, pp. 21–41.

Tannen, D. (1985). Relative focus on involvement in oral and written discourse. In D.R. Olson, N. Torrance, and A. Hildyard (Eds.), *Literacy, Language, and Learning: The Nature and Consequences of Reading and Writing*. Cambridge: Cambridge University Press, pp. 124–147.

Tannen, D. (1986). Introducing constructed dialogue in Greek and American conversational and literary narrative. In F. Coulmas (Ed.), *Direct and Indirect Speech*. Berlin: Mouton, pp. 311–332.

Tannen, D. (1987). Repetition in conversation: towards a poetics of talk. *Language*, 63, 574–605.

Tannen, D. (1990a). Ordinary conversation and literary discourse: coherence and the poetics of repetition. In E. Bendix (Ed.), *The uses of linguistics. Annals of the New York Academy of Science*, 583, 15–32.

Tannen, D. (1990b). Silence as conflict management in fiction and drama: Pinter's Betrayal and a short story. In A.D. Grimshaw (Ed.), *Conflict Talk: Sociolinguistic*

28 *John P. Rae et al.*

Investigations of Arguments in Conversations. Cambridge: Cambridge University Press, pp. 260–279.

Tannen, D. (1992). How is conversation like literary discourse? The role of imagery and details in creating involvement. In P. Downing et al. (Eds.), *The Linguistics of Literacy*. Amsterdam: John Benjamins, pp. 31–46.

Tannen, D. (1998). 'Oh talking voice that is so sweet': the poetic nature of conversation. *Social Research*, 65, 631–651.

te Molder, H., and Potter, J. (2005). *Talk and Cognition: Discourse, Mind and Social Interaction*. Cambridge: Cambridge University Press.

Ten Have, P. (2007). *Doing Conversation Analysis: A Practical Guide*. London and Thousand Oaks: Sage.

Toolan, M. (1985). Analysing conversation in fiction: the Christmas dinner scene in Joyce's Portrait of the Artist as a Young Man. *Poetics Today*, 8, 393–416.

Toolan, M. (1990). *The Stylistics of Fiction: A Literary-Linguistics Approach*. London: Routledge.

Wilkinson, S., and Kitzinger, C. (2006). Surprise as an interactional achievement: reaction tokens in conversation. *Social Psychology Quarterly*, 69, 150–182.

Woods, W.L. (1938). Language study in schizophrenia. *The Journal of Nervous and Mental Disease*, 87, 290–316.

Wooffitt, R., and Holt, N. (2011a). Introspective discourse and the poetics of subjective experience. *Research on Language and Social Interaction*, 44, 135–156.

Wooffitt, R., and Holt, N. (2011b). *Looking in and Speaking Out: Introspection, Communication, Consciousness*. Exeter, UK: Imprint Academic.

Wooffitt, R., Fuentes-Calle, A., & Campbell, R. (2020). Small stories with big implications: Identity, relationality and aesthetics in accounts of enigmatic communication. Narrative Inquiry. Advance online publication DOI: https://doi.org/10.1075/ni.20013.woo

Part 1
Studies in Poetics
Talk-In-Interaction

1 Poetics and Performativity in the Management of Delicacy and Affiliation

Ian Hutchby

Gail Jefferson and the 'Wild Side' of Conversation Analysis

Conversation analysis (CA) is a method that has become known for its power to identify robust and reproducible sequential structures that underpin the management of intersubjectivity in everyday language use. Often, when we think of CA's approach to the organization of sequences and the constitutive turn-types that fill the 'slots' in those sequential structures, the canonical example is the adjacency pair sequence (Schegloff and Sacks, 1973). Sacks's last set of recorded lectures were centrally concerned with developing a formal analytic account of adjacency pairs (Sacks, 1992, vol. 2, pp. 521–569); while Schegloff's (2007) later monograph focused much of its attention on how adjacency pairs, and their attendant 'pre-expansion' and 'post-expansion' sequences, are at the heart of talk-in-interaction as an organized phenomenon.

However, since Sacks's earliest, foundational lectures, CA has simultaneously pursued a deep analytical concern not just with the structural aspects of turn-sequencing in talk-in-interaction, but also with the much more nuanced, contingent, situated nature of the actions that actual people in actual talk situations are engaging in, even as they produce and reproduce those observable patterns and devices.

This combination of the structural and the contingent permeates Sacks's *magnum opus*, the *Lectures on Conversation*, which Gail Jefferson edited for publication some years after his untimely death (Sacks, 1992). In his extensive introductions to the two volumes, Schegloff (1992a; 1992b) traces the many ways in which Sacks's work developed between 1964 and 1972, arguing that one of the main developments was away from a more 'culturalist' set of concerns in the early years towards a more structuralist bent in later lectures, especially in Sacks's formal account of the adjacency pair concept in the final Spring 1972 series. This may be so; but what is also clear is that he began in the first lecture with an investigation of how sequentially organized activities (later to become known as 'repair') are marshalled in pursuit of a specific, contingent activity (calling a suicide prevention centre and avoiding the requirement to give your name), and ended, in the final lecture published in the collection, similarly with a concern as to how sequential resources can underpin contingent activities: this time laughing

DOI: 10.4324/9780429328930-3

32   *Ian Hutchby*

together in expressions of sorrow or joy (on which see also Jefferson, Sacks, and Schegloff, 1987).

Jefferson's work, including but not limited to the paper 'On the Poetics of Ordinary Conversation', represents a stand-out case of this combination of the generic and the contingent, the structural and the temporal, in the analysis of talk-in-interaction. One place in which this can be seen quite clearly is in her work on repair and correction in conversation (Drew and Bergmann, 2018). From the earliest publications of work that would come to be known as CA (for example, Schegloff, 1968; Sacks, 1972; Schegloff and Sacks, 1973; Sacks, Schegloff, and Jefferson, 1974; Schegloff, Jefferson, and Sacks, 1977), CA was coming to be seen as a highly structuralist approach which focused somewhat neutrally on the 'conversational order', seemingly as a reality *sui generis*. By contrast, in her solo work, Jefferson zeroed in more closely on the more contingent questions of what people were actually *doing* as they were designing their turns and producing their sequences. The difference in approach is summarized by Drew and Bergmann (2018, p. 6) thus:

> For Jefferson participants in a conversation do not act as linguists or philologists: they are not interested in the correction of some conversational hitch or disturbance just for the sake of correction. For speakers, error correction is, as [Jefferson, 1974] puts it . . . 'an interactional resource'. Conversational episodes in which speakers correct themselves are interactional spaces in which, under the cover of a neutral concern for the conversational order, other and more delicate things can be pursued.

Hence:

> Whereas the [Schegloff, Jefferson, and Sacks] 1977 paper focused on structures and sequences of repair, Jefferson focused on the interactional uses and affordances of repair/correction.

The difference is particularly evident in the only paper co-authored by the three main founding figures in which Jefferson was listed as first author: the 1987 publication of 'Notes on laughter in pursuit of intimacy' (Jefferson, Sacks, and Schegloff, 1987).

In fact, Jefferson herself begins the 'Poetics' paper by making a similar distinction between approaches to doing CA. As is often (though not exclusively) the case in Jefferson's papers, she prefaces the actual analysis with some fairly informal remarks on how she came to be thinking about the topic that will be analyzed, or otherwise contextualizing the paper. In this particular case, she refers to first giving the paper at a conference in 1977, when

> the field of Conversation Analysis was coming to be identified almost exclusively by reference to the Sacks et al paper 'A simplest systematics for the organization of turn-taking for conversation', published in 1974. As an

Poetics and Performativity   33

antidote to that drastically constricted version of the field, I decided to present the wild side: stuff which we'd pretty much kept to ourselves and played with as a hobby. The stuff was wild, not only in its content, but in its lack of organization or development. It was, and still is, a big heap divided into not terribly descriptive or generative sub-heaps.

(Jefferson, 1996, p. 2)

Although Jefferson was, of course, a co-author of the same Sacks, Schegloff, and Jefferson (1974) paper, it is in this remarkably candid distinction, between the latter's 'drastically constricted' version of CA and the 'wild side' of CA, that the beauty and originality of Gail Jefferson's contributions to what is now the vast international field of CA can best be appreciated.

'On the Poetics of Ordinary Conversation' is, then, a self-confessed contribution to the wild side of CA; a side that Harvey Sacks was actively exploring in his later lectures, from 1970 onwards (Sacks, 1992, vol. 2). It is here that, as Schegloff (1992b, p. x) puts it,

A concern with storytelling in conversation which first emerges in the Spring 1968 term is much more fully developed, beginning with considerations of sequential organization but extending into quite new analytic directions. Observations about sound patterning and other 'literary' aspects of word selection emerge for the first time, and are taken up in several of the lecture sets.

Indeed, Jefferson quotes a note in which Sacks speculates on the possibility of 'word selection by reference to sound patterns' and asks her to 'check this out': a request that, a few years later, results in the conference presentation of 'Poetics' (Jefferson, 1996, p. 2). (As an aside, in editing Sacks's collected *Lectures*, Jefferson includes the term 'poetics' in a number of the lecture headings she provides; however as she remarks in a footnote, 'The term "poetics" doesn't occur in the lectures; it is used in this and several subsequent lecture-heads to capture such phenomena as "sound-related" terms, puns, etc.' (Sacks, 1992, vol. 2, p. 261).)

Of course, this is not to say that all of Jefferson's published work dealt with the wild side. Far from it. Many of her papers were focused around systematic and meticulous analyses of specific conversational phenomena and their variations, based on the rigorous collection of large corpora of data extracts (Jefferson, 1972; 1984a; 1984b; 1986; 1987; 1988). The key point is that even here, her analytical sensibility consistently leans, not towards the structural features of the 'devices' themselves, but towards the intricate details, the subtle delicacies of the interactional projects people are pursuing in and through such devices, the contingencies of what people are *doing* in the living, breathing moment.

In this chapter, the aim is to illustrate some further aspects of the 'wild side' of CA, using a small set of examples of poetic and performative talk. Like Jefferson herself, who, as Drew and Bergmann (2018, p. 10) point out, was 'quite aware of the fact that she dealt with phenomena and asked questions for which there

34   *Ian Hutchby*

was insufficient evidence to substantiate strong analytic claims', the aim is not to build a collection of similar instances out of which to fashion any systematic analysis of a generic phenomenon. Nevertheless, the singular instances are there to be observed; what people appear to be using performative features to do in their specific interactional circumstances is open to be analysed. As we will see, there may be a way to consider these examples as a kind of minimal collection of 'something similar going on in talk-in-interaction', but they each also stand alone, possible exemplars not of one type of thing, but of many.

The Dramatization of Talk

With typical acuity, Erving Goffman, in his book *Frame Analysis*, observed that 'often, what talkers undertake to do is not to provide information to a recipient but to present dramas to an audience' (Goffman, 1974, p. 508). Goffman described the use of playful and exaggerated behaviour in such phenomena as 'mockeries and say-fors', in which nonnatural performances of speaking may be adopted by a speaker in the form of ventriloquizing the thoughts or remarks of another—usually an entity which cannot speak in its own right, such as a pet or a baby (Goffman, 1974, pp. 534–537).

More recently, Holt (2007) took up similar themes in a more detailed empirical analysis of 'enactments': episodes in talk-in-interaction where speakers collaboratively construct fictionalized versions of reported speech to present a humorous scenario, usually based upon a caricature of one participant or another. Here speakers 'say-for' imagined embodiments of themselves or their interlocutor to suggest how they might react in a hypothetical version of events. Enactments involve a range of phenomena, including exaggerated prosody, burlesque and parodic reported speech, collaborative laughter, and so on.

A related set of studies has examined the slightly different question of how speakers using direct or indirect reported speech introduce affect, or to put it another way, take up personal stances on the talk they are recounting from the past (Günthner, 1999; Ivanova, 2013; Klewitz and Couper-Kuhlen, 1999; Niemelae, 2005; Soulaimani, 2018). These studies have further highlighted the multimodal dimensions of this 'stance-taking' process, showing that speakers utilize various resources, from prosody to gesture, body positioning and facial expression, to engage in specific interactional work with, or upon, the speech that is being reported.

Drawing on some of these ideas, the following analysis adapts the notion of 'poetics' to refer not only to such things as word-selections, sound-connections, and lexical patterns, but also to the prosodic enunciation of words, and the use of vocal, facial, and bodily modulations in the production of narrative components and receipt items. Thus, a link is proposed between *poetics* and *performativity* in talk-in-interaction.

The analysis examines various types of interactional activity in which hearably performative, nonnatural speech phenomena can be found; activities such as complaining, apologizing, empathizing, or recounting a potentially embarrassing

Poetics and Performativity   35

personal story. A common thread is proposed in that the poetic and performative phenomena identified seem to be bound up, in various ways, with speakers' management of *delicate* actions. Further, in that these activities involve delicacy, there is also a suggestion that a speaker's use of performative phenomena is bound up with seeking the recipient's affiliation or alignment.

Performed Retelling in a Complaint Narrative

As Goffman (1981) pointed out in his analysis of 'footing', speakers ('animators') may use their own words, the words of others, or indeed invented words attributed to others, in various ways in designing their utterances, especially when recounting stories (Coulmas, 1986; Holt and Clift, 2007; Buchstaller and van Alphen, 2012). In certain circumstances, through exaggerated prosodic and paraverbal turn-design features, speakers can additionally convey that what they are producing is a *performance* of, rather than an accurate reproduction of, something that was said by another in the past. In doing so, they appear to exhibit or take up a particular stance in relation to the utterance they are reporting; a stance that can be critical, or mocking, humorous, or playful.

This kind of *performed retelling* can be seen initially in the following extract from a radio phone-in programme. The topic of the call, as appropriate for this particular setting, is based around a position-taking: here, a complaint about the behaviour of dog owners in the neighbourhood who fail to clean up after their dogs have fouled the pavements and verges. The phenomena of interest do not occur until the segment of reported speech in lines 24–26; however, both the preceding and the subsequent talk are important in the caller's attempt to construct an affiliative environment for what seems like a planned performative 'punchline'.

```
(1)  [Hutchby:2.2.89:4]
1    Host:    And good morning tuh Lin:da frum Ruislip. Good
2             morni[ng.
3    Caller:       [Good mor:ning Brian. .hhh We've godda real
4             problem he:re with dogs fouling our footway.=
5    Host:    =Oh, some[thing important now.
6    Caller:           [.phhh
7             (.)
8    Caller:  Pahd'n?
9    Host:    Something important this time.=Right.
10   Caller:  eYe:s:. h Well i' i:s to us: anyway.
11   Host:    Yes[:,
12   Caller:     [I'm:: a-er mother of two small boys, .hh an'
13            I've now got tuh the situation where we ca:n't,
14            gedout uv our ca::r on the pa:vement si:de e- c-
15            becuz it's so ba::d. .hhhh As I said we've gotta
16            gra:ss verge u- u- s- outside our house, .hh an'
17            the local dog owners, ↑walk their ↓dogs ↑past my
18            ↓house, (.) .h they ↑do: their bizni:ss, right
19            outside, .hh an' ↓walk a↑wa↓y.
20            (0.5)
```

36   Ian Hutchby

```
21 Caller:   .hh One da::y, I akchilly sa:w a lady=e- ow:ner, allow
22           her dog, tuh do its bizniss ↑ri:ght in the middle
23           of my: gateway. .hhh An' when I remonstrated with
24→          the la:dy, .h she told me thut her dog 'as got t'do
25→          its bizniss somewhe:↑re, it ↓might ↑as ↓well: ↑be
26→          ↑↑the:re.
27 Host:     M:m[:,
27 Caller:      [.phhh
28           (.)
30 Caller:   A-e(i)s you c'n imagine I wuz absolutely:=livvid(h),
```

The caller's main gist here concerns her outrage at the inconsiderateness of local dog owners who allow their dogs to do their 'business' on the grass verges, with the clear implication that this constitutes a health risk for her two small children.

In line with the general strategy adopted on this particular talk radio show (Hutchby, 1996), the host's first move is to offer a sceptical or ironic response to the caller's topic: 'Oh, something important now' (line 5). This kind of withering dismissiveness is a factor with which talk radio callers frequently have to contend. However, in this case, the caller's response is interesting in terms of her attempt to build a sympathetic environment in which to produce her ultimate complaint.

One way of seeing her 'Pahd↑n:?' in line 8 may be as an indication of the caller's surprise at the rapidity with which the host's sceptical stance is adumbrated. In English, 'Pardon?' is an example of an open-class repair initiator, similar to 'What?' (Drew, 1997). But it can also act quite differently as a marker of irate objection to a prior turn (sometimes appearing in the form 'I beg your pardon?'). It is not absolutely clear which of these actions the caller is doing with her 'Pahd↑n:?' in line 8. But it is noticeable that the host backs down somewhat in his reiterative turn in the following line 9. First, he drops the turn-initial 'Oh', one use of which is as a marker of irony, especially in argumentative contexts (Hutchby, 2001). Second, he tags on a particle, 'Right', which can be heard (even if not intended) as situating himself in a position of attentiveness: hence treating the caller's proposed topic as, after all, something worth listening to. The caller subsequently underlines this, emphasizing that for herself and her family, and by implication a broader constituency of 'citizens' or 'mothers with small children', it is indeed an important issue.

Moving on to the key segment in which she describes her encounter with one particular dog owner, it becomes even more notable that the caller is careful to build into the description contextual features which invite the recipient to evaluate negatively the kind and extent of rudeness that she presents herself as having been subjected to. Thus, she states that 'One da::y, I akchilly sa:w a lady=e- ow:ner, allow her dog, tuh do its bizniss ↑ri:ght in the middle of my: gateway'. This both foregrounds the dog owner's culpability for an uncivil action, and emphasizes the caller's integrity. The phrase 'I akchilly sa:w' again is able to reference at least two types of action. It could be that she 'just happened' to glimpse this particular person, or it could be that this sighting was in fact the culmination of a period of surveillance, in the hope of catching someone in the act. Whichever it might

Poetics and Performativity 37

be, the phrase, 'all<u>o</u>w her d<u>o</u>g, tuh <u>d</u>o its <u>b</u>izniss ↑ri<u>:</u>ght in the middle of my<u>:</u> gateway', stresses the woman's responsibility for this transgression: the dog is 'allowed' to do its business rather than being forced to go to a more appropriate spot. It also foregrounds her inconsiderateness: it is not just on the grass verge, but '↑ri<u>:</u>ght in the middle of my<u>:</u> gateway'.

For present purposes, it is the final part of the caller's turn, in which she uses indirect reported speech to characterize the woman's impolite behaviour in a face-to-face encounter, that is most significant. Having first reported that she 'r<u>e</u>monstrated with the la<u>:</u>dy', in lines 24–26, the caller purports to quote the woman's response. However, the speech is not reported in what could be described as a natural way. The transcript shows the caller adopting a marked 'sing-song' prosody as she reports this response (marked by upward and downward arrows that aim, albeit crudely, to match the shifting pitch of her voice): 'she <u>t</u>old me thut her dog 'as g<u>o</u>t t'do its bizniss s<u>o</u>mewhe:↑re, it ↓m<u>i</u>ght ↑as ↓w<u>e</u>ll: be ↑↑th<u>e</u>:re'. Reporting the speech in this nonnatural, parodic way, the caller seems to embody or enact a burlesque of what the woman is reported as saying: a verbal caricature which, in its inflection, highlights the very rudeness or inconsiderateness of such a statement.

The use of exaggerated prosody here is one example of a performed retelling: a stretch of reported speech designed to indicate that this is not how the originator 'actually' spoke the words, but how the current speaker intends the words that were spoken to be *interpreted* (in this instance, negatively). The performance highlights the 'anyone can see' nature of this example of rude behaviour. The caller is thus engaged in using reported speech to take up a position on the event she is recounting.

The fact that the caller intends her reporting to be heard in this way can be derived from the following turns. In line 7, the talk show host responds in a way that exhibits a lack of willingness to collaborate in the complaint that is being constructed. He merely offers a continuer (Schegloff, 1982), which on one level conveys an indication that the caller's story has yet to reach an adequate conclusion or punchline. On another level, the sheer flatness or blankness of this continuer, placed where it is in relation to the caller's telling of her story, clearly demonstrates that the host is declining to align with the complaint, and refusing to pick up on or collaborate in the theatre of its production. Orienting to this lack of uptake, in line 10, the caller proceeds to furnish him in overt terms with the kind of hearing she has evidently been expecting him to achieve via her performed retelling: 'A-e(i)s you c'n im<u>a</u>gine <u>I</u> wuz absolutely:=<u>l</u>ivv<u>i</u>d(h)'.

In this talk radio setting, then, we find a first indication of how the performativity of talk can not only be fitted to a specific kind of activity, but also, in some sense, fitted to a speaker's expectations about the relevant kinds of activities for a particular setting. The caller's role in making a talk radio call is to adopt a position on some issue, which the caller here does by constructing a complaint about the blunt inconsiderateness of the woman dog owner. However, even (or perhaps especially, given the host's propensity for scepticism) in the talk radio context, complaining is a delicate activity which relies for its

38 Ian Hutchby

effectiveness on the affiliation or alignment of the recipient. The caller builds her turn throughout, and in detail, in such a way as to encourage that alignment, topping it off with a performative, 'you must be with me on this' enunciation of the woman's excuse. Yet in this instance, her interactional work falls on stony ground as the host's blank response pops her balloon.

By contrast, in the following example, this time from an ordinary telephone conversation, the complainant succeeds in eliciting affiliation from her recipient, as she recounts a story about having been insulted at a local church charity sale. The key factors of interest here are, first, the way that Lesley, the complainant, sets up and cultivates the ground for her recipient, Joyce, to assess the kind of affiliative response that might be relevant to this story; and second, the exquisitely poetic relationship between the story's initial setup and its ultimate conclusion.

```
(2)  [Holt:Xmas 85]
1→   Lesley:  I'm broiling about something hhhheh[heh .hhhh
2    Joyce:                                      [Wha::t.
3    Lesley:  Well that sa:le. (0.2) At- at (.) the vicarage.
4             (0.6)
5    Joyce:   Oh ye-:s,
6             (0.6)
7    Lesley:  u (.) ihYour friend 'n mi:ne was the:re
8             (0.2)
9    Joyce:   (h[h hh)
10   Lesley:   [mMister:, R:,
11   Joyce:   Oh y(h)es, (hm hm)
12            (0.4)
13→  Lesley:  And em: .p we (.) really didn't have a lot'v cha:nge
14→           that (.) day becuz we'd been to Bath 'n we'd been:
15→           Christmas shoppin:g, (0.5) but we thought we'd better
16→           go along t'th' sale 'n do what we could, (0.2) we
17→           hadn't got a lot (.) of s:e- ready cash t'spe:nd.
18            (0.6)
19   Lesley:  In any case we thought th' things were very
20            expensive.
21   Joyce:   Oh did you.
22            (0.9)
23   Lesley:  AND uh we were looking round the sta:lls 'n poking
24→           about 'n he came up t' me 'n he said Oh: hhello
25→           Lesley, (.) still trying to buy something f'nothing,
26→  Lesley:  .tch! .hh[hahhhhhhh!
27→  Joyce:            [.hhoohhhh!
28            (0.8)
29→  Joyce:   Oo[: : :[:L e s l e y]
30→  Lesley:    [OO:. [ ehh heh heh ]
31            (0.2)
32   Joyce:   I:s[n 't]      [he
33   Lesley:     [What] do y[ou sa:y.
34            (0.3)
35   Joyce:   Oh isn't he drea:dful.
36   Lesley:  eYe::s.
37            (0.6)
```

```
38   Joyce:    What'n aw::ful ma:[::n
39   Lesley:                      [Ehh heh heh heh
40   Joyce:    Oh honestly. (.) I cannot stand the man it's [just-
41   Lesley:                                                [I
42             thought well I'm goin t' tell Joyce that,
```

There is something poetic, in Jefferson's (1996) sense, in the way Lesley introduces her desire to tell the story in line 1: a kind of 'mis-saying'. The phrase 'I'm broiling about something' is interesting in that 'broiling' does not seem to be the correct word to use. 'Broil' is a largely American term (Lesley and Joyce are English) meaning to cook food under, or over, direct intense heat. Whereas what Lesley is using the term to indicate, it transpires, is something more like a state of indignant agitation or a pent-up desire to get this story out to her friend.

It seems possible, therefore, that Lesley's mis-saying in fact arises from a merger of two different but, in this context, more appropriate words: br(ewing) and (b) oiling. In a similar but much more abstract sense to extract (1)'s 'We've godda real problem he:re with dogs fouling our footway', Lesley attempts to find wording that will indicate exactly what kind of story it is that Joyce is being asked to listen to: a story about the kind of thing that one might retain an internal feeling of 'brewing' or 'boiling' about until the opportunity to tell it arises—which it now has. (Indeed, at the end of the extract [lines 41–42], Lesley expressly indicates her intention to select Joyce as a recipient of this story, probably because Joyce herself seems to be acquainted with 'ihYour friend 'n mi:ne . . . mMister:, R:,' [lines 7–10].)

As in extract (1), Lesley then proceeds to furnish background details which present a favourable context for her own activities at the time (lines 13–17). She and her companion (possibly her husband) had been Christmas shopping. As a result, they didn't have much money left to spend, but they went to the charity sale in order to do their bit as (or perhaps to be seen as) good citizens.

Then comes the punchline. 'Mr R' is described 'coming up to' Lesley and delivering his insult, 'still trying to buy something f'nothing,'—broadly glossed as the social gaffe of trying to hunt for bargains at a church charity sale. Not only that, but the word 'still' implies that this is something Mr R takes it Lesley has been guilty of before, if not repeatedly.

Almost immediately we find the two women simultaneously engaging in nonlexical expressions of indignation: first of all, sharp and extended intakes of breath (lines 26 and 27), followed, after a short pause, by loud, extended expulsions of air formed into 'Ooo'-sounds (lines 29 and 30). These verbalizations relate onomatopoeically to the sense in which such an insult or social squelch can be felt almost physically. More than that, they indicate Joyce's understanding of the kind of story Lesley has recounted for her. Notice, for example, that it is Joyce, the recipient, who by a small margin is the first to embark on the irate 'Oo:::: Lesley' response, Lesley's own 'OO:. ehh heh heh' coming a moment later in overlap.

But the poetic resonance lies most neatly in the relationship between the phrase with which the story was introduced, and these verbalizations at its conclusion. In other words, Lesley having described herself almost as having been keeping a lid

40 *Ian Hutchby*

on her state of heated internal agitation with the term 'broiling', these verbalized expulsions of air are in their way onomatopoeic expressions of that lid having finally been blown off.

Apologizing and Empathizing

If the previous extracts show a speaker reporting a purportedly real encounter in the pursuit of a complaint about that encounter, the next extracts show speakers dramatizing their talk by adopting fictional roles or identities that enable them to manage delicate situations, such as apologizing to a recipient, or empathizing with a recipient's romantic troubles.

Consider the opening in Extract (3), from a telephone conversation between two middle-aged female friends.

```
(3)  [Power Tools]
1              ((ring))
2     Margy:   Hello:,
3     Edna:    Hello Margy?
4     Margy:   ↑Ye:[s,
5→    Edna:        [.hhhh We do pai:::nt↑ing, a:ntiqu↑i::ng,=
6     Margy:   =I(h)s tha:t ri:ght.=
7     Edna:    =Ehhhh[hhhhhhhh[.hh].hh!
8     Margy:        [hmh hmh [hmh]
9              (.)
10→   Edna:    ihh-hn:n-hn-.hh-hn [keep] people's pa:r↑too:::ls
11    Margy:                       [.hhh]
12    Margy:   Yehhhhh:↑hheeh[(.hhh)
13    Edna:                  [I:'m sorry about that
```

The call appears to begin in a fairly standard way with an identification-recognition sequence (Schegloff, 1979) in lines 1–4. Then, Edna's 'reason for the call' turn (Schegloff, 1986) after she has established that Margy is the answerer (line 5) is decidedly odd. She presents, without any initial contextualization, a small dramatization in which she embodies the figure of a salesman advertising some kind of interior decoration service: 'We do pai:::nt↑ing, a:ntiqu↑i::ng . . .'.

The fact that this is intended to be hearable as a humorous parody is found not just in the fact that, as friends, Margy and Edna both know that Edna is not involved in the interior decoration business, but also, as in Extract (1), in the exaggerated prosody of the utterance, in particular the use of elongated phrasing and marked upward intonation. Again, the enunciation is hearably nonnatural, or performed. In fact, such features seem to be used by Margy to display her early recognition of this as a joke. Notice, for example, her slight laughter in lines 6 and 8 (punctuated by more pronounced laughing from Edna in line 7) that occurs before the point of the joke has been revealed, or its punchline delivered.

It transpires, as we see, that Edna has called to apologize for her husband's failure to return a borrowed power tool, which Margy's husband had consequently had to go and ask to have back. Like complaints, apologies are

Poetics and Performativity 41

delicate actions in which achieving the appropriate alignment of the recipient is an important matter. But whereas, in the talk radio extract earlier, the caller could not count on, and did not receive, any sympathetic alignment from the combative host, here the use of a parodic call opening serves to situate the recipient (Margy) in a humorous and hence, as Edna hopes, forgiving mode.

Here, the way that the call is opened, in lines 1–4, becomes additionally significant. Following a standard summons-answer sequence of [((ring))]—[Hel<u>lo</u>:,], the caller's (Edna's) first turn initially presents itself as a recognitional opening: that is, having recognized Margy's identity from her line 2 voice sample 'Hel<u>lo</u>:,', Edna responds with a voice sample of her own: 'Hello Mar<u>gy</u>?' Notice, however, the try-marked (Sacks and Schegloff, 1979) intonation, indicated by the question mark. Although it seems that Edna recognizes Margy as the answerer, her question intonation opens a different kind of response slot for Margy than would a differently intoned 'Hello Margy!', for example. A suitable next turn to 'Hello Margy!' would be a similarly recognitional 'Hi Edna!', whereas a suitable next turn to the try-marked 'Hello Mar<u>gy</u>?' is the acknowledgement that Edna in fact produces in line 4, '↑<u>Ye</u>:s,'.

In other words, purely through a shift in intonation, the opening sequence enables the caller to position herself such that she can propose *not* to have been recognized, even though she has established the identity of the answerer. This, as Hopper (1993, pp. 207–211) has pointed out, is a key strategy adopted by telemarketers in their attempt to prevent answerers from immediately hanging up on them:

```
(4)   [UTCL A35.24]
1      Ans:   Hello?
2      Call:  Mister ↑Smalley,
3      Ans:   Yes
4      Call:  This is Missy Weevil, sir I'm calling you from
5             Ward Life Insurance Company in Chicago?
6      Ans:   Uh huh
7      Call:  ↑How do you do sir.
8      Ans:   Just fine.
9      Call:  Great. How was your Christmas?
10     Ans:   Just fine.
```

By opening her call with an invitation to the answerer to confirm his name, the cold caller here draws him into an interactional sequence even though, as seemingly indicated by his minimal responses, he is less than enthusiastic about becoming involved in a conversation with her.

It is not known whether Edna, in extract (3), has any experience of telemarketing; nevertheless, the same technique is used in a way that turns out to enable her to take on the elaborate fictional identity that she has decided to adopt in both mitigating, and, through the use of humour, seeking her recipient's alignment with, the apology that she has been forced to make via this call.

One last interesting feature of the performative apology strategy is that it relies on the extremely commonplace use of lists of three (Jefferson, 1990) as a rhetorically effective interactional device. While the first two parts of

42   *Ian Hutchby*

the list, 'painting' and 'antiquing', purport to be a description of services rendered, both their intonation, and the fact that there are only two parts, project
the existence of a third. As noted, the joke is already partly recognized in the
laughter that accompanies parts one and two of the list. But it is in the third
part, similarly intoned but framed by playful laughter, 'ihh-hn:n-hn-.hh-hn
keep people's pa:r↑ too:::ls', that both the third part of the list, and the apology, are finally revealed in the form of the joke's punchline.

In the following extract, again from a telephone conversation between friends,
Hyla has previously been complaining, with a sympathetic ear from Nancy, about
a boyfriend who moved away to college promising to write to her, but from whom
she is still waiting to hear.

```
(5) [HG: 26]
1      Nancy:     I know see that's w't I don't understan'
2                 that's why I still think he might write you,
3                 (0.3)
4      Nancy:     It jis'takes 'm awhi:le,
5                 (.)
6→     Hyla:      khh-hh-h-He writes one word a day,hhih[hn
7      Nancy:                                          [Yeahhh
8                 (.)
9→     Nancy:     Dea:r? hh nex'day. Hyla,=
10     Hyla:      =.u.u .hhh
11                (.)
12→    Nancy:     Ho:w?
13                (.)
14     Hyla:      .hhhi:[nh]heh-heh,
15→    Nancy:           [A:]re?
16                (.)
17→    Nancy:     ↑You:.=
18     Hyla:      =.eh- .uh,
```

Again, here we are in the environs of a delicate activity, that of troubles-telling—
another activity which can often rely for its success on managing the alignment
of a recipient. As Jefferson (1988) showed, in ordinary conversation the role of a
troubles-recipient is, in general, to empathise with the troubles-teller: the interactional focus should be on the teller and his or her experience. Problems can arise
if, for example, the recipient attempts too swiftly to offer advice.

As the extract begins, Nancy is in the process of furnishing a sympathetic, and
hence also collaborative environment in which Hyla can discuss her troubles.
She indicates that, rather than abandoning Hyla, the boyfriend is still likely to
write, except it 'jis' takes 'm awhi:le,'. Following this Hyla, as the troubles-
teller, embarks on a harsher, or more extrematized, evaluation of the boyfriend's
epistolary absenteeism: 'He writes one word a day' (line 6). It is this negative
characterization that provides Nancy with an appropriate space to empathize
by performing the imagined process of letter-writing through a parodic say-for
(lines 9–17).

Here, then, what is being performed is writing, rather than speech; although the writing, and more particularly the joked-about speed of it, is being parodized *in* speech. Nancy is using a parodic version of letter-writing to engage in a potentially delicate activity: sympathizing with her friend's concerns about her boyfriend, while avoiding the possibility of upsetting her by being too dismissive or insulting. As in the previous extract, the recipient, Hyla, displays both her understanding of the joke, and her appreciation of it, by inserting laugh particles in between each of the imagined daily additions to the missive.

The previous extracts have shown, in different ways, that speakers can be found to use exaggerated, parodic, performative, or otherwise nonnatural speech design features in their management of situations involving some kind of interactional delicacy: managing a complaint, apologizing for a faux pas, or empathizing with a friend's problematic romance. Production of these kinds of performative talk, which can be done using direct or indirect reported speech, invented speech, or even by verbalizing the nonverbal act of writing, seems either to rely upon, or to provide an interactional space for, affiliation by the recipient. It is through the building of an affiliative environment that the speaker's delicate activity can be undertaken without interactional friction. Depending on the context, however, this may or may not succeed. In ordinary conversation, collaboration and cooperation seem more likely, whereas in the talk radio materials, where scepticism and argument are more prevalent, a caller may find themselves denied any hoped-for affiliation.

Parodic Second Versions

In the final set of extracts, a participant on a TV talk show uses a range of paraverbal phenomena in the course of talking about the revelation of two secrets: first, how she decided to reveal to her husband that she was gay; and second, how she revealed her secret love for another woman.

The potential for embarrassment and the need for delicacy are particularly great here; not only because the speaker, anonymized as 'Jane', is revealing a highly personal story in front of a studio audience and on television, but also because, as it will turn out, both her husband 'Mike' and her new partner 'Hilly' are themselves present in the studio audience.

The key feature of interest here is that the speaker typically produces *two different versions* of her own account. The first version is presented as a serious and accurate account of what happened during the revelation. The second version seems to be occasioned by the host's reaction to the first, and uses parodic speech and burlesque facial expressions to introduce playful distance between Jane herself and the events or statements being reported.

In Extract (6), the host initiates a sequence in which Jane is invited to recount how she first revealed her secret to Mike:

44 *Ian Hutchby*

(6) [ITV2 7.3.07]

On stage: Host; Jane. Onscreen caption: 'Jane left her husband because she's gay'

VERBAL TRACK		VISUAL TRACK
1	Host: How did you tell him.	*Close up (CU) on host*
2	(1.2)	
3	Jane: We wen' out t'dinner en	*CU on Jane*
4	(3.2)	*Jane moves face towards*
5	Host: °Mfhh°	*audience, looks upwards,*
6	(0.2)	*adopts comical expression*
7	Jane: En I tol:d 'im I s' y'ew	*Jane looks back*
8	d'you know Mike wut- I think,	*towards host*
9	after lots of soul searching	
10	en lots of reading en lots	
11	of prayin:g I p- (.) I do	*Jane eye-to-eye contact*
12	belie:ve that I'm a lesbian,	*with host*
13	(2.9)	*Jane pulls 'worried' face*
14	Host: Was that hard fer you t'do?	
15	Jane: Very painful to do.	*CU Jane*

In response to the host's question, Jane first reports that 'we wen' out t'dinner' (line 3), then pauses, and then reproduces her words to Mike using direct reported speech (lines 7–12). The content of that turn presents her account to him as a serious and considered one ('after lots of soul searching en lots of reading en lots of prayin:g'), and both this preamble, and the final revelation ('I do belie:ve that I'm a lesbian'), are uttered using direct eye-to-eye gaze with the host and a 'serious' facial set. This represents the *standard gaze configuration* adopted by speakers on the show. Its significance for the present analysis derives from the way that the guest's means of dramatizing her narrative, in subsequent extracts, typically involve moving her face *out of* this standard gaze configuration to perform a range of audience-directed expressive actions that accompany the second versions of her telling.

This is first observable, in fact, during the pause in lines 4–6 of the extract, which lasts in total about 3.5 seconds, including the slight snort in line 5. As can be seen from the 'visual track' description, having begun with gaze directed at the host during the utterance 'We wen' out t'dinner en', Jane embarks upon the pause, then engages in a series of face and head movements in which she (a) averts her gaze, (b) turns her face towards the audience, (c) purses her lips into a kind of halfway grin, (d) directs her gaze upwards and into middle-distance, and finally (e) adopts a comical, semi-vacant smile gazing at the space above the audience's heads.

Collectively, what this set of movements seems to be doing is indexing a slight, and temporary, shift in footing, a slight mocking of the seriousness of the account she has just undertaken. It can be seen as a nonverbal display of what, verbally, might be formulated as, 'I don't believe I'm about to say this in front of you people' (the audience). The host's muffled laugh in line 5 is potentially an indication of her own orientation to this framing.

Poetics and Performativity 45

Parodic paraverbal phenomena thus accomplish a bracketing of the seriousness with which Jane began her report of the revelation and to which she returns as she resumes speaking in line 7 of the transcript. At this point, the facial orientation and eye contact have returned to the standard gaze configuration, and a fully serious facial expression has been re-established by the end of the turn in line 12.

Although brief, this set of movements is significant in terms of the talk show guest's management of delicacy and affiliation in this highly public, performative setting. Once an issue as personal as sexual identity has been introduced into discussion, its inter- and intrapersonal consequences may quickly come to the fore. Using paraverbal phenomena to produce bracketings, reframings, or otherwise shift footing is a way that a speaker can performatively distance themselves from the emotional labour that may be involved here.

Another aspect of this is that, like the earlier speaker 'doing complaining' on talk radio, here the speaker is somehow gearing up for 'doing entertaining', in the sense that the story is produced for an audience—in this case, both a co-present audience in the studio as well as a non-present overhearing audience. Later extracts will show that Jane's bracketings and parodic reframings are similarly produced with facial orientation towards the co-present studio audience, while the serious versions of events are produced using the standard gaze towards the host.

Thus, in the next extract, Jane responds to the host's surprised or even slightly sceptical reaction to her account of the husband's remarkably sympathetic receipt of her news by actively changing the story, using verbal and paraverbal performances to parodize her own previously serious account.

(7) [ITV2 7.3.07]
On stage: Host; Jane.

```
VERBAL TRACK                                    VISUAL TRACK
1    Host: How did 'e take it initially.=       CU host
2    Jane: Initially, he: u-he ses yihknow      CU Jane
3          what I love you:, .hhh I support
4          you,=whatever you need to do,
5          I want you to be happy:, (.)
6          .h[hh I wantche du- yihknow,
7→   Host:   [Rilly.
8          (0.9)
9    Jane: guw- [Do what you need t'do=
10→  Host:      [This was his first rea-        CU host
11   Jane: =[Tha:t was his first=
12   Host: =[his firs'-
13   Jane: =reac[tion w-we w-
14→  Host:      [At dinner?                     CU host
15         (0.2)
16   Jane: Yeh- we:ll, .hh i'was akchully       CU Jane
17         a:fter dinner I chickened
18         out at dinner, .h an' then we
19         went tuh the booksto:re, .h an'
20         then we kinda sat on the ker:b.      Jane moves face
21         (1.0)                                away from host,
```

46   *Ian Hutchby*

```
22→ Jane:  .h I wuz like I go:tta te:ll you     adopts sideways-on
23          somethin:g. This w'z like o:n the    comical expression
24          ke:rb. (1.8) At Borders.=
25   Host:  =An' your husband sa:id. (0.5) At    CU host
26          Borders. [Goo:d,                     Host looks theatrically
27   Jane:           [Ye::s.                     towards audience
28   Aud:   eh heh hih hih [hah
29   Host:                 [And your husband
30          sa:id, (0.3) I-
31   Jane:  He said it's gonna be okay. (0.4)    CU Jane
32          I love you, we'll get through it.
33          (0.8)
34→ Jane:  An' I thought, Ah don'know if you    Jane moves face to
35          heard me.                            front, adopts quizzical
36   Aud:   Heh [ha hah                          expression
37   Host:      [hmm hmm hm
```

The question in line 1 elicits a straight account of Mike's supportive response, again using direct reported speech. However, as the host produces her turns 'Rilly' (line 7) and 'At dinner?' (line 14), with prosody designed to convey some level of disbelief, Jane immediately moves into a second, very different, account of what happened, where it happened, and what was said at the time.

Jane reports that she had actually 'chickened out' at dinner, and that after a visit to the bookstore they had 'kinda sat on the ker:b'. At this point we find another use of reported speech, 'I wuz like I go:tta te:ll you somethin:g'. The camera shows Jane's facial orientation shifting again towards the audience in front, that is, the direction she had moved in during the 3.5-second pause earlier. In this instance, eye contact with the host is retained, but as the head orientation moves, this becomes increasingly sideways on and thus comically absurd. The expression adopted is also jocose, and contrasts noticeably with the 'standard' gaze.

The words as reported here, 'I wuz like I go:tta te:ll you somethin:g', are different both in tone and content to the 'soul searching' account given in Extract (6). While in the original revelation account, Jane herself seemed to be playing the account 'straight'—embodying both verbally and paraverbally the account being reported—here she is using facial and prosodic manipulation to introduce distance between herself and the account she is reporting. Her use of the phrase 'I wuz like' to mark the reported speech 'I go:tta te:ll you somethin:g' is itself significant here. As work on the quotative form 'I was like' (or generically, *be+like*) has shown, it is often used in a context where the speaker wishes not just to report spoken words, but to express an attitude or stance with regard to the words reported (Golato, 2012; Tagliamonte, 2005; Tagliamonte and D'Arcy, 2005). Jane uses the phrase to reframe her account in a performed retelling designed to maintain affiliation with the host by implicitly acknowledging the latter's potential scepticism.

Similar features can be found in lines 34–35, just after Jane reiterates her husband's sympathetic response to her news. Here, the face is presented fully towards the audience, with the facial expression adopting emblems of puzzlement or

Poetics and Performativity   47

perplexity (eyebrows down; eyes cast downwards and sideways; chin pulled back towards throat) as she performs an internal dialogue that, once again, introduces playful distance between the teller and the account presented: 'An' I thought, <u>A</u>h don'know if you h<u>ea</u>rd me.' This engenders an audience response in the form of laughter.

Later in the same show, Jane's ex-husband, Mike, has joined her on the sofa in front of the audience, and the host brings in Hilly, Jane's current girlfriend, who is shown sitting in the audience. At the start of Extract (8), Hilly, in answer to a question from the host, produces a 'straight' account of how Jane revealed to her that she had strong feelings for her. Similar performative, sequential, and paraverbal features are found in the telling of serious and parodic versions of the same events.

```
(8)  [ITV2 7.3.07]
On  stage:  Host;  Jane;  Mike;  In  audience:  Hilly;  Onscreen  caption—
'Hilly,  Jane's  partner'
VERBAL TRACK                                        VISUAL TRACK
1    Hilly:  So: um, (0.8) Jane- just ca:lled       CU Hilly
2            me one day an' said yihkno:w, (.)
3            I just have to tell you that,
4            (0.2) you're the one.
5            (1.0)
6    Hilly:  An:d um (.) mthh hh .hh
7            (0.8)                                   CU host, looking
8    Hilly:  An:d uh- uh huh hh                      confused
9            (0.2)
10   Mike:   Huh huh [huh hh
11   Hilly:          [I said ↑rilly::. eh huh        CU Hilly
12   Host:   You di[:d?                              Host looks at Jane
13   Jane:         [Sorry ↑do w-
14           (.)
15   Jane:   ↑Do what you wanna do with that         CU Jane, holding
16           information talk t'y'later.             imaginary phone
17           Kchk!                                   Jane mimicks hanging up
```

As in the previous episode, the features to take note of are, first, the host's response to this, which again is one of questioning surprise, and second, Jane's own overtly fictionalized account of how the event unfolded.

Although Hilly's account in lines 1–4 uses direct reported speech, the words she quotes seem more likely to be a gloss of what was said rather than a verbatim quote. Nevertheless, she produces this utterance as a 'straight' telling, with no marked prosodic or paraverbal inflection. The straightness of the telling, indeed, can be seen to occasion the host's reaction: a rapid looking back and forth between Jane and Hilly followed slightly later by a surprised 'You d<u>i</u>:d?' directed at Jane (line 12).

In lines 13–16, Jane responds to this by producing a parodic second version of events in which she adopts an exaggerated facial expression with gaze to the front, eyes widened and raised towards the ceiling, and the use of her hand enacting the phone itself held to her left ear. The parody is extended here as,

48   *Ian Hutchby*

following the performed reporting of '↑D<u>o</u> what you wanna do with th<u>at</u> information talk t'y'later', Jane mimics with her hand the rapid hanging up of the phone in its cradle accompanied by the onomatopoeic 'K<u>chk</u>!' (line 17).

Playfulness and humour are once more used to reframe the seriousness of a prior account which has occasioned a hearably, and in this case, with the rapid looking back and forth, visually surprised reaction from the host. The performance on Jane's part is particularly marked, as both the words spoken and the mimed action of hanging up are nonnormative: this is manifestly not how ordinary telephone conversations between friends are ended (Schegloff and Sacks, 1973), perhaps especially not ones in which the caller has called to declare their love for the recipient.

As this sequence proceeds, the host continues to pursue an account from Jane regarding this second revelation of unrequited love for Hilly. This culminates in one more, quite exquisite episode of verbal and gestural synchrony in a performed retelling:

```
(9)  [ITV2:  7.3.07]
On stage: Host; Jane; Mike
VERBAL TRACK                              VISUAL TRACK
1  Host:  An' so you called 'er up
2         en [said what.
3  Jane:     [I loved 'er f- I loved    CU Jane, eye
4         'er fer seven years.          contact with host
5  Host:  Yeh.
6  Jane:  But I could never tell her that
7         because it was inappropriate,
8         es I was in a relationship, a:nd
9         'n she was in a relationship.
10        .hh But when the coast was clear
11        fer me:,
12 Host:  You called 'er up [and said
13 Jane:                    [I said I-    Jane and Mike
14        m-yihkn- I don' know where       Jane brushes hand
15        you're at in your relationship   across her lap
16        but ↑I ↓lur:ve ↓you::            Jane faces audience, adopts
17        (.)                              'puppy dog' expression
18 Hilly: Ehhhh huh huh
19 Jane:  >↑That's all I gotta say ↓bye.< Jane mimics hanging up
```

Initially, Jane returns in this excerpt to a serious account of events, describing how she loved Hilly for seven years but felt unable to reveal that while they were both in relationships. This is accompanied visually, once again, with the standard gaze configuration of eye-to-eye contact with the host.

From line 13 onwards, she then shifts into direct reported speech, relaying her announcement when, as the host puts it, 'You called 'er up and said . . . '. This reported speech (lines 13–16) consists of two clauses: first, 'I don' know where you're at in your relationship'; and second, 'but ↑I ↓lur:ve ↓you::'. The latter clause embodies probably the most serious part of the whole story other than Extract (6)'s 'I do believe that I'm a lesbian'. Yet it is produced in

Poetics and Performativity 49

a noticeably nonnatural verbal format, with the rather self-conscious pronunciation of '↑I ↓lur:ve ↓you::'—which also uses the kind of exaggerated pitch changes noted in previous extracts. The camera shows at this point Jane moving her face towards the front, perhaps focusing on Hilly sitting in the audience before her, and adopting a humorous 'puppy dog' expression.

But it is in the moment just prior to this, as she enunciates the phrase 'I don' know where you're at in your relationship', that the least obvious, but perhaps most exquisite example of performative talk is to be found. As she says the words, the camera switches momentarily to a longer shot showing both Jane and Mike sitting next to each other on the stage. Jane can be seen making a swift brushing movement with her right hand across her skirt, looking down at her lap, as if brushing off some fleck of dust she has noticed. Next to her on the sofa, Mike can be seen looking directly at her hand as she does this. The brushing hand movement seems to act as some kind of gestural onomatopoeia, an enacted embodiment of her literally brushing away the previous relationship, with Mike, and so clearing the way for her embarkation on the next, with Hilly.

Conclusion

This chapter began by foregrounding CA's central concerns not just with the structural aspects of turn-sequences, but the nuanced and contingent interactional projects that living, breathing humans are found to be engaging in once we look closely at the organization of talk. Jefferson's work on poetics, and what she called the wild side of CA, is rooted in a deep interest in noticing the details, sometimes mundane, sometimes bizarre, sometimes almost unnoticeable until noticed, of how interactants go about doing the things they do when talking with one another.

The chapter proposed an extended use of the term 'poetics' to mean not only word-selections, sound-connections, and lexical patterns, but also the prosodic enunciation of words, and the use of vocal, facial, and bodily modulations in the production of narrative components and receipt items. Examining data from a radio phone-in, from ordinary telephone conversation, and lastly from a televised entertainment talk show, the analysis showed various ways in which these nonnatural, performative phenomena can be deployed in pursuit of a range of nuanced and contingent projects. Primarily, they were shown to be involved in the management of potentially delicate activities: mounting a case for a complaint, finding an indirect way to launch an apology, empathizing with a friend's troubles in romance, or recounting a potentially embarrassing story about revealing secret feelings to a partner. In each of these environments, a speaker can be thought to desire affiliation and perhaps also collaboration from a recipient. Whether or not that is forthcoming is itself, of course, a contingency. Nevertheless, speakers have been shown to do considerable work in the attempt to create such environments for the activities they have it in mind to undertake. In this, the use of exaggerated, performative, and above all, parodic speech phenomena can be seen to be significant.

50   *Ian Hutchby*

Works Cited

Buchstaller, I., and van Alphen, I. (Eds.) (2012). *Quotatives: Cross-Linguistic and Cross-Disciplinary Perspectives*. Amsterdam: John Benjamins.

Coulmas, F. (Ed.) (1986). *Direct and Indirect Speech*. Berlin: De Gruyter.

Drew, P. (1997). 'Open' class repair initiators in response to sequential sources of troubles in conversation. *Journal of Pragmatics*, 28, 69–101.

Drew, P., and Bergmann, J. (2018). Introduction: Jefferson's 'wild side' of conversation analysis. In P. Drew and J. Bergmann (Eds.), *Repairing the Broken Surface of Talk: Managing Problems in Speaking, Hearing and Understanding in Conversation*. Oxford: Oxford University Press, pp. 1–26.

Goffman, E. (1974). *Frame Analysis*. Cambridge, MA: Harvard University Press.

Goffman, E. (1981). *Forms of Talk*. Philadelphia: University of Pennsylvania Press.

Golato, A. (2012). Impersonal quotation and hypothetical discourse. In I. Buchstaller and I. van Alphen (Eds.), *Quotatives: Cross-linguistic and Cross-disciplinary Perspectives*. Amsterdam: John Benjamins, pp. 3–36.

Günthner, S. (1999). Polyphony and the 'layering of voices' in reported dialogues: an analysis of the use of prosodic devices in everyday reported speech. *Journal of Pragmatics*, 31, 685–708.

Holt, E. (2007). 'I'm eyeing your chop up mind': Reporting and enacting. In E. Holt and R. Clift (Eds.), *Reporting Talk: Reported Speech in Interaction*. Cambridge: Cambridge University Press, pp. 47–80.

Holt, E., and Clift, R. (Eds.) (2007). *Reporting Talk: Reported Speech in Interaction*. Cambridge: Cambridge University Press.

Hopper, R. (1993). *Telephone Conversation*. Bloomington: Indiana University Press.

Hutchby, I. (1996). *Confrontation Talk: Arguments, Asymmetries and Power on Talk Radio*. Mahwah: Lawrence Erlbaum Associates.

Hutchby, I. (2001). Oh, irony and sequential ambiguity in arguments. *Discourse and Society*, 12, 147–165.

Ivanova, O. (2013). Constructing social norms: the pragmatics of multimodal quotation boundaries in spoken Swahili. *Journal of Pragmatics*, 57, 82–99.

Jefferson, G. (1972). Side sequences. In D. Sudnow (Ed.), *Studies in Social Interaction*. New York: Free Press, pp. 294–338.

Jefferson, G. (1974). Error correction as an interactional resource. *Language in Society*, 3, 181–199.

Jefferson, G. (1984a). Notes on some orderlinesses of overlap onset. In V. D'Urso and P. Leonardi (Eds.), *Discourse Analysis and Natural Rhetoric*. Padua, Italy: Cleup Editore, pp. 11–38.

Jefferson, G. (1984b). On stepwise transition from talk about a trouble to inappropriately next-positioned matters. In J.M. Atkinson and J. Heritage (Eds.), *Structures of Social Action: Studies in Conversation Analysis*. Cambridge: Cambridge University Press, pp. 191–222.

Jefferson, G. (1986). Notes on latency in overlap onset. *Human Studies*, 9, 153–183.

Jefferson, G. (1987). On exposed and embedded correction in conversation. In G. Button and J.R.E. Lee (Eds.), *Talk and Social Organization*. Clevedon: Multilingual Matters, pp. 86–100.

Jefferson, G. (1988). On the sequential organization of troubles talk in ordinary conversation. *Social Problems*, 35, 418–442.

Jefferson, G. (1990). List construction as a task and resource. In G. Psathas (Ed.), *Interaction Competence*. Washington, DC: University Press of America, pp. 63–92.

Poetics and Performativity 51

Jefferson, G. (1996). On the poetics of ordinary talk. *Text and Performance Quarterly*, 16, 11–61.

Jefferson, G., Sacks, H., and Schegloff, E.A. (1987). Notes on laughter in pursuit of intimacy. In G. Button and J.R.E. Lee (Eds.), *Talk and Social Organisation*. Clevedon: Multilingual Matters, pp. 152–205.

Klewitz, G., and Couper-Kuhlen, E. (1999). Quote-unquote? The role of prosody in the contextualization of reported speech sequences. *Pragmatics*, 9, 459–485.

Niemelae, M. (2005). Voiced direct reported speech in conversational storytelling: sequential patterns of stance taking. *SKY Journal of Linguistics*, 18, 197–221.

Sacks, H. (1972). An initial investigation of the usability of conversational data for doing sociology. In D. Sudnow (Ed.), *Studies in Social Interaction*. New York: Free Press, pp. 31–74.

Sacks, H. (1992). *Lectures on Conversation* (2 volumes). G. Jefferson and E.A. Schegloff (Eds.). Oxford and Cambridge, MA: Basil Blackwell.

Sacks, H., and Schegloff, E.A. (1979). Two preferences in the organization of reference to persons in conversation and their interaction. In G. Psathas (Ed.), *Everyday Language*. Hillsdale: Lawrence Erlbaum Associates, pp. 15–21.

Sacks, H., Schegloff, E.A., and Jefferson, G. (1974). A simplest systematics for the organization of turn-taking for conversation. *Language*, 50, 696–735.

Schegloff, E.A. (1968). Sequencing in conversational openings. *American Anthropologist*, 70, 1075–1095.

Schegloff, E.A. (1979). Identification and recognition in telephone conversation openings. In G. Psathas (Ed.), *Everyday Language*. Hillsdale: Lawrence Erlbaum Associates, pp. 23–78.

Schegloff, E.A. (1982). Discourse as an interactional achievement: Some uses of 'uh huh' and other things that come between sentences. In D. Tannen (Ed.), *Analyzing Discourse: Text and Talk*. Washington, DC: Georgetown University Press, pp. 71–93.

Schegloff, E.A. (1986). The routine as achievement. *Human Studies*, 9, 111–151.

Schegloff, E.A. (1992a). Introduction. In H. Sacks (Ed. G. Jefferson), *Lectures on Conversation* (Volume 1). Oxford: Blackwell, pp. ix–lxii.

Schegloff, E.A. (1992b). Introduction. In H. Sacks (Ed. G. Jefferson), *Lectures on Conversation* (Volume 2). Oxford: Blackwell, pp. ix–lii.

Schegloff, E.A. (2007). *Sequence Organization in Conversation*. Cambridge: Cambridge University Press.

Schegloff, E.A., Jefferson, G., and Sacks, H. (1977). The preference for self-correction in the organization of repair in conversation. *Language*, 53, 361–382.

Schegloff, E.A., and Sacks, H. (1973). Opening up closings. *Semiotica*, 7, 289–327.

Soulaimani, D. (2018). Talk, voice and gestures in reported speech: towards an integrated analysis. *Discourse Studies*, 20, 361–376.

Tagliamonte, S. (2005). So who? Like how? Just what? discourse markers in the conversations of young Canadians. *Journal of Pragmatics*, 37, 1896–1915.

Tagliamonte, S., and D'Arcy, A. (2005). When people say 'I was like': the quotative system in Canadian youth. *University of Pennsylvania Working Papers in Linguistics*, 10, 257–272.

2 A Walk on the Wild Side

Exploring Associations Across Topic Transition in Interaction

Elizabeth Holt

Jefferson's article 'On the Poetics of Ordinary Talk' explored a phenomenon first investigated by Sacks, which she referred to as 'most roughly, that occasionally, talk appears to be produced at least in part by reference to, e.g. sounds and associations' (1996, p. 1). She outlined a range of different kinds of associations, including sound-rows (e.g., where the same sound is repeated several times within a turn or across turns), and category-selected components, including co-class puns, where two members of the same category are referred to, but one is not used in reference to the category to which they are co-members. Jefferson presented an array of instances which persuasively suggest that sometimes turns are constructed—words selected, matters raised—due, at least in part, to various kinds of associations with prior talk.

This offers an alternative to the accepted understanding (in both lay and academic approaches to language study, such as linguistics) of how talk is formulated. Saussure's (1959) model captures this idea, where thoughts are encoded into sound-patterns and transmitted to a hearer, who then decodes the sounds into thought, as represented by the Figure 2.1.

The model suggests that the origin of what is said lies in the speaker's brain, and thus, speech is driven by expressing private thoughts. What models such as this, and lay conceptions of the way talk is produced, tend to overlook is the extent to which thoughts that lead to utterances are themselves influenced by preceding interaction, which is itself generative, influencing the selection of words and matters. Thus, a more accurate representation would depict the participants as fully immersed in the sequential environment, with less emphasis on the brain as the origin of individually generated thoughts.

According to Schegloff:

> What occurs in interaction is not merely the serial externalization into some joint arena of batches of talk hatched in private (socialized) intensions, and filled out with the docile artifacts of "language" (as in many versions of speech act theory, discourse analysis and the like). This treats the mind/brain as the scene of all action.
>
> (1989, p. 140)

DOI: 10.4324/9780429328930-4

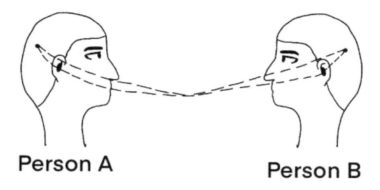

Person A   **Person B**

Figure 2.1 Based on Saussure's model of speech exchange.

He goes on to point out that what we say is shaped by the structure of social interaction: 'interaction is that for which the talk is conceived; its character is shaped by the structure of opportunities to deliver the message' (Schegloff, 1989, p. 140). Jefferson's and Sacks' work on poetics suggests a further way in which talk is profoundly shaped by interaction: that what is said (both in terms of the selection of words and phrases, and the content/subject of the talk) is triggered, at least in part, by associations (either conscious or subconscious) arising from preceding talk.

Sacks' (1995, vols. 1 & 2) discussion of tying structures and topic is also relevant to exploring how the words used and matters raised are generated by associations and connections in interaction. For instance, in one lecture he considered the process of identifying rules to explain how, within a conversation, people arrive at the words they use (1995, vol. 2, p. 341). Similarly, he discussed the emergence of topics showing how, for example, second stories can arise from the telling of a first story (see, e.g., 1995, vol. 2, pp. 305–308). His recognition of the importance of tying structures is central to understanding both the way turns-at-talk are designed to fit with prior ones, and how topic results from these processes (see Sacks, 1995, vol. 1, pp. 540–542, 716–738). Tying structures are the means participants use to display their understanding of prior talk, and in so doing forge connections and coherence across turns-at-talk. He considered the implications these have for how memory is organized and occasioned in talk (see, e.g., 1995, vol. 2, p. 299), pointing out that people can rely on interaction to occasion things to say, rather than, for example, having a list that is worked through. He argued that word-choice is highly 'historically sensitive': aspects such as prior sounds, contrasting words, and evocations of categories have an important influence on the choice of subsequent words.

54   *Elizabeth Holt*

However, his discussion often suggests a kind of purposefulness to the way these associations occur. For example, in one lecture, he said:

> we can ask, is it possible that in searching for words, people use a *history sensitive* procedure? That is, do they engage in employing recent words as a source for finding new words.
>
> (Sacks, vol. 2, p. 342)

Verbs in phrases such as '*use* a historically sensitive approach' and '*engage* in *employing*' carry connotations of deliberateness. But this imputation arises from the unavoidable implication of conscious intent conveyed by the language: people do what they do (generally) not as a result of deliberate, conscious choice, but because they must employ and are fully immersed in the interactional 'tools' and structures of their culture, which centrally organizes both their contributions to interaction and the resulting ways in which their brains function. People do not use a historically sensitive approach due to any conscious choice, but because part of the way that interaction and our brains function is to be aware of, and formulate contributions based on, prior interaction.

Taking into account the work on poetics and Sacks' observations on tying allows for a holistic view of associations across sequences and of how these arise. Jefferson demonstrates that we should consider not only how matters are introduced in either connected (i.e., tied) ways or more disjunctively, but also the kinds of associations that may lead to them being raised in the first place. Tying structures and the kinds of associations we see in her poetics article are closely related: tying focuses on how participants connect turns to prior talk; poetics focuses on how prior talk may influence the selection of words, phrases, or matters. The former suggests conscious 'work', while the latter suggests we are subconsciously influenced by preceding sounds, categories, etc. in formulating turns. But a different model of how talk is generated can encompass both, and moves away from this inappropriate distinction. In other words, what we say in interaction does not necessarily arise from our individual thoughts, but from ongoing sequences of action; and is not simply thoughts encoded in language, but contributions to action, generated by the structures and organisations provided for us by our culture, including ones that enable us to create and display the fit between a current turn or matter and a preceding one.

Jefferson referred to the aim of the chapter on poetics as 'to present the wild side: stuff which we'd pretty much kept to ourselves and played with as a hobby. The stuff was wild, not only in its content, but in its lack of organization and development' (1996, p. 2). Focusing on these associations is the 'wild side' also because the connections are rarely explicitly oriented to by speakers. Studying them can lead to speculation about cognitive aspects of language formulation, going beyond

A Walk on the Wild Side 55

the bounds of Conversation Analysis. Further, they can appear to be the product of coincidence (see Sacks, 1995, vol. 2, pp. 291–292). However, if they are part of a general pattern of tying mechanisms, it is feasible that while some are usually unnoticed (such as sound-rows) and even 'disguised' (Jefferson, 1996, p. 36), others are more obvious, sometimes oriented to by speakers and contributing to creating coherence across turns and sequences (such as the repetition of a word across turns or talking about matters related by co-membership of a category). In this chapter, I consider poetics along with tying mechanisms to argue that they are part of both the way participants design actions and how they arrive at those actions, and so, should be considered along with focusing on what participants are doing in turns.

In considering the legacy of Jefferson's work on poetics and how it may influence future research, this chapter is an initial pass at exploring how it may contribute to the analysis of the way sequences are constructed, and the connection between this and the cognitive and social practices that underpin their production. I begin by exemplifying some of these associations and their role in creating coherence within and between sequences and how talk about some matter may trigger subsequent talk. I then move to focus on various types of association around topic transitions, since this is where the relationship between a turn and prior talk is recurrently attended to as speakers initiate shifts in more or less connected ways. I end with an analysis of instances where participants appear to work to disguise the touched-off nature of the matters they introduce, suggesting orientation to the appropriacy or otherwise of revealing the historical sensitivity or their tied nature.

Poetics and Other Associations

A fundamental finding arising from the work on poetics is that the selection of a word or matter in formulating a turn may, in part, be influenced by various kinds of associations with prior talk, covering sound- and category-formed components, including puns. In this section, I present examples from my dataset to illustrate associations resulting from both phonetic and semantic connections.

The first instance contains a number of sound-flurries and other sound-associations. Dana, a friend of Gordon, and Lesley, his mother, are talking about how he is getting on at university. Repeated sounds are indicated using italics, while rhyming connections are in bold.

```
(1) [Holt: SO88(II): 2:4:1-2]
29    Les:                  [.t Oh good. c'z he w'z a bi'
30           deispondent when we w'r there(p)
31    Dan:    Yeah. He'd just had iz firs' piece of work
32           ripped apart but I think now eez gettin'
```

56   Elizabeth Holt

```
33                    use to it an::d .hhh it's uh[(    )
34      Les:                                         [.h Ye:s uh:m
35                    'n I: think (.) p'raps uh he took it to
36                    heart . .h[hhh
37      Dan:                    [Yeah
38      Les:          Ehm (0.4) .t.kh ↑Ri:ght. Well. He said to let
39                    you know that- (0.2) to drop in any time.=
40      Dan:          =[Yeh.
41      Les:          =[eh↑heh heh heh he:[h..hhhh
42      Dan:                              [Well I'll pop over
43                    the[n.((smile))
44      Les:             [ihYes.
45                    (.)
46      Les:          .hh O[kay .hh ↑If you could (.) le' (.) me have that=
47      Dan:               [(    )
48      Les:          =book u-so:[me (.) back sometime becuz I promised it=
49      Dan:                     [Yeah
50      Les:          =to- to: Peter.
51                    (0.3)
52      Dan:          Oh yea[h.
53      Les:                [uh::: becuz he's looking up colleges as well.
54      Dan:          Yea[h
55      Les:             [.hhh[]
56      Dan:                  []I[(s this) um
57      Les:                     [S:e-
58                    (0.3)
59      Dan:          (I didn't) go recently becuz I've bee:n .hh
60                    bouncing between: dean:s an:-
```

In the extract there are multiple sound-flurries. Up until line 36, in particular, there is repeated use of the t-sound (note, however, that in some words, although the letter is included in the spelling, it is rarely pronounced: these have not been italicized). Other sound-flurries occur in more limited sections. In line 30, Lesley describes Gordon as '*de↓spondent*'. This repeats the d-, s-, and t-sounds that have been prevalent in prior turns, but also begins a flurry of p-sounds: 'He'd jus*t* *had* iz firs' *pi*ece of work ri*pp*ed a*p*art'. There is a rhyme between this and the next turn, with Dana saying 'ripped apart' and Lesley saying 'took it to heart'. There is also a rhyming association between 'drop' (line 39) and 'pop' (line 42). Line 48 begins a flurry of b-sounds that extends to line 60, joined with a row of ee-sounds in Dana's turn at lines 59–60, which results in the rhyme in 'been' and 'deans'.

In the following extract, there are both phonetic and semantic associations. Joan and Lesley are discussing financial problems. After saying that they are both doing competitions in order to earn money, Lesley refers to an acquaintance's method for bringing in some extra finance by making decorations out of hard-baked dough. The Pools is a competition based on predicting football results, and ERNIE is the name of the computer that randomly selects savings bonds for prizes.

A Walk on the Wild Side   57

```
(2) [Holt:X(C)2:1:2:9-10]
1   Joa:    I: [↑in the mea]:ntime I'm [relyin' on the pools'n
2           Ern[ie.
3   Les:       [↑(        )-]
4   Les:    Oh: ye- I've done a few compe↓titions hheh[ha
5   Joa:                                              [↑Ye:s I'm:
6           doing competi↓tion so[rt'v thi:ng °(        )°
7   Les:                          [How ↑'bout Helene's idea. she's
8           doing this uhm (0.5)dou:gh.
9              (.)
10  Joa:    ↑Yes she ↑i:s. isn't she.
11             (.)
12  Les:    I ↑think they're having- (0.2) I think they're having
13          a sticky ti:me [aren't they.]
14  Joa:                   [ Oh: are the]y?
15          (0.5)
16  Les:    Y[es.
17  Joa:    [Oo:: dear,=
18  Les:    =Think s[o,
19  Joa:            [Well we're all in the same boa:t, I'm
20          quite miserable this Christmas.
```

Lesley assesses the family's financial situation as 'having a sticky ti:me' (line 13). Thus, there is a punning relationship between 'dough' and 'sticky'. Further, 'dough' is a common colloquialism for money, so connects to the ongoing discussion in this way too. Notice also the repeat of the 'done' and 'doing' in previous turns, the d-sound possibly also having an influence on the selection of 'dough'.

Analysis of these two extracts supports the work on poetics in suggesting that phonetic and semantic associations can influence the selection of subsequent words and phrases. Holt's investigation of idiomatic phrases (1991, chap. 4) provides further evidence and suggests that it is possible to distributionalize their occurrence in terms of the sequential organizations of talk. Holt found that a number of these phrases formed puns on previous talk as a result of a congruence between a literal meaning of the phrase and an element of prior talk. These idiomatic expressions recurrently occurred at topic terminations (Drew and Holt, 1998). The following is a case in point.

```
(3) [Holt:2:3:9]  (Holt, 1991, p. 130)
1   Ste:    Ye[ah well there you are: nob'ddy has a (.) perfect=
2   Les:      [.TCH!
3   Ste:    =life s[o
4   Les:           [ehhh heh[heh .hh
5   Ste:                    [.tch
6   Ste:    Well he didn't either 'ee had a bad start (I mean)
7           'ee had iz (0.3) .t.k.hh father shot by the Nazis 'nd
8           iz uh .hh mother died in: Auschvitz
9           yih kno:w [so
10  Les:              [Oh really:?=
```

58 Elizabeth Holt

```
11  Ste:    =So eez [had the: (   ]   )-
12  Les:            [Oh 'z a Je:w] is he Je:w?
13           (.)
14  Ste:    Oh yeah.
15           (.)
16  Ste:    He's had k- eez a Czechoslovakian Jew
17           so [eez had k- eez had=
18  Les:        [Yes
19  Ste:    =quite a- checkered career already=
20  Les:    =eh heh
21  Ste:    .hhhh[Yeah
22  Les:         [Ye:h.
23           (0.2)
24  Les:    .h[hh Alri:ght. Well I:'ll ↑get my husband then:=
25  Ste:      [.TCH!
26  Les:    =to get in touch with the add↓ress.=
27  Ste:    =Thanks [very[mu:ch.
```

It is possible that in casting around for an idiom to summarize the talk and bring it to a close, Steven may be influenced by the previous use of 'Czechoslovakian' in his selection of 'checkered career', and, as a result comes up with this expression as a summary of prior talk.[1] Idiomatic phrases are highly historically sensitive in that they draw from the previous talk to provide a summary, but the recurrence of punning associations suggests that less obvious connections (e.g., between a literal meaning of the phrase and some element of the topic) may also influence their selection.

Having shown how categories and sounds in talk can lead to the selection of associated words and phrases, Jefferson turns her attention to what she calls 'triggered topics', where sounds and categories may 'select something like a train of thought, to generate what can turn out to be a considerable chunk of conversation' (1996, p. 36). She analyses the following extract where a sound—'part'—leads to talking about a 'party'.

(4)[TCI(b):16:11-12] (Jefferson, 1996, p. 37)
```
1    Joa:    =[My biggest thing is tryintuh figure out howtuh
2            cut the neck en around th'ears.
3    Lin:    Yea[h,
4    Joa:       [That's the hard phha(h)a(h)art=
5    Lin:    =Yeah,=
6    Joa:    =.m.hhhhh without makin it look yihknow c'z I
7            c'n take the scissors'n cut right around iz
8            ears but then yih c'n rilly tell it.=
9    Lin:    =[Yeah.]
10   Joa:    =[too:.]So,
11   Lin:    Ye[ah,
12   Joa:      [.t.hhhh that's (.) the part. I gotta figure
13            out howtih do:,hh
14   Lin:    Yah how much didju git et yer gift'n gadget
15            party,
16           (.)
```

```
17    Joa:        .hhhhhhh uh::: u-sevendy I think it wa:s=
18    Lin:        =Hm:. .hh I hadda pretty good party .hhhh
19                uh quite a few people came,
```

Jefferson (1996, p. 37) pointed out that the possibly pun-generated word 'part' (line 4) may engender talk about the party, beginning in lines 14–15. She suggested that Linda designs her turn to show that it is an ordinary topic change rather than a sound-generated one, arguing that 'it may be the case that if it's *not* the sort of triggering that is accepted as rational and legitimate, then it is not acknowledged to have been the triggering' (unlike triggerings that may be acknowledged through something like 'speaking of X'). Jefferson argued that the introduction of the new topic is carefully managed in order to tell the recipient how to hear it and not to hear it as 'a noise fathering a thought' (1996, p. 36). She pointed out that the compacted 'Yah' in line 14. which initiates the new topic may be used to 'show the agenda'd character of the new topic; to show if anything, that she was hardly listening to what Joan was saying' (1996, p. 36).

Analysis of these extracts supports the finding that words are selected and even matters raised as a result of associations with preceding talk. Considering different kinds of associations, including both those explored in Jefferson's chapter and the tying techniques identified by Sacks, allows us to see both how coherence is created across talk—i.e., how sequences are made to cohere—and how various kinds of associations can lead to their generation.

Associations and Topic Transitions

Sacks (1995, vol. 2, pp. 343–344) and Jefferson (1996) suggested that poetic connections do not occur with uniform distribution across conversations, but are associated with specific positions within sequences. According to Sacks,

> my feeling is that you ought to be allowing the possible development of a picture in which at some point in utterance sequences people are partially assembling their talk . . . out of what they've already built. They're doing some sorts of recombinations and are exceedingly sensitive to historical development and extensions on what they've said so far. And this is not talking about it in terms of what they topically say, but, for whatever they say, in terms at least of where they get the words they're using.
>
> (1995, vol. 2, p. 324)

He suggested that they may cluster towards the ends of topics. Jefferson analyzed an instance where the sound-flurry ends at a sub-topic shift and another where it ends at a topical boundary, suggesting that they may respect topic boundaries. Thus, it is pertinent to investigate the relationship between associations and topic boundaries, in terms of whether historical sensitivity is

60   *Elizabeth Holt*

recurrent towards the end of topics, associations cross boundaries, and whether there is any distinction between the kinds of associations (e.g., relating to poetics or content) that are more or less likely to cross boundaries.

Around these boundaries, participants often most clearly orient to the connection between matters as they work to introduce something in a way that is either tied to previous talk, or disjunctive with it. A productive approach is thus to analyse associations across turns-at-talk where transitions are managed. Therefore, I now turn to an examination of various kinds of topic changes, focusing on how connections and coherence are forged and, alternatively, how speakers introduce new matters in ways that frame them as unconnected to prior talk. I begin by showing that participants can initiate new matters in more or less connected ways—presenting the two ends of the spectrum, from stepwise to disjunctive transitions.

Topic Transitions and Tying Mechanisms

Sacks' interest in tying came from the recognition that the notion of topic in conversation is problematic: although we might presume that the fact that conversations are organized into topics is straightforward, in fact, identifying topics is fraught with difficulties (Schegloff, 1990, p. 52). Sacks, instead, began with the question how do persons 'show respect for topic' (1995, vol. 1, p. 538). Rather than trying to identify the content of sequences of talk as a way of pinning down the topic, he concluded that topical organization is a consequence of these tying structures. Sacks gave the example of 'pro-terms' (such as the replacement of a noun with 'it' in a following turn) as one of these tying structures. By employing such tying structures, participants orient to topic, and, as Sidnell noted, it is therefore 'possible to locate a set of practises in conversation by which topics are generated, maintained, pursued and so on' (2010, p. 226).

Topic transitions in conversation rarely have clear-cut boundaries; rather, the participants link each new matter to the previous, such that a range of matters may be discussed without any overt termination of one prior to the introduction of a next one. This is stepwise movement (Sacks, 1995, vol. 2, p. 566; Jefferson, 1984), or topic shading (Schegloff and Sacks, 1973). In this way, the relevance of matters ('why that now?') is made clear (Sacks, 1995, vol. 1, p. 542). The next extract exemplifies stepwise transition. It comes from the near the beginning of a weekly catch-up call between Lesley and her mother. Just before, Mum explains that she has rung on an unusual day because she will be going to church the following evening. This leads on to talk about the weather.

```
(5)[Holt:1:8 1-2]
1   Les:    Oh:- You know we had snow this evening,
2   Mum:    So did we::.
3   Les:    Ye::[s.
```

A Walk on the Wild Side 61

```
 4  Mum:            [We had th'most awful hai:l storm this afternoo:n
 5  Les:    Oh:.
 6  Mum:    Wz like u-half crow::ns c[oming dow]n.
 7  Les:                            [Y e : :s.]
 8  Les:    Ye:s.
 9           (0.3)
10  Mum:    Terrible weather fer this time a'the ye[a:r,]
11  Les:                                           [I kn]o:::w,
12           (0.3)
13  Les:    I [mean flowers are not coming out are the:y.
14  Mum:      [Mm:.
15  Mum:    ↑No::. No:.
16           (0.7)
17  Mum:    Got couple of daffodils out in the ga[:rden] ( )
18  Les:                                          [Oh I ]haven't,
19           (.)
20  Mum:    Hm:. .h An' s'm crocuses [b't[ not a lot at a:l[l.
21  Les:                             [.h [Yes            [.h
22  Les:    Well we have snowdrops'n the cro:cuses look all
23           battered,
24           (.)
25  Mum:    Ye[s.
26  Les:      [An' I've got a few scyllas ou:t.=
27  Mum:    =Isn'it a shame.
28  Les:    Ye:s.
29           (.)
30  Mum:    that you:- look forward to'm they come out'n then they
31           get- battered tuh pie[ces.
32  Les:                          [Ye:s.
33  Mum:    Mm[:.
34  Les:      [I, I pruned a few roses t'day'n gave them some
35           manu:re,
36           (0.6)
37  Mum:    ( ) good.
38  Les:    Ah:,hh (1.6) But then Mar- ah:-:,h (_) then I've run
39           out've it s:o anyway m-uh- aa-Mark's coming home
40           t'morrow so .hh he'll mix me suh mo:re if
41           he [thinks:
42  Mum:       [(          ) compound it was?=
43  Les:    =Yes.
44           (0.9)
45  Mum:    T'morrow ni:ght?
46           (.)
47  Les:    Uh: five uh'clock t'morrow.
48  Mum:    .hh E:vening.
49           (0.3)
50  Les:    Yes.
51  Mum:    (          ), oh ( [          )
52  Les:                      [So I expect they:'ll be: um:
53           travelin:g (0.5) Well what happen:s they usually get
54           up about two uh' clock in the morning,
55  Mum:    Oh: yes.
56           (1.1)
57  Mum:    Ye:h when Miriam goe:s she (.) she hastuh set off at
```

62   Elizabeth Holt

```
58                three uh'clock in the mo:rn[ing,
59   Les:                                  [Ye:s.=
60   Mum:    But it's (.) it is a nuisance.
61           (0.6)
62   Les:    .t Yes well they had to .hh[h
63   Mum:                                [Ye:s.=
64   Les:    =But they didn't (0.7) e-have to: get there til:
65           (1.2) three at u-three thirty. uh .h It was
66           gon't'be o:ne thirty but (.) that seemed too early.
67           so they made it three thirty
68           (1.8)
69   Mum:    'T's'n awful time t'get up isn'it.
70   Les:    Ye(h)es
```

At line 13, talk of the bad weather leads Lesley to observe that the flowers are not coming out. Following this, there are several turns relating to the flowers in their gardens (lines 17–26). Lesley talks about pruning the roses and giving them manure, then mentions that she has now run out of manure. There is a lull with a pause, an assessment from Mum, Lesley's 'Ah:,hh', a long pause, and then Lesley continues on the subject of manure with 'But then Mar- ah:-:,h ( ) then I've run out've it s:o anyway m-uh- aa-Mark's coming home t'morrow so .hh he'll mix me suh mo:re if he thinks:', using the pro-term 'it' and ellipsis after 'more'. Thus, by way of talking about manure, she refers to her husband Mark and his return home on the following day (he is currently abroad). Mum appears to ask something relating the manure in line 42, then after a small lull topicalizes the news of Mark's return with the elliptical 'T'morrow ni:ght?'. There then follows talk about Mark's return, specifically in terms of the time of leaving. In lines 57–58, Mum mentions that her granddaughter also has to leave early in the morning when she goes abroad (possibly also skiing), but Lesley gives a minimal response and Mum produces a general assessment. In line 62, Lesley returns the talk to her husband (and son, who has gone with him) by comparing their early departure for the return with their leaving arrangements.

Thus, over these turns, the speakers move from talking about the weather and the spring flowers in their gardens, to the return of Lesley's husband and son, and then to their outward journey. The reference to Mark making up more manure on his return acts as a pivot between talk about the garden and his return, pro-terms and ellipsis connecting it to prior talk. But nowhere is the coherence of turns disrupted, and therefore nowhere does it become salient to wonder why a participant refers to a certain matter at any point; the relevance of each new subject accrues from its connection with prior talk.

It is not always the case that new turns are tied to previous ones and that coherence is maintained across talk; interactional affordances accrue to dislodging the tying and creating breaks in the coherence in order to introduce new matters or sequences. These occur at disjunctive topic transitions (Drew and Holt, 1998). They are less common than stepwise transitions and,

A Walk on the Wild Side 63

according to Sacks, may be an indication of a less successful conversation (Sacks, 1995, vol. 2, p. 566). In disjunctive transitions, speakers include turn-initials that indicate that the new turn is not related to the prior talk. These include 'anyway', 'well', 'but', and 'by the way'. In Extract (6), there is a disjunctive turn beginning with 'Anyway' at line 15. Prior to and at the start, Lesley is telling her mother about the death of an acquaintance at the age of seventy-nine. This is followed by talk about recently experiencing a 'good evening'.

```
(6)  [Holt:X(C)85:1:1:6]
1    Les:    ...He wz a (0.2) .p a buyer for the hoh- i- the
2            only horse hair fact'ry left in England.
3    Mum:    Good gracious,
4            (0.3)
5    Les:    And he wz their buyer,
6            (.)
7    Mum:    Hm:::
8    Les:    .t
9    Mum:    Hm:.
10   Les:    So he had a good inni:ngs did[n't he.
11   Mum:                                 [I should say so:
12           Ye:s.
13           (0.2)
14   Mum:    Marvellous,
15   Les:    .tk .hhhh Anyway we had a very good evening on
16           Saturda:y.
```

Talking about a death in interaction can be delicate and, even though Lesley ends on a positive idiomatic summary of his life (Drew and Holt, 1998), transitioning to talking about a good time may need to be handled carefully (Holt, 1993). Thus, introducing the new topic in a highly disjunctive fashion may result from sensitivity to the nature of these matters. (Notice, however, a poetic connection between 'good innings' and 'good evening').

Many topic shifts fall somewhere between the extremes of disjunctive and stepwise transitions. Often a topic pivots on a single turn, word, or phrase (Holt and Drew, 2005; Sacks, 1995, vol. 2, p. 300). There is a noticeable shift in focus, but the coherence is not dislodged, as tying links the new matter to the previous. Connections are recurrently created through the use of repeated words or phrases, use of pro-terms and ellipsis. In Extract (7), the repetition of 'move' contributes to creating coherence as speakers transition to talking about a new matter. Joan has been discussing her family's financial problems resulting from the fact that her husband has not been paid his bonus.

```
(7) [Holt:X(C)2:1:2:5]
1    Joa:    [you[know why:, we're just haffing
2            to (.) cut th'corners everywhere now,
4    Les:    iYes:.[ Yes I ]qui[te agree.]
```

64 Elizabeth Holt

```
 5   Joa:         [y'kno:w]      [ or even ]↑mo:ve, wh(h)o kno:ws
 6   Joa:    .he: .eh-[.e .hh
 7   Les:         [Oh you ↑mus[n't mo:ve,
 8   Joa:                     [eh e-he
 9            (.)
10   Joa:    ↑Oh::: ↓well,
11            (.)
12   Joa:    get a smaller place
13            (.)
14   Joa:    I wouldn't mind doin' that (it's less work) but the
15           other two aren't interested.
16   Les:    Oh I ↑love your hou[:se,
17   Joa:                       [Yehh:: Yes I like it very much.
18           But um (0.4) it keeps us poo:r.
```

At the start of this extract, Joan uses a summary idiomatic phrase 'just haff-ing to (.) cut th'corners everywhere now'. Lesley comes in with an elaborate affiliation, while Joan overlaps her with a continuation 'y'kno:w or even ↑mo:ve, wh(h)o kno:ws', followed by a few beats of laughter. In so doing she introduces a new matter connected with her trouble—that they may need to move to save costs. In line 7, Lesley topicalizes this with 'Oh you ↑musn't mo:ve,'. Thus, she repeats 'move' (rather than saying, e.g., 'you mustn't' or 'you mustn't do that'). This becomes the focus of the talk as Joan responds with reasons for moving to a smaller house, and Lesley positively assesses their current house.

Here, a transition from one related matter to the next is managed through a pivotal turn that begins with a summary idiom and then brings in a new matter that is a possible solution to the problem. The mention of moving becomes the focus of ongoing talk. The repetition of 'move' contributes to constituting this as a connected, but nevertheless new matter—i.e., use of ellipsis or a pro-term (as in 'you mustn't' or 'you mustn't do that') linking it more thoroughly to prior talk.

But along with these tying mechanisms, notice, too, the poetic link between the prior talk and the new one: in summarising the economizing measures that Joan and her family are having to take, she arrives at an apposite metaphorical depiction of downsizing—'cut the corners'—just prior to introducing this as a further measure they are considering.

In this instance, there is a connected transition. There is no dislodging of the tying as there is in Extract (6), but nor is there such a gradual stepwise transition as in Extract (5).

In summarizing their financial difficulties, Joan possibly arrives at the idiom 'cut the corners', which may remind her of a possible solution (or upshot of their difficulties)—moving house. There is a poetic link between the metaphorical cutting of corners and a literal meaning of the expression—reducing the size of your house being a literal 'cutting of corners'. Thus, tying and poetic associations contribute to the connected transition from one matter to the next, and it is possible that the idiom may play a role in the generation of a new matter.

A Walk on the Wild Side   65

In order to explore further how various kinds of associations influence the way matters are raised and designed and how speakers orient to issues of coherence across transitions, in the next section, I consider how these are introduced and tied to prior turns, the poetic links that reveal the way participants are historically sensitive to previous talk, and how they make use of the resources available to generate further talk.

Associations and Topic Transitions

In this section, I analyze a range of associations across different kinds of topic transitions. Considering various kinds of associations (including poetic connections and tying mechanisms) enables us to begin to see how these play a part in respecting topics at points where participants orient to these matters as they move from one to the next in more or less disjunctive ways.

I begin with an example of stepwise transition, managed, in part, through the use of several co-class members ('address', 'letter', 'write to', and 'visit') as well as a punning co-class connection between 'flooding' and 'damn',[2] contributing to the maintenance of coherence across this transition. Dana is a friend of Lesley's son, Gordon. He and most of their other friends have just left the area to move to university. Lesley and Dana talk about where several friends have gone and whether Gordon has their new addresses. At the start of the extract, they are talking about Norm, who has just moved to his new accommodation.

```
(8) [Holt: SO88(II): 2:4:6]
1   Dan:  So: (.) an' Gordon is quite chuffed about all this
2         (0.2) an' I think Norm's goin' to write t'him
3         (.)
4   Les:  He-[Oh good.
5   Dan:     [He's got the address. anyway
6   Les:  eeY[es.
7   Dan:     [And um
8         (0.4)
9   Dan:  he's sending out ay- all these little um (0.3)
10        change'v address cards=
11  Les:  =Oh Norm is,
12        (.)
13  Dan:  Yeah.
14  Les:  Oh how s[ w e e t]
15  Dan:          [He's in:c]redibly organ[ized['n
16  Les:                                  [.hh [hYe:s. Ye:s.
17  Dan:  So, (.) an' so I'm geh:- gett'n all these letters
18  Dan:  flooding in 'n I'm-
19        (0.2)
20  Les:  ↑tehh!
21  Dan:  t(h)ry(h)na keep u(h)p wi[th it.
22  Les:                           [ehh↑heh heh[eh-heh-eh-heh]=
23  Dan:                                       [I've got so many]=
```

66 Elizabeth Holt

```
24   Les:   =[.hhhhhh
25   Dan:   =[damn people to wri:te[to
26   Les:                          [↑Oh: ye:s. Yes[lovely.
27   Dan:                                          [(    )
28   Les:   And visit hheh ha huh-[e h - h u h .hhhh].t]
```

Over this sequence, there is a stepwise transition from talk about Norm and whether Gordon has his new address to Dana going to visit those who have left (following the extract, they move to talking about visiting Gordon). Within the sequence there are a series of shifts of focus: for instance, after talking about Norm sending out notifications of his new address, Dana moves to discussing the fact that she is getting lots of letters 'flooding in'. In lines 23 and 25, she does a non-fully serious complaint with 'I've got so many damn people to write to' (Glenn and Holt, 2019). Thus, there is a co-category connection between 'flooding' and a homophone of 'damn'. There are also co-category members throughout this sequence—'address', 'letters', and 'people to write to', the final one making possible a contextually created opposition with 'visit'. Repetition of words helps to provide coherence, including 'address' in lines 5 and 10, which connects the reference to Gordon having Norm's new address to the mention of him sending out notifications. Pro-terms also maintain the coherence, including the use of 'he's' (line 15) linking back to the references to Norm, and 'it' in line 21, which implicitly connects to the mention of the letters and the implication that she needs to respond.

Various associations thus contribute to maintaining the coherence across these turns as the speakers manage a change in topic from Gordon having Norm's address to Dana going to visit Gordon. These associations arise from both the tying mechanisms, and from other kinds of historical sensitivity of speakers to their own and previous speaker's turns. But the question arises: do any of these kinds of associations occur in disjunctive transitions, where a new matter is introduced in a way that is not tied to the prior one? As we saw previously, Sacks and Jefferson suggest that sound-flurries may respect topic boundaries. The following extract suggests that, though a speaker may work to introduce a new matter in an unconnected way, sound-flurries indicate some association. The excerpt comes at the end of the call between Lesley and Dana. Lesley initiates closing-relevant talk by mentioning that she will tell Gordon that she and Dana have been in touch when she next speaks to him.

(9) [Holt:S88:2:10:6–7]
```
1   Les:   .hhhh ↑Oh:goo:d. Well↑ (.) anyway I'll be able
2           t'tell Gordon I've ↓heard from you the:n,?
3   Les:   .hh[hh
4   Dan:      [Right.
5          (.)
6   Les:   And uh:m I'll send 'im your ↓love sh[all I:?
7   Dan:                                       [(  ) Yah.
8   Les:   O:ka:y a[n:d uh ]
```

```
 9  (Ski):                [mgh mgh]-m[ghh.
10  Dan:                       [I'll (.) Tell 'im I'll (0.2) 'n
11           kee-hee-keep im on 'iz toes tell 'im I'll call 'im
12           sometime
13  Les:     ↑ehhh hhe ↓hu:h ha ha-e-hu-e .hhh hhh [Oka(h)y
14  Dan:                                           [(      )
15  Les:     .hh He'll behave 'imself then. ((smile voice))
16           .hhh[h ↑a-]
17  Dan:         [ R i ]:[ght.
18  Les:                 [Ahh hhah, And em: .tch ↓Yes. Oh so we'll
19           ↑↑see you sometime Dana,
20           (.)
21  Dan:     Yeahp.
22           (.)
23  Les:     eh-We'll ↑keep the kettle ↓on.
24           (0.3)
25  Les:     ↑Bye bye the[n
26  Dan:                 [Bye:,
```

After asking whether she should send Gordon Dana's love (line 6), Dana agrees
and continues with 'I'll', which may be the start of 'I'll call him sometime', but
she breaks off and adds "'n kee-hee-keep 'im on 'iz toes'. Thus, there is a repetition of the k- and e-sounds. The k-sound occurs again in 'call'. Lesley does
a breathy acknowledgment, says 'Oka(h)y' then adds to the joke with 'He'll
behave imself then'. In line 18, after the breathy acknowledgement, Lesley produces 'And em:', thus apparently maintaining coherence to produce a connected
turn. However, she breaks off, then does a '.tch' and '↓Yes.'. She then initiates
the new matter in a more disjunctive way, mainly through the unit-initial 'Oh'.
She maintains the closing relevance by referring to seeing Dana (repeating
'sometime') in line 19. However, this is a formulaic-sounding invitation. Earlier
in the call, she has invited Dana to visit. The invitation is strengthened in line
23 with 'We'll ↑keep the kettle ↓on.', which also refers to the fact that Dana
would be calling on Lesley, and gives some clues about the type of visit (i.e.,
dropping in for a cup of tea, rather than a more formal visit, etc.). In doing so,
Lesley repeats 'keep' and repeats the k-sound in 'kettle'. Thus, it is possible
that, in adding to her formulaic invitation, Lesley is influenced by the previous
repetition of these sounds, creating a sound-flurry association across talk that
is constituted as disjunctive. Furthermore, there is a sound-flurry involving an
s-sound in Lesley's initiation of the new matter (note that Dana is a pseudonym
and the actual name begins with s) which occurs within the launch of the new
sequence.

There are certain connections between the matters: in both, Lesley looks ahead
to future arrangements (common in closing-relevant talk [Button, 1990, 1991]),
and in lines 10–12, Dana refers to when she will contact Lesley's son, which potentially links with when she will next see Lesley. Further, in lines 11 and 12, Dana
says 'I'll call im sometime', which sounds similar to 'I'll call in sometime' (earlier
in the call Lesley invites her saying 'please ca:ll:'). Thus, associations across the

68 *Elizabeth Holt*

extract suggest some coherence, despite the somewhat disjunctive introduction of the invitation.

A look at a longer excerpt from Extract (1) also suggests that while some sound-flurries may indeed end at topic boundaries, other kinds of associations continue, thus contributing to making this a somewhat less disjunctive transition than would otherwise have been the case.

```
(1) [Continuation]
38   Les:   Ehm (0.4) .t.kh ↑Ri:ght. Well. He said to le⌐
39          you know that- (0.2) to drop in any time.=
40   Dan:   =[Yeh.
41   Les:   =[eh↑heh heh heh he:[h..hhhh
42   Dan:                      [Well I'll pop over
43          the[n.((smile))
44   Les:      [ihYes.
45          (.)
46   Les:   .hh O[kay .hh ↑If you could (.) le' (.) me have that=
47   Dan:        [( )
48   Les:   =book u-so:[me (.) back sometime becuz I promised it=
49   Dan:             [Yeah
50   Les:   =to- to: Peter.
51          (0.3)
52   Dan:   Oh yea[h.
53   Les:         [uh::: becuz he's looking up colleges as well.
54   Dan:   Yea[h
55   Les:      [.hhh[]
56   Dan:          []I[(s this) um
57   Les:              [S:e-
58          (0.3)
59   Dan:   (I didn't) go recently becuz I've bee:n .hh
60          bouncing between: dean:s an:-
61   Les:   .pltchAh that's alright we've been away a:nyway
62   (Dan): °( [ )°
63   Les:        [It'd be nice to see you
64          again,  .hhh[hhhh]↓.hhhhhhh
65   Dan:               [Okay]right I'll pop round some(time)
66          (.)
67   Dan:   I can't guarantee ↓when becuz
68   Les:   ↑OH no that's alrigh[t,
```

In line 46, Lesley does a shift to request the return of a book she has leant to Dana (a guide to universities). She does this in a somewhat disjunctive way: there is a short pause, then the disjunct marker following an inbreath ('.hh Okay'). It is possible that this could have been done in a more connected way, for e.g., 'when you do pop in can you bring the book' or 'talking of popping in . . .'.[3] However, this might imply that Lesley had been somewhat devious in getting Dana to agree to come over (if indeed this is what the previous talk does), in a non-serious way, but then: (a) treating it a serious acceptance and (b) potentially implying that the invitation was made in order to secure the return of the book.

A Walk on the Wild Side 69

Interestingly, at this juncture, the p- and t-flurries continue, but then stop at line 50, where Lesley mentions the name of the person she has promised the book to—'Peter' (original name). At this point, a new flurry is initiated with multiple uses of b-sounds, starting from the first mention of the book—'*b*ook u-s<u>o</u>:me (.) *b*ack s<u>o</u>me*t*ime *b*ecuz'—and continued in Dana's account—'*b*ecuz I've *b*ee:n .hh *b*oun<u>c</u>ing *b*etween: dean:s'. Notice that in line 65 Dana says 'I'll *pop* round some(*t*ime)', thus repeating her 'pop' from line 42 and Lesley's 'time' from line 39 and 'sometime' from line 48. Thus, there are poetic alignments in Dana's turns at a point where Lesley's request introduces potential social misalignment.

Thus, this extract suggests that, although some flurries may be limited to a few turns, others can extend through longer segments and even cross topic boundaries. Other associations also cross topic boundaries—e.g., the repeat of 'pop' and 'time'—as participants may be influenced by prior talk, whether or not it is constructed as part of the same topic. This could be the case in this extract, where, although Lesley uses a disjunct to dislodge the tying between the joking invitation and her request for the book, there are connections between them that may, in part, result in these associations.

The final extract in this section demonstrates that a complex web of associations can provide coherence across, and may play a part in generating, a topic shift and that participants orient to the connection of new matters in managing these transitions. In Excerpt (10), Lesley begins to introduce a related matter in a highly connected way, but breaks off to do it more disjunctively. Joan and Lesley have been discussing their money troubles and various ways of trying to improve their financial situations. At the start of the extract, Joan is exploring the possibility of earning some money through knitting.

```
(10)[Holt:X(C)2:1:2:8-9]
1    Joa:   [I mean I c]'n knit 'n (.) an' do that
2           sorta thing. 'n I know someb'dy 'oo made a lot with a
3           knittin' machine.
4           (.)
5    Les:   iYes.
6           (0.4)
7    Joa:   Made it a proper business: you know (            ),
8           .hhhh (0.2) But ↑ba:sic'ly (0.7) u-h you know, u-it
9           js wouldn't ↑suit me that sorta thing I doh- I think
10          I- if I wz at ho:me I'd be doin' (.) house↑work. 'n I
11          wouldn' be able a'get (.) stuck into[it.
12   Les:                                       [No:. I know ah-
13          it's the seh- .hhh I- I [make silhouettes you know.=
14   Joa:                           [(      )
15   Les:   =[an'
16   Joa:   =[Do you,
17          (.)
18   Joa:   Yes,
19   Les:   And they look (.) really an↑ti[que
20   Joa:                                 [ukh-hih ukhh
```

70   Elizabeth Holt

```
21              (0.9)
22  Les:    But um
23              (0.7)
24  Les:    't's ↑not worth my while selling them[becuz
25  Joa:                                          [Ohh no:[:.
26  Les:                                                  [people
27          c'n ↑buy them for about four pounds fifty in[the shops.]
28  Joa:                                                 [That's it.]
29  Joa:    That's i[t, (yeah.)
30  Les:            [you know made by machine.
31              (.)
32  Joa:    That's it.
33  Les:    Mm[:.
34  Joa:      [Ye:h,
```

Joan raises the possibility of earning money through knitting, before discarding it due to working at home not suiting her. In line 12, Lesley affiliates with 'No:. I kno̱w'. After the cut off 'ah-', she then moves on with 'it's the seh-'. As Jefferson points out in a footnote on the transcript, this could be the start of 'It's the same' or 'It's the selling' (which she goes on to discuss in line 24). However, she breaks off, takes an audible in-breath, and then says 'I- I make silhouettes you know', thus introducing the matter in a less connected way. She then goes on to follow a similar format to Joan's previous telling: stating something she can do (a craft skill), but then pointing out why this is not a viable option for earning extra income.

Lesley possibly begins to introduce the matter as connected to the previous (especially if she was saying 'It's the same', though even 'It's the selling of them' frames the new matter as connected), but repairs to convey it as less connected (though still not disjunctively introduced, so still suggesting some connection with the prior talk). If it is the first possibility, it may be that Lesley realizes what she is saying is not quite the same—Joan's problem was not to do with not being able to sell the products at enough to make much profit. If it was the second possibility, it could be that she repairs in order to introduce the most salient fact first—i.e., she creates silhouettes, before moving on to discuss problems in selling them.

However, there are other associations here that may play a role in the selection and design of the introduction of this matter. One concerns the mention of 'machine' in 'knitting machine' (line 3). Lesley frames her problem in earning money from a craft activity as stemming from the fact that silhouettes can be purchased from the shops for a small amount of money because they are 'made by machine' (line 30). This formulation of the problem seems odd: something like 'mass produced' or 'printed' would be more appropriate. It is possible that Lesley is influenced by the mention of 'machine' earlier in the sequence: she may be aware (subconsciously or otherwise) of a rather different kind of link—i.e., the knitting machine facilitates the successful business, but machine-produced silhouettes mean that she cannot compete in price.

A Walk on the Wild Side 71

These connections concern the content of the talk, but there are also poetic associations that may contribute to the selection and delivery of this topic. In the turn immediately before Lesley's shift, there is a flurry of s-sounds in Joan's turn (lines 7–11). In introducing the new matter, there is also repeated use of s-sounds in Lesley's turn, including beginning 'seh-' and 'silhouettes'. Repetition of words from Joan's turns also characterizes Lesley's telling, including 'know' (lines 12, 13 and 30, connecting with Joan's use in 2, 7, and 8) and 'made'/'make' (Lesley's 'make' in line 13, reflecting Joan's 'made' in lines 2 and 7). (Notice also the sound-row in line 27, repetition of f- and fo-sounds possibly leading to the selection of this hypothetical price.)

Thus, there are a range of connections, both in terms of the content and the delivery of the talk across this transition. Lesley initially introduces the new matter in a way that frames it as very closely connected with Joan's talk, but then repairs to portray it as less so. However, the repetition of sounds and words contributes to the coherence of the talk in terms of its relation to Joan's telling about an acquaintance's success, and her own problem in doing the same. While Lesley can be seen to attend to matters of connection in line 13, most probably in terms of content, other associations may exist on a lower level of potential attention. So, while they may do work on more noticeable aspects of coherence (especially ones to do with content), others such as sound-association may go unnoticed, and potentially give some insight into connections across sequences of talk, even where speakers introduce the new matter in a disjunctive way.

In sum, analysis of various kinds of associations across transitions suggests that in introducing new matters speakers may be influenced by prior talk in terms of the selection of words, categories, and sounds, and that they may contribute to creating coherence even across topic boundaries and breaks in the conversation.

Resisting Associations

However, these often-tacit associations do not mean that we are trapped in talking about matters raised in prior talk, or in designing our turns in ways that manifest these connections. Jefferson argued that we are not at the mercy of triggered topics:

> It may be that the triggering mechanisms are not something inevitable and irresistible, something that we're just not in control of. It's possible that you can have *selective* triggering.
>
> (1996, p. 39)

Jefferson analyzed an extract which suggests that if a topic is triggered at an inappropriate place in the conversation, it can be suppressed. In a call where reference

72 *Elizabeth Holt*

to children dressed in turtlenecks is followed by talk about eating a lot of turkey, Jefferson pointed out that, at the beginning of the call, mention of a turkey dinner is not followed by a move to this matter.

Furthermore, the fact that topics may be triggered, but participants introduce them in ways that disguise their triggering, means that participants can do subtle work to make use of triggering associations without simply introducing matters in ways that may reveal their origin. In Jefferson's terms, they frame them in ways that tell the recipient not to hear them as triggered by the prior talk. To explore this further, I turn now to consider two extracts where it is possible that topics are triggered by preceding talk (talk about particular matters—in the first, taking someone on holiday, and in the second, mention of gardens). However, it appears that in both cases, the speakers work to initiate them as disjunctive topic introductions rather than touched off by prior talk.

Lesley and Robbie are both stand-in (supply) teachers. Robbie is currently teaching a class that was previously taught by Lesley. Just prior to the extract, they are talking about the lack of dictionaries in the classroom, and at the start, Lesley suggests that Robbie purchase some for the class.

```
(11)  [Holt:M88:1:5:12-13]
1    Les:  [You'll haf to be innovative'n::d .hhhh ↑pur↓chase
2          some.↓
3          (0.4)
4    Rob:  Ah yes I'm doing a lot'v ↓things on my (h)ow:n I've
5          got two: drapes up but u-one I bought'n one's u-part
6          a'my son's curtain .hh becuz it's a
7          red (.) with[a (     )
8    Les:              [.t ↑Oh ↑↑you
9          got dra:pes up. Oh w[ell done.
10   Rob:                      [Oh I got drapes ↓up. I think
11         it's disgraceful they ↓haven't got↓ I mean if we're
12         goin t' have drapes we've got (0.3) we've actually
13         had th(h)at trellis i:n,
14         (.)
15   Rob:  it'll be jolly good in th'
16         g(hh)a[r(h) dheh ↑hehn ↑heh heh]=
17   Les:        [I  t  ↓ w i : : l l ↓ ]=
18   Les:  =↓Ye:s that's true↓
19   Rob:  Yes
20         (0.2)
21   Les:  [Hm.
22   Rob:  [↑But what abou:t u:m:
23         (0.9)
24   Rob:  Ye- ↑What about ↓you now. How're ↓you.
25   Les:  .hh ↑Oh fi: neh-we:ll: nah:- yes I am: fair↓ly
26         fi:ne,
27         (0.5)
28   Rob:  Oh[↓:.
29   Les:    [m-Uh:m
30         (0.9)
```

A Walk on the Wild Side 73

```
31  Rob:   Dare I ask how:    the house is or sh'l I not.
32         (0.5)
33  Les:   Uh:m::: no eh- neyss not at the moment ehh ↑hheh hheh
34         [heh
35  Rob:   [Oh::: drat
36  Les:   Hm:.
37  Rob:   It-it's (0.2) it's- as you al:ready ↓know it's ba:d
38         time to[↓try 'n[(          )
39  Les:          [.hhhh  [I ↓know I know but I'm quite happy:
40         so:
41  Rob:   ↑Good.  ↑(f'you)[it's a ↑love↓ly house'n garden an'=
42  Les:                   [Yeh.
43  Rob:   =you've got lots t'd[o 'n
44  Les:                       [.hhhh There's ↑too ↑much t'do=
```

The word at line 16 'g(hh)ar(h)dheh' is 'garden' interspersed with laughter particles. It is possible that it reminds Robbie of a matter relating to Lesley—that she is currently trying to sell her house—and that she begins to ask about this. However, she then breaks off and asks a more general how-are-you question instead.

Following Lesley's suggestion that she 'be innovative'n::d .hhhh ↑pur↓chase some', Robbie confirms that she is, and refers to a change she has made to the classroom where she has purchased a drape and added another. She then goes on to mention another alteration she has made to the appearance of the classroom concerning a trellis—likely to be a wooden lattice, often used to secure plants against fences or walls in a garden. In saying 'it'll be jolly good in th' g(hh)ar(h) dheh', she appears to be saying that it will be useful in the garden once it is finished with in the classroom. Lesley affiliates with this, and then there is a slight lull with a minimal response from Robbie and a short pause. Robbie then says '↑But what abou:t u:m:'. Thus, she appears to raise a new matter which is other-oriented. It is done as somewhat connected to prior talk, in that there are no markers of disjunction (e.g., 'Anyway'). 'But' suggests a departure, but one that is not totally unrelated. The design of the question is suited to asking about a specific matter (e.g., 'What about your allergies?', 'What about your house, is it sold yet?'). At precisely the point where she arrives at the subject of the questions, she breaks off and produces a hesitation marker. There is then a long pause. Robbie produces 'Ye-' which could be the start of 'Yes', and then repeats the question,[4] this time completing it and adding 'How're ↓you.'.

Lesley does a positive response, breaking off to do a troubles-premonitory (Jefferson, 1980) response (which may relate to her current allergy attack, introduced a little later in the call). Robbie says 'oh', then a long pause develops before she says, 'Dare I ask how: the house is or sh'l I not', referring to Lesley's problems in trying to sell it. Following Lesley's response that suggests her attempts are not going well, Robbie refers to problems in the housing market generally. Then, at line 41, in response to Lesley's more positive gloss on the situation, she assesses it as 'a ↑love↓ly house'n garden', thus mentioning the garden as well as the house.

74 Elizabeth Holt

Mentioning 'garden' in line 16 may remind Robbie of the situation regarding Lesley's house-selling. She begins to introduce this as a next topic, but then repairs to do a more general how-are-you enquiry. Evidence that she had the related matters of house and garden in mind (possibly sparked off from her mention of 'garden' in line 16) comes from the fact that she later produces the collocation 'house and garden'. Therefore, it may be that Robbie resists doing an enquiry about the house-selling in a more obviously touched-off manner. Why she does this can only be a matter of speculation, but interestingly, when she does ask about the house in line 31, she phrases it in a way that orients to the delicacy of the topic, possibly verbalising the hesitancy that led to the alternative state-enquiry.[5]

Similarly, in the next extract, talk about one matter appears to lead the speaker to introduce a new matter, but she does not do it in a connected way. At the start of this call, Lesley asks Joan 'How much for the lovely table decoration'. Joan says that it is a Christmas present (i.e., that Lesley does not need to repay her for it) and that she was delighted to give it to her as a thanks for the frozen food and for taking their son on holiday. (Their sons are good friends and the initial reason for the friendship between the families.) They then move on to discussing Joan's cat, and the invitation that Joan's son has made to Lesley's son regarding a social event in the near future. They then move towards closing, returning to the reason-for-call—the Christmas present. Joan then initiates a new topic, regarding the fact that they will no longer be able to go on holiday abroad this year, given their financial situation. They were planning to take Lesley's son with them.

```
(12)   [Holt:X(C)2:1:2:3-4]
1    Joa:   Alright the:n tha[nks a  lot Lesle[y
2    Les:                    [.hh          [eeYe:- uh-we:ll
3           u-hu- ↑Well ↓thank you very much f'my Christmas
4           [present,
5    Joa:   [↑Oh:: pleasure,
6           (0.2)
7    Joa:   Pleasure
8    Les:   [e h h ha ha ]
9    Joa:   [heh-heh-heh-h]a-ha .eh: .eh .hh I mean we're only too
10          delighted. to. (0.2) you having tay- .hhh Now while
11          you're on the pho↓:ne, Lesle[y,
12   Les:                               [Yes.
13          (.)
14   Joa:   Fred's g'nna contact you .hhh But we were hoping t'go
15          to ↓Spain next yea:r,=
16   Les:   =Oh[ y  e  s. don't]
17   Joa:      [(an' we told ]Tim) but between you 'n I 'n the
18          gatepost Fred's got no bon↓us from iz fi:rm this ye[ar
19   Les:                                                      [No:
20   Les:   well that's happ'n to us t[oo:.
21   Joa:                             [So: u- (0.3) UNfortunately
22          I mean the money that- (0.3) an' it's usually quite a
23          substantial [one. an' (we/'ee) ju]st ha(v/s)en't got=
```

24	Les:	[I k n̲ o̲ w .]
25	Joa:	=a[ny[thing to sp̲a̲re.]
26	Les:	[.h[I thi̲n̲k we're a̲]:ll in the sa̲me b̲oat ⌊this yea̲:r
27	Joa:	Ye̲::s.

In lines 1–7, the conversation appears to be moving to a close, partly through the repeat of 'pleasure' and the short pause, where no 'unmentioned mentionables' (Schegloff and Sacks, 1973) are introduced. Joan extends the topic of the present by, most likely, again referring to one of the reasons for giving it: 'I mean we're o̲nly too de̲lighted. to). (0.2) (yo̲u having tay-)' appears to be the start of another reference to the fact that Lesley and her family took Joan's son on holiday. However, Joan cuts off at the start of the mention of what is likely to be 'taken him on holiday' and produces a disjunctive topic change. In fact, this is a 'conversation restart' (Jefferson, 1984, p. 193). The topic launch—'.hhh Now while you're on the pho↓:ne, Lesley,'—frames this as a distinct matter. She then goes on to explain that they will not be able to go abroad (and therefore take Lesley's son away). That they can no longer take him on holiday is not said explicitly, but Lesley orients to this in her response—'O̲h y e s. do̲n't' (likely designed to end in 'worry') which Joan overlaps. Thus, it appears that Lesley orients to this as an account for not being able to take him abroad, coming in quickly to reassure Joan that it is not a problem.

That the speakers are orienting to unexpressed shared knowledge about the offer is further underlined by her introduction of the topic with 'Fre̲d's g'nna contact you .hhh But we we̲re hoping t'go̲ to̲ ↓Spain next yea̲:r', and '(an' we to̲ld Tim)', implying that this news has special relevance for Lesley and her family (rather than being, for example, introduced as a troubles-telling on the part of Joan).

Therefore, a possibility here is that talk about Lesley having taken her son away reminds Joan of the fact that they are no longer able to take Lesley's son to Spain. However, she does not introduce this matter as a touched-off or related topic (e.g., 'Talking about taking him away . . .'). Instead, she breaks off from saying 'tay-'—just as she is about to refer to taking him on holiday—then does a conversation restart, which frames the new matter as distinct and unrelated to the previous.

Again, it is only possible to speculate on why she may do this, but one reason may be that, while the matters are connected in terms of being about taking the other's son on holiday, Lesley has taken Joan's son away, whereas Joan is no longer able to take Lesley's son abroad. Thus, introducing it in a connected manner would emphasize the disparity in the situations and the fact that they are not going to take Lesley's son away, even though Lesley took Joan's on holiday.

Jefferson (1996, p. 43) argued:

> So it doesn't look as if these processes are constantly suppressed in normal thought progression. Rather, they are embedded in and obscured by a range of syntactic, sequential and interactional structures. Most of them, then, become

76   *Elizabeth Holt*

unnoticeable. And the few that are noticed, for whatever reasons we come to notice them, can be explained away as exceptions.

The two instances analyzed here suggest that while prior talk (mention of gardens and taking someone on holiday) may lead to the generation of next topics, speakers do not suppress their introduction, but work to introduce it in a way that disguises the relationship.

Conclusion

Contrary to common pre-conceptions about how talk tends to be generated (i.e., as largely driven by individual thoughts arising in people's minds), analysis of interaction reveals that it is often sequentially occasioned: prior talk can generate subsequent talk (both in terms of words used and matters raised) due to associations that we tend to overlook as being generative in this way.

In this chapter, I have considered poetics alongside other kinds of connections, therefore situating it as one type amongst various talk-generating and coherence-creating associations. Thus, this broader category includes the type of associations analyzed by Sacks and Jefferson that are generally unnoticed and may even be obscured (e.g., sound-triggered topics), along with ones that are sometimes explicitly oriented to in talk. This has shown that structures underpinning the phenomena revealed by Jefferson can be identified in sequences involving other kinds of associations leading to touched-off matters as well as, for example, that participants can introduce topics in disjunctive ways, even when there is a link to prior talk that may have reminded them of the new matter and/or could be used to introduce the new matter in a connected way.

CA focuses on why people design their contributions in the way they do in terms of the action these contributions perform in light of the ongoing action-sequence. But the current analysis and the work of Jefferson and Sacks on poetics, tying, and how matters are introduced highlight the fact that we also should consider how previous talk may influence the design of subsequent turns in a number of ways (some more obvious, some less so). In searching for a way to do a particular action or in arriving at the next contribution, participants are highly 'historically sensitive' to both their own and others' words, and this is central to the formulation of their actions. This supports an alternative model of the origin of talk: one that captures how an important part of how we arrive at and design contributions to talk is sequentially and contextually driven.

Notes

1. Stephen appears to be unaware of the pun and does not acknowledge it. Lesley may notice it, as suggested by the short laugh at line 20. But this is unusual in the collection—most are not explicitly oriented to.
2. My thanks to Phil Glenn for bringing this to my attention.

A Walk on the Wild Side   77

3. It becomes clear elsewhere in the call that the return of the book involves Dana bringing it to Lesley (i.e., dropping in to Lesley's house). Later in the call, Lesley says that wanting the book back is an excuse to get Dana to drop in, therefore showing orientation to the delicacy of the potential implication that she is only inviting Dana in order to secure return of the book.
4. An extremely 'wild possibility' is that she realizes that the form can be adapted to a more general state-enquiry at the point where she says 'Ye-', then she recycles that, but goes on to add a more common formulation afterwards ('How're ↓you').
5. It is also possible that the formulation of this turn, alluding to potential troubles, is orienting to the troubles-premonitory response in lines 25–26—i.e., on hearing Lesley has some kind of trouble, she casts around for a possible reason and arrives at knowledge of her house-selling activities. This would mean that the topic is not touched off by the earlier mention of 'garden' and its resulting association—house and garden—but is more locally occasioned.

Works Cited

Button, G. (1990). On varieties of closings. In G. Psathas (Ed.), *Interaction Competence.* Washington, DC: University Press of America, pp. 93–147.

Button, G. (1991). Conversation-in-a-series. In D. Boden and D.H. Zimmerman (Eds.), *Talk and Social Structure: Studies in Ethnomethodology and Conversation Analysis.* Cambridge: Polity Press, pp. 251–277.

Drew, P., and Holt, E. (1998). Figures of speech: figurative expressions and the management of topic transition in conversation. *Language in Society*, 27, 495–522.

Glenn, P. and Holt, E. (2019). *Tossed in Laughables at Topic Termination.* Unpublished conference presentation, LANSI, New York.

Holt, E. (1991). *Figures of Speech: An Exploration of the Use of Idiomatic Phrases in Conversation.* Unpublished thesis, submitted to The University of York.

Holt, E. (1993). The structure of death announcements: looking on the bright side of death. *Text*, 13(2), 189–212.

Holt, E., and Drew, P. (2005). Figurative pivots: the use of figurative expressions in pivotal topic transitions. *Research on Language and Social Interaction*, 38(1), pp. 35–61.

Jefferson, G. (1980). On "trouble-premonitory" response to inquiry. *Sociological Inquiry*, 50(3–4), 153–185.

Jefferson, G. (1984). On stepwise transition from talk about a trouble to inappropriately positioned matters. In J.M. Atkinson and J. Heritage (Eds.), *Structures of Social Action: Studies in Conversation Analysis.* Cambridge and New York: Cambridge University Press, pp. 191–222.

Jefferson, G. (1996). On the poetics of ordinary talk. *Text and Performance Quarterly*, 16(1), 1–61.

Sacks, H. (1995). *Lectures on Conversation* (2 volumes). G. Jefferson (Ed.). Oxford: Blackwell.

Saussure, F.D. (1959). *Course in General Linguistics.* C. Bally and A. Sechehaya (Eds.) in collaboration with A. Riedlinger and W. Baskin (Trans.). New York: Philosophical Library.

Schegloff, E.A. (1989). Reflections on language, development and the interactional character of talk-in-interaction. In M. Bornstein and S. Bruner (Eds.), *Interaction in Human Development.* New York: Erlbaum, pp. 139–153.

78 *Elizabeth Holt*

Schegloff, E.A. (1990). On the organization of sequences as a source of "coherence" in talk-in-interaction. In B. Dorval (Ed.), *Conversational Organization and Its Development*. Norwood, NJ: Ablex, pp. 51–77.

Schegloff, E.A., and Sacks, H. (1973). Opening up closings. *Semiotica*, 7, 289–327.

Sidnell, J. (2010). *Conversation Analysis: An Introduction.* Chichester, West Sussex, UK: Wiley-Blackwell.

3 On Doing Things Through Topical Puns and Near-Synonyms in Conversation[1]

John P. Rae

In spontaneous talk, speakers occasionally make unusual word-choices. In his play, *The Rivals*, Sheridan's character, Mrs Malaprop, unknowingly utters expressions that sound superficially like her intended word (Sheridan, 1775).[2] For example:

> But the point we would request of you is, that you will promise to forget this fellow—to illiterate him, I say, quite from your memory.
>
> (Act 1, Scene II)

> Oh, there's nothing to be hoped for from her! she's as headstrong as an allegory on the banks of Nile.
>
> (Act III, Scene III)

There is an extensive literature on malapropisms in psychology (e.g., Fay and Cutler, 1977; Vitevitch, 1997) and philosophy (Davidson, 2005; Unnsteinsson, 2017). Davidson (2005) argues that our ability to understand malapropisms (and other idiosyncratic usages) has important implications for how language and communication should be theorized. Put simply (and in terms that Davidson does not use), rather than reasoning bottom-up from a speaker's words, to an important extent, we reason top-down, wholistically, from our grasp of what the speaker is trying to convey. This, Davidson points out, blurs the distinction between understanding how language works and understanding how the world works. Addressing malapropisms and related errors can be a practical concern in interactions involving knowledge differences, such as doctor-patient interactions (Berger and Cartmill, 2017).

In malapropisms we have *homophony* without synonymy—that is, similarity in sound without similarity in meaning. However, synonymy is a vexed concept. In some contexts, two words can have the same meaning, yet there can be shades of difference between them that can become important in other contexts. For example, in some cases, a psychotherapist might suggest alternative expressions to those used by a client, perhaps to encourage fuller expression of feelings (Rae, 2008). Whether a word is a synonym, or a near-synonym, can be a matter of taste and judgement. Consider the following examples, in which the focal words are shown in bold.

DOI: 10.4324/9780429328930-5

80 *John P. Rae*

```
(1)  Photographs [JR:FN]³ Socket
((Having browsed through a set of photographs, Krishna hands them
to Sean, without replacing them in fully in their cardboard cover.))
01   K: →     Put them in the socket
```

```
(2)  Organic Farming [JR Broadcast Radio, pseudonymized] Digress
25   VB:   .pt I'd agree with a lot of what Susan's
26         just been saying.
27   VB:   <I think the only area where I kind of s-
28   →     start to digress °so you were talking about this idea
29         y'know produce ever more f:ood to feed
30         thee a growing population °h I was speaking
```

```
(3)  Rail Enquiry Service [JR call-in radio] Timetable
07   C:    Right °h em: (.) e- it's about thee ergh thee national rail
08         en↑quiry service. I'm a freelance singer? and so (.) I
09   →     don't have a ↑regular timetable °hh I have to travel at (.)
10         (tp) sh:ort notice to v- v:very many places ↓I'm based in
```

In Extract (1), we have 'socket' where 'sleeve' or 'pocket' might be expected;[4] in Extract (2), 'digress' rather than 'disagree'; in Extract (3), 'timetable' rather than 'schedule'. At first sight, these might appear to be cases where there is nothing more than some looseness in the speakers' word-choices. The processes and issues involved in word-selection have been discussed in a number of disciplines, including computational linguistics (e.g., Edmonds and Hirst, 2002) and have been a major focus in psycholinguistics (e.g., Levelt, 1993; Levelt, Roelofs, and Meyer, 1999; Pickering and Garrod, 2013). Word-selection has also been a sustained focus of work in Conversation Analysis (CA), which has characteristically explored speakers' word-choices and the interaction context in which they occur. Examples are the granularity of descriptions (Schegloff, 2000), ways of referring to persons (Schegloff, 1996), descriptions of locations (Schegloff, 1972; Drew, 1978), and category terms (Schegloff, 2007).[5] In this chapter I will argue that, at least in some cases, near-synonyms are amenable to analysis, and that Jefferson's (1996) study of poetics in conversation provides resources for this.

Contextual Influences on Word-Choice

In her report on the multiple ways in which a speaker's word-choices appear to be occasioned by context, in particular by elements within the speaker's own talk, Jefferson touches on near-synonyms, remarking that 'Sometimes a word occurs that seems a bit special, maybe out of character, maybe not register-fitted to the surrounding talk.' (Jefferson, 1996, p. 19). She provides three examples, reproduced here as Extracts (4)–(6). In Extract (4), she suggests that 'momentarily', which is rather formal or institutional for a domestic phone call in which 'soon' might be expected, is potentially touched off by the name of the party being referred to: 'Terry'.[6] (In Jefferson, 1996, square brackets are used to show focal elements; here they are additionally shown in bold.)

(4) [GN-FN] (Jefferson, 1996, p. 19) momentarily
01 Martha: I called **[Terry]** and told her to come over around nine
02   thirty.
03 Jan: It's nine thirty now.
04 Martha: Well then she'll be here momen[**tari**]ly.

Jefferson presents Extract (5) as part of her discussion of how numbers occur in talk; however, she also suggests that 'asinine', a rather unusual word for a teenager in a context when 'stupid' might have been used, might be linked to the number 'ninety'.

(5) [GTS:11:2:65] (Jefferson, 1996, p. 20) asinine
01 Roger: We mebe g(h)o **[ninedy]** miles o(h)n a Friday night.
02   Going nowhere.
03   An' my dad thinks it's asi[**nine**].

Whilst Extracts (4)–(5) are examples of connections involving similar sounds, Jefferson reports a case where the connection involves related meanings. In Extract (6), Laverne describes an encounter with an underaged drinker in a bar where she works. She reports herself saying that she was 'affronted' (line 14), rather than using a more vernacular expression, such as 'offended'.

(6) [Frankel:TC:1:1:3] (Jefferson, 1996, p. 57) affronted
01 Laverne: So one a'the- u-one a'the other guys came up
02   →   **[behind]** me they alweez do:. Yihknow they-
03   whenever you take a drink away fr'm a gi:rl.
04   °hh (.) you alweez have a bouncer with you.
05   °hh jest in ca:se the guy- (0.2) who's with
06   'er decides t'come °t°hh stand up en hitche.
07 Esther: (0.3)
08 Laverne: M-hm,=
09   = °p°hhhhhhh So: she goes w'l ah'on't see w't
10   cher so c'ncerned about you didn't seve it
11   tih me:,
12   (1.0)
13 Laverne: °t°hh So I looked at at 'er en I s'd Cathy, I said
14   →   said °hh I feel personally **[affronted]**, °hh
15   thetchu w'do it in a place that! work °hh
16   →   en put m~ in a **[position]** like you jis put me in.

Jefferson notes that 'affronted' (line 14) is related to both 'behind' (line 2) and 'position' (line 16). This case offers two significant features for the present analysis. First, the relationship between the focal word and the element to which it is related is *semantic* rather than *phonological*—that is, it concerns the meaning of the words rather than how they sound. Second, the relationship is not solely to a preceding word (here, 'behind') but also to an upcoming word, 'position'.

The cases examined here ('soon'/'momentarily'; 'stupid'/'asinine'; 'offended'/'affronted') are close synonyms, but with differences in register. A case of an incorrect near-synonym appears in Sacks' treatment of proverbial expressions

82   *John P. Rae*

in conversation in his lectures. Sacks' analysis concerns the '*punning relationship*' (1992, p. 421, emphasis in the original) between Louise's figure of speech 'something to look up to' (lines 15–16) and the actual positioning of the pictures of the Beatles (on the bedroom ceiling) in the fragment shown as Extract (7).

```
(7) Group Therapy Session (Sacks, 1992, vol. 2, pp. 420-421)
01 Ken:     Wuh- d- her whole room jus' got it wallpapered. She jus'-
02          jus- got done rewallpapering it about a month ago,
03 Louise: -with the pictures of the Beatle//s
04 Ken:     No. A- a month ago Mom had it done in this gra:sscloth, like
05          junk y'know it looks like//Hawaiian-
06          (1.5)
07 Louise: Yeah I know we have it.
08          (1.5)
09 Ken:   →She came in there the other night with a Scotch tape an'
10          every inch of the room. You couldn'- The roof I think she's
11          got done, in Beadle pictures. An she lays there in bed at night,
12          (2.5)
13 Roger:  She's doing that because all her friends are (doin' it).
14          (    //    ) over th'Beadles
15 Louise: Mm they need some kind idol y'know, something to//
16          look up to
17 Ken:    I:dol! They look like little kangaroos://::s.
18 Louise: Hheh!
```

Sacks draws attention to two features of the sequential environment in which Louise's punning idiomatic expression occurs: the conclusion of a telling and the production of an error. The error concerns Ken's lexical choice, 'roof' rather than 'ceiling', in line 10. The location of the pictures is within the room, not on the building, making 'ceiling' correct (Merriam Webster, 'Definition of ceiling 1a: the overhead inside lining of a room') rather than 'roof' ('Definition of roof 1a(1): the cover of a building'). In the course of his analysis of this, Sacks remarks that Ken quite commonly makes similar errors and that, commonly, Louise corrects him. The production of Ken's error is not the focus of Sacks' treatment here; however, there are some aspects of the context that might be relevant in the occurrence of this error. First, there is the sound-connection between 'roof' (line 10) and the just previous 'room' (also line 10). Second, we can further note that relevant sounds also occur in Ken's subsequent unflattering description of the Beatles: 'They look like little kangaroo::s' (line 17, emphasis in the original).[7] Here then, we have a situation where, in place of a word that might be expected, a related word to 'ceiling', not quite a synonym, is produced—that is, 'roof'; moreover, there are contextual features (in this case sounds) that appear to relate to that word-choice. Here, the contextual connection could be to a previously occurring feature ('room') or a future one ('kangaroos'), or both.

The primary thrust of Jefferson's analysis of 'momentarily' and 'asinine' and 'affronted' in Extracts (4)–(6) is not that these words are unusual, but rather, that there are associations between them and other words in the surrounding talk. Jefferson's point is in the interestingness of these word-choices, given their relationship to sounds that have recently occurred (see similarly, Schegloff, 2007, in connection to work on the analysis of category terms). However, we can also note that connections can be identified between the speaker's activity of the moment and these word-choices. We can see that some management of relationships might be at work. For example, in responding 'Well then she'll be here momentarily', Martha might be reaching for a somewhat formal framing of matters; perhaps alluding to the patience that is often required in navigating organizational matters. Similarly, the formality of 'affronted' could be alluding to speaker's institutional, and statutory, responsibilities. In choosing 'asinine', Roger could be seeking to portray something of the loftiness of the paternal criticisms to which he is subject (of course, he might even be quoting the expression used by his father). Rather than challenging Jefferson's analysis, such observations are consistent with it, and suggest that there are connections in the speakers' word-choices between other expressions in their talk and the activities in which they are engaged.

Jefferson's analysis of poetics includes a consideration of how near-synonyms can occur in conversation. She demonstrates how a speaker's word-selection can apparently be influenced by sound or meaning relations with words in the surrounding talk. However, prior to considering the relevance of this for the cases of 'socket', 'digress', and 'timetable' in Extracts (1)–(3), it will be relevant to consider another vexed topic: speech errors and speakers' motivation.

Speech Errors, Word-Selection, and Motivation

In Jefferson's study, a number of sound-related exchange errors involve the *anticipation* of a sound-feature (this is known as 'feature anticipation' in psycholinguistic terminology). For example, in Extract 8, the forthcoming 'dropback' (a technical term in American football) is apparently anticipated in the attempted production of 'deep', resulting in the nonword 'dreep'.

```
(8) [Football broadcast] (Jefferson, 1996, p. 6) dreep-deep
01  Announcer:     Staubach goes back in a [dr]eep - [dee]p
02                 [dr]opback.
```

Jefferson refers to these as CV-CCV alternations (or reversals) (C=consonant, V=vowel), and notes that they are very common.[8] In her discussion of such errors, Jefferson considers two historic studies, both landmarks in their own ways: Meringer and Mayer's (1895) work on misspeaking and misreading,[9] and Freud's chapter 'Slips of the Tongue' (1901/1938). Jefferson comments on the nature and popularity of Freud's account:

> When I first started playing around with speech errors in 1968 or thereabouts, anybody I talked to about the thing came up with Freudian Slips,

84   *John P. Rae*

and that seemed enough for them. So I took a look at Freud's article, "Slips of the Tongue," published in 1901. The article begins by citing previous work on the subject by the linguists Meringer and Mayer in their 1895 article "Slips in Reading and Speaking." They had such categories as "transpositions," "anticipations," "perseverations," "contaminations" and "substitutions," and explained the phenomena in neurological terms such as "innervation" and "excitatory process." Freud pretty much replaced those sorts of accounts with the single account, "unconscious motives." It's beginning to look as if his attempted replacement is better treated as a possible addition to the sorts of accounts given by Meringer and Mayer. Sometimes a cigar is just a cigar, and sometimes, maybe most times, a CV-CCV reversal is just a CV-CCV reversal.

(Jefferson, 1996, p. 9)

It is worth revisiting some of these specifics and in particular considering what came to be known as 'Freudian slips'. Freud had a long-standing interest in speech. Before developing what became known as psychoanalysis, Freud wrote a book on aphasia (1953/1891). 'Slips of the Tongue' is actually a chapter of another book, *The Psychopathology of Everyday Life*. As the title suggests, one reason for this book's importance is that it broadens the application of psychoanalysis from clinical situations to everyday situations. In the chapter, Freud considers Meringer and Mayer's book in some detail. It would be more accurate to say that Freud's position was that Meringer and Mayer's account was incomplete. The place of Freud's treatment has been discussed in detail. Ellis (1980) offers an account from the perspective of psychology, arguing that multiple processes are involved in speech errors. Dressler (2009) provides a more recent account from the linguistic perspective. There appears to be evidence that Freud was correct about a number of things—for example, speech errors can by affected by attention, and motivation can be relevant in terms of how hard a speaker concentrates.

Jefferson presents a number of examples of instances that were suggested to be Freudian slips by participants at the time of their occurrence. Extract (9) involves the utterance of the post-flight pleasantries following a conspicuously bumpy landing.

```
(9)  [GJ:FN]  (Jefferson, 1996, p.  7) fright-flight
01  Stew:    On behalf of the who[l]e f[r]ight- f[l]ight c[r]ew I'd like
             to thank you for Flying Air California.
```

Jefferson comments 'Freudian Slip! Lots of nudging and grinning among us passengers. But then I thought, no, it's one of those sound-selection things' (1996, p. 7). Jefferson continues, 'It seems to me all these cases have to do with various sound-productional mechanisms, but *some* get seen by speakers and/or recipients as having to do with something altogether different, some sort of psychological mechanism' (1996, p. 8)—that is, a deeper psychological

Topical Puns and Near-Synonyms 85

mechanism than the one concerned with sound-production. Nevertheless, she goes on to say, 'This is not to say that matters psychological/sociological don't show up in funny ways in people's talk. For example, it's possible that in the following instance someone is trying to avoid what he can foresee as a dangerous CV-CCV reversal, and that maneuver results in the omission of the dreaded consonant from a word in which it did belong' (1996, p. 8). She offers as an example the fragment shown in Extract (10).

```
(10)  [Football broadcast] (Jefferson, 1996, p. 8) pay-play
01    Announcer:    Jones was not open on that [pay]- [play],
                    both [backs] in their [block]ing).
```

Here, in psycholinguistic terminology, a *feature deletion error* occurs such that 'play' is initially produced as 'pay' and is then promptly corrected. Jefferson proposes that the initial production of 'pay', rather than the intended 'play', could be a consequence of the announcer working to avoid the production of 'blacks' in place of 'backs', the two backs in question both being African-American men. She further notes that in the next turn the announcer comments on the players' Oakland Raiders black uniforms, and suggests that this an instance of a *suppression-release phenomenon* (see Introduction). It is notable in this example that the proposed concern of the speaker (the ethnicity of the players) does not reside in the talk, but is a visible feature of the setting. This is commented on by a question from a member of the audience at Jefferson's 1977 talk (Nevile, 2015), on which Jefferson (1996) is based. The relevance of this case for the present analysis is that the proposed phenomenon (avoiding mentioning the players' ethnicity) has not previously surfaced in the talk. That is, the speaker's word-choice apparently anticipates a yet-to-be mentioned semantically-salient issue (see, similarly, Schegloff, 2003a; 2003b). In this example, Jefferson provides evidence of how the speaker's concerns can find expression in their talk. In this case, something that the speaker is seeking to avoid saying shows itself.

Jefferson's work on poetics was apparently conducted independently of work on speech errors in psychology, in particular Victoria Fromkin's *Speech Errors as Linguistic Evidence* (1973; see also, Boomer and Laver, 1968; Butterworth, 1982; Garnham, Shillcock, Brown, Mill, and Cutler 1982). Jefferson perhaps makes a veiled allusion to this tradition in the 1977 talk with a reference to 'experiments'. (Nevile, 2015, lines 140–141).[10] Many of the phenomena identified in Jefferson (1996) have been well studied in psychological research. Moreover, models such as Dell's spreading activation model offer good explanations of them (Dell, 1986; Dell and Oppenheim, 2015).[11] Based on the multiple connections found in neural networks, this model proposes that entities at different levels in the speech production process (such as concepts, words, and the phonemes from which they are built) are interconnected. For example, consider the case of word-selection in Jefferson's example 'The arti[c]le thetchu [q]uote here refers to Roman [C]atholicism in what [kuh] - in what areas?' (Jefferson,

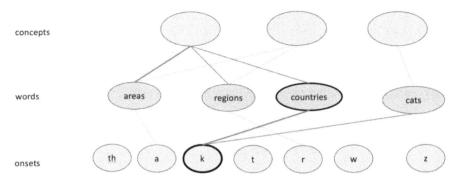

Figure 3.1 Simplified Spreading Activation Model for 'kuh' in 'The arti[c]le thetchu [q]uote here refers to Roman [C]atholicism in what [kuh]—in what areas?'

1996, p.5). Here the speaker is selecting a word that, in terms of its semantics, expresses the concept of, say, geographical areas, so there is *top-down activation* such that the probability of producing near-synonyms such as 'areas', 'regions', 'countries', or 'zones' is raised. However, the multiple occurrences of /k/ in the speaker's talk leads to *bottom-up activation* of words starting with that sound, even if they are not semantically related (e.g., 'countries', 'cats'). In the sentence that is underway, spreading of activation occurs, and the simultaneity of the top-down semantic activation relating to geographic regions and the bottom-up phonological activation relating to the sound /k/ leads to the activation of 'countries'. The speaker starts to produce this word, but then other processes (perhaps involving self-monitoring) activate 'areas'; consequently, we get 'countries' (started and then cut-off) and then the production of 'areas' (Fig. 3.1).

Research into unusual lexical choices in psycholinguistics, philosophy, and CA has shown particular interest in cases in which the word-choice is incorrect, or where correction is relevant. Jefferson remarks, 'I start with errors because they are places where the conversation's surface is already broken, so we can see a little way inside and begin to catch sight of the phenomena' (Jefferson, 1996, p. 5). In addition to accounting for speech errors, spreading activation models can account for puns. For example, the previous mention of a word can increase the probability of the selection of a related word. Across her paper, and particularly for meaning-related instances, in the vast majority of the cases that Jefferson presents, the stimulus word *precedes* the focal word. For example, in Extract (11), the topical pun 'steered' follows 'agricultural'.

(11) [Lamb Interviews] (Jefferson, 1996, p. 17) steered
```
01  Mrs A:    I wanted to go to an [agricultural] college but my
              mother [steered] me away from that
```

Such occurrences can be thought of as the outcome of well-known priming effects in which one process (choosing a word or expression) is influenced by a just-previous activity (Lashley, 1951). There is nothing particularly wild or strange about such processes. However, analyzing them can become tendentious or wild—for example, if we were to propose (without corroborating evidence) that here the speaker is (perhaps unconsciously) using cattle-related tropes in reference to their mother. On the other hand, Extract (12) provides an example whereby the pun anticipates the production of the word (a person's name) and is apparently primed by it. Here, Jefferson describes a phone call in which a speaker, on being asked a question (line 3), rather than answering, adds an increment to their previous turn (line 4) before acquiescing and answering the question (end of line 4). Jefferson points out that at just the place where the speaker refrains from answering, where they suppress answering, something of the name is released into surface of the speaker's talk.

```
(12) GJ:FN  (adapted from Jefferson, 1996, pp. 19–20)
1   Norm:   He'll be a little after one. He's
2           [At my house now.
3   Gail:   [What's his name.
4   Norm:   Barring any unforeseen trouble. His name's Bart
```

In his treatment of poetics, Hopper (1992) uncouples the idea of a Freudian slip from the idea of suppression in his consideration of Extract (13). The context, as sketched by Hopper, is this: 'a teacher berates his wife on her insensitivity to his rough day' (1992, p. 116). The speaker uses a related, but incorrect word, and then self-corrects.

```
(13) [UTCL C15:Scott] (Hopper, 1992, p. 116) preaching
01  Frank:  I had a very difficult preaching- teaching clinic today.
```

Hopper observes, 'This substitution of "preaching" for "teaching" exploits multiple associations between the two terms. This instance could also be characterized as a Freudian slip, one whose associative qualities fit the speaker's moralistic stance' (1992, p. 117).

However, there are cases of puns where a relationship to a project of the speaker is more pertinent. For example, Jefferson (1996) gives Extract (14) as an example of a topical pun, with the expletive 'damn' fitted to the topic of 'reservoirs' through being a homonym of 'dam'.

```
(14) [GJ:FN] (Jefferson, 1996, p. 17) damn
01  Beth:   They're not doing anything to catch the rainfall.
02          They're not building [reservoirs]. They just don't give
03          a [dam]n.
```

The idiom 'they don't give a damn' does more than merely use a reservoir-related term ('dam'). Rather, the expression is consistent with the speaker's complaint:

88   *John P. Rae*

they (the authorities responsible for such matters) are not constructing any dams. In this way, the speaker's concerns can be seen to show up in their talk, irrespective of suppression being part of the picture.

Whilst Jefferson warns against drawing on Freudian explanations of speech phenomena, she acknowledges and demonstrates how speakers' concerns can surface in their talk. She proposed a suppression-release mechanism, whereby something that the speaker is avoiding saying finds expression in their talk. However, more mundane cases involve speakers' concerns showing up in their talk without suppression apparently being relevant.

Speakers' Projects and Word-Choice

Drawing on Jefferson's (1996) analysis of how a practical concern of the moment can influence the production of a speaker's talk, in particular their word-choices, we can revisit the examples of unusual word-choices with which we began. In Extract (1), Krishna's instruction concerns the secure and proper placement of the photographs in their cardboard pocket sleeve. In the context of fitting something into a place that exists for that, 'socket' has relevant connotations that go beyond expressions such as 'pouch' or 'sleeve'.

```
(1)  Photographs [JR:FN] Socket
((Having browsed through a set of photographs, Krishna hands them
to Sean, without replacing them in fully in their cardboard cover.))
01   K:  →      Put them in the socket
```

In Extract (15), an extension of Extract (2), the speaker formulates a disagreement by digressing (lines 27–48). Saying 'digress', rather than 'diverge' or 'differ', turns out to foreshadow a digression.

```
(15) Organic Farming [JR Broadcast Radio, pseudonymized] Digress
((Opening question 01-02 is apparently inserted into the recording of
an interview.))
01 PR:  Well first I asked Susan about how worried farms are about
02      losing some of the chemicals they've had in the past.
03 SK:  There is a a huge opportunity out there, °h we've got
04      all sorts of scientists botanists: entomologists: looking
05      at the next °h frontier if you like of crop protection
06      °h er using er biology, using the plants to help
07      themselves there's some really exciting things
08      that I think will be °h coming (.) out in the next
09      three °h to five years maybe longer but you're
10      right if you don't have the tools that you already
11      have and if those go:? an' if they go (.) because of (.)
12      politics rather than science an' good
13      research then that is a really worry.
14      y'we have the luxury in this part of the
15      world of never worrying when you go the shops that
16      there's going to be empty shelves that isn't
```

```
17        the case for some parts
18        of the world and it's the products that our members supply
19        to conventional and organic farming that make sure
20        we have that sustainable food supply.
21   PR:  °tlhh Val Brown. Organic farmers do use some chemicals
22        f- far fewer than in the conventional systems are-
23        are you concerned about the
24        changing attitudes to these chemicals.
25   VB:  .pt I'd agree with a lot of what Susan's
26        just been saying.
27   VB:  <I think the only area where I kind of s-
28     →  start to digress °so you were talking about this idea
29        y'know produce ever more f:ood to feed
30        thee a growing population °h I was speaking
31        at the ((name of region)) climate
32        change (.) conference in
33        ((name of city)) on Tue:sday °h about how organic
34        farming itself (.) the systems it follows how
35        it is already an adaptation
36        to climate change °h and I think as part
37        of that we've all got to learn
38        to (.) have a slightly different diet?
39        Perhaps eat less meat but better
40        <better quality meat °h an' waste (.)
41        (l) far less food that we do now
42        an' I think then (.) that if we do those
43        thing as well the actual need
44        to drive intensification (in) food production
45        is not quite such a stark
46        sor'uv picture tha-
47        as (.) many people currently believe it is? an I think
48        we've gotta do all those things together.
```

In Extract (16), an extension of Extract (3), involving a freelance singer, what turns out to be at issue is his irregular schedule and his need to get accurate train timetable information. By using 'timetable' rather than 'schedule' to refer to his own arrangements, he foreshadows (perhaps unintentionally) the forthcoming topic of train timetables.

```
(16) Rail Enquiry Service [JR call-in radio, pseudonymized] Timetable
03   S:   ... let's take our first ↑call >°h< which comes from
04        William Moran °hh William good afternoon.
05   C1:  ↑Good afternoon. hh
06   S:   Go ahead
07   C1:  Right °h em: (.) e- it's about thee ergh thee national rail
08        en↑quiry service. I'm a freelance singer? and so (.) I
09        don't have a ↑regular timetable °hh I have to travel at (.)
10        (tp) sh:ort notice to v- v:very many places ↓I'm based in
11        London. hh and I have noticed on ↑more than one occasion
12        that when I phone °h um thee oh eight four five number?
13        >°h< that if I have to phone a↑ga↓in just to confirm some
14        information:. I get completely different reply.
```

90 *John P. Rae*

In each case then, the somewhat unusual word is intimately fitted to the speakers' concerns, as is subsequently evident in their talk, or to other contextual features.

Analyzing these near-synonyms as a merely a result of some slack in the word-retrieval process fails to capture the fittedness of the word to the speaker's current project—for example, 'pouch' is related to 'pocket', but lacks the sense of offering a secure fitting given by 'socket'; 'programme' or 'diary' are related to 'schedule', but lack the connection to transport; 'diverge' is related to 'disagree', but does not fit with going into tangential matters. The precise senses in which near-synonyms depart from closer synonyms can speak to the speaker's current project.

Table 3.1 Relationship Between the Target Word and the Word Produced

Potential Target Word	Context	Word Produced
'pocket'	Fitting something into a place designed to receive it in order to secure it	'socket'
'disagree'	Stating a point of difference through starting a digression	'digress'
'schedule'	Difficulties with rail travel given one's work schedule	'timetable'

Near-Synonyms and Puns as Resources for Interaction

A conspicuous addition to the published version (Jefferson, 1996) of the 1977 talk (Nevile, 2015) is an appendix examining two phone calls made by the same person, Emma, in the aftermath of the assassination of Robert Kennedy. Jefferson opens with a very strong caveat.

> I've always figured that this case is so improbable that presenting it would simply impeach anything else I might say. Even at the Boston conference where my aim was to show the loopy side of Conversation Analysis, I left it out. But at this point I don't see that there's anything to be gained by being self-protective, so here it is.
>
> (Jefferson, 1996, p. 49)

In both calls, Emma attempts to share with her recipients the coincidence that the location where Kennedy's funeral casket was loaded onto an aircraft is the same place as her point of departure for a previous holiday in Hawaii, such that she recognised the airport buildings now appearing, tragically, on the news. In the course of her subtle exploration of Emma's talk and its opaqueness to her recipients, Jefferson suggests, 'It may be that Emma is indeed pointing to a feature of the landscape, but a landscape accessible only to her; an *internal landscape*' (Jefferson, 1996, p. 54; emphasis added).[12] This intersects with a

Topical Puns and Near-Synonyms 91

theme in Woods (1938), which Jefferson refers to earlier in her paper—that is, the idea that neurotypical people may experience the clang connections that occur in the talk of people with schizophrenia, but they do not voice them. People with schizophrenia differ, Woods suggests, in that they aren't attempting to communicate; Jefferson notes that in CA terms, their utterances are not recipient-designed.

Whilst speakers may sometimes struggle to share their experiences, the internal landscape can surface in a speaker's conduct and be available for others. In the cases examined here ('socket', 'timetable', 'digress'), the glimpses of the speakers' minds at work potentially affords the recipient insights into the speakers' concerns and foreshadows, or speaks to, where the speaker is going. This surfaces in a literal way in the following example, a case involving a connection with an object that is visible in the environment, rather than an expression in talk. On the spur of the moment, Bill has chosen to accompany a relative on their walk to an appointment. Following some talk about the route, it is known that Bill noticed a discarded banana skin in the road near where they are about to cross, and resolved to move it to a safe place. At this point he made the remark shown in Extract (17).

```
(17) [JR:FN] peel off
01 Bill:    I'll peel off when we get to the park
```

Of all the expressions that could be used to refer to ending their joint walk (e.g., 'I'll head off'), Bill produces 'peel off'. ('When vehicles, people, or animals peel away/off, they separate from the group or structure they were part of and move away in a different direction' https://dictionary.cambridge.org/dictionary/english/). This expression speaks of the banana skin (or peel) and perhaps moving it off the road.[13] Speaking to his internal landscape potentially identifies something in the shared landscape. This wording thereby provides a hint that he is going to break his stride to deal with the banana skin or that, when he does, this is not completely unexpected. A number of studies have identified how in co-present settings, the reorganization of participation involved in such things as making or taking a phone call (Rae, 2001), getting ready to dance in a dance class (Broth and Keevallik, 2014), or walking away (Broth and Mondada, 2013) involves the production of preparatory movements that can allow co-participants to see what might be underway and how to conduct themselves with respect to that incipient trajectory of action.

Connections between word-choices and previous and forthcoming matters occur in literature, a language-use situation where there is scope to go back and re-edit what is being presented. Here are two examples from Melville's *Moby Dick* (Melville, 1851), a retrospective one and prospective one; both concern the character Queequeg. Both involve offensive terms, which are possibly intended to portray the narrator's own prejudices at this stage in the story. In Chapter 7, the narrator, Ishmael, steps into a chapel and notices the members of the congregation are 'steadfastly eyeing several marble tablets, with black borders, masoned into the

92   *John P. Rae*

wall on either side the pulpit'. These are memorials naming lost relatives, giving the approximate location and date of loss. Ishmael narrates:

> Shaking off the sleet from my ice-glazed hat and jacket, I seated myself near the door, and turning sideways was surprised to see Queequeg near me. Affected by the solemnity of the scene, there was a wondering gaze of incredulous curiosity in his countenance. This savage was the only person present who seemed to notice my entrance; because he was the only one who could not read, and, therefore, was not reading those frigid inscriptions on the wall.
>
> *(Moby Dick, chapter 7, www.gutenberg.org/files/2701/*
> *2701-h/2701-h.htm)*

Merriam-Webster's dictionary gives the following definitions and synonyms for 'frigid': '1 b: lacking warmth or ardor [synonym] INDIFFERENT [e.g.] "had an emotionally frigid father" and 'and 2d: lacking imaginative qualities [synonym] INSIPID [e.g.] "writing precise and frigid" poetry'. However, in the context of this narrative, and the previous mention of 'sleet' and 'ice', the following meaning of 'frigid' is salient: '1a intensely cold'. Melville's word-selection thereby creates a connection between Ishmael's frozen appearance and the memorials; a synonym such as 'indifferent' or 'unfriendly' would not have made this connection.[14]

Conversely, word-choices can provide readers with resource to anticipate where the narrative is going. In a previous chapter, Ishmael's first encounter with Queequeg is described:

> he turned round—when, good heavens! what a sight! Such a face! It was of a dark, purplish, yellow colour, here and there stuck over with large blackish looking squares. Yes, it's just as I thought, he's a terrible bedfellow; he's been in a fight, got dreadfully cut, and here he is, just from the surgeon. But at that moment he chanced to turn his face so towards the light, that I plainly saw they could not be sticking-plasters at all, those black squares on his cheeks. They were stains of some sort or other. At first I knew not what to make of this; but soon an inkling of the truth occurred to me. I remembered a story of a white man—a whaleman too—who, falling among the cannibals, had been tattooed by them. I concluded that this harpooneer, in the course of his distant voyages, must have met with a similar adventure.
>
> *(Moby Dick, Chapter 3, www.gutenberg.org/files/*
> *2701/2701-h/2701-h.htm)*

Here we have the connection, this time punning, between 'inkling' and tattoos, a connection which synonyms such as 'vague notion' would have lacked. In fact, in this context, following the previous description of geometric shapes as 'black squares on his cheeks', the word 'inkling' is a punning clue.[15] It is possible that Melville's writing here is an instance of written productions reflecting spontaneous conversational practices (Person, 2016). In literature and in conversation, word-choice can allow the reader, or recipient, to share associations the writer, or speaker, is making.

Topical Puns and Near-Synonyms   93

The analysis offered here has sought to revisit Jefferson's (1996) examination of poetic phenomena involved in word-selection in talk-in-interaction, and to explore how it can be drawn on to examine near-synonyms in conversation. The treatment offered here is exploratory and is limited to a small number of cases. Nevertheless, it indicates that near-synonyms can be more than merely approximate word-choices; they can be relevant for the organization of joint experience and action in interaction. Future work with larger corpora, particularly with video recordings of co-present interactions, is needed. Further work could also give fuller consideration to the intersections between Jefferson's observational analysis and work in computational linguistics (e.g., Edmonds and Hirst, 2002) and psycholinguistics (e.g., Levelt, 1993; Levelt, Roelofs, and Meyer, 1999; Pickering and Garrod, 2013). One approach would be to integrate CA with experimentation (Kendrick, 2017). This could be relevant in determining whether or not speakers' word-choices are unusual.

The connection between the word-selections made in both near-synonym constructions and topical puns in spontaneous talk can be deeper than phonological or semantic association, but rather, can involve a relationship to the speaker's course of action. Such word-selections can capture a key aspect of the speaker's concerns and potentially make it available to the listener. In this way, something which might be seen as a merely a quirk of the speaker's psychology or language can contribute to making the speaker's concerns socially available. As a consequence, speakers' puns or near-synonyms could play a part in the achievement of shared understanding or joint action.

Notes

1. An earlier version of this paper was presented as a contribution to a panel on 'Poetics, the "Wild" Side of CA: Twenty Years after Jefferson', organized by Raymond F. Person, Jr., at the 15th International Pragmatics Conference, 16–21 July 2017, Belfast. I'm grateful for the discussion on that occasion. I'm also grateful to Ray Person and Robin Wooffitt for helpful comments and suggestions.
2. See also Bowles (this volume) for a similar literary example from Charles Dickens.
3. Extracts denoted by 'FN' are from field notes, rather than recordings. Whilst CA characteristically draws on recordings of interactions, field notes, though of lower evidential value, can be of value for illustrative purposes.
4. 'Socket' could potentially be a *blend* (Meringer and Mayer, 1895) of 'pocket' and 'sleeve'.
5. Bilmes (2011) provides a critical discussion and synthesis of category terms in conversation.
6. Here, 'Terry' is the actual name, not a pseudonym. Jefferson discusses the analytical problems posed by pseudonymization. The word 'momentarily' illustrates some of the difficulties in deciding whether or not one word is a synonym of another. In US English, 'momentarily' is a synonym for 'soon' (i.e., 'in a moment'). However, in British English, its primary meaning is 'briefly' (i.e., 'for a moment'). This can lead to wry amusement—or concern—for speakers of British English on a flight when the cabin crew announces that the plane will be 'in the air momentarily').
7. Perhaps a critical comment on the coiled energy suggested by the slightly crouching position in which the band members are shown in Harry Hammond's (1920–2009) famous black and white photograph of The Beatles, backstage at the BBC Old Paris Cinema 1963 (Image ID 2006AF8509 © Victoria and Albert Museum, London).

94 *John P. Rae*

8. Although Jefferson uses the term 'reversal', the examples that she presents do not involve the production of the two putatively reversed elements. Hence, in psycholinguistic terminology, these are anticipations rather than exchanges.
9. Anwar (1981/1982) demonstrates that Medieval Arabic linguists made extensive studies of speech errors.
10. In the 1977 talk, a questioner raises parallels with an experiment in which participants were unable to hear their answers to questions by being played loud white noise through headphones (Mahl, 1972). In responding, Jefferson remarks that cases in her collection involve situations, such as sports commentating, where speakers, in a sense, are alone with their own speech. Another questioner suggests that Cooper and Ross's (1975) study of what are often called fixed binomials (e.g., 'ladies and gentlemen' rather than 'gentlemen and ladies') might be relevant.
11. Spreading activation processes are drawn on by Hopper (1992) in his discussion of the relationship between 'preaching' and 'teaching'. Bowles (this volume) also discusses Bergen's (2004) spreading activation account of phonesthemes.
12. A related point is made by Wooffitt and Holt (2011) in their analysis of talk-aloud protocols in psychology experiments. The relationship between conversation and cognition is explored from a number of perspectives in te Molder and Potter (2005).
13. Another expression for one party separating from another party also involves a potential connection to bananas ('to split').
14. Such a retrospective connection achieves a form of 'tying'; see Holt, this volume.
15. Note the pun on 'ink', and thereby the connection to tattooing contained in 'inkling'. The description 'stained' in the previous sentence is a further clue. A potential clue occurs two paragraphs previously with a mention of staining and quills, and use of the word 'tinkling', when prior to having the opportunity to inspect the man, Ishmael scrutinizes an item of clothing left in the room that he has been designated to share with Queequeg: 'I can compare it to nothing but a large door mat, ornamented at the edges with little tinkling tags something like the stained porcupine quills round an Indian moccasin'.

Works Cited

Anwar, M.S. (1982). The legitimate fathers of speech errors. In K. Versteegh, E.F.K. Koerner, and H.-J. Niederehe (Eds.), *The History of Linguistics in the Near East*. Amsterdam: John Benjamins, pp. 13–29. (Original work published 1981)

Bergen, B.K. (2004). The psychological reality of phonaesthemes. *Language*, 80, 290–311.

Berger, I., and Cartmill, J.A. (2017). Correcting malapropisms: strategies to bridge cultural and socioeconomic gaps. *International Journal of Human Rights in Healthcare*, 10, 84–94. https://doi.org/10.1108/IJHRH-12-2015-0040

Bilmes, J. (2011). Occasioned semantics: a systematic approach to meaning in talk. *Human Studies*, 34, 129–153. https://doi.org/10.1007/s10746-011-9183-z

Boomer, D.S., and Laver, J.D.M. (1968). Slips of the tongue. *British Journal of Disorders of Communication*, 3, 2–12. https://doi.org/10.3109/13682826809011435 [In Fromkin, 1973.]

Broth, M., and Keevallik, L. (2014). Getting ready to move as a couple: accomplishing mobile formations in a dance class. *Space and Culture*, 17, 107–121. https://doi.org/10.1177/1206331213508483

Broth, M., and Mondada, L. (2013). Walking away: the embodied achievement of activity closings in mobile interaction. *Journal of Pragmatics*, 47, 41–58.

Butterworth, B. (1982). Speech errors: old data in search of new theories. In A. Cutler (Ed.), *Slips of the Tongue and Language Production*. Berlin: Walter de Gruyter, pp. 73–108.

Cooper, W.E., and Ross, J.R. (1975). World order. In R.E. Grossman, L. James San, and T.J. Vance (Eds.), *Papers from the Parasession on Functionalism*. Chicago: Chicago Linguistic Society, pp. 63–111.

Davidson, D. (2005). *Truth, Language, and History*. Oxford: Oxford University Press.

Dell, G.S. (1986). A spreading-activation theory of retrieval in sentence production. *Psychological Review*, 93, 283–321. https://doi.org/10.1037/0033-295X.93.3.283

Dell, G.S., and Oppenheim, G.M. (2015). Insights for speech production planning from errors in inner speech. In M. Redford (Ed.), *Handbook of Speech Production*. Oxford: Wiley-Blackwell, pp. 404–418.

Dressler, W.U. (2009). Freud vs. Meringer on slips of the tongue. In P. Giampieri-Deutsch (Ed.), *Geist, Gehirn, Verhalten: Sigmund Freud und die modernen Wissenschaften*. Würzburg: Königshausen & Neumann, pp. 159–171.

Drew, P. (1978). Accusations: the occasioned use of members' knowledge of religious geography in describing events. *Sociology*, 12, 1–22.

Edmonds, P., and Hirst, G. (2002). Near-synonymy and lexical choice. *Computational linguistics*, 28, 105–144.

Ellis, A.W. (1980). On the Freudian theory of speech errors. In V.A. Fromkin (Ed.), *Errors in Linguistic Performance*. New York: Academic Press, pp. 23–132.

Fay, D., and Cutler, A. (1977). Malapropisms and the structure of the mental lexicon. *Linguistic Inquiry*, 8, 505–520.

Freud, S. (1938). *The Psychopathology of Everyday Life. Jokes and the Release and the Unconscious*. J. Strachey and A. Richards (Eds.) and A. Tyson (Trans.). Middlesex: Penguin. (Original work published in 1901).

Freud, S. (1953). *On Aphasia: A Critical Study*. E. Stengel (Trans). Madison, CT: International Universities Press. (Original work published in 1891).

Fromkin, V.A. (Ed.) (1973). *Speech Errors as Linguistic Evidence*. Berlin: Walter de Gruyter.

Garnham, A., Shillcock, R.C., Brown, G.D., Mill, A.I., and Cutler, A. (1982). Slips of the tongue in the London-Lund corpus of spontaneous conversation. In A. Cutler (Ed.), *Slips of the Tongue and Language Production*. Berlin: De Gruyter Mouton, pp. 251–263. https://doi.org/10.1515/9783110828306

Hopper, R. (1992). Speech errors and the poetics of conversation. *Text and Performance Quarterly*, 12, 113–124.

Jefferson, G. (1996). On the poetics of ordinary talk. *Text and Performance Quarterly*, 16, 11–61.

Kendrick, K.H. (2017). Using conversation analysis in the lab. *Research on Language and Social Interaction*, 50, 1–11. https://doi.org/10.1080/08351813.2017.1267911

Lashley, K.S. (1951). The problem of serial order in behavior. In L.A. Jeffress (Ed.), *Cerebral Mechanisms in Behavior: The Hixon Symposium*. New York: Wiley, pp. 112–146.

Levelt, W.J. (1993). *Speaking: From Intention to Articulation*. Boston: MIT Press.

Levelt, W.J.M., Roelofs, A., and Meyer, A.S. (1999). A theory of lexical access in speech production. *Behavioral and Brain Sciences*, 22(1), 1–38. https://doi.org/10.1017/S0140525X99001776

Mahl, G.F. (1972). People talking when they can't hear their voices. In A.W. Siegman and B. Pope (Eds.), *Studies in Dyadic Communication*. Elmsford: Pergamon, pp. 211–264. https://doi.org/10.1016/C2009-0-14566-X.

Melville, H. (1851). *Moby-Dick; or, The Whale*. Retrieved from: www.gutenberg.org/files/2701/2701-h/2701-h.htm

Meringer, R., and Mayer, K. (1895). *Versprechen und Verlesen: Eine psychologischlin guistische Studie*. Stuttgart: Göschenische Verlagshandlung.

96 *John P. Rae*

Nevile, M. (2015). *Transcription of Gail Jefferson*. Boston University Conference on Ethnomethodology and Conversation Analysis, 9 June 1977. Retrieved from: https://emcalegacy.info/jefferson.html

Person, R.F., Jr. (2016). *From Conversation to Oral Tradition: A Simplest Systematics for Oral Traditions*. London: Routledge.

Pickering, M.J., and Garrod, S. (2013). An integrated theory of language production and comprehension. *Behavioral and Brain Sciences*, 36, 329–347.

Rae, J.P. (2001). Organizing participation in interaction: doing participation framework. *Research on Language and Social Interaction*, 34, 253–278.

Rae, J.P. (2008). Lexical substitution as a therapeutic resource. In A. Peräkylä, C. Antaki, S. Vehviläinen, and I. Leudar (Eds.), *Conversation Analysis and Psychotherapy*. Cambridge: Cambridge University Press, pp. 62–79.

Sacks, H. (1992). *Lectures on Conversation* (2 volumes). G. Jefferson and E.A. Schegloff (Eds.). Oxford and Cambridge: Basil Blackwell.

Schegloff, E.A. (1972). Notes on a conversational practice: formulating place. In D. Sudnow (Ed.), *Studies in Social Interaction*. New York: The Free Press, pp. 75–119.

Schegloff, E.A. (1996). Some practices for referring to persons in talk-in-interaction: a partial sketch of a systematics. In B.A. Fox (Ed.), *Studies in Anaphora*. Amsterdam: John Benjamins, 437–486.

Schegloff, E.A. (2000). On granularity. *Annual Review of Sociology*, 26, 715–720.

Schegloff, E.A. (2003a). The surfacing of the suppressed. In P.J. Glenn, C.D. LeBaron, and J. Mandelbaum (Eds.), *Studies in Language and Social Interaction: In Honor of Robert Hopper*. Mahwah, NJ: Lawrence Erlbaum Associates, pp. 241–262.

Schegloff, E.A. (2003b). On ESP puns. In P.J. Glenn, C.D. LeBaron, and J. Mandelbaum (Eds.), *Studies in Language and Social Interaction: In Honor of Robert Hopper*. Mahwah, NJ: Lawrence Erlbaum Associates, pp. 452–460.

Schegloff, E.A. (2007). A tutorial on membership categorization. *Journal of Pragmatics*, 39, 462–482. https://doi.org/10.1016/j.pragma.2006.07.007

Sheridan, R.B. (1775). *The Rivals*. Retrieved from: www.gutenberg.org/ebooks/24761

te Molder, H.E., and Potter, J.E. (2005). *Conversation and Cognition*. Cambridge: Cambridge University Press.

Unnsteinsson, E. (2017). A Gricean theory of malaprops. *Mind & Language*, 32, 446–462.

Vitevitch, M.S. (1997). The neighborhood characteristics of malapropisms. *Language and Speech*, 40, 211–228.

Woods, W.L. (1938). Language study in schizophrenia. *The Journal of Nervous and Mental Disease*, 87, 290–316.

Wooffitt, R., and Holt, N. (2011). Introspective discourse and the poetics of subjective experience. *Research on Language & Social Interaction*, 44, 135–156.

4 The Poetics in Jefferson's Poetics Lecture

Robin Wooffitt, Darren Reed, Jessica A. Young, and Clare Jackson

Introduction

We begin with two quotations. The first comes from Gail Jefferson's lecture on the poetics of ordinary conversation, presented at the 1977 Boston University Conference on Ethnomethodology and Conversation Analysis.[1] The second comes From Robert Hopper's (1992) paper on speech errors and poetics, published in *Text and Performance Quarterly*.

> by the way (1.0) if you ever think you're gonna lecture on this stuff you have t' be very careful because you start doing it
>
> (Jefferson, 1977, lines 689–670)

> We approach embodied interactive phenomena by way of evidence that speech errors make manifest. This evidence shows figures of speech operating in everyday interaction, *and reveals fragments of the great poem speaking us into being*.
>
> (Hopper, 1992, p. 122, emphasis added.)

The argument and observations in this paper attempt to bridge these two statements.

Anyone who has lectured on, or written about, conversational poetics knows just how right Jefferson was. For example, the authors of this chapter have numerous experiences of discussing data to identify a specific poetic phenomenon, while at the same time reproducing that very phenomenon in their talk or text. It is curiously hard *not* to do. And once intellectual interest in these phenomena is piqued, it is virtually impossible not to notice them as they occur in data or in everyday life. While Jefferson's comment identifies a practical consequence of an academic concern for conversational poetics, Hopper's remarks, which come at the end of his paper, seem to point to something of deeper significance. He implies that poetic forms may have a constitutive and foundational role in social interaction (see Holt, this volume). Our empirical observations (we hope) reveal further 'fragments of the great poem', and thereby support Hopper's contemplation about the foundational role of poetics in our lives.

DOI: 10.4324/9780429328930-6

98 *Robin Wooffitt et al.*

Our data are the video recording and transcript of Jefferson's 1977 lecture. We began to examine Jefferson's lecture as part of a small weekly data session some years ago. We selected her lecture as it provided both audio and video data, and the relation between talk and bodily movement was an interest of the group. But beyond that, there was no expectation that her talk would yield such rich data on conversational poetics. That it does provides evidence in support of both Jefferson's and Hopper's arguments.

We have examined her lecture as data in this chapter for several reasons. There is a neat and appealing reflexivity in exploring poetic phenomena in her talk on conversational poetics. Her observation that if 'you're gonna lecture on this stuff you have t' be very careful because you start doing it' virtually compels anyone interested in conversational poetics to study this lecture. The study of conversational poetics in academic lecturing stands as an extension to studies of conversational poetics and their relationship to rhetorical figures in ancient oral traditions from other cultures (Person, 2016; this volume).

There is a final, more substantial reason behind using Jefferson's lecture. Sociology has not in any significant sense engaged with poetics. There have been some attempts to advocate for a more lyrical or aesthetic sociology (such as Abbott, 2007), or an exploration of the theoretical foundations for a sociology of art and aesthetics (for example, Swingewood, 1987), but beyond that, there is little, other than a literature on art and music more generally (for example, Brown, 1977; Stevenson, 2017). There have been further CA studies of poetics which pick up themes from Sacks' lectures and Jefferson's 1996 paper (Beach, 1993; Hopper, 1992; Wooffitt and Holt, 2011a; 2011b) and there is work on poetics from other disciplines concerned with discourse and communication (Norrick, 2000/2001; Tannen, 1987; 1990; 1998). But there is no significant or sustained concern with a sociological poetics. We want to argue that Jefferson's work, and her extension of Sacks' original observations on conversational poetics, provides the basis for a sociological exploration of poetics. It is a particular kind of sociology, to be sure: CA is regarded as a departure from the substantive and methodological canon of the discipline, certainly in the UK. But for those us who are committed to the empirical investigation of social interaction achieved through talk, CA is quintessentially sociological (Hutchby and Wooffitt, 2008; Maynard, 2013). In that sense, a CA examination of poetics is a sociological engagement, and Jefferson's work has to be central to that. Her place in that sociology of poetics should be as significant as Hymes' (1998) work on ethnopoetics in anthropology, and Jacobson's (1987[1961]) work on poetics and linguistics. By focusing on the content and structure of Jefferson's lecture on poetics, we hope to give a platform to and evidence for that argument.

In the spirit of the playful features of poetics, and Jefferson's disclosure that CA has a wild side, our approach departs from the rigour that is typically associated with papers reporting CA research. We do not, for example, identify and track the distributionalized contours of a specific phenomenon across a collection of instances. Neither do we offer next-turn proof procedures to substantiate our

The Poetics in Jefferson's Poetics Lecture   99

claims. Nor do we investigate deviant cases to refine our empirical claims. Instead, we examine (usually) discrete instances of a range of phenomena. In the spirit of exploration that informs Sacks' lectures on poetics and Jefferson's lecture and paper, we push our arguments as far as they will go—far more than we would in a more conventional paper intended for dissemination in an academic journal. We recognize that this leaves us open to the charge that we are letting our imaginations run ahead of us, and claiming order and design where there is mere happenstance. Sacks recognized the same potential critique: that the sound associations and other poetical relationships he was identifying in his data were speech events that were not robust, sequentially organized interactional phenomena. But he persevered, nonetheless. His rationale:

> Well, is there anything to it. . . . Well who knows? Noticing it, you get the possibility of investigating it. Laughing it off in the first instance, or not even allowing yourself to notice it, of course it becomes impossible to find out whether there is anything to it. . . . Now there is a tremendous temptation on the part of people doing social science in general, to not notice a possible fact unless they already have an explanation for it. And . . . that's awfully silly, and it's of rather more interest to get in a position to be able to notice possible facts for which the question is, then, what in the world could explain that?
>
> (Sacks, 1992, vol. II, p. 292)

Our analysis of poetic forms in Jefferson's lecture is undertaken in the spirit of intellectual openness expressed in that quote, and which is exemplified by Sacks' analysis of conversational organization more generally. We begin with some observations on basic sound-runs, and then develop the argument that Jefferson's lecture contains some more complex poetic forms: short-form micro poetics, and formal poetics and rhetorical figures.

Sound-Runs

Consider the following excerpt from Jefferson's talk (which has been amended from Nevile's transcription).

```
190   now I'm gonna be looking a:t talk (0.9)
191   u::m (2.0) pretty much (0.8) it's figured that (0.5) all these
192   mar:vellous sounds (0.7) are the providence of- (0.3) poets (0.8)
193   who make it their business (0.7) to work out (0.2) to seek out (0.5)
194   to really endeavor to find jus' the word (0.7)
195   I'm gonna read you a- (0.5) this is gonna be (0.4) a translation
196   done by a committee (0.4) of a poem by Paul Valéry (0.6)
197   that's (.) at the top (.) Harvey has a collection of (0.3)
198   sound phenomena (0.3)
199   and at the top of it (0.3) is this poem (0.2) by Paul Valéry and it
200   goes (0.8)
```

100   *Robin Wooffitt et al.*

```
201   I'm looking for a word said the poet (0.6)
202   a word which should be: (0.4)
203   feminine (0.3) of two syllables (0.4)
204   having P or F (0.6) with a muted ending (0.5)
205   and synonymous with splitting (.) to segregation (0.4)
206   and not scholarly (0.3) not rare (0.5)
207   six conditions at least (.) exclamation point (0.8)
208   that's the poem (0.8) tha::t's the poet's job (0.4) °alright°
209   (0.7)
210   now you look over at pathology (0.2) which is the other domain (0.7)
211
212   an' psychotic talk the clangs and associations (0.6) about
213   which (.) people's um (1.1) people say well (0.2)
214   you have all these crazy things going o:n (0.6)
215   now Woods made a very nice observation (0.7)
216   when he says (0.6) he says this about a particular pathological
217   activity an' I'm jus' gonna adapt it to: (0.5) across the board for
218   any of them (1.2)
219   there is probably nothing pathological about them as a purely
220   subjective phenom- as purely subjective phenomena (0.6)
221   introspective observation will verify that we are prone t' do
222   them (0.7)
223   what is pathological is the tendency to incorporate such autistic
224   productions (0.5) without any endeavor to translate them into a form
225   which considers the needs of a listener (1.2)
226   Woods complained (0.7) he has a lovely complaint throughout
```

There is a dominant 'P' sound-run here (with a less pronounced 'V'-run). The 'P'-run is 'pretty' (191), 'providence' (192), 'poets' (192), 'poem' (196), 'Paul' (196), 'poem' (199), 'Paul' (199), 'poet' (201), 'P' (204), 'point' (207), 'poem' (208), 'poet's' (208), 'pathology' (210), 'people's' (213), 'people' (213), 'particular pathological' (216), 'probably' (219), 'pathological' (219), 'purely' (219), 'purely' (220), 'prone' (221), 'pathological' (223), and 'pro-ductions' (224).[2]

In each of these cases, the 'P'-sound occurs in word-initial position. In addition, there are numerous words which contain a 'P'-sound in a subsequent, noninitial position, such as 'top' (197 and 199), 'splitting' (205) (though this does come from the quoted poem), 'adapt' (217), 'introspective' (221), 'incorporate' (223), and finally 'complained' and 'complaint' (226). We include these as Jefferson was also minded to see words containing a particular sound as evidence of the operations of a run (Jefferson, 1990, p. 69; 1996, p. 13).

We can speculate as to the trigger for this run. Jefferson is getting to part of her talk where she talks about a poem, which explicitly refers to words beginning with the letter 'P', written by a poet whose first name is Paul. Whatever the reason, though, there is evidence that this run is oriented to and sustained. Its occurrence is an achievement. There are, for example, occasions in which a self-repair is initiated on part of the talk that contains a word beginning with 'P'. The self-repair may require the repetition of part of the repaired talk that leads to a repeat of a 'P'-word.

The Poetics in Jefferson's Poetics Lecture 101

```
219   there is probably nothing pathological about them as a purely
220   subjective phenom- as purely subjective phenomena (0.6)
```

Here, the repair (the omission of the article 'a') ensures that 'purely' is repeated. Alternatively, the repair may lead to a minor modification of a word beginning with 'P', as in the following case, which again contributes to the ongoing 'P'-run.

```
213   which (.) people's um (1.1) people say well (0.2)
```

There is a more protracted repair in lines 216–217, in which additional material exhibits further instances of the ongoing sound-run.

```
215   now Woods made a very nice observation (0.7)
216   when he says (0.6) he says this about a particular pathological
217   activity an' I'm jus' gonna adapt it to: (0.5) across the board for
218   any of them (1.2)
219   there is probably nothing pathological about them as a purely
```

In this excerpt, Jefferson begins to report a claim by Woods about features of talk by persons with schizophrenia. The insertion after the repair in line 216 clarifies that she is taking a general principle from this specific case. This act of logical extension may have been conveyed in various ways. However, the design of her turn, and the use of the phrase 'particular pathological', not only has its own melodic tone, but sustains the overarching 'P'-run.

In each of these cases of self-repair, the consequence is the production of repeats of 'P'-words, or the inclusion of additional 'P'-words.

The 'P'-run is also maintained through some more conspicuous word-selection choices. The phrase 'autistic productions' (223–224) is a case in point. Here 'productions' seems to imply intent, and therefore seems ill-fitted for a turn in which Jefferson is referring to moments in talk that are the result of a medical condition, and not something the speaker would intend to happen.

However, given the prominence of a 'P'-run in the immediately prior context, 'what is pathological is the tendency to incorporate . . .', then the choice of 'production' is entirely fitted.

In the following excerpt, there is a word-selection error which is not repaired. Jefferson says:

```
191   … all these
192   mar:vellous sounds (0.7) are the providence of- (0.3) poets (0.8)
```

Here Jefferson is noting that it is the task of the poet to 'craft sounds'. She says this is the 'providence' of poets. But it is likely that she was intending to say 'provenance', which, in its invocation of origins, appropriate ownership, and authority, fits better with the point that she is making.

The difference between the two words is minor: they have the same number of syllables, both begin with 'prov', and both end with 'nce'. (Incidentally,

102 *Robin Wooffitt et al.*

'provenance' replaces 'providence' in the written version published in *Text and Performance Quarterly* [Jefferson, 1996, p. 4] and is retained in the reprinted version in Drew and Bergmann's edited collection of her papers on repair and correction [Jefferson, 2018, p. 130]). Given the structural similarities, and the correction in the published versions of the paper, it would be easy to view her use of 'providence' as an understandable and momentary slip of no further analytic interest. However, prior to the sequence of talk in which we have identified a 'P'-run (that is, prior to line 190), Jefferson has been talking about the work of Woods, which she clearly admires. And towards the end of this 'P'-run, she returns to discussion of his work. 'Woods' contains a strong 'D'-sound, and stands as a referential and (to a lesser extent) acoustic context for the temporary flurry of 'P'-sounds. This perhaps provides a poetic logic for the apparent word-selection error: 'providence' supplies the 'D'-sound that connects with her ongoing concern with Woods' work, whereas 'provenance' does not.

We mentioned earlier that in the run of 'P'-sounds there is a simultaneous but less marked run of 'V'-sounds. Again, we can speculate that the trigger for this was the topic of that specific part of Jefferson's talk. She is describing how she came to work on poetics. She was guided by observations from Harvey (Sacks), and she is about to report the translation of the poem by Valéry.

The 'V'-run is comparatively infrequent. Moreover, it is comprised of more words that contain the sound, rather than begin with it: 'marvellous' (192), 'providence' (192), 'endeavour' (194), 'Valéry' (196), 'Harvey' (197), 'Valéry' (199), 'over' (210), 'observation' (215), 'verify' (221), and 'endeavour' (224). In this little cluster, though, we see more evidence of work to maintain the run, such as repetition of the poet's name, and selection of the word 'endeavour'. The second use of 'endeavour' seems out of place in the broader semantic context, echoing the conspicuous selection of some of the words in the 'P'-run. But the first use of 'endeavour' (line 194) has additional interesting features. It arrives in lines 193–194.

```
193   who make it their business (0.7) to work out (0.2) to seek out (0.5)
194   to really endeavor to find jus' the word (0.7)
```

Here, Jefferson is embarking on the utterance: 'who make it their business . . . to find jus' the right word', which includes a three-part list, 'to work out', 'to seek out', and 'to endeavour'. The list seems superfluous. However, lists normatively come in threes (Jefferson, 1990; Person, this volume). This means that, once initiated, there are three opportunities for further word-selection to capture the poets' efforts at word-selection, which itself constitutes a reflexively poetic moment. It is in the third opportunity presented by the list that Jefferson alights on 'endeavour' to capture the poet's concerns with finding the right word. This maintains the discernible 'V'-run, while illustrating precisely the effort and labour her three-part list seeks to convey.

There are, then, sound-runs (predominantly alliterative) in Jefferson's lecture. This is not a surprise, given that it is recognized that poetic phenomena are often

The Poetics in Jefferson's Poetics Lecture   103

reproduced in our discourse on them. In the next two sections, however, we see evidence of the operation of more structural poetic forms.

Short-Form Micro Poetics

In some parts of her lecture, Jefferson produces momentary spates of talk that seem to exhibit an organization similar to formal poetics, be it in terms of length, tempo, word-choice, and so on. Sometimes we have to dig to find these, as in the first case in the following section. About halfway through her talk, Jefferson is illustrating occasions in which the exact opposite category-selection than the clearly intended one pops into the talk, for example, where 'mother' is said where 'father' was the target (see lines 638–640 of Nevile's transcript). The specific case she is building towards concerns a political interview with the US Postmaster General, in which he inadvertently criticizes the Republicans, rather than the intended targets, the Democrats. She says of this datum:

```
653  He's attempting (0.6) to do a criticism of the Democrats…
```

We were struck by the design of this turn. 'He's attempting to do . . .' seems conspicuous. Surely the more natural formulation would be 'make a criticism, or 'offer a criticism': but 'do' a criticism?

It might be that this was a vernacular phrase common in the US at the time, or it may have been idiosyncratic to Jefferson. But it is odd to our ears. Our sense of the oddness of this phrase is supported by recognition of the way that in certain speech events, the use of 'to do' or its variants is used humorously to introduce an action. The first author noticed this trend recently on football chat sites, where submissions would defend a player who was sent from the field for abusive language with claims to the effect that 'he only did a swear'. The use of 'did/do' in these cases minimizes the offensive action. (An example of this use of 'did'/'do' can be found here: www.football365.com/news/england-player-ratings-wales-grealish-coady-calvert-lewin.)[3] We do not think Jefferson was using 'to do' in the ironic or anachronistic way we have observed in contemporary examples of this formulation, but there is another reason why 'to do' works here, rather than 'make' or 'offer'. Some components of this turn constitute a short poem:

> *do a criticism*
> *[of the] Democrats'*

Broken down, we can see the poetic elements more clearly in this:

| **Do** | *a* | **CR***iticism* |
| **Dem** | *o* | **CR***ats* |

Both 'lines' begin with a strong 'D'-sound; after the first syllable there is a vowel, and the final part of each begins with the 'CR'-sound. That poetic configuration

104   *Robin Wooffitt et al.*

would be lost with the more conventional ways to formulate an intention to offer a criticism.

There is a similar poetic form in an earlier part of the talk, in which Jefferson is providing the historical context of the work on poetics. She is reporting that Sacks had written a note to himself to ask her to look at some data in which there seemed to be a particular clustering of sounds which might be of analytic interest. She then rounds off this historical account.

```
115   okay so that's: where for me it got started (0.3) I have a feeling
116   it's been going on for ever and ever (0.7)
117   ah Harvey had clearly been reading (0.2) all sorts of stuff about it
118   (.) without an interest i- (.) in it (0.4)
```

In the last two lines, Jefferson conveys the way that Sacks' interest in conversational poetics seemed to be incidental to the main focus of his work. She then says:

```
119  it's not new with us (.) it doesn't reside with us
```

Again, broken down, it becomes apparent that this is another instance of momentary poetic expression:

> *it's not new with us*
> *it doesn't reside with us*

There are similarities in the design of these two components that lead to a certain poetic parallelism between them (see Frog, this volume):

1. They are approximately the same length (5–7 syllables)
2. Both begin with it's/it
3. Both components are negatively framed (i.e., 'it's [it is] not new . . .', 'it doesn't [does not] reside . . .')
4. Both are completed by the phrase 'with us', thereby placing CA (or CA as it was at that time) at the perspectival centre.

The present tense construction of 'it's not new with us' seems to herald a shift in the focus of Jefferson's talk, in that she is about to shift the topic from an account of how she came to collect instances of conversational poetics, to discussion of another researcher's ongoing work on talk of people with schizophrenia. It also seems to capture that conversational poetics is (or had been) known to Sacks and colleagues for some time. The turn component 'it doesn't reside with us' seems to acknowledge that the phenomena was not at that point central to their research on interaction. Despite this logic, we felt the second component was curiously designed. To us, the use of the verb 'reside' seems conspicuous. To reside is to live in a place, which seems a clumsy metaphor to convey the lack of importance of poetics in CA research. However, again, there are acoustic contexts in the immediately prior talk,

The Poetics in Jefferson's Poetics Lecture   105

and in the immediately subsequent talk, that may have triggered selection of this verb.

There is a run of 'R'-sounds in the anecdote detailing how Jefferson came to learn of Sacks' preliminary observations. From line 99 on, there is 'remembered' (99 and 100), 'written' (102), 'read' (106 and 107), 'repetition' (108), 'rephrased repetitions' (109–110), and 'reading' (117). Interspersed through this run are additional words with strong 'R'-sounds (occasionally given prominence through Jefferson's accent): 'addressed' (100), 'handwritten' (twice in 105), 'clearly' (117), and phrases such as 'turn up a corpus' (113–114) and 'for ever and ever' (116). The design of the anecdote about Sacks' note floods the talk with 'R'-sounds: the note was hand*written*, she couldn't *read* it, she thought it was about *repetitions*, but in fact he was interested in *rephrased repetition*. Given this acoustic context, the choice of 'reside with us' (119) may be a continuation of the active run established in the prior talk.

The choice of 'reside' may have anticipated what was coming next in Jefferson's talk. The next thing she says is

```
120   u::m (1.2) Judy Davidson….
```

Then, a few seconds later, she introduces Woods' work into the talk. Starting in line 127, there is a cluster of 'D'-sounds that seems to herald the first mention of Woods. Describing how she began to read relevant literature, Jefferson says: 'So Ju*d*y brought in some stuff and I starte*d* rea*d*ing it, which I *d*on't usually *d*o, and what happene*d* was that I *d*evelope*d*. . .' (127–130). 'Reside' may therefore constitute both a continuation of the 'R'-run and a precursor to the 'D'-run that is launched around the names Judy Davidson and Woods.

From line 821 onwards, Jefferson describes how, when working with Arlene Terasaki, they came upon something that, in her words 'strikes you as a little bit funny, just something special or interesting' (827–829). When confronted with something unusual, she recommends 'tracking back through the data' (830) to see if there is some root for the oddity in prior talk.[4] Terasaki had found the use of the word 'affronted' of particular interest in the data they were both concerned with, as it did not seem to fit with the talk in which it was produced. Investigation revealed that prior to the use of 'affronted', 'behind' had been central to the talk. Jefferson considered the relevance of the categorical pairing of 'behind/front', established by 'behind', to provide a least a plausible explanation for the out-of-place 'affronted'. We had found 'it doesn't reside with us' to be 'a little bit funny/special/interesting', and examination of the prior talk suggested the strong influence of the 'R'-run that 'reside' continued. This degree of influence on word-selection also supports our claim that 'reside' anticipates that Jefferson's talk is approaching reference to Judy Davidson, and later, Woods.[5]

There may be another anticipatory element at play. Jefferson clearly admires Woods' work. As a conversation analyst, it is no surprise that she is sympathetic

106 *Robin Wooffitt et al.*

to his decision to study naturally occurring discourse, rather than data generated from some experimental setting. She says:

```
142   b't this guy was very much in favour o:f (1.2) what he called the
143   living language
```

Woods' phrase, the 'living language', was sufficiently important for Jefferson to repeat it in her lecture.

This resonates with Schegloff's (2004) paper on the way in which tunes whistled absentmindedly can musically articulate ongoing matters of concern connected to immediate external or environmental considerations. He reports his first noticing of a form of the phenomenon:

> It started—at least I first noticed it—one day in the late 60's or early 70's, while I was walking the two blocks from the bus stop at Broadway and 86th St. in New York City to our apartment house. I 'caught myself' incessantly whistling a fragment of a melody from a then-popular tune. It was driving me crazy. What was that?!! When I finally figured out the words—in fact, the words that are carried by that fragment of the melody which I had been repeating—I was taken aback. Although I no longer recall either the melody or the words, they virtually named a matter I knew myself to be concerned with, but had not been aware I was concerned with just then. It was like the surfacing of a 'leak' from a stream of 'subconsciousness.'
>
> (Schegloff, 2004, p. 19)

Schegloff's observations raise the possibility that tacit word-selection procedures are so intimately entwined with matters of ongoing concern that they may reflect a homophonic grasp at the word 'living'. That is: to reside is to live in a place. Could it be that the selection of 'reside' anticipates the phrase Woods used to capture his data: the *liv in* (g) language?

Formal Poetics and Rhetorical Figures

In this section, we examine more formal poetic organizations and rhetorical figures that are to be found in parts of Jefferson's lecture.

Our interest in rhetorical figures reflects the fact that when they occur, they seem to be vehicles for the continuation of poetic forms. We noticed earlier, for example, that at one point in her talk, Jefferson produces a three-part list, with the third part, 'to endeavor', contributing to an ongoing 'V'-run.

```
193   who make it their business (0.7) to work out (0.2) to seek out (0.5)
194   to really endeavor to find jus' the word (0.7)
```

Later, in the midst of the 'P'-run we discussed in an earlier section, Jefferson begins to report some of Woods' arguments based on his analysis of the talk of people

The Poetics in Jefferson's Poetics Lecture   107

with schizophrenic symptoms. She reports that Woods argued that the 'clangs and associations' (157) that interested him should not be treated as pathological; what was unusual was that these peculiarities of talk were not interactionally fitted. In CA terms, there was no recipient design. This is how Jefferson articulates this observation:

```
219   there is probably nothing pathological about them as a purely
220   subjective phenom- as purely subjective phenomena (0.6)
223   what is pathological is the tendency to incorporate such autistic
224   productions (0.5) without any endeavor to translate them into a form
225   which considers the needs of a listener
```

This takes the rhetorical form: position X is wrong (subjectively, the peculiarities are *not* pathological); but position Y is right (interactionally, the peculiarities *are* pathological). It is, then, a form of contrast structure common to political speeches (Atkinson, 1984; Heritage and Greatbatch, 1986) and advertising (McQuarrie and Mick, 1996).

Contrast structures are rhetorically most effective when the two opposing positions are adjacent (Heritage and Greatbatch, 1986), but that is not the case with Jefferson's contrast structure; in our presentation previously, we edited out a short addition. The actual sequence is this:

```
A:    there is probably nothing pathological about them as a purely
      subjective phenom- as purely subjective phenomena (0.6)

      introspective observation will verify that we are prone t do
      them (0.7)

B:    what is pathological is the tendency to incorporate such autistic
      productions (0.5) without any endeavor to translate them into a
      form which considers the needs of a listener
```

As in contrast structures in political rhetoric, the production of the first part projects the relevance of the second. The first part establishes an expectation that the turn will continue in a particular way. In this case, however, the expected second part is not produced at the end of the first; there is additional talk expanding on the first: 'introspective observation will verify that we are prone t do them'. This is plainly not the second part of the contrast, and so the expectation that the second will be produced still obtains.

Talk embedded into two-part devices may do pragmatic and inferentially oriented work, paralleling the interactional work that is managed through insertions in sequential organisations (for a review, see Stivers, 2013). For example, Wooffitt (1991) found that people reporting paranormal experiences often use a format to introduce their first awareness of the phenomenon they were reporting. This format is 'I was just doing X . . . when Y', where the X component details the circumstances at the time, and the Y component reports the actual paranormal event. (So, a first encounter with a violent spirit entity is described

108　*Robin Wooffitt et al.*

as 'I was going through the doorway (0.7) I was just (.) jammed against the door post'; Wooffitt, 1991, pp. 269–270). Wooffitt noted that, on occasions, there was talk embedded between the X and Y components. In each case, these additions were designed to underpin the claimed factual status of the experience. He argued that explicit claims to the facticity of the reported event are inferentially sensitive, in that they can be taken to be evidence of the opposite of what is claimed (a sceptical response captured in the line from Hamlet: 'the lady doth protest too much'). Embedding evidential talk between the two parts of the 'X when Y' device, while the expected production of the second is still relevant, minimizes its manifestly inferential objectives.

There is evidence, then, that the moment between the two parts of rhetorical figures provides a resource to accomplish or develop pragmatic objectives. It is a site in which work can be done in support of an ongoing discourse project. Jefferson's embedded talk in her contrast structure does not do the same kind of explicitly evidential work, but it does allow her to continue the ongoing 'P'-run, as she reflects on the ubiquity of poetic phenomena: she says we are 'prone to do them'.

If we can see the emergence of basic rhetorical figures, such as three-part lists and contrast structures, and short-form poetic organizations, are there any other formal structures evident in her lecture? We think there is one more, though it comes not in the main body of her talk, but during the question-and-answer session at the end of her lecture.

A member of the audience (identified as QU5 in Nevile's transcript, and just Q in both Jefferson's 1996 paper and the version printed in Drew and Bergmann, 2018) begins a turn at line 1326 with reference to the work of a psychotherapist that bears on the topic of Jefferson's talk. He describes the work, which was examining the effect of reduced capacity to self-monitor one's speech on the features of the talk. He concludes by reporting that that study discovered that 'this sort of stuff' (line 1335, presumably referring to poetic phenomena) occurred more frequently the less participants could monitor their own talk. The following extract picks up from the end of QU5's turn (58 minutes and 40 seconds in the video recording).

```
1335 Q   their own speech (0.2) the more this sort of stuff (C.3) came up
1336 GJ  wonderful (0.2) oh that's fabulou[s]. [(mmm )     [(            )]
1337 Q                                  [a]nd A:Lso (0.2)[other things](.)
1338     like ah=
1339 GJ  =wait a minute I have t' e-yo- y' have t be suspicious (.) of
1340     comments like that (.) that means I hav- I have something to say on
1341     it when a recipient says oh that's terrific (0.6) give them room
1342     (.) °'cause they wanna talk° u:::m (1.3) the kind of talk I do when
1343     I (.) do a lecture in class is: (.) loose to the point of: (0.2)
1344     lunacy (0.2) that is I will jus say whatever happens to occur to me
1345     (1.4) thank you very much
```

There is some confusion about who has rights to speak in lines 1336 and 1337. Clearly QU5 has heard Jefferson's 'oh that's fabulous' as turn ending. There are grounds for this inference. During the question the camera had been on QU5. It

The Poetics in Jefferson's Poetics Lecture   109

only pans back to Jefferson as she is saying 'that's fabulous'. But when she comes into shot Jefferson has turned away from her audience, stepped back to her right and has her left hand cupped over her mouth. At this point she is nearly facing the blackboard. So, QU5 can see that Jefferson has physically disengaged with the audience (and him), and has imposed a physical barrier over her mouth. This is further evidence that her turn had ended after 'fabulous'. Her brief reflective 'mmm' (which might mitigate that inference) is also obscured by the volume at which QU5 continues his turn with 'also' (line 1337). There is some other vocal sound from Jefferson (itself barely audible), which might be a further, but softer, 'mm'. It is at least possible that the combination of Jefferson's physical movement, and relative volumes of Jefferson's continuation post-'fabulous' and QU5's 'and'-prefaced turn (in 1137), led him to infer that he was in the clear to speak further.

It transpires, though, that he was not. Jefferson's 'wait a minute' is interjacently positioned (Jefferson, 1986), in that it is not in the vicinity of a TCU, and ends QU5's turn (see Szczepek-Reed, 2017, on 'meta cut-offs'). It is not, however, a turn which is designed to attend to conversational material which, for procedural reasons, has to be addressed immediately (for example, new information from QU5). We know this because, having gained the floor, Jefferson launches a turn which establishes her rights to ongoing speakership. There is a self-repair, from 'I have to' to 'you have to'. Then there is a recommendation to be 'suspicious' of turns like 'oh that's terrific' as they indicate a speaker has more to say on a topic. (Incidentally: she has just said 'oh that's fabulous'. Yet when referring to that *kind* of phrase, she says 'oh that's terrific'. There is a poetic logic to the substitution of 'fabulous' with 'terrific', in that the latter is a constitutive component of a short-lived constellation of 'R'-sounds: 'recipient', 'terrific', and 'room'. In addition, 'terrific' contributes to a fractured and distributed three-part list of 'F'-sounds: 'fabulous', 'wonderful', 'terrific'.) Jefferson's turn also exhibits a pedagogic tone towards QU5, as Jefferson tells him why he was wrong to continue speaking: he needs to recognize that, when someone says something like 'oh that's wonderful' they have more to say, 'cause they wanna talk'.

Having set up that she has more to say on the topic, and in so doing establishing a form of conversational norm (which, by implication, QU5 has failed to observe), Jefferson does not immediately return to the topic she has just established is her interactional right. Instead, she launches into an account of her teaching practices. This may be a way of modulating or softening the element of correction metered out in her prior talk. This is because she explicitly draws attention to her unorthodox lecturing style to undergraduates, the implication being that her 'loose' style of university lecturing is evident here, too, in an academic conference, and that this 'loose' style somehow explains QU5's error in (according to Jefferson) inappropriately continuing his turn when she had not completed hers.

This 'concessionary' component of her turn is here:

```
1342   the kind of talk I do when
1343   I (.) do a lecture in class is: (.) loose to the point of: (0.2)
1344   lunacy (0.2) that is I will jus say whatever happens to occur to me
```

110 *Robin Wooffitt et al.*

After this there is a gap of (1.4), during which time someone in the audience makes a remark, which is heard by Jefferson, but which is too quiet for transcription. She says 'thank you very much', and there is a ripple of laughter in the audience. This suggests that the audience hears this as an ironic receipt of a playful turn, possibly a deprecating agreement with her admittedly chaotic lecturing style. Jefferson then returns to the topic of poetic phenomena occurring when speakers experience diminished sensory awareness.

The report of her teaching style in lines 1342–1344, is, then, an interleaved account of her teaching style, and has many poetic qualities. There is repetition: 'I do', 'I do'. There is the 'L'-run in 'lecture', 'loose', and 'lunacy', the last two of which also establish the 'OO'-sound. There may be an association between 'lunacy' and Woods' interest in the talk of people with schizophrenia. Overall, there is a melodic tone and rhythm to this sequence.

It is, of course, a little story about her. It is designedly nonserious; it is offered as an amusing and *exaggerated* insight into her teaching delivery style. One might refer to one's lecturing style as informal, and perhaps even loose—but to the point of 'lunacy'? Furthermore, this word evidently does not fit the moment, as anyone who ever heard Jefferson talk in any academic setting will recall that she was supremely in control of her subject and her audience. 'Lunacy' seems overly harsh, even in the context of self-deprecation. The production of an 'L'-run and a 'loo'-run provides one reason why that conspicuous word-selection was made. There may be another reason, but to develop our argument, it is necessary to reproduce this segment from Jefferson's lecture in a more conventional poetic form.

We recognize that an objection might be that reproducing her words in this way on the page simply imposes the poetic form. However, this is conventional practice in the analysis of narrative and other forms of discourse in ethnopoetics. As Hymes notes, 'Oral discourse . . . is an organisation of lines' (1990, p. 45). Moreover, it is taken to be a key analytic technique in exposing what might otherwise be latent and unnoticed poetic structures (see, for example, Blackledge, Creese, and Hu, 2016; Blommaert, 2006; Hymes, 1994; 2006; Staats, 2008).

Here is the sequence as a poem.

the kind of talk I do when I (.) do a lecture in class
is: (.) loose to the point of: (0.2) lunacy(0.2)
that is I will jus say
whatever happens to occur to me

What Jefferson has produced in these lines, is a clerihew. According to Wikipedia (https://en.wikipedia.org/wiki/Clerihew, accessed 11/10/2020), a clerihew is a

whimsical, four-line biographical poem invented by Edmund Clerihew Bentley. The first line is the name of the poem's subject, usually a famous person put in an absurd light, or revealing something unknown or spurious about them . . . the rhymes often forced.

Here are some examples of clerihews (again from Wikipedia):

> Sir Christopher Wren
> Said, "I am going to dine with some men.
> If anyone calls
> Say I am designing St. Paul's"

> John Stuart Mill,
> By a mighty effort of will,
> Overcame his natural bonhomie
> And wrote Principles of Political Economy

> Sir Henry Rider Haggard
> Was completely staggered
> When his bride-to-be
> Announced, "I am She!"

The segment in which Jefferson describes her lecturing style exhibits most of the features that define a clerihew. Obviously, our arrangement of her story into four lines is a deliberate decision to match this to the definition of a clerihew. There are, however, other features of this segment that very closely match the standard features of a clerihew. It is an (auto)biographical poem about a famous person: Gail Jefferson! From the start, Jefferson was a key player in establishing the style of work now recognized as CA, and even in 1977 her work was influential beyond the CA community. So, although the famous subject of the poem is not named in the first line, it is established that she is referring to herself. The poem casts her in a vaguely absurd light, in that her lecturing style is loose to the point of lunacy, by implication, potentially no more than stream of consciousness. As such, this reveals something about her which was previously unknown. It is also self-depre-cating and captures the mildly deflating tone of a clerihew. Finally, there is little that rhymes formally. Although in a clerihew it is typically lines 1 and 2, and 3 and 4 that rhyme, in this case, lines 2 and 4 achieve a weak form of rhyme in 'lunacy' and 'me'. We are not suggesting that Jefferson composed a clerihew based on a literary form that Edmund Clerihew Bentley invented; however, with the intuition of a poet, Bentley invented a literary form based on the poetics of ordinary talk, of which Jefferson's spontaneous clerihew is an example.[6]

There is another poetic feature here. Earlier in the talk, Jefferson has shown how some poetic speech errors seem to cluster in talk that deals with potentially sensitive matters, or matters which might be interpersonally delicate: a focus on skin colour, for example. In the formal paper version of the talk (Jefferson, 1996), she eventually dismisses this reading of poetic speech errors. However, there may be something in this sequence of her talk that points to a matter of interpersonal significance. This clerihew inserts itself into her talk at precisely the point of a sensitive matter: Jefferson has chastised a member of the audience for break-ing an interactional expectation or norm. Moreover, this is at a CA conference,

112 *Robin Wooffitt et al.*

where it might be expected that the audience members would be knowledgeable of the norms that underpin interaction. So when Jefferson mildly chastises QU5 for interrupting her, and not recognising that she has more to say, she publicly draws attention to a specific interactionally inappropriate act *and* his broader professional credentials, framed as a pedagogical moment. The clerihew acknowledges the sensitivity in this pedagogical moment. It is self-deprecating, thereby defusing any possible grievance QU5 may have for being publicly corrected. It casts her lecturing style in a way that could account for a misunderstanding about who has rights to speak, thereby mitigating the procedural error she has just exposed. And it does this placatory work immediately, in that it is inserted prior to the topically relevant talk projected by her pedagogically framed calling out of what she has identified as QU5's interactional misstep.

Here is a final observation, which speaks to a broader, yet in this case ironic, poetic moment. Robert Hopper produced a transcript of Jefferson's 1977 lecture, and parts of that transcript are included in the published version. These capture the question-and-answer session at the end of the talk. Included is QU5's question, and Jefferson's response. In a standard orthographic transcription, Hopper conveys the interactional perturbation that is captured in lines 1336 to 1339 in our transcription. His transcript continues and records Jefferson's response.

GJ: Wait a minute. You have to be suspicious when a recipient says oh that's terrific. It means they're going to talk. About monitoring: What I've been noticing . . .

(Jefferson, 1996, p. 48)

The transcript captures Jefferson's immediate response, and then moves to her remarks on the interactional contexts which seem disproportionately to facilitate poetic phenomena; the clerihew is omitted. We do not know whether Hopper excluded this from his original transcript, or whether Jefferson subsequently cut it when preparing the talk for publication; neither do we know why it was cut. Regardless, the result is the same. An exquisite example of a complex, yet spontaneous conversational poetic form was excluded from a ground-breaking paper that established the character and pervasiveness of conversational poetic phenomena.

Conclusion

Jefferson's 1977 lecture sets out a research agenda for an interactionally focused analysis of the way that poetic phenomena weave through the talk out of which human sociality is forged, negotiated, and maintained. She describes some of those phenomena, enticing us to look again at our own data to see if they are to be found there. But more than that, her talk is a demonstration of those phenomena, and others besides, some of which, as we have seen, do not make it into the formal written version of the talk.

Jefferson's work on poetics merits comparison with others whose work has begun to reveal the poetical substrates of our everyday language. Her distinctive

The Poetics in Jefferson's Poetics Lecture   113

contribution, though, is to ground her observations in relation to what Schenkein called 'the conversation analytic mentality' (1978, p. 1), a focus on the interactional rootedness of turn-design and word-selection. This is notably lacking in the theoretical linguistic argument developed by Jacobson (1961), whose poetic functions are described in terms of principles of cognitive exchange divorced from the messiness of actual talk-in-interaction. Similarly, the kind of ethnopoetic anthropological research initiated by Hymes (1998) similarly fails to capture the breathing language in the flow of social encounters (though, to be fair, much of Hymes' work examined narratives as instruments by which cultural norms were passed across generations). But in addition to the focus on the interactional bedrock of poetic phenomena, Jefferson's talk, both in its content and its delivery, shows us how poetic phenomena can arise spontaneously in the flow of talk, outside of examples of these phenomena she presented. The seamlessness with which they manifest in her talk, and indeed, shape moments of her engagement with her audience, is perhaps an indication of an underlying poetic orientation that has more influence on turn-design than we previously imagined. Her lecture provides a tour of poetic moments, both designedly and spontaneously, which cumulatively begin to reveal, in Hopper's eloquent phrase, the great poem speaking us into being.

Acknowledgements

We are grateful to Ray Person and John P. Rae for their insightful and helpful comments on an earlier version of this chapter.

Notes

1. The lecture was transcribed by Maurice Nevile (2015). The video recording of this presentation has also been digitized, and both the video recording and transcript are available at (http://emca-legacy.info/jefferson.html).
2. Using Excel 'pivot tables', John P. Rae provided a statistical analysis of the frequency of 'P' in this data. His findings:

   Words starting with P in the Valéry passage (lines 190–226) 10.6%
   Words starting P in the rest of the talk 2.5%

   He concluded that there are more than three times as many words starting with P in the Valéry passage compared to the rest of the talk. This is statistically significant: Chi-square $(1, 8990)=61.59$, p < .001.
3. There is a line of postcards that further exemplifies this practice. In each case, an old black and white photograph of people is embellished with speech bubbles. The first invites another character to 'Do a swear', resulting in an anachronistic, inappropriate, yet creatively vulgar statement from the other (examples can be found here: www.brainboxcandy.com/rude-cards/).
   The humorous function of the cards is in part a result of the conspicuously designed invitation to vulgarity. We are, therefore, (moderately) confident in identifying something unusual or marked about Jefferson's use of 'to do' in this example.
4. In her written version of the talk, Jefferson states 'What we're learning to do is to track back into the talk and see if we can find a possible source for some striking word' (Jefferson, 1996, p. 19).

114 *Robin Wooffitt et al.*

5. This raises a question: *how long does the influence of a poetic formulation last?* There is some evidence to bear on this from Wooffitt and Holt's (2011a; 2011b) study of introspection in a parapsychology experiment on extrasensory perception. As part of the experimental protocol, participants were asked to report out loud any thoughts, images, ideas that came to mind in a 30-minute period (to ensure they would focus on their conscious experience, participants were subject to partial sensory deprivation). These reports of their inner mental states were recorded. There were some intriguing poetic phenomena in these data. One instance, revolving around a speech error, provides insight as the durability of poetics. One participant reports that she is 'wondering if my boyfriend's got safe homely'. 'Safe homely' is a speech error, an attempt at 'got home safely'. There is no self-correction, so it appears that the participant had not noticed her error. There follows a period of 26 seconds in which she says absolutely nothing. Then she says: 'Remembered I left my bedroom window open'. The poetic relationship is clear: there is, first, an error, a reference to 'safe homely'; in the second, there is an explicit concern about a *safe home*: an open window invites concerns about intruders, burglary, theft, and so on. The error anticipates—and partially reproduces in an almost literal form—the anxiety expressed later. It is difficult to determine which came first: perhaps there had been a nagging anxiety about her bedroom window all day, and it found expression in the 'safe homely' error. Or perhaps the mistake was unmotivated by underlying concerns, and actually triggered the anxiety about her home. But the poetic relationship between the error and the later remark seems clear, and spans over 26 seconds.
6. We are grateful to Ray Person for this observation and phrasing.

Works Cited

Abbott, A. (2007). Against narrative: a preface to a lyrical sociology. *Sociological Theory*, 25(1), 67–99.

Atkinson, J.M. (1984). Public speaking and audience responses: some techniques for inviting applause. In J.M. Atkinson and J. Heritage (Eds.), *Structures of Social Action: Studies in Conversation Analysis*. Cambridge: Cambridge University Press, pp. 370–409.

Beach, W.A. (1993). The delicacy of preoccupation. *Text and Performance Quarterly*, 13, 299–312.

Bergmann, J.R. and Drew, P. (2018). Introduction: Jefferson's "Wild side" of conversation analysis. In P. Drew and J. Bergmann, (Eds.) *Repairing the Broken Surface of Talk: Managing Problems in Speaking, Hearing, and Understanding in Conversation*. Oxford: Oxford University Press, pp. 1–26.

Blackledge, A., Creese, A., and Hu, R. (2016). The structure of everyday narrative in a city market: an ethnopoetics approach. *Journal of Sociolinguistics*, 20(5), 654–676.

Blommaert, J. (2006). Applied ethnopoetics. *Narrative Inquiry*, 16(1), 181–190.

Brown, R.H. (1977). *A Poetic for Sociology: Toward a Logic of Discovery for the Human Sciences*. Cambridge: Cambridge University Press.

Heritage, J., and Greatbatch, D. (1986). Generating applause: a study of rhetoric and response at party political conferences. *American Journal of Sociology*, 92(1), 110–157.

Hopper, R. (1992). Speech errors and the poetics of conversation. *Text and Performance Quarterly*, 12(3), 113–124.

Hutchby, I., and Wooffitt, R. (2008). *Conversation Analysis: Principles, Practices and Applications* (Second edition). Oxford: Polity Press.

Hymes, D. (1990). Ethnopoetics. *Text*, 10, 45–47.

The Poetics in Jefferson's Poetics Lecture   115

Hymes, D. (1994). Ethnopoetics, oral-formulaic theory and editing texts. *Oral Tradition*, 9(2), 330–370.

Hymes, D. (1998). When is oral narrative poetry? Generative form and its pragmatic conditions. *Pragmatics*, 8(4), 475–500.

Hymes, D. (2006). Ethnopoetics. *Theory, Culture and Society*, 23(2–3), 68–69.

Jacobson, R. (1987) [1961]. Linguistics and poetics. In R. Jakobson (Ed.), *Language and Literature*. Cambridge, MA: Harvard University Press, pp. 62–94.

Jefferson, G. (1977). *Boston University Conference on Ethnomethodology and Conversation Analysis* [video recording]. Retrieved from: https://ca.talkbank.org/browser/index.php?url=Jefferson/Poetics/Poetics.cha

Jefferson, G. (1986). Notes on 'latency' in overlap. *Human Studies, 9*, 153–183.

Jefferson, G. (1990). List construction as a task and resource. In G. Psathas and R. Frankel (Eds.), *Interactional Competence*. Hillside, NJ: Lawrence Erlbaum Associates.

Jefferson, G. (1996). On the poetics of ordinary talk. *Text and Performance Quarterly*, 16, 1–61.

Jefferson, G. (2018). On the poetics of ordinary talk. In P. Drew and J. Bergmann (Eds.), *Repairing the Broken Surface of Talk: Managing Problems in Speaking, Hearing, and Understanding in Conversation*. Oxford: Oxford University Press, pp. 127–206.

Maynard, D.W. (2013). Everyone and no one to turn to: intellectual roots and contexts for conversation analysis. In J. Sidnell and T. Stivers (Eds.), *The Handbook of Conversation Analysis*. Chichester: Blackwell, pp. 11–31.

McQuarrie, E.F., and Mick, D.G. (1996). Figures of rhetoric in advertising language. *The Journal of Consumer Research*, 22, 424–438.

Nevile, M. (2015). *Transcription of Gail Jefferson*. Boston University Conference on Ethnomethodology and Conversation Analysis, 9 June 1977.

Norrick, N.R. (2000/2001) Poetics and conversation. *Connotations*, 10, 243–226.

Person, R.F, Jr. (2016). *From Conversation to Oral Tradition: A Simplest Systematics for Oral Traditions*. New York and Abingdon: Routledge.

Sacks, H. (1992). *Lectures on Conversation* (2 volumes). G. Jefferson and E.A. Schegloff (Eds.). Oxford and Cambridge, MA: Basil Blackwell.

Schegloff, E.A. (2004). Whistling in the dark: notes from the other side of liminality. In *Texas Linguistic Forum, 48: Proceedings of the Twelfth Annual Symposium about Language and Society*. Austin, TX: Department of Linguistics, University of Texas, Austin, pp. 17–30.

Schenkein, J. (1978). Sketch of the analytic mentality for the study of conversational interaction. In J. Schenkein (Ed.), *Studies in the Organisation of Conversational Interaction*. New York: Academic Press, pp. 1–6.

Staats, S.K. (2008). Poetic lines in mathematics discourse: a method from linguistic anthropology. *For The Learning of Mathematics*, 28(2), 26–32.

Stevenson, N. (2017). E.P. Thompson and cultural sociology: questions of poetics, capitalism and the commons. *Cultural Sociology*, 11(1), 11–27.

Stivers, T. (2013). Sequence organisation. In J. Sidnell and T. Stivers (Eds.), *The Handbook of Conversation Analysis*. Chichester: Wiley Blackwell, pp. 191–209.

Swingewood, A. (1987). *Sociological Poetics and Aesthetic Theory*. New York: St Martin's Press.

Szczepek-Reed, B. (2017). "Can I say something?": meta turn-taking in natural talk. *Pragmatics and Society*, 8(2), 161–182. https://doi.org/10.1075/ps.8.2.01szc

Tannen, D. (1987). Repetition in conversation: towards a poetics of talk. *Language, 63*, 574–605.

116 *Robin Wooffitt et al.*

Tannen, D. (1990). Ordinary conversation and literary discourse: coherence and the poetics of repetition. In E. Bendix, (Ed.) *The Uses of Linguistics. Annals of the New York Academy of Science*, 583, 15–32.

Tannen, D. (1998). 'Oh talking voice that is so sweet': the poetic nature of conversation. *Social Research*, 65(3), 631–651.

Wooffitt, R. (1991). 'I was just doing X . . . when Y': some inferential properties of a device in accounts of paranormal experiences. *Text*, 11, 267–288.

Wooffitt, R., and Holt, N. (2011a). Introspective discourse and the poetics of subjective experience. *Research on Language and Social Interaction*, 44(2), 135–156.

Wooffitt, R., and Holt, N. (2011b). *Looking In and Speaking Out: Introspection, Communication, Consciousness*. Exeter, UK: Imprint Academic.

Part 2

Studies in Poetics

Literature

5 The Poetics of Mrs Gamp's Conversation—Are They Dickens's 'Slips of the Pen'?

Hugo Bowles

This chapter will explore how both sides of the equation are visible in the work of Charles Dickens. On the one hand, many of the features of the poetics of conversation identified by Gail Jefferson in her seminal 1996 paper are strongly foregrounded in the conversational style of Dickens's characters; yet, on other occasions, the very same poetic effects may also appear as unconscious 'slips of the pen', and do not necessarily appear to be the product of deliberate 'endeavor' on Dickens's part. This suggests that the poetics of conversation may not be based on a binary of '*unconscious* poetics of conversation v *conscious* (i.e., deliberately arranged) literary poetics', but that authors can be subject to the same instinctive influence of sounds and associations in their written production as speakers are in conversation.

Poetic Deviation and Poetic Reproduction

One of the benefits of applying Conversation Analysis (CA) to literary texts is that it shows how fictional discourse is socially situated, and 'how characters' social relations are dynamically enacted by their interactions, rather than merely being illustrated by them' (Thomas, 2012, p. 4). CA is also one of many analytical methods that can show where writers have deliberately deviated from a conversational norm; Thomas (2012) has outlined these deviations in fictional dialogue and Herman (1995) has done the same for drama. Pragmatically speaking, deviation from a conversational norm in literature (poetic deviation) can take a number of forms. It might be an incongruity of conversational behaviour interpretable as violations of principles of cooperation and politeness (Short, 1989, pp. 150–154), a mismatch between the talk and its context, such as using a formal register in a situation when an informal register is expected, or non-conformity with literary conventions.

However, although CA-informed analyses of deviation can be helpful, the poetics of conversation described in Jefferson (1996) presents a challenge to the view that literary effects are entirely based on deviant *writing*. Literary critics and stylisticians will generally notice poetic deviation in a literary text and assume that the writer has sought to achieve it by writing in a way which distorts a normal linguistic pattern. However, evidence from ordinary conversation

DOI: 10.4324/9780429328930-8

120   *Hugo Bowles*

indicates that poetic deviation in talk may not be deliberate. Jefferson's data shows that the poetic features of talk are usually not noticed by speakers and listeners during the interaction itself. She shows, for example, that when speakers produce alliterative sequences, which she terms 'sound-rows', one sound may act as a trigger for deployment of another sound, and that speakers are usually unaware that this has taken place. It is therefore worth exploring the hypothesis that writers, like speakers, may not notice the poetic features of their own writing and, by implication, may not always be engaging in acts of conscious manipulation while they are writing. Instead, they may quite simply be accessing the poetic mechanisms that underpin their own conversational abilities and unconsciously reproducing them.

Taking this idea of *unconscious reproduction* as a starting point, this chapter seeks to explore the question of whether poetic effects can appear as naturally in the construction of fictional dialogue as they do in ordinary talk. The first two sections of the chapter will illustrate how poetic features are displayed in the speech of the Dickensian character Mrs Gamp, distinguishing between features that seem to be the product of deliberate foregrounding and those which may be unconsciously reproduced. The third—and more speculative—section relates the analysis of character speech to Dickens's own working practices as a writer in order to explore the question of how poetic effects come to be cognitively accessed and expressed. At a conscious level, creative writers obviously make deliberate use of traditional poetic features in their work, but this chapter will argue that they may also access them unconsciously and internally in the same way that speakers do. This third section of the chapter will therefore include evidence of how Dickens 'heard' and vocalized his characters' voices, and how this hearing may have influenced his creative processes. The hypothesis is that since Dickens was trained in his youth to listen to and transcribe speech, and was also very strongly affected by his own internal dialogues while he was writing, they may have made it easier for him to access and represent poetic features of his characters' talk, both consciously and unconsciously.

Dickens's Fictional Speech

Dickens's techniques for presenting conversation have been extensively analyzed in terms of their grammatical construction and stylistic effects (Fludernik, 1993), their role as a narrative device (Lambert, 1981), and the part they play in the historical development of fiction in the 19th century (Page, 1988; Chapman, 1994). Dickens's representations of speech and thought are particularly interesting because of their novelty and variety. As Leech and Short (2007) have shown, writers of fiction can vary the degree to which a narrator or character is perceived to be in control of the action of a novel by using forms of speech representation that vary from direct forms that are more controlled by the speaking character, to highly indirect forms that are more controlled by the narrator; the same categories apply to speech in non-literary texts (Semino and Short, 2004). Lambert (1981) argues that, in Dickens's work, direct speech tends to be reserved for more

The Poetics of Mrs Gamp's Conversation 121

important characters and is used to foreground their importance in the book as a whole, while free indirect speech is used for the speeches of characters who are antagonistic to the main characters, allowing Dickens to 'cast ironic light on what they say' (Leech and Short, 2007, p. 269). Although there is a great deal of direct speech in Dickens's novels, the author frequently intrudes on his main characters' speech by interrupting it with lengthy speech tags, which Lambert calls 'suspended quotations'. Consider the following sentence from Dickens's 1843 novel Martin Chuzzlewit (MC):

> 'I have seen a deal of trouble my own self', said Mrs Gamp, laying greater and greater stress upon her words, 'and I can feel for them as has their feelings tried . . .'
>
> (Charles Dickens, *Martin Chuzzlewit*, chapter 19)

Here, the flow of Mrs Gamp's speech is interrupted, as Dickens inserts a speech tag describing the manner in which she spoke. This suspended quotation, which Dickens uses far more frequently than other writers of his era, enables him to combine the liveliness of Mrs Gamp's direct speech with information about her intonation, as well as reinforcing the idea that she is an alcoholic (see the following). From an authorial perspective, it suggests a conflict between Dickens's desire to give his characters free rein to express themselves through direct speech and a need to insert himself into the narrative as often as possible. This division between lively, free-flowing direct speech and tightly controlled reporting of the speech has implications for the role of the poetics of conversation in Dickens's creative process (to be discussed in Section 3). We will look first at the direct speech itself and how Dickens presents it in the lively discourse of Mrs Gamp.

Mrs Gamp's Speech Style

The fictional character Mrs Gamp appears in only four chapters of MC, but she is one of Dickens's most recognizable and best-loved creations. Her character is based on a description of a nurse given to Dickens by his friend, Angela Burdett-Coutts. Dickens suggests in the preface to MC that he saw her as a realistic character in terms of the nursing role she was supposed to be performing in the novel. She was, in the words of Dickens's preface to MC, 'four-and-twenty years ago, a fair representation of the hired attendant on the poor in sickness'. However, his depiction of her as a nurse is not a realistic portrayal but a carefully constructed caricature. Mrs Gamp is nursing the sick, often on their deathbeds, while at the same time breaking a number of social taboos. She drinks far too much, overcharges her employers, castigates her co-worker, and mistreats her patients, once even taking over the bedroom of her patient Jonas Chuzzlewit and making him sleep on a mattress on the floor. Dickens alleviates her disturbing behaviour through the comic design of her speech, particularly her clumsy attempts to talk her way into and out of difficult situations.

122   *Hugo Bowles*

Mrs Gamp is instantly recognizable to Dickens's readers because of the way that she talks. Her popularity, like that of Sam Weller the coachman in *Pickwick Papers*, owes a great deal to the Cockney-infused idiolect which Dickens created for her, and which defines her conversational style.

This idiolect, described in detail by Golding (1985), is an elaborate construction that mixes traditional and novel forms of literary representation. On the one hand, it shows many of the typical ways in which 19th-century authors represented Cockney dialect (Chapman, 1994, pp. 42–50), including the use of the 's' ending for the first person ('what I sometimes has to do'; 'I says'), the use of 'as' as a relative pronoun ('the last case **as** ever I acted in'), and double negatives ('**don't** ask me to take **none**'). Dickens adds extra syllables to words ('serpiant') and uses dialectal forms such as 'chimley' for 'chimney' and 'dispoged'[1] for 'disposed' to illustrate Mrs Gamp's unusual pronunciation. Syntactically, her word-order is haphazard, as are her inflections, particularly noun-verb agreement, comparatives, and superlatives ('better', 'awfullest'). In terms of semantics, Mrs Gamp has a habit of consistently choosing the wrong word. This sometimes takes the form of straightforward malapropism,[2] such as 'torters of the Imposition', 'witness for the persecution', and 'mortar' instead of 'motto' (see Golding, 1985, p. 104, for further examples) or adding to and distorting collocations ('according to the best of my ability'). From a pragmatic point of view, Mrs Gamp's error-strewn discourse makes it very hard to follow what she is saying, and contributes to a general impression of incoherence.

From an interactional perspective, Mrs Gamp politely steamrollers her listeners. According to Andrews (2013), Mrs Gamp is one of Dickens's 'monologue specialists' who dominates the discourse space through soliloquy. Her speech is unusually self-referential and is often made up of single, long turns. She is extremely industrious in turning conversations into monologues by using a kind of structural clothing that involves her interlocutors in what she is saying, while at the same time reducing them to silence. Mrs Gamp's ability to seize the conversational floor is shown in her first interaction in direct speech. This takes place when she is being engaged by her potential employer, Pecksniff, to watch over the body of Anthony Chuzzlewit before his funeral. She begins her job interview with an anecdote describing her reaction to seeing her husband's corpse in hospital. This is responded to by Pecksniff with a tricky question:

Example (1)

'You have become indifferent since then, I suppose?' said Mr Pecksniff. 'Use is second nature, Mrs Gamp.'

'You may well say second nater, sir', returned that lady. 'One's first ways is to find sich things a trial to the feelings, and so is one's lasting custom.'

Mrs Gamp responds to Pecksniff's opening question by adroitly picking up Pecksniff's comment about use being second nature and politely turning it around

The Poetics of Mrs Gamp's Conversation   123

('one's first ways . . .'). This reasserts her suitability for the role while underscoring her dominant position in the conversation.

There is a similar exchange with Pecksniff later in the chapter:

Example (2)

But here he was interrupted by Mrs Gamp, who, divested of her bonnet and shawl, came sidling and bridling into the room; and with some sharpness demanded a conference outside the door with Mr Pecksniff.

'You may say whatever you wish to say here, Mrs Gamp', said that gentleman, shaking his head with a melancholy expression.

'It is not much as I have to say when people is a-mourning for the dead and gone', said Mrs Gamp; 'but what I have to say is TO the pint and purpose, and no offence intended, must be so considered.'

Here Dickens uses two speech act descriptors to qualify Mrs Gamp's intervention as initially hostile ('but here he was interrupted by Mrs Gamp' and 'with some sharpness demanded a conference outside the door'). The conversation then moves into direct speech as Pecksniff declines Mrs Gamp's request to talk outside. Mrs Gamp glosses over his refusal by picking up his 'say what you wish to say' topic in order to introduce a form of polite disagreement ('it's not so much as I have to say . . . but. . . .'). However, having reasserted her authority over the exchange, she makes no conversational point at all except to say, without a trace of irony, that what she says is 'to the pint (point) and purpose'. Mrs Gamp's strategy in the two extracts of 'you may say x, but I say y' is to shift the topic of conversation and, by failing to provide a new topic in the same turn, to leave no conversational space for her interlocutors to intervene because they do not understand what they are supposed to be responding to.

Having taken control of the conversation, Mrs Gamp uses storytelling to maintain it. In Example (3), while she is engaged in negotiations with Pecksniff about her role in watching over the body, she takes on the delicate task of asking him to supply her with a bottle of liquor while she is nursing.

Example (3)

'You have become indifferent since then, I suppose?' said Mr Pecksniff. 'Use is second nature, Mrs Gamp.'

'You may well say second nater, sir,' returned that lady. 'One's first ways is to find sich things a trial to the feelings, and so is one's lasting custom. If it wasn't for the nerve a little sip of liquor gives me (I never was able to do more than taste it), I never could go through with what I sometimes has to do. "Mrs Harris," I says, at the very last case as ever I acted in, which it was but a young person, "Mrs Harris," I says, "leave the bottle on the chimley-piece, and don't ask me to take none, but let me put my lips to it when I am so dispoged, and then I will do what I'm engaged to do, according to the best of my ability."'

124 *Hugo Bowles*

Here Mrs Gamp justifies her request for a bottle of liquor by using an anecdote of a previous nursing job during which she had made a similar request to her friend Mrs Harris. However, having explained to Pecksniff that she needs liquor to calm her nerves, she launches straight into the story ('"Mrs Harris", I says at the very last case as every I acted in . . .') without any kind of preface. Structurally, the 'Mrs Harris . . .' sequence is a direct speech monologue (Mrs Gamp's orders to Mrs Harris) within a direct speech monologue (Mrs Gamp talking to Pecksniff). The fact that there is no reported reply from Mrs Harris implies that her request to leave the bottle by the chimney was granted, which in turn makes Mrs Gamp's request to Pecksniff seem all the more reasonable. Mrs Harris's embedded silence is crucial to Mrs Gamp's conversational goal. Her lack of counter-argument against Mrs Gamp in the embedded narrative acts as a barrier against possible counter-arguments in the current conversation. Andrews neatly describes this conversational technique as being 'to pre-empt the responses of the real interlocutor the better to enable Mrs Gamp to monopolize the conversation' (Andrews, 2013, p. 56).

Another of the reasons why Mrs Gamp is an engaging character is that Dickens uses her state of intoxication as an implied explanation for the zany way in which she speaks. Sometimes he makes an explicit connection between the amount she drinks and the way she talks:

Example (4)

'I don't know as it ever would have done, sir,' Mrs Gamp replied, with a solemnity peculiar to a certain stage of intoxication. 'Now that the marks,' by which Mrs Gamp is supposed to have meant mask, 'is off that creetur's face, I do not think it ever would have done.

Here Dickens underscores the link between Mrs Gamp's speech and her state of mind for the benefit of the reader. First, he links her intonation to her drunkenness ('Mrs Gamp replied, with a solemnity peculiar to a certain stage of intoxication') and then deliberately explains the malapropism of 'marks'/'mask' to the reader, hinting by association that it has been caused by drinking too much. It is an accurate portrayal; according to Jefferson, words can be wrongly selected as a consequence of some speech pathologies because of associations determined by similarities in sound. The slips from /n/ to /l/ in 'chimley' and from /z/ to /dʒ/ in 'disposed' are typical of the disarticulation of consonants found among experimental subjects in an intoxicated condition (Collins, 1980; see also Chin and Pisoni, 1997, for a review of the literature on speech and alcoholism). Mrs Gamp's lack of consideration of her listeners, allied to her loose grammar and weird logic, also has much in common with the impaired speech of patients suffering from vascular dementia or even psychosis. These patients can be 'grossly insensitive to the needs of the listener' (Kempler, 1995) particularly with regard to topic management, and their speech presents a decrease both in informational content and in coherence.

Mrs Gamp's Conversational Poetics

So far, the analysis has adopted a traditional pragmatic approach to character speech in order to show how Dickens presents Mrs Gamp's conversational style so that readers can infer aspects of her character from its surface features. However, alongside these overt, easily interpretable items, there are more subtle poetic features at work in the text. Jefferson (1996, pp. 3–4) has commented on the way psychotics do not design their talk with the needs of their listeners in mind. Their lack of inhibition, which makes the workings of poetics in conversation more accessible to analysis, also applies to Mrs Gamp. Lurking beneath the obvious lexicogrammatical distortions on the surface of her idiolect, one can find many of the subtle poetic features identified by Jefferson. These will now be analyzed in detail.

Mrs Gamp's Syntactic Sound-Formed Errors

Syntactic errors in Mrs Gamp's word-selection can often be traced back to sound-triggers. Sound-preservation is one of the areas which strongly influences Mrs Gamp's word-choice. In Example (5), the areas where Mrs Gamp's unusual syntactic choices appear to be triggered by a particular sound are marked in bold:

Example (5)

'You may say whatever you wish to say here, Mrs Gamp,' said that gentleman, shaking his head with a melancholy expression.

'It is not much as I have to say when people is **a-mourning** for the dead and gone,' said Mrs Gamp; 'but what I have to say is to the pint and purpose, and no offence intended, must be so considered. I have been **at a many** pla**ces** in my time, gentlemen, and I hope I know**s** what my dut**ies is**, and how the same should be performed; **in** course, if I did not, **it** would be very strange, and very wrong in **sich** a gentleman as Mr Mould, **which** has undertook the highest families in this land, and given every satisfaction, so to recommend me as he does. I have seen a deal of trouble my own self,' said Mrs Gamp, laying greater and greater stress upon her words, 'and I can feel for them as has their feelings tried, but I am not a Rooshan or a Prooshan, and consequently cannot suffer Spies to be set over me.'

In this extract, there are three different sound-triggers that have led to speech errors:

- *I know*s *what my dut*ies is

Here there is a lack of agreement between plural subject ('duties') and third-person singular ('is'). Although lack of agreement is a common feature of Cockney dialect representation, the selection of 'is' rather than 'are' is facilitated by the

126   *Hugo Bowles*

/z/-/ɪz/ sound-row from 'knows' (/z/) to 'duties' (/ɪz/) culminating in the selection of the ungrammatical 'is'.

- *. . . is a-mourning*
- *I have been AT A many places in my time*

Here there are two lexicogrammatical errors—one is the choice of the preposition 'at' instead of 'to', and the other is the addition of the article 'a' in 'a many'. Both these errors can be accounted for by '**is a-mourning**' acting as a sound-trigger: by selecting 'a' to precede 'many', Mrs Gamp echoes the onset syllable of 'a-mourning' (əm); by selecting 'at', she echoes the onset vowel /ə/[3] of 'a-mourning' and combines it with the onset /t/ sound of the word she should have used ('to').

- *very wrong in* **sich** *a gentleman* **as** *Mr Mould,* **which has** *undertook*

In this example, selection of the ungrammatical relative pronoun '**which** . . . **has**' rather than 'who . . . has' is suggested by the sound-run from the preceding dialectal '**sich** . . . **as**'.

In Example (6), as Mrs Gamp continues her one-sided conversation with Pecksniff, there is an even more intricate interplay of sound-selection revealed by Mrs Gamp's grammatical errors. The words involved in the sound-rows are shown in italics and the key grammatical errors marked in capitals:

Example (6)

It is not a easy matter, gentlemen, to live when you are left a *wider*[4] *woman;* particular when your feelings *works* upon you to that extent that you often find yourself a-going out on terms which is a certain loss, and never can repay. *But* in *whatever way* Y*OU EA*RNS your *bread, you* may have *rules and regulations of your own* which cannot be *BROKE THROUGH.*

In this extract, the grammatical errors 'you earns' (lack of agreement) and 'broke through' (unnecessary addition of 'through') are the culmination of intersecting sound-rows that precede the errors. There are three sound-rows: combinations with /w/ (row (6a)), combinations with /b/ (row (6b)), and combinations with /r/ (row (6c)). The rows are also interlocking—the /b/-row begins halfway through the /w/-row and the /r/-row/ halfway through the /b/ row. What is interesting is that the errors occur at the end of each of the rows, which suggests that they are brought about by pre-formed sound-rows.

(6a)	/w/	/w/	/wɜː s/		/w/	/w/	/wɜː z/
	wider	woman	works		whatever	way	**you earns**
(6b)	/b/	/br/	/br/				
	but	bread	**broke**				

The Poetics of Mrs Gamp's Conversation 127

(6c)　　/ju:/ /ru:/ /re/　　　　/rəu/　/ru:/
you rules regulations your own **through**

Sound-row (6a) has an interesting parallelism. It can be divided into two halves, each of which is introduced by two words beginning with /w/—'wider woman' and 'whatever way'. The third word of each half extends the /w/ to /wɜ:/ in '<u>wo</u>rks' and 'yo<u>u ea</u>rns'; after the initial 'you', the verb 'earns' seems to have been selected in order to mirror 'works', leading to the ungrammatical 'you earns'. The lack of agreement is not jarring to the reader because of the rhythmical parallelism of the row.

In (6b) and (6c), Mrs Gamp's error ('broke through the rules' instead of 'broke the rules') cuts across both rows, combining 'broke' at the end of the /b/+/br/+/br/ sequence with 'through' at the end of the /u:/+/ru:/+/re/+/ru:/ sequence. If 'broke' is a correct sound-triggered choice, 'through' is an incorrect addition, induced by the need for a third monosyllabic word to be placed at the end of the /ju:/-/ru:/ sound-chain.

Gist-Preserving Errors

A gist-preserving error is described by Jefferson as an error of speech in which 'the wrong item captures not only the sense of the correct item, but also its alliteration' (p. 5). In the example she uses, one of the speakers (McGee) is trying to recall the exact words of a previous utterance:

Example (7) (Jefferson, 1996, p. 5)

McGee:　　What was it he said something about substituting sideburns for sense
Delegate:　Beards for brains
McGee:　　Beards for brains. Right.

Here McGee remembers the original phrase 'beards for brains' as 'sideburns for sense'. In his attempt to remember the phrase, he inserts a semantic equivalent for 'beards' (sideburns) and a semantic equivalent for 'brains' (sense) into the original structure 'x for y', producing the correct 'gist' of the phrase but the wrong form. Mrs Gamp is also fond of using idioms and proverbs to illustrate or reinforce a particular point that she is making but, like McGee, although she remembers the basic idea that the idiom is designed to express, she has trouble remembering its exact wording and resorts to semantic substitution to preserve its gist. In the following example, she is trying to bolster her status in the eyes of her interlocutor by quashing a suggestion that money is her main motivation for working long hours. To illustrate her point, she comes up with a mangled biblical quotation:

Example (8)

Rich folks may ride on camels, but it an't so easy for 'em to see out of a needle's eye.

128　*Hugo Bowles*

The original quotation from the Good News Bible is 'it is easier for a camel to go through the eye of a needle, than for a rich man to enter into the kingdom of God' (Matthew 19:24, KJV), but Mrs Gamp cannot remember it correctly. To compensate, she uses keywords from the idiom (rich, camel, needle, eye) and constructs a sentence around them, presumably in the hope that the keywords have preserved enough of the gist of the original quotation for the listener to be able to reconstruct it.

Jefferson's description of speakers like McGhee as 'struggling with a grab bag full of idioms in bits and pieces' (1996, p. 28) could easily be applied to Mrs Gamp. Her mangling of clichés and proverbs is related to what Jefferson calls the management of 'fractured idioms' (p. 26). In this case, collocations or idioms are fractured when the speaker tries to refer to an idea suggested by a previous speaker by selecting a word from a collocation that has already been used in the conversation. Mrs Gamp's fracturing of the 'eye of the needle' proverb follows Jeffersonian principles. Just as McGee's 'sideburns for sense' maintained somewhat the alliteration of 'beards for brains', Mrs Gamp's selection of 'camel' and 'needle' maintains the alliterative syllabic /l/ in final position, and her addition of the /r/-onset monosyllabic 'ride' seems to be sound-selected by the 'rich' at the start of the phrase.

The reconstruction of the idiom is also significant in a context of poetics. Jefferson's example shows McGee's fractured idiom being noticed and repaired by the Delegate, while Mrs Gamp's has to be repaired by her readers. It is the reader who has to supply the meaningful connections in a message that has been seriously derailed by bad grammar and loose semantics. Arguably, it is the poetics of the discourse that helps the reader to do this work of reconstruction. Although Mrs Gamp's speech is riddled with sound-assisted mistakes, their poetic harmony renders the ungrammatical features not only acceptable to the reader, but also rather charming.

Sound-Triggered Collocational Errors

Alongside Mrs Gamp's more glaring malapropisms, there are collocational errors which have their origin in sound-formation:

Example (9)

I am not a Rooshan or a Prooshan, and consequently cannot suffer spies to be set over me

Here, the reader's eye is drawn to the unusual spelling of <Rooshan> and <Prooshan> and focuses less on the strange formality of the words 'consequently' and 'suffer' and the collocational error 'set over'. In one of Sacks's examples of sound-related lexical choice (Sacks, 1992, p. 307), a speaker uses the word 'roof' because he has used the word 'room' a few seconds earlier; in this case, assonance has overridden accurate semantics in the word-search, and the progression of the /ru:/ phoneme selects the wrong word. Mrs Gamp produces something similar in the clause 'and consequently cannot suffer spies to be set over me'; here the unusual verb 'set' seems to have been selected by the sound-run /s/. This sound-selection preserves the gist of what she means (she does not want people to spy on her when

The Poetics of Mrs Gamp's Conversation   129

she is working) as long as the listener is prepared to work to understand the strange collocation 'to set spies over'.

The 'set over' collocation is a *post-formed* mistake caused by a preceding sound-run. Example (10) shows a *pre-formed* collocational mistake, caused by a post-formed sound-run:

Example (10)

in course, if I did not, **it** would be very strange

This is an example of a sound-formed error in which the collocational mistake '**in** course' precedes a correctly formed hypothetical clause 'if . . ., it . . .'. An /ɪ/ sound-row stretches across the utterance. The 'in course' mistake may be caused by this /ɪ/ sound, generated as an echo in Mrs Gamp's mind from the pre-formed 'if . . .' clause.

Chiasmus

Wales (2014, p. 54) defines chiasmus as 'a rhetorical term to describe a construction involving the repetition of words or elements in reverse order (ab:ba)'. An example of chiasmus would be John F Kennedy's phrase 'let us never negotiate out of fear but let us never fear to negotiate', with the words 'fear' and 'negotiate' repeated in reverse order. However, chiasmus does not only involve grammatical structures or individual words, but can include even small units of language like morphemes or phonemes. Keyser (2011), for example, notes patterns of phonemic chiasmus in Poe's poem *The Raven* (Poe, Quinn, and O'Neill, 1992), such as the line 'the raven, never flitting . . . shall be lifted' with the phoneme sequence /f/ and /l/ in 'flit' reversed as /l/ and /f/ in 'lifted'.

In relation to the poetics of conversation, chiasmus involves phonemic repetition and reversal, as in Poe's example, and although Jefferson does not include reversed sound-repetition in her descriptions of conversational data, it is quite possible that poetic patterns of sound-reversal occur in conversation and are involved in the mechanisms of sound-triggering that she describes. In one of Mrs Gamp's anecdotes about viewing her dead husband's body in hospital, we find two elaborate examples of it within the same sentence:

Example (11)

'Ah!' repeated Mrs Gamp; for it was always a safe sentiment in cases of mourning. 'Ah dear! When Gamp was summoned to his long home, and **I see him a-lying in Guy's Hospital with a penny-piece on each eye**, and his wooden leg under his left arm, I thought I should have fainted away. But I bore up.'

In this sentence, the focus is on Mrs Gamp's description of her husband's body in 'I see him a-lying in Guy's Hospital with a penny-piece on each eye'. In this phrase, the words 'Guy's' and 'piece' are entirely superfluous; Mrs Gamp could have kept the same image by simply using the words 'hospital' and 'penny' ('lying in hospital'; 'with a penny on each eye'). On closer inspection, the selection of the redundant words 'Guy's' and 'piece' seems to have been triggered by an interlocking pattern of three sound-rows: /aɪ/, /ɪŋ/ and /i:/.

Let us first consider the selection of the word 'Guy's' in Figure 5.1:

Figure 5.1 Patterning of /aɪ/ and /ɪŋ/

The dominant sound-row /aɪ/ runs across the phrase, bracketing it with 'I' at the start and 'eye' at the end and with the /aɪ/ in '**ly**ing' and '**Gu**y's' in the middle. Two /ɪŋ/-sounds are attached to the central /aɪ/-sounds, but in opposite ways: /aɪ/ is followed by /ɪŋ/ in 'ly*ing*' and /ɪŋ/ is followed by /aɪ/ in 'in Guy'. This reversal of sounds means that 'lying in Guy' forms a chiasmus and the selection of the redundant word 'Guy's' at the end of the chiasmus seems to be a poetic addition, with the /ɪŋ/ of 'lying' triggering the first syllable of 'in [G][uy]' and /aɪ/ the triggering the second.

Turning to the selection of the word 'piece' in Figure 5.2, we find the following pattern:

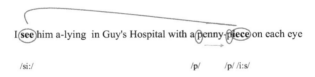

Figure 5.2 Patterning of /p/, /s/ and /i:/

Here we have a similar double sound-trigger involved in the selection of the redundant word 'piece'. The sound-row /i:/ is prevalent across the phrase, running from 'see' to 'piece' to 'each'. The onset /p/ of 'penny' triggers the onset /p/ of 'piece', while the /s/ and /i:/ of 'see' trigger the /i:/ and /s/ of '-iece' (/i:s/), with which 'see' forms a chiasmus.

These two interlocking examples of chiasmus within the same phrase show that, although Jefferson does not herself explicitly refer to chiasmus in her description of sound-selection, intricate patterning of sounds triggered through chiasmus (in this case involving /aɪ/, /ɪŋ/ and /i:s/) can produce unusual word-selection that goes unnoticed.

Rhythm and Blank Verse

Another of the features of Mrs Gamp's idiolect is the cadence of her monologues, a great many of which are spoken in the iambics of blank verse. In Example (12), Mrs Gamp is in the process of flattering the daughters of her employer Mr Mould. When Mr Mould claims not to know what his children are thinking, Mrs Gamp

The Poetics of Mrs Gamp's Conversation   131

objects and justifies it by launching into a tangential story of how Mr Gamp had treated their son when he had had too much to drink. The phrases in blank verse are shaded in grey.

Example (12)

'Oh yes, you do know, sir!' said Mrs Gamp, 'and so does Mrs Mould, your 'ansome pardner too, sir; and so do I, although the blessing of a daughter was deniged me; which, if we had had one, Gamp would certainly have drunk its little shoes right off its feet, as with our precious boy he did, and arterward send the child a errand to sell his wooden leg for any money it would fetch as matches in the rough, and bring it home in liquor; which was truly done beyond his years, for ev'ry individge penny that child lost at toss or buy for kidney ones; and come home arterwards quite bold, to break the news, and offering to drown himself if sech would be a satisfaction to his parents.—Oh yes, you do know, sir,'

The story is framed rhetorically by Mrs Gamp's objection 'Oh yes you do know sir', which occurs at the start and at the end of the monologue. The pattern of this phrase is iambic, with three metrical feet of two syllables each, the first of which is unstressed and the second stressed. The final stressed syllable of the third foot is a single monosyllabic word. This pattern sets the rhythm for the rest of the story, in which it is repeated 14 times, as shown in Table 5.1.

Table 5.1 Blank Verse Rhythm in *Martin Chuzzlewit*

Foot 1 (Iambus)		Foot 2 (Iambus)		Foot 3 (Iambus)	
Unstress	*Stress*	*Unstress*	*Stress*	*Unstress*	*Stress*
oh	yes	you	do	know	sir
and	so	does		Mrs	Gamp
your		'ansome		pardner	too
if	we	had	had	one,	Gamp
would		certainly		have	drunk
	shoes	right	off	his	feet
as	with	our		precious	boy
to	sell	his		wooden	leg
		money	it	would	fetch
as		matches	in	the	rough
	done	beyond		his	years
that		child	lost	at	toss
or	buy	for		kidney	ones
quite	bold	to	break	the	news
and		offering		to	drown
oh	yes	you	do	know	sir

132   *Hugo Bowles*

Mrs Gamp's standard pattern—a trio of iambics ending with a final clunking monosyllabic word—resembles what Tannen (2007, p. 76) describes as a listing rhythm. The overall effect is of a content-free list of clauses tacked on to one another, while the metronomic rhythm is designed to brook no interruption. There are no intonational spaces into which an interlocutor can insert themselves.

Blank verse rhythm is also underscored by Mrs Gamp's predilection for repetitive or redundant phrases linked by the connector 'and': 'dead and gone', 'past and over', 'ant no better and ant no worse', 'often and often says to me'. However, she is creative in this redundant phrasing, extending it to syntactic parallelism such as 'young you are and will be', 'very strange and very wrong', 'brought reg'lar and draw'd mild', 'his way bein' quiet and his hours early', or the more alliterative clichés 'black and blue' and 'rules and regulations'. She also exploits this alliterative combination technique to produce her own inventions such as 'pint (point) and purpose' and 'births and berryins (buryings)'.

The link between the use of a blank verse rhythm in literary texts and speech is a strong one. Historically, blank verse has often been used by writers to give literary texts a conversational style. Dickens described his own tendency to write in blank verse as follows:

> I am perfectly aware that there are several passages in my books which, with very little alteration—sometimes with none at all—will fall into blank verse, if divided off into Lines. It is not an affectation in me, nor have I the least desire to write them in that metre, but I run into it, involuntarily and unconsciously, when I am very much in earnest *I even do so in speaking.* [my italics].

> Charles Dickens, Letter to Charles Watson,
> 25 April 1844 (House, Storey, and Tillotson, 1974)

This suggests that blank verse iambics was the default rhythm that Dickens fell back into when he got carried away with what he was writing. It was the style he adopted when he was going with the flow of his thoughts rather than consciously manipulating them. What is particularly interesting in this self-report is that Dickens describes the blank verse phenomenon as occurring *in his own speech* as well. It seems, then, that the blank verse of Mrs Gamp's monologues may be reflecting an involuntary stream of verbal consciousness in Dickens's own head.

However, although the iambic rhythm of blank verse is strongly influential in verbal thinking and the production of speech and writing, this is not to say that the rhythm of Mrs Gamp's monologue has not been stylized by Dickens. What the use of blank verse achieves in the story of Mrs Gamp's bizarre behaviour is that, by virtue of its very blandness, it is able to foreground those features which do not conform to the rhythm. For example, the strange formality of 'satisfaction' is enhanced by the fact that it is a polysyllabic word in a sea of monosyllables and that it has a trochaic structure (stress-unstress-stress-unstress) that

The Poetics of Mrs Gamp's Conversation   133

reverses the rhythm of Mrs Gamp's standard iambics. The word 'individgle' in the expression 'every individgle penny' stands out because of its unusual phonetic spelling and the fact that it fractures the standard 'every *single* penny' idiom by replacing 'single' with 'individgle'. But it also stands out because it is trochaic and disturbs the rhythm of the phrase. Overall, this passage is an interesting example of the poetics of conversation *being reflected in* a literary monologue (the blank verse) and of the writer *deviating from it* for stylistic effect.

The Poetics of Conversation and the Creative Writing Process

The influence of sound looms large in the emergence of poetics in conversation, but I would argue that it also has a strong effect on poetics in writing, because of the role that sound plays in the writing process itself and the internal conversations that writers have with themselves. In this section, I make some suggestions as to how talk creates the poetic sense of sound that writers go on to elaborate in their work.

Voices and Creative Writing

The local, cognitive environment in which writers do their thinking prior to and during their writing is an important aspect of the writing process that is often overlooked. Writing tends to be a solitary activity in which the writer is surrounded by his or her thoughts. As writers think about and compose their work, they are in a verbal echo-chamber which includes different kinds of sound.

The first kind of sound-triggering may be prompted by the voices of imagined characters. Dickens admitted to hearing voices, as his close friend George Lewes testified: 'Dickens once declared to me that every word said by his characters was distinctly heard by him' (Lewes, 1872). Mrs Gamp was one of the characters whose voice was most forceful in Dickens's head. In the early 20th century, an American writer on spiritualism wrote, without providing a source, that Mrs Gamp's voice was 'whispering to him in the most inopportune places—sometimes even in church—that he was compelled to fight her off by force' (Peebles, 1903, p. 36).

Another kind of sound is the writer's own voice, perhaps ventriloquizing a character's voice. While writers are thinking, they may talk to themselves out loud or read back what they have written. Dickens did both. Not only would he hear the words of his characters in his head, he would also rehearse them out loud. After hearing a voice, Dickens would sometimes act out what the voice was saying before he wrote it down. Dickens's daughter Mamie described this process as a 'facial pantomime':

> The facial pantomime was resumed, and then turning toward, but evidently not seeing me, he began talking rapidly in a low voice. Ceasing this soon,

134 *Hugo Bowles*

however, he returned once more to his desk, where he remained silently writing until luncheon time.

(Mamie Dickens, 1885, pp. 47–48)

Dickens's actions prior to writing would therefore involve hearing, miming, and vocalizing the talk of his characters, all of which suggests that he wanted to hear what the talk sounded like before writing it down. Dickens's eldest son Charley gives us a more detailed description of what the pantomime entailed:

Many a mile have I walked with him thus—he striding along with his regular four-miles-an-hour swing; his eyes looking straight before him, his lips slightly working, as they generally did when he sat thinking and writing; almost unconscious of companionship, and keeping half a pace or so ahead

(Collins, 1981, p. 121)

The phrase 'lips slightly working' refers to what has been described as 'inner speech', which has been observed to take place when people read (for an excellent summary, see Rayner et al., pp. 187–213). Inner speech is a form of internal dialogue in which sounds are mentally represented and produced by the reader, either by soundlessly moving the lips (sub-vocalization) or by sounding them out (actual vocalization). This kind of vocalization was something that Dickens was used to doing because he had been a shorthand writer in his youth and would have had to do a great deal of sounding out of possible words when converting his difficult shorthand script into longhand (Bowles, 2019, ch. 4). He may well have adapted this vocalizing-transcribing habit to his creation of character speech, preferring to hear and vocalize his character speech and transcribe it verbatim in his head before committing it to paper. This process is something that his training had prepared him for and which he himself describes in one of his letters:

I never commit thoughts to paper until I am obliged to write, being better able to keep them in regular order, on different shelves of my brain, ready ticketed and labelled to be brought out when I want them.

(*Knickerbocker Magazine* (14), New York, 1839, p. 196)

In his writing of character speech, Dickens thus seemed to rely on his own idiosyncratic rehearsal process and the prodigious memory for verbatim speech that he had acquired through shorthand training.

The idea of writers' engaging in a dialogue with themselves is starting to interest cognitive psychologists. Since the 1990s, research on inner speech mainly focused on the psychology of reading and, in psychiatry, the hearing of voices by schizophrenic patients. Much of this research presumed that hallucinations were the product of a single voice. More recent research has explored inner speech as essentially dialogic—'dialogue between different internalized voices' (Fernyhough,

The Poetics of Mrs Gamp's Conversation 135

2016, p. 137). The interesting question is how this inner speech connects to the poetic features on the page.

The Sound-Triggering Process—Inner Speech and Spreading Activation

Jefferson is content to record instances of poetic sound-triggering but does not explore how or why this occurs at a cognitive level. Given recent advances in the cognitive sciences, it may now be possible to develop Jefferson's observations and examine ways in which sounds might be triggered during the writing process. Traditional literary criticism examines how writers are influenced by other writers in their development of theme, plot, and style, and how their word-selection may be mitigated by a desire to imitate literary styles and conventions. However, stylistic influences are also exerted at a local level by the vocal environment in which writers immerse themselves and by the local cognitive context of the words they are using. I would like to suggest that there are two cognitive mechanisms at work in this local environment.

Firstly, since the poetics of conversation are sound-formed, the trigger for the activation of non-interactional poetic effects in literary speech may be the inner speech of the writer, either through sub-vocalization or actual vocalization. As well as providing a triggering mechanism, I would argue that the more writers hear the voices of their characters and the more they internalize the voicing and try to reconstruct proposed word-usage through mental rehearsal, the wider and more active the verbal echo chamber will become.

Secondly, the mechanism of *spreading activation* will intensify the diffusion of poetic features in the echo chamber. Spreading activation is a model for the association of items stored in the brain and is based on the idea that activation of one item will immediately activate all the items that are associated with it. So, to take the example of lexical comprehension, if a word beginning with the phoneme /p/ is heard, all words beginning with /p/ will be accessed by the hearer through spreading phonological and semantic activation. The same applies to writing. Spreading activation will associate information that is the current focus of the writer's attention, such as sounds in the writer's local cognitive environment, with information stored in the writer's memory, such as words and meanings associated by the writer with those sounds. This kind of spreading activation has been shown to be influential in word-selection and in the construction of phonesthemes (Bergen, 2004) and has been hypothesized by Hopper (1992) to play a role in the poetics of conversation.[5] Put simply, the spreading activation model suggests that sounds that have just been heard by a speaker are better triggers because they are more readily available for re-use.

Dickens's construction of character speech epitomizes this process. His pre-writing vocalization seems to have involved rehearsal of the speech of his characters rather than narrative. The constant repetition of imagined verbal scenarios in his theatrical conversations with himself prior to writing strongly suggests that his verbal writing environment was a place where the poetics of conversation could have exerted a strong influence on character speech because the vocalized internal dialogue would have accentuated the poetic mechanisms. Mrs Gamp's speech is a good example. On Peebles's account, at least, Mrs Gamp's voice was a particularly insistent one in Dickens's head. Dickens's propensity for intense, self-absorbed vocalization of character talk prior to writing may be reflected in her highly poetic monologues, filled with the same blank verse that he himself involuntarily and unconsciously used when speaking in earnest.

Sound and the Tyranny of Letters

One of the consequences of inner vocalization prior to writing is that it enables the writer to absorb sounds without turning them into words. Sacks (1992) argued that we cannot not think about what people ask us to think about, or respond to it, in a way which is not influenced by the way they have already spoken. Walter Ong has applied a similar argument to writing and reached a similar conclusion. Describing the 'tyranny' of standard lettering, he argues that we are unable to think of a word purely in terms of sound, and that we have to attend to the letters:

> A literate person, asked to think of the word 'nevertheless', will normally (and I strongly suspect always) have some image, at least vague, of the spelled-out word and be quite unable ever to think of the word 'nevertheless' for, let us say, sixty seconds without adverting to any lettering but only to the sound.

> (Ong, 2002, p. 12)

I would suggest that as a consequence of the propensity for vocalization that he had acquired in his youth, Dickens was better equipped to think of words in terms of their sound and, as a result, more able to resist the tyranny of letters. He became particularly adept at separating the spoken word from its written counterpart by using phonetic spelling or changing a word such as Mrs Gamp's <suppose> to <suppoge> in order to give an idea of its pronunciation. This kind of orthographic change also enables Dickens's readers to escape the tyranny of standard lettering by attending to the sound of a word rather than its spelling.

Dickens also uses unorthodox representations of talk to make the previously unnoticed influence of the previous speaker a bit more noticeable. He does this by using deliberate non sequiturs, by showing crazy speech, distortions of speech patterns, by breaking down the standard patterns of speech, and by breaking up words. In this sense, a creative writer like Dickens, whose representations of speech frequently show spelling and syntactic rules being broken almost by default, is the equivalent of Sacks's pathological speaker who breaks the rules of ordinary conversation, while at the same time revealing to the world what those rules actually are.

Conclusion

If one accepts that conversation itself is poetic, deviation from a conversational norm is not the only possible description of poetic effects in literary texts. Since the existence of poetic effects in literature may be reproductions of poetic mechanisms that are *already present* in ordinary talk, a writers' skill may in fact be partly *imitative*, i.e., instinctively reproducing the natural creativity of what they hear around them. It may therefore be possible to distinguish writers' *instinctive imitation* of poetic features of conversation from their *creative manipulation* through foregrounding and deviation. The novelty of this idea is the suggestion that the presence of poetic features in fictional characters' direct speech may not be the product of *conscious* stylization by the writer. A writer of literary dialogue may reproduce poetic features of conversation *without being aware of them*, and in this respect he or she would be acting in written form in a way that is no different from a speaker in ordinary conversation.

This chapter has tentatively suggested two cognitive mechanisms which enable this kind of unconscious literary reproduction to take place. Poetic effects may first be triggered by the sound of a writer's thoughts if the writer is in the habit of verbalizing them before writing. As in conversation, these 'sound effects' tend to go unnoticed; indeed, it may be the very fact that the writer does not pay attention to them that allows them to occur. The hypothesis is that sounds connect by association with sound-related words stored in the writer's memory through spreading activation and that this cycle of internal voicing, sound association, and spreading activation accentuates the poetic mechanism. Jefferson's claim (1996, p. 4) that what distinguishes poetic pathological talk from creative writing is the amount of 'endeavor' involved in the latter may not always be the case. Poetic effects can certainly be contrived, but they may also appear as unconscious 'slips of the pen'.

Notes

1. The representation of /z/ as /dʒ/ in the words <suppoge> may also be an imitation of a residue of early 19th-century upper-class speech. In the mouth of Mrs Gamp, this kind of 'genteel' Cockney could be interpreted as a form of upper-class affectation (Chapman, 1994, pp. 45–47).
2. Malapropism is also known as catachresis—a 'lexical deviation based on ignorance of the true word' (Wales, 2014, p. 258).
3. The pronunciation of these initial sounds is inferred by the reader. My argument is that a reader will infer the same unstressed sound in the onset of <a-mourning>, <at>, and <a many>.
4. Here the word 'wider' is intended to represent the word 'widow' with a non-standard pronunciation. Dickens probably intends it to show Cockney dialect, though on other occasions, he uses the phonetic spelling <widder>.
5. Note that Hopper explicitly begins his article with a reference to Jefferson's poetics lecture, which he transcribed and encouraged her to publish it later in the same journal. In fact, many of his examples come from Jefferson's lecture and handout.

138 *Hugo Bowles*

Works Cited

Andrews, M. (2013). *Dickensian Laughter*. Oxford: Oxford University Press.

Bergen, B.K. (2004). The psychological reality of phonaesthemes. *Language*, 80(2), 290–311.

Bowles, H. (2019). *Dickens and the Stenographic Mind*. Oxford: Oxford University Press.

Chapman, R. (1994). *Forms of Speech in Victorian Fiction*. Harlow: Longman.

Chin, S.B., and Pisoni, D.B. (1997). *Alcohol and Speech*. San Diego: Academic Press.

Collins, P.J. (1980). A comparison of the oral syntactic performance of alcoholic and non-alcoholic adults. *Language and Speech*, 23, 281–288.

Collins, P. (Ed.) (1981). *Dickens: Interviews and Recollections* (Volume 1). London: Macmillan.

Dickens, C. (1968). *Martin Chuzzlewit*. Harmondsworth: Penguin.

Dickens, M. (1885). *Charles Dickens by His Eldest Daughter* [Mary Dickens]. London: Cassell.

Fernyhough, C. (2016). *The Voices Within: The History and Science of How We Talk to Ourselves*. New York: Basic Books.

Fludernik, M. (1993). *The Fictions of Language and the Languages of Fiction*. London: Routledge.

Golding, R. (1985). *Idiolect in Dickens*. Basingstoke: Macmillan.

Good NewsBible. (2010). New York: Harper Collins.

Herman, V. (1995). *Dramatic Discourse: Dialogue as Interaction in Plays*. London: Routledge.

Hopper, R. (1992). Speech errors and the poetics of conversation. *Text and Performance Quarterly*, 12(2), 113–124.

House, M., Storey, G., and Tillotson, K. (Eds.) (1974). *The Letters of Charles Dickens*. Oxford: Clarendon.

Jefferson, G. (1996). On the poetics of ordinary talk. *Text and Performance Quarterly*, 16(1), 11–61.

Kempler, D. (1995). Language changes in dementia of the Alzheimer type. In R. Lubinski (Ed.), *Dementia and Communication*. San Diego: Singular, pp. 98–114.

Keyser, S.J. (2011). Reversals in Poe and Stevens. *Wallace Stevens Journal*, 35(2), 224–239.

Lambert, M. (1981). *Dickens and the Suspended Quotation*. New Haven: Yale University Press.

Leech, G., and Short, M. (2007). *Style in Fiction*. Harlow: Pearson.

Lewes, G.H. (1872). Dickens in relation to criticism. *Fortnightly Review*, 17, 141–154.

Ong, W. (2002). *Orality and Literacy: The Technologizing of the Word*. London and New York: Routledge.

Page, N. (1988). *Speech in the English Novel*. London: Methuen.

Peebles, J.M. (1903). *What is Spiritualism?* Peebles Institute Print.

Poe, E.A., Quinn, A.H., and O'Neill, E.H. (1992). *The Complete Tales and Poems of Edgar Allan Poe: With Selections from His Critical Writings*. New York: Barnes & Noble.

Rayner, K., Pollatsek, A., Ashby, J., and Clifton, C. (2012). *The Psychology of Reading*. New York: Psychology Press.

Sacks, H. (1992). *Lectures on Conversation* (Volumes 1 and 2). Oxford: Blackwell.

Semino, M., and Short, M. (2004). *Corpus Stylistics: Speech, Writing and Thought Presentation in a Corpus of English Writing*. London: Routledge.

Short, M. (1989). Discourse analysis and the analysis of drama. In R. Carter and P. Simpson (Eds.), *Language, Discourse and Literature*. London: Unwin, pp. 139–170.

Tannen, D. (2007). *Talking Voices*. Cambridge: Cambridge University Press.

Thomas, B. (2012). *Fictional Dialogue: Speech and Conversation in the Modern and Postmodern Novel*. Lincoln and London: University of Nebraska Press.

Wales, K. (2014). *A Dictionary of Stylistics*. Abingdon: Routledge.

6 Dialogic Syntax in Ancient Greek Conversation

Anna Bonifazi

1. Introduction

Gail Jefferson connects the core ideas of her 1996 article to Harvey Sacks' observations about 'rephrased repetitions' (Jefferson, 1996, p. 2; see Sacks 1992) and about other features that sound poetic to the extent that '[o]ccasionally talk appears to be produced at least in part by reference to e.g. sounds and associations' (Jefferson, 1996, p. 1). Crucially, these phenomena usually are 'disguised by the clothing of sentence structure' (Jefferson, 1996, p. 5, with reference to Woods, 1938, pp. 294, 297). The selection of certain words in monologic as well as dialogic discourse seem to make reference to 'some categorial business' (Jefferson, 1996, p. 15): the selection can be triggered by sound phenomena or by categorial associations based on, e.g., homonymy, register/idiom, semantic domains such as colours, body-parts, and even correspondences in the sequence organization of utterances. What is more, the selection can generate chains of associations, and those chains may turn out to characterize large chunks of conversations (Jefferson, 1996, p. 36). About sound-triggered topics across turns-at-talk, Jefferson mentions the following example about Barbara, Claire, and Jean sitting around a kitchen table; Barbara gets up and rummages through a cupboard:

```
(1) (Jefferson, 1996, p. 30)
Claire:              ((To Barbara)) What are you doing.
Barbara:      -->    I'm looking fo::r, -- I'm looking fo:r,
                     ((brief silence))
Claire:              ((To Jean, with whom she has a lunch date))
              -->    I'm looking forward to Saturday, I hope I'm
                     feeling well enough.
```

The expression 'I'm looking forward' appears to be triggered by the previously repeated chunk 'I'm looking for'. All in all, sound-selection and category-selection, however unconscious, seem to influence word choice in following talk-in-interaction; they play a role in the construction of turns-at-talk.

Besides being found in everyday conversation, sound- and category-selection are found in institutional talk. Among others, Arminen (2005; discussed in

DOI: 10.4324/9780429328930-9

Dialogic Syntax in Ancient Greek 141

Person, 2016, pp. 27–31) claims that in institutional settings, such as clinics, classrooms, courtrooms, etc., a number of features of everyday conversation are simply adapted. Person (2016, pp. 63–67) expands on this claim by pointing out that institutional talk encompasses forms of speech orally transmitted generation by generation, that is, oral traditions. In oral traditions, sound patterning and categorial parallelism are not only present, but even exaggerated. They are instrumental to the use and re-use of traditional forms of speech, as they can be economically acknowledged, memorized, and reproduced. For example, traditional phraseology in different oral traditions implies a generous use of prosodic and metrical repetitions, as well as lexical and/or semantic affinities reinforcing the structural role of recurrent descriptions and motifs (Person, 2016, pp. 81–87). Even literary representations of conversation, Person's argument continues, can be seen as adaptations of conversational practices (2016, p. 175); 'literary' devices such as alliterations and ring-compositions ultimately resemble strategies already present in spontaneous turns-at-talk.

This last point is where this piece begins. The analyses that I will present in the following sections suggest that what makes dialogues look good and work well in literary works (at least as far as the selected corpus of ancient Greek literary works are concerned) is first and foremost the poetics of natural conversation. In line with Jefferson 1996, I focus on sound- and category-selection that is manifested through unfolding turns of speaking. My argument goes beyond the fundamental idea that re-created or even totally made-up conversations ought to resemble, and to be recognized as, natural dialogues. I propose a further step by positing that the ordinary side of literary talk is poetic in itself, to the extent that it makes use of dialogic syntax.

Section 2 introduces the notion of dialogic syntax. Section 3 presents the analysis of dialogic syntax in dialogic passages from quite different ancient Greek discourse types. Section 4 offers some conclusions.

2. The Dialogic Syntax Framework, and Its Applications Up to Now

In an article published in 2014, John Du Bois explores and assesses the fundamental properties and advantages of a framework that he calls 'dialogic syntax'. The word 'syntax' in this phrase is not to be taken in the conventional sense, but rather as a term referring to a 'mapping relation' (2014, p. 393). The word 'dialogic' does not refer just to conversation, but it signposts the broader concept of 'dialogic resonance', defined as 'the catalytic activation of affinities across [overt] utterances' (2014, p. 359). Such resonance is prototypically manifested in dialogues, but it occurs also in monological discourse. The idea of linguistic aspects recurring across utterances is not new (see, most notably Harris, 1952). However, Du Bois' framework expands on past approaches by articulating the spectrum of grammatical affinities that natural language use reveals—from

142   *Anna Bonifazi*

prosodic echo to similar clausal constituents, from semantic analogy or contrast to pragmatically equivalent utterances—and by theorizing how those affinities have 'consequences for meaning' (2014, p. 366)—for example, whenever structural parallelism influences inferential work (more on this in the following section).

The analytical device making dialogic resonance surface from actual language use is called 'diagraph', defined as 'a higher-order, supra-sentential syntactic structure that emerges from the structural coupling of two or more utterances' (2014, p. 359). For instance, let us consider Du Bois' analysis of dialogic syntax in an excerpt from the Santa Barbara Corpus of Spoken American English, consisting of a snippet from a conversation between a young couple:

```
(2)(Du Bois, 2014, p. 384)¹
1    Jennifer:   Look at ^you being smart.
2                (1.0)
3    Dan:        (H) @
4                (0.7)
5                I'm not ¿^smart?
6                (0.3)
7    Jennifer:   You're ^stupid.
8                (0.9)
9    Dan         Don't ^call me ^stupid.
```

Each column displays a set of items resonating with each other. From this simple diagraph Du Bois (2014, p. 387) derives a series of mapping abstractions that the participants to the conversation seem to handle quite smoothly. For example, in column C, two forms of 'to be' are mapped onto each other ('m', 'morphologically finite inflection', and 'being', 'morphologically non-finite inflection'). Furthermore, 'you being smart' (pragmatically connoted as an ironic assessment) is mapped to 'I'm not smart' (pragmatically connoted as 'ironic reversal'). If we would sketch a dialogic syntax account of Example (1) from Jefferson 1996, several aspects of resonance would emerge: not just sound affinities, but also the symmetry of the first-person pronoun, the echoed present continuous verb form, and—not least—the same conversational spot (turn start). Symmetrically, if we would describe Du Bois' Example (2) in Jefferson's terms, we would say that deictic personal pronouns and forms of 'to be' are category-triggers, whereas the reiteration of 'sm'(art) and 'st'(upid) represent sound-triggers.

Up to now, the mechanisms of dialogic syntax have been studied in several modern languages beside English, including German, French, Finnish, Hebrew, and Japanese (Du Bois and Campbell, forthcoming, pp. 5–6). Du Bois and Campbell claim that dialogic syntax can also be used as a way to study less familiar or endangered languages, to the extent that it 'offers tools uniquely suited to the demands of language description and documentation' (Du Bois and Campbell, forthcoming, pp. 27–28). If produced resonance and interpreted resonance are a sign of active collaboration by interlocutors while

Dialogic Syntax in Ancient Greek   143

co-constructing dialogic turns, then—the authors argue—the study of language use has to encompass the study of the activation and reception of affinities across utterances.

This paper does not represent the first application of the dialogic syntax framework to the Ancient Greek language. Drummen 2016 shows how diagraphs can illustrate the relation between different kinds of resonance and particle use in Classical tragedy and comedy. Even though Drummen's main focus is on particle use, and the contribution of metrical resonance is not considered, the author uncovers dialogic syntax features by means of an unprecedented linguistic analysis. More recently, Hof 2020 presents a close reading of the prologue of the play *Ajax* by Sophocles (5th century BCE; lines 1–133) by drawing on the core ideas of Du Bois' dialogic resonance. The analysis aims to highlight the pragmatic significance of resonating words in the utterances of the goddess Athena and the hero Odysseus, dialogic partners of the prologue. No diagraphs and no grammatical observations accompany this study; however, the attention to resonance allows Hof to centre the (often antagonistic) interaction and the engagement of the conversation participants on the retrieval of terms dynamically interwoven across different turns-at-talk.[2] The present paper is the first attempt to treat different kinds of ancient Greek conversations as objects for dialogic syntax analyses. As such, it defamiliarizes literature-oriented approaches to the texts: instead of considering words as a *product* devised a priori, it privileges unmediated attention to words *producing* sense in the making. The affinities pointed out are of phonological, morphological, syntactic, semantic, pragmatic, and metrical nature. In Jefferson's terms, they constitute sound- and category-triggers of 'poetic' conversation.

3.   Dialogic Syntax in Conversational Passages Occurring in Six Different Discourse Types

The following selection aims to reflect as diverse range of examples as possible. Subsection 3.1 analyzes a passage from a novel (prose), and in particular a minimal dialogue (14 words over two turns) between father and daughter; its literary significance lies in the moment of the story the brief dialogue belongs to, that is, one of the most important recognition scenes towards the end of a long novel. Subsection 3.2 analyzes a passage of philosophical dialogue from Plato's *Symposium* (prose again), and in particular six turns uttered by five speakers, which means a five-party conversation; its literary significance lies in the thematization of drinking as 'the' joint activity that is going to underlie the rest of the conversation about love (the 'symposium', lit. 'drinking together'), carried out not by common people but by Athenian intellectuals. Subsection 3.3 analyzes a passage from historiography (prose again), and in particular an excerpt (seven turns) from a very long dialogue between two groups of people in opposition to each other; its literary significance lies in the compression of collective voices into single utterances ('The Athenians replied . . .'), and in the scholarly supposition that

144 *Anna Bonifazi*

the author, Thucydides, entirely made this dialogue up. Subsection 3.4 analyzes a passage from lyric (sung poetry), in particular a dialogue of two turns between a hero, making a plea while crying aloud, and a god; its literary significance lies in the almost mystic moment of the ode in which the two turns are embedded. Subsection 3.5 analyzes a passage from Homeric epic poetry, in particular the last four turns of the exchange between a dying hero and his killer (not exactly a realistic setting for an elaborate conversation); its literary significance lies in the climactic moment of the epic poem represented by this very exchange between pivotal characters, and by the inclusion (somehow expected by the audience) of traditional narrative motifs. Finally, subsection 3.6 analyzes a passage from Classical comedy (poetry again), in particular a long sequence of turns where two slaves talk to each other; its literary significance lies in the sophisticated lexical choices and poetic rhythm that make the dialogue as clever as hilarious. All in all, I have chosen as artful dialogic sequences as possible, so that there is maximal exposure to arguments that may counter or at least challenge the core idea of dialogic syntax, which is that dialogue features the activation of affinities across utterances in a particularly clear way. As the analyses will show, that core idea can only be fully confirmed, regardless of the different formats, contexts, and meanings.

While preparing the diagraphs, I noticed that in addition to the classical slow reading required for philological analyses, reading the passages aloud and paying attention to sounds was essential, not only for metrical lines but also for prose. On the one hand, I connect this to the salience of sound in the ancient performative settings (full performance for lyric, epic, and comedy; reading aloud for the historiography of Thucydides, philosophical dialogues and novels). On the other hand, I connect it to the 'auditory imagery', to use Chafe's term (in Chafe, 1988), that reported conversations trigger *qua* direct speech—people's voices.

As for the following tables, the layout of texts is slightly modified with respect to the original, to visually highlight the dialogic parts (e.g., third-person words appear in italics), and to locate metrical affinities in the poetic passages. For the sake of space, all diagraphs except the first one appear in the Appendix; they include transliterations and literal translations of the selected Greek words. Grammatical explanations are incorporated in the analysis. Words in grey are words that have already occurred once in previous columns of the same diagraph. Due to length limits, 'internal' resonance, that is resonance within individuals turns, is not analyzed.

3.1. *Novel: Chariton (1st century CE), Callirhoe 8.6.8*

Almost at the end of the novel *Callirhoe* (often recalled as the first European novel transmitted to us), one of the crucial recognition scenes involves the female protagonist Callirhoe and her father, Hermocrates, ruler of Syracuse, after quite complicated travels and adventures. The father leaps aboard the ship carrying his own daughter and her husband, eventually, to safety.

Dialogic Syntax in Ancient Greek 145

Text 3.1 (Greek edition: Blake, 1938; translation: Goold, 1995):

Ἑρμοκράτης δὲ ἀνεπήδησεν ἐπὶ τὴν σκηνὴν καὶ περιπτυξάμενος τὴν θυγατέρα "ζῆς, τέκνον," εἶπεν "ἢ καὶ τοῦτο πεπλάνημαι;" "ζῶ, πάτερ, νῦν ἀληθῶς, ὅτι σε ζῶντα τεθέαμαι." δάκρυα πᾶσιν ἐχεῖτο μετὰ χαρᾶς.

Hermocrates leaped on board and rushed to the tent; embracing his daughter he cried, "My child, are you really alive or am I deceived in this, too?" "Yes, father, I am, and really so now that I have seen you." Everybody wept for joy.

Diagraph 3.1

	A	B	C	D
Hermocrates (father)	*zês* you live	*téknon* child [voc.]	*kaí toûto* right away	*peplánēmai* I am deceived
Callirhoe (daughter)	*zô* I live *zônta* (you) living/ alive	*páter* father [voc.]	*nûn* now	*tethéamai.* I have seen you

Column A singles out the use of the same verb 'to live' in the same tense and in the same turn position (*zês* 'you live'; *zô* 'I live' at the onset of each turn). An additional participial form from the same verb (*zônta*) resonates with them. The three words highlight the central point of the essential exchange, i.e., to have survived death and dangers. Column B shows resonance on the lexical level of kinship terms *téknon* 'daughter' and *páter* 'father' (category-triggering), and on the pragmatic level of vocatives explicitly addressing the respective interlocutors. The items in column C resonate semantically: 20 times in the same novel (and not unfrequently in Classical Greek) *kaí toûto* (lit. 'and this [thing]') works as a fixed phrase meaning 'immediately, right away',[3] and *nûn* means 'now'. Finally, in column D, the two verb forms *peplánēmai* and *tethéamai* map onto each other in many ways: both occur in turn-final position; they rhyme with each other (-*mai*, -*mai*); they share the same number of syllables (4); they are both first-person forms; they are both in perfect tense, thus expressing the result of a process that started in the past and still continues in the present ('I went astray, and now I am deceived' + 'I saw you, and I am still looking at you'); and semantically and cognitively, they reflect opposite experiences (wandering off vs. gazing at/observing/recognizing), thus stressing analogy by contrast. Overall, several sound- and category-triggers activate resonance in this short exchange.

3.2. Philosophical Dialogue: Plato (5th–4th Century BCE), Symposium 176a–176d

Unlike novels, where direct speech is typically embedded into third-person narration, Plato's dialogues directly display direct speech organized in large frames

146 *Anna Bonifazi*

of conversations about philosophical matters. As McCabe puts it (2019, p. 102), they are 'not merely verbatim reports of actual events, but artful presentations of conversation'. The dialogue *Symposium* is a polyphonic praise of Eros presented by notable men (including Socrates and the playwright Aristophanes, among others) at a banquet. The following passage is taken from the initial part of the dialogue, where Apollodorus, one of Socrates' students, reports to a few friends (including Plato, apparently) the discussion preceding the proper exchange about love. The discussion revolves around how much to drink during the symposium after dinner. The reported conversation occupies sections a to d of page 176 (in the standard division following the manuscript pages). The participants in the conversation are five illustrious intellectuals: Pausanias, Aristophanes, Eryximachus, Agathon, and Phaedrus. By being the one who reports the dialogue, Apollodorus is the implicit grammatical subject of the Greek verb *éphē* '(he) said', repeated four times in the passage. As a consequence, all the speaking verbs referring to what the conversation participants utter are in the infinitive form—see *lógou . . . katárchein* 'to start the conversation' in 176a, *phánai* 'to say' in 176a, *eipeîn* 'to talk' in 176b, and again *phánai* 'to say' twice in 176b and once in 176c.

Text 3.2 (Greek edition: Burnet, 1901; translation: Fowler, 1925):

176.(a) *Μετὰ ταῦτα, ἔφη, κατακλινέντος τοῦ Σωκράτους καὶ δειπνήσαντος καὶ τῶν ἄλλων, σπονδάς τε σφᾶς ποιήσασθαι, καὶ ᾄσαντας τὸν θεὸν καὶ τἆλλα τὰ νομιζόμενα, τρέπεσθαι πρὸς τὸν πότον· τὸν οὖν <u>Παυσανίαν</u> ἔφη λόγου τοιούτου τινὸς κατάρχειν.*

Εἶεν, ἄνδρες, *φάναι*, τίνα τρόπον ῥᾷστα πιόμεθα; ἐγὼ μὲν οὖν λέγω ὑμῖν ὅτι τῷ ὄντι πάνυ χαλεπῶς ἔχω ὑπὸ τοῦ χθὲς πότου καὶ δέομαι ἀναψυχῆς τινος—οἶμαι δὲ καὶ ὑμῶν τοὺς πολλούς· παρῆστε γὰρ χθές—σκοπεῖσθε οὖν τίνι τρόπῳ ἂν ὡς ῥᾷστα πίνοιμεν.

(b) *Τὸν οὖν <u>Ἀριστοφάνη</u> εἰπεῖν,*
Τοῦτο μέντοι εὖ λέγεις, ὦ Παυσανία, τὸ παντὶ τρόπῳ παρασκευάσασθαι ῥᾳστώνην τινὰ τῆς πόσεως· καὶ γὰρ αὐτός εἰμι τῶν χθὲς βεβαπτισμένων.
Ἀκούσαντα οὖν αὐτῶν ἔφη <u>Ἐρυξίμαχον</u> τὸν Ἀκουμενοῦ
Ἦ καλῶς, *φάναι*, λέγετε. καὶ ἔτι ἑνὸς δέομαι ὑμῶν ἀκοῦσαι πῶς ἔχει πρὸς τὸ ἐρρῶσθαι πίνειν, <u>Ἀγάθων<ος></u>.
Οὐδαμῶς, *φάναι*, οὐδ' αὐτὸς ἔρρωμαι.

(c) Ἕρμαιον ἂν εἴη ἡμῖν,
ἦ δ' ὅς,
ὡς ἔοικεν, ἐμοί τε καὶ Ἀριστοδήμῳ καὶ Φαίδρῳ καὶ τοῖσδε, εἰ ὑμεῖς οἱ δυνατώτατοι πίνειν νῦν ἀπειρήκατε· ἡμεῖς μὲν γὰρ ἀεὶ ἀδύνατοι. Σωκράτη δ' ἐξαιρῶ λόγου· ἱκανὸς γὰρ καὶ ἀμφότερα, ὥστ' ἐξαρκέσει αὐτῷ ὁπότερ' ἂν ποιῶμεν. ἐπειδὴ οὖν μοι δοκεῖ οὐδεὶς τῶν παρόντων προθύμως ἔχειν πρὸς τὸ πολὺ πίνειν οἶνον, ἴσως ἂν ἐγὼ περὶ τοῦ μεθύσκεσθαι οἷόν ἐστι τἀληθῆ λέγων ἧττον ἂν εἴην ἀηδής. ἐμοὶ γὰρ δὴ τοῦτό γε οἶμαι (d)

Dialogic Syntax in Ancient Greek 147

κατάδηλον γεγονέναι ἐκ τῆς ἰατρικῆς, ὅτι χαλεπὸν τοῖς ἀνθρώποις ἡ μέθη ἐστίν· καὶ οὔτε αὐτὸς ἑκὼν εἶναι πόρρω ἐθελήσαιμι ἂν πιεῖν οὔτε ἄλλῳ συμβουλεύσαιμι, ἄλλως τε καὶ κραιπαλῶντα ἔτι ἐκ τῆς προτεραίας.
Ἀλλὰ μήν,
ἔφη φάναι ὑπολαβόντα <u>*Φαῖδρον*</u> *τὸν Μυρρινούσιον,*
ἔγωγέ σοι εἴωθα πείθεσθαι ἄλλως τε καὶ ἅττ᾽ ἂν περὶ ἰατρικῆς λέγῃς· νῦν δ᾽, ἂν εὖ βουλεύωνται, καὶ οἱ λοιποί. (e) *ταῦτα δὴ ἀκούσαντας συγχωρεῖν πάντας μὴ διὰ μέθης ποιήσασθαι τὴν ἐν τῷ παρόντι συνουσίαν, ἀλλ᾽ οὕτω πίνοντας πρὸς ἡδονήν.*

176 (a) *After this, it seems, when Socrates had taken his place and had dined with the rest, they made libation and sang a chant to the god and so forth, as custom bids, till they betook them to drinking. Then* <u>*Pausanias*</u> *opened a conversation after this manner*:
"Well, gentlemen, what mode of drinking will suit us best? For my part, to tell the truth, I am in very poor form as a result of yesterday's bout, and I claim a little relief; it is so, I believe, with most of you, for you were at yesterday's party: so consider what method of drinking would suit us best."
(b) *On this* <u>*Aristophanes*</u> *observed*:
"Now that, Pausanias, is a good suggestion of yours, that we make a point of consulting our comfort in our cups: for I myself am one of those who got such a soaking yesterday."
When <u>*Eryximachus*</u>, *son of Acumenus, heard this*;
"You are quite right, sirs," *he said*; "and there is yet one other question on which I request your opinion, as to what sort of condition Agathon finds himself in for drinking."
"No, no," *said* <u>*Agathon*</u>, "I am not in good condition for it either."
(c) "It would be a piece of luck for us, I take it,"
the other went on,
"that is, for me, Aristodemus, Phaedrus, and our friends here, if you who are the stoutest drinkers are now feeling exhausted. We, of course, are known weaklings. Socrates I do not count in the matter: he is fit either way, and will be content with whichever choice we make. Now as it appears that nobody here present is eager for copious draughts, perhaps it will be the less irksome to you if I speak of intoxication, and tell you truly what it is. The practice of medicine, I find, has made this clear to me—(d) that drunkenness is harmful to mankind; and neither would I myself agree, if I could help it, to an excess of drinking, nor would I recommend it to another, especially when his head is still heavy from a bout of the day before."
Here Phaedrus of Myrrhinus interrupted him, saying:
"Why, you know I always obey you, above all in medical matters; and so now will the rest of us, if they are well advised."

148   *Anna Bonifazi*

> *Then all of them, on hearing this,* (e) *consented not to make their present meeting a tipsy affair, but to drink just as it might serve their pleasure.*

According to the diagraph extracted from this passage (see diagraph 3.2 in the Appendix), the first four columns display deictic resonance between markers of 'I' (A)—'we' (B)—'you' singular (C)—'you' plural (D) that consist of personal pronouns, inflected verb forms,[4] and vocatives; in Jefferson's terms, this is category-triggering resonance. The fact that column A is the only one reporting hits for each of the six turns is relevant: in the reported dialogue, 'I' markers constitute the primary means to connect the utterances to each of the different speaking 'I' and each of the voices. The abundance and persistence of resonating items in columns A, B, C, and D reflect the conversational involvement of the five parties both as individuals and as a group. The dialogic syntax behind column E highlights category-triggering again, as the conversational and pragmatic resonance concerns the fundamental matter motivating the discussion. Two questions raised by Pausanias in 176a strongly echo each other (the first is direct: *tína trópon hrâista piómetha* lit. 'in which way shall we drink most conveniently?'; the second is indirect: *tíni trópōi àn hōs hrâista pínoimen* lit. '[please consider] in which way we shall drink most conveniently'). Aristophanes replies in 176b by retrieving the point through several resonating terms (the noun 'way'; the lexeme *hrâst-* for '[most]convenient/easy', and the lexeme *pín-* for 'to drink'): *tò pantì trópōi paraskeuásasthai hrāistṓnēn tinà tês póseōs* lit. 'to provide by all means some recovery from the drinking'. Later, in 176b Eryximachus expresses in the form of indirect question, again, *pôs ékhei pros tò errôsthai pínein* lit. 'how he [Agathon] feels about being eager to drink'. The theme of drinking (see column F) surfaces from multiple occurrences of terms not only denoting 'drinking [wine]' in a neutral sense (see the sound- and category-triggering verbs *piómetha, pínoimen, pínein, pieîn,* and the nouns *pótou, póseōs,* all sharing the same etymological root) but also drunkenness (see the verb *methúskesthai* and the related noun *méthē*), the idea of soaking in wine (see the substantivized participle *bebaptisménōn* lit. '[among] those who have been baptized in wine'), and being devoted to drinking-bouts (see the participle *kraipalônta*). Column G reports the mapping between 'yesterday' (see *khthés* uttered three times), and 'the day before' (*tês proteraías*), which is the day where all the speakers had drunk too much. In column H, *khalepôs ékhō* 'I am in a bad state' and *khalepón* 'harmful' in a ring-fashion wrap up a series of expressions semantically similar, as they reveal lack of strength and no eagerness to drink a lot (*oud'érrōmai* 'I am not in good health';[5] *apeirḗkate* 'you give up'; *oudeís . . . prothúmōs ékhein* 'nobody is eager [to drink a lot]').[6] The last three columns include resonance confined to the last two turns (i.e., the second turn by Eryximachus and the turn by Phaedrus). This is no coincidence: the selection of affinities reflects the final (and decisive) steps of the argumentation. The recall of medical studies (*iatrikês* twice in 176d, see column I) determines necessary recommendations (*àn sumbouleúsaimi* 'I would recommend', and *àn*

Dialogic Syntax in Ancient Greek 149

eû bouleúōntai 'if [they] would be well advised', both in 176d, see column J). The echo of the construction *állōs the kaí* 'and especially' (twice in 176d, see column K) seals the alignment (and the agreement) between the views of the speakers concluding the discussion.

3.3. Historiography: Thucydides (5th century BCE), Histories 5.91–97

The last passage in prose is taken from the famous (and long) dialogue of the Melians (*Histories* 5.85–113), where Thucydides dramatizes a failed negotiation between the Athenians and the inhabitants of the island of Melos in 416 BCE, during the Peloponnesian War. The Athenians had invaded the island; before sieging it, they recommend its inhabitants to accept subjugation in order to minimize suffering. The Melians refuse and get sieged. The exceptional form of the dialogue (where usually opposing speeches would be presented) articulates in 29 alternating turns the collective voice of some Athenian spokesmen and the collective voice of Melian counsellors. The piece is famous for representing the 'basic essence of imperialism' (Romilly, 1963 [1947], p. 397) and the Athenians '"brainwashing" the Melians by a dialectical destruction of their intellectual and moral foundations' (Bosworth, 2006, p. 313n.3). The following excerpt is made of seven relatively short turns discussing the advantages of subjugation.

Text 3.3 (Greek edition: Jones and Powell, 1942; translation: Hammond, 2009):

[5.91.1] ΑΘ. Ἡμεῖς δὲ τῆς ἡμετέρας ἀρχῆς, ἢν καὶ παυθῇ, οὐκ ἀθυμοῦμεν τὴν τελευτήν· οὐ γὰρ οἱ ἄρχοντες ἄλλων, ὥσπερ καὶ Λακεδαιμόνιοι, οὗτοι δεινοὶ τοῖς νικηθεῖσιν (ἔστι δὲ οὐ πρὸς Λακεδαιμονίους ἡμῖν ὁ ἀγών), ἀλλ' ἢν οἱ ὑπήκοοί που τῶν ἀρξάντων αὐτοὶ ἐπιθέμενοι κρατήσωσιν. [5.91.2] καὶ περὶ μὲν τούτου ἡμῖν ἀφείσθω κινδυνεύεσθαι· ὡς δὲ ἐπ' ὠφελίᾳ τε πάρεσμεν τῆς ἡμετέρας ἀρχῆς καὶ ἐπὶ σωτηρίᾳ νῦν τοὺς λόγους ἐροῦμεν τῆς ὑμετέρας πόλεως, ταῦτα δηλώσομεν, βουλόμενοι ἀπόνως μὲν ὑμῶν ἄρξαι, χρησίμως δ' ὑμᾶς ἀμφοτέροις σωθῆναι.

[5.92] ΜΗΛ. Καὶ πῶς χρήσιμον ἂν ξυμβαίη ἡμῖν δουλεῦσαι, ὥσπερ καὶ ὑμῖν ἄρξαι;

[5.93] ΑΘ. Ὅτι ὑμῖν μὲν πρὸ τοῦ τὰ δεινότατα παθεῖν ὑπακοῦσαι ἂν γένοιτο, ἡμεῖς δὲ μὴ διαφθείραντες ὑμᾶς κερδαίνοιμεν ἄν.

[5.94] ΜΗΛ. Ὥστε [δὲ] ἡσυχίαν ἄγοντας ἡμᾶς φίλους μὲν εἶναι ἀντὶ πολεμίων, ξυμμάχους δὲ μηδετέρων, οὐκ ἂν δέξαισθε;

[5.95] ΑΘ. Οὐ γὰρ τοσοῦτον ἡμᾶς βλάπτει ἡ ἔχθρα ὑμῶν ὅσον ἡ φιλία μὲν ἀσθενείας, τὸ δὲ μῖσος δυνάμεως παράδειγμα τοῖς ἀρχομένοις δηλούμενον.

[5.96] ΜΗΛ. Σκοποῦσι δ' ὑμῶν οὕτως οἱ ὑπήκοοι τὸ εἰκός, ὥστε τούς τε μὴ προσήκοντας καὶ ὅσοι ἄποικοι ὄντες οἱ πολλοὶ καὶ ἀποστάντες τινὲς κεχείρωνται ἐς τὸ αὐτὸ τιθέασιν;

150   *Anna Bonifazi*

[5.97] ΑΘ. Δικαιώματι γὰρ οὐδετέρους ἐλλείπειν ἡγοῦνται, κατὰ δύναμιν δὲ τοὺς μὲν περιγίγνεσθαι, ἡμᾶς δὲ φόβῳ οὐκ ἐπιέναι· ὥστε ἔξω καὶ τοῦ πλεόνων ἄρξαι καὶ τὸ ἀσφαλὲς ἡμῖν διὰ τὸ καταστραφῆναι ἂν παράσχοιτε, ἄλλως τε καὶ νησιῶται ναυκρατόρων καὶ ἀσθενέστεροι ἑτέρων ὄντες εἰ μὴ περιγένοισθε.

[5.91.1] *Ath.* Even if our empire is brought to an end, we are not anxious about the consequences. It is not ruling powers like the Spartans who are vindictive to their defeated enemies (and in any case we are not dealing with the Spartans now): the greater cause for fear is if their own subjects turn on their previous rulers and gain control. [5.91.2] But that is a danger you can leave to us. Right now we want to make clear to you that we are here in the interests of our own empire, yes, but what we shall say is designed to save your own city. Our desire is to take you under our rule without trouble: it is in both our interests that you should survive.

[5.92] *Mel.* And how could it be in our interest to be your slaves? How does that compare with your interest in being our masters?

[5.93] *Ath.* Because submission offers you the alternative to a much more terrible fate: and because we gain by not destroying you.

[5.94] *Mel.* So can we not be friends rather than enemies? Would you not accept our inactive neutrality?

[5.95] *Ath.* Your friendship is more dangerous to us than your hostility. To our subjects friendship indicated a weakness on our part, but hatred is a sign of our strength.

[5.96] *Mel.* And do your subjects see the logic of this? Do they then make no distinction between those who have no dependent connection and the rest who are mostly your colonies, and in some cases have revolted and been put down?

[5.97] *Ath.* Well, they certainly think that neither category is short of a case in justice, but they see it as a matter of power—if the independents survive, it is because we are too frightened to attack them. So quite apart from the resulting extension of our empire your subjection will give us greater security. It is particularly important that we, as a naval power, should not let islanders get away from us, especially you in your weak position.

If we take into account the diagraph (see the Appendix, diagraph 3.3) we may focus first on columns E, F, and G. They report dialogic resonance concerning circumstances that may occur (see *én*, *án*, and *ei* meaning 'if' in conditional clauses, in E), negations (including the negative particles *ou(k)*, *mé*, and forms of the pronoun *oudéteros/médéteros* 'neither of the two', in F), and conjunctions used to make progress with the argumentation (*hósper kaí* 'like, for example', twice, and *hóste* 'so that', twice, in G). In column H I have gathered the etymologically related terms *hupakoûsai* 'to obey' at 93, and *hupḗkooi* 'subjected people' (plural noun) twice at 91.1 and 96, and also a term that is

Dialogic Syntax in Ancient Greek 151

opposite in sense but similar in sound: *ápoikoi* 'settlers' lit. '[those] away from home', 96, who by being politically independent represent the counterpart of subjected people. Columns J and I highlight category-triggered contrasts as well as sound-echo: column I shows that what could be advantageous for the Melians from the Athenians side (*khrēsímōs . . . sōthênai* 'it is convenient that you are being saved', 91.2) is retrieved by the Melians in terms of what could be advantageous for the Athenians from the Athenian (!) side (*khrḗsimon . . . douleûsai* 'being convenient to become slaves', 92, echoing not only the same form *khrēsim*- but also the infinitive form of the respective verbs). Column J shows that both parties mention the strongly opposed notions of friendship and enmity (*phílous . . . polemíōn* 'friends . . . [war] enemies', the Melians in 94; *philía* 'friendship', *ékhthra* 'enmity', *mîsos* 'hate', the Athenians in 95). While up to now resonance proves to be balanced between the two groups, resonance in columns A, B, C, and D reveals strong asymmetries. As for A and B, 14 'we' markers (A) and eight 'you' (plural) markers (B)—including personal pronouns and inflected verbs—are uttered by the Athenians, against just two and two, respectively, uttered by the Melians. Column C spotlights a ratio of 5:1 terms lexically related to the same idea of 'ruling' and 'be in command' (*árkhein* is the verb, and *arkhê* the noun). Column D shows a subtler affinity retrieved through the various turns of talk: the historian lets both parties align by using no fewer than six passive forms of verbs ('those who have been conquered', 'let [this] be left', 'to be saved', 'to be elucidated', 'to be subdued', and 'to be subjected [to someone]'. This level of dialogic syntax stresses the concept of subjugation at the grammatical level. All this confirms the overall conversational design of the excerpt, which is utterly asymmetrical: the Melians' turns are short and invariably consisting of three questions, whereas the Athenians articulate only answers, and over a longer sequence of utterances. Finally, even though dialogic syntax within the same turn of talk is not consistently checked in this paper, a few repetitions in the utterances by the Athenians in this passage are worth mentioning: *deinoí*, 5.91.1—*tà deinótata*, 5.93; *epì sōtēríai*—*sōthênai*, both in 5.91.2; *dēlṓsomen*, 5.91.2—*dēloúmenon*, 5.95; *astheneías . . . dunámeōs*, 5.95—*dúnamin . . . asthenésteroi*, 5.97; *perigígnesthai*—*perigénoisthe*, both in 5.97. These repetitions challenge the general idea of Thucydides' fondness for lexical variation. The present contrary evidence may suggest that lexical repetition contributes to the realism of the dialogic format that the historian wants to recreate.

3.4. *Lyric: Pindar (6th–5th century BCE),* Nemean 10.76–88

This is the first of three passages where the arrangement of words and the metrical shape of the performative output are interdependent. Ancient Greek lyric, epic, and comic verses are inherently open to metrical resonance beside all the other possible levels of resonance, the principle being that the same sound(s) in the same metrical place (e.g., at the end of verses or after cae-suras) causes resonance, affinity, and analogy. Substantial inspiration for

152　*Anna Bonifazi*

the following analyses comes from Sweetser 2006, an article exploring the cognitive blends suggested by rhymes and meter in the verse-play *Cyrano de Bergerac* by Edmond Rostand. Similar sounds and similar metrical positions suggest connections that are not signalled otherwise, and let spectators and readers draw inferences about most significant analogies as well as contrasts. Even though the present argument does not directly thematize the cognitive side of the poetics of conversation, I stress a point of alignment: sound-selection turns out to be particularly relevant to the dialogic syntax of the conversation in fundamentally the same way. Sound effects and metrical affinities (open to prosodic and even melodic realizations, in these ancient texts) trigger analogies and juxtapositions instrumental to the central messages of the poetic compositions.

As for Pindaric epinician odes, the music and the dance accompanying the realization of the songs celebrating athletic victories represent further levels of potential resonance (here not analyzed, due to the consistent attention to words, and to the lack of specific evidence about melodic and choreographic schemas). The central metrical resonance that is taken into account in the following analysis is strophic response, a term identifying the correspondence of metrical patterns across stanzas (or strophes).[7] For the sake of space and clarity, strophic response is indicated in the text by a few words in boldface, and it is explained in the analysis. The short dialogue between Pollux (Polydeukes in Greek), half-brother of Castor, and his father Zeus takes place once Castor has died and Pollux pleads with Zeus to let him die as well. It consists of just one turn for each fictional character, and it corresponds to the adjacency pair 'request and counter-proposal'. The dialogue is part of the narration of a famous myth linking the victor's family to the worship of Castor and Pollux. As I say elsewhere (see Bonifazi, 2001, pp. 182–186), reported direct speech in Pindaric mythical episodes is to be taken as a climactic moment of the epinician performance.

Text 3.4 (Greek edition: Maehler, 1971; translation: Race, 1997):

(. . .)	[Strophe 5]
θερμὰ δὴ τέγγων δάκρυα στοναχαῖς	(75) cf. 81
ὄρθιον φώνασε· **Πάτερ Κρονίων**, τίς δὴ λύσις	(76) cf. 82
ἔσσεται πενθέων; καὶ ἐμοὶ **θάνατον** σὺν	(77) cf. 83
τῷδ᾿ ἐπίτειλον, ἄναξ.	
οἴχεται τιμὰ **φίλων τατωμένῳ**	(78) cf. 84
φωτί· παῦροι δ᾿ ἐν πόνῳ πιστοὶ βροτῶν	
καμάτου μεταλαμβάνειν.' ὣς	(79) [Antistrophe 5]
ἤνεπε· Ζεὺς δ᾿ ἀντίος ἤλυθέ οἱ,	
καὶ τόδ᾿ ἐξαύδασ᾿ ἔπος· ᾽Εσσί μοι υἱός·	(80)
τόνδε δ᾿ ἔπειτα πόσις	

Dialogic Syntax in Ancient Greek   153

σπέρμα θνατὸν ματρὶ τεᾷ πελάσαις   (81) cf. 75
στάξεν ἥρως, ἀλλ' ἄγε τῶνδέ τοι ἔμπαν αἴρεσιν   (82) cf. 76
παρδίδωμ'· εἰ μὲν **θάνατόν** τε φυγὼν καὶ   (83) cf. 77
    γῆρας ἀπεχθόμενον
αὐτὸς Οὔλυμπον θέλεις <ναίειν ἐμοὶ>   (84) cf. 78
  σύν τ' Ἀθαναίᾳ κελαινεγχεῖ τ' Ἄρει,

ἔστι σοι τούτων λάχος· εἰ δὲ κασιγνήτου πέρι   (85) [Epode 5]
μάρνασαι, πάντων δὲ νοεῖς ἀποδάσσασθαι ἴσον,   (86)
ἥμισυ μέν κε πνέοις γαίας ὑπένερθεν ἐών,   (87)
ἥμισυ δ' οὐρανοῦ ἐν χρυσέοις δόμοισιν.'   (88)
(. . .)

                                                            [Strophe 5]
Hot indeed were the tears he shed; he groaned   (75) cf. 81
and cried aloud, "Father, son of Kronos, what release   (76) cf. 82
will there ever be from sorrows? Grant me death   (77) cf. 83
    along with him here, lord.
Honor disappears when a man loses his friends,   (78) cf. 84
    and few mortals remain faithful in time of toil

to share the labor." *Thus he spoke.*   (79) [Antistrophe 5]
    And Zeus came before him
and proclaimed these words: "You are my son.   (80)
But this man was conceived afterwards   (81) cf. 75
    by your mother's husband, when that hero came   (82) cf. 76
    to her
and sowed his mortal seed. But come, I nonetheless
grant you this choice: if you prefer to escape death   (83) cf. 77
    and hateful old age,
and come by yourself to live on Olympos with   (84) cf. 78
    me and
with Athena and Ares of the darkened spear,

that destiny is yours. But if you strive on   (85) [Epode 5]
    behalf of your
brother, and intend to share everything equally   (86)
    with him,
then you may live half the time beneath the earth   (87)
and half in the golden homes of heaven."   (88)

As we see in the diagraph (see diagraph 3.4 in the Appendix), Column A captures
a fundamental semantic resonance clarifying the kinship relation between the
interlocutors: father (*páter Kroníōn* 'father', 76, followed by the patronymic
Kroníōn 'son of Chronos' stressing the genealogic link further) and son (*huiós*

154   *Anna Bonifazi*

'son', 80). Columns B and C recap the 'you'- and 'I'-markers, respectively. Together with *páter* 'father', 76, the words *epíteilon, ánax* 'fulfill the desire, lord' (imperative + vocative), 77, are the only 'you' expressions by Pollux. Yet, they are pragmatically central as they encode the explicit request to Zeus: namely, to grant him death together with his half-brother. Not differently from analogous columns in previous diagraphs, 'you'- and 'I'-markers encompass personal pronouns and verb forms (plus the possessive adjective *teâi* 'your' related to Pollux's mother, 81). The five 'you' verb forms uttered by Zeus show his focus on his interlocutor's present and future hypothetical situation: *essí* 'you are' [my son], 80; *théleis* [if] 'you want', 84; *márnasai* [if] 'you strive', 86; *noeîs* [if] 'you intend', 86; *pnéois* 'you could breathe', 87. Column D captures an essential resonance underlying the entire conversation: *epíteilon* '[please] fulfill the desire', 77, is the verb encoding the first part of the adjacency pair (the request), while the verb *pardídōm'* 'I grant', 83, encodes the start of the second part (the counterproposal: instead of death, Zeus grants Pollux either the possibility to live with him forever, or the possibility to live one day on the earth as a mortal, and one day in heaven as a god).

The last three columns single out category- and sound-selection at once. Column E concerns proximal deictic references: *sùn tôd'* 'with this one' uttered by Pollux at 77, and *tónde* 'this one' uttered by Zeus at 80 and referring to the corpse of Castor; *tônde* 'of these [things]' uttered by Zeus at 82 refers to the alternatives that he is about to pronounce. Column F concerns the pivotal term 'death', *thánaton*, in the accusative case, pronounced in 77 and 83, which are responsive lines (see the following). Column G shows the mapping of three forms of the verb 'to be' actually meaning 'to exist', even if the subjects are different: the third-person indicative future *éssetai* 'will be/exist' uttered by Pollux, 77, is mapped onto the second-person indicative present *essí* 'you are' uttered by Zeus, 80, and a further third-person form indicative present, with accent retraction because it occurs at verse beginning (like *éssetai*): *ésti* 'there is/exists', uttered by Zeus in 85.

As for the metrical mapping of affinities (see words in boldface in the text), we need to take into account that the two turns occupy the last strophe (almost entirely), the whole last antistrophe, and the first part of the last epode of the ode.[8] Strophes and antistrophes are supposed to share the same metrical verse schemas; in other words, each line in a strophe has a responsive line in the antistrophe. Line 81, uttered by Zeus—*spérma thnatòn matrì teâi pelásais* lit. 'mortal seed [accusative] having approached your mother'—shares several syllabic sounds with its responsive line 75, which introduces the words of Pollux (before the conversation starts): *thermà dè téngōn dákrua stonakhaîs* lit. 'shedding warm tears with groans'. Furthermore, the responsive lines 76 and 82 include a comparable, resonating pragmatic boundary: *páter Kroníōn* '[You], father, son of Chronus' in 76 fulfils the communicative function of opening Pollux's speech, while the two discourse markers *all' áge* in 82 open Zeus' counterproposal. Beside the occurrence of the same word 'death' in the same grammatical case in the two responsive lines 77 and 83 (mentioned previously), responsive lines 78 and 84 offer a

Dialogic Syntax in Ancient Greek   155

semantic contrast. Line 78 points out human solitude (honour is gone if a man has no friends), whereas line 84 prospects divine company (Pollux in Olympus may enjoy the company of Zeus, Athena, and Ares). Overall, metrical resonance significantly increases the dialogic syntax represented in the diagraph, and it reminds us of a crucial point made by Du Bois (and others): structural parallelism influences inferential work.

3.5. Epic: Homeric Poetry (8th–5th century BCE), Iliad 22.331–360

The second passage in meter is equally extraordinary, but for a different reason. The following Iliadic moment reports the final sequence of turns between the Achaean hero Achilles and his main adversary, the Trojan hero Hector, whom Achilles has just struck dead.[9] The dialogue between the two has actually started along with the start of the duel (see the three turns at lines 250–259, 261–272, and 279–288),[10] followed by a pause during action (lines 289–330). While the first lines look plausible in a realistic account of the final exchange between the two archenemies, after line 327, we know that Hector is fatally wounded, and on the literal level of human physicality he can hardly speak at that moment. However, the Homeric poet puts in his mouth lucid as well as poignant words, and the syntax does not seem to reflect any break or stumble. The passage clearly exemplifies an unreal, and wholly epic moment of lyric grandeur corresponding to a climactic moment (perhaps the most climactic moment) of the conflict between Achaeans and Trojans. And yet, once again, the dialogic syntax of natural conversations is unfailingly present, much beyond the 'catch-word technique' identified by Irene de Jong in Homeric dialogues.[11] The selected text includes the last four turns before Hector dies: *Iliad* 22.331–336 (Achilles); 338–343 (Hector); 345–354 (Achilles); and 356–360 (Hector).

Text 3.5 (Greek edition: Allen, 1931; translation: Lattimore, 1951):

ἤριπε δ' ἐν κονίῃς· ὃ δ' ἐπεύξατο δῖος Ἀχιλλεύς·	(330)
Ἕκτορ ἀτάρ που ἔφης Πατροκλῆ' ἐξεναρίζων	
σῶς ἔσσεσθ', ἐμὲ δ' οὐδὲν ὀπίζεο νόσφιν ἐόντα	
νήπιε· τοῖο δ' ἄνευθεν ἀοσσητὴρ μέγ' ἀμείνων	
νηυσὶν ἔπι γλαφυρῇσιν ἐγὼ μετόπισθε λελείμμην,	
ὅς τοι γούνατ' ἔλυσα· σὲ μὲν κύνες ἠδ' οἰωνοὶ	(335)
ἑλκήσουσ' ἀϊκῶς, τὸν δὲ κτεριοῦσιν **Ἀχαιοί.**	
τὸν δ' ὀλιγοδρανέων προσέφη κορυθαίολος Ἕκτωρ·	
λίσσομ' ὑπὲρ ψυχῆς καὶ γούνων σῶν τε **τοκήων**	
μή με ἔα παρὰ νηυσὶ κύνας καταδάψαι **Ἀχαιῶν,**	
ἀλλὰ σὺ μὲν χαλκόν τε ἅλις χρυσόν τε δέδεξο	(340)
δῶρα τά τοι δώσουσι πατὴρ καὶ **πότνια μήτηρ,**	
σῶμα δὲ οἴκαδ' ἐμὸν δόμεναι πάλιν, ὄφρα πυρός με	

156 *Anna Bonifazi*

Τρῶες καὶ Τρώων ἄλοχοι λελάχωσι θανόντα.
τὸν δ᾽ ἄρ᾽ ὑπόδρα ἰδὼν προσέφη πόδας ὠκὺς Ἀχιλλεύς·
μή με κύον γούνων γουνάζεο **μὴ** δὲ **τοκήων·** (345)
αἲ γάρ πως αὐτόν με μένος καὶ **θυμὸς** ἀνήη
ὤμ᾽ ἀποταμνόμενον κρέα ἔδμεναι, οἷα ἔοργας,
ὡς **οὐκ** ἔσθ᾽ ὃς σῆς γε κύνας κεφαλῆς ἀπαλάλκοι,
οὐδ᾽ εἴ κεν δεκάκις τε καὶ εἰκοσινήριτ᾽ ἄποινα
στήσωσ᾽ ἐνθάδ᾽ ἄγοντες, ὑπόσχωνται δὲ καὶ ἄλλα, (350)
οὐδ᾽ εἴ κέν σ᾽ αὐτὸν χρυσῷ ἐρύσασθαι ἀνώγοι
Δαρδανίδης Πρίαμος· **οὐδ**᾽ ὧς σέ γε **πότνια μήτηρ**
ἐνθεμένη λεχέεσσι γοήσεται ὃν τέκεν αὐτή,
ἀλλὰ κύνες τε καὶ οἰωνοὶ κατὰ πάντα δάσονται.
τὸν δὲ καταθνῄσκων προσέφη κορυθαίολος Ἕκτωρ· (355)
ἦ σ᾽ εὖ γιγνώσκων προτιόσσομαι, **οὐδ**᾽ ἄρ᾽ ἔμελλον
πείσειν· ἦ γὰρ σοί γε σιδήρεος ἐν φρεσὶ **θυμός.**
φράζεο νῦν, **μή** τοί τι θεῶν μήνιμα γένωμαι
ἤματι τῷ ὅτε κέν σε Πάρις καὶ Φοῖβος Ἀπόλλων
ἐσθλὸν ἐόντ᾽ ὀλέσωσιν ἐνὶ Σκαιῇσι πύλησιν. (360)

But he dropped in the dust, and brilliant Achilleus (330)
  vaunted above him:
'Hektor, surely you thought as you killed Patroklos you
  would be
safe, and since I was far away you thought nothing of me,
o fool, for an avenger was left, far greater than he was,
behind him and away by the hollow ships. And it was I;
and I have broken your strength; on you the (335)
  dogs and the vultures
shall feed and foully rip you; the Achaians will
  bury Patroklos.'
In his weakness Hektor of the shining helm spoke to him:
'I entreat you, by your life, by your knees, by your parents,
do not let the dogs feed on me by the ships of the Achaians,
but take yourself the bronze and gold that are there (340)
  in abundance,
those gifts that my father and the lady my mother will
  give you,
and give my body to be taken home again, so that
  the Trojans
and the wives of the Trojans may give me in death
  my rite of burning.'
But looking darkly at him swift-footed Achilles answered:
'No more entreating of me, you dog, by knees or parents. (345)
I wish only that my spirit and fury would drive me
to hack your meat away and eat it raw for the things that

Dialogic Syntax in Ancient Greek   157

you have done to me. So there is no one who can hold
   the dogs off
from your head, not if they bring here and set before
   me ten times
and twenty times the ransom, and promise more in addition,   (350)
not if Priam son of Dardanos should offer to weigh out
your bulk in gold; not even so shall the lady your mother
who herself bore you lay you on the death-bed and
   mourn you:
no, but the dogs and the birds will have you all for their
   feasting.'
Then, dying, Hektor of the shining helmet spoke to him: (355)
'I know you well as I look upon you, I know that I
   could not
persuade you, since indeed in your breast is a heart
   of iron.
Be careful now; for I might be made into the gods' curse
upon you, on that day when Paris and Phoibos Apollo
destroy you in the Skaian gates, for all your valour.'   (360)

Let us focus on the diagraph (see diagraph 3.5 in the Appendix). Column A singles out the dialogic verbalization and variation of second-person (singular) markers from both sides: vocative expressions (*Héktor*, 331; *népie* 'fool', 333; *kúon* 'dog',[12] 345; all of them uttered by Achilles); imperative verbs (*éa* 'let', 339; *dédexo* 'accept', 340; *gounázeo* 'entreat by kneeling', 345, all uttered by Achilles; *phrázeo* 'be careful', 358, by Hector); the imperatival infinitive *dómenai* 'give', 342 by Hector; other indicative and past-tense verbs in second person (*éphēs* 'you said', 331, *opízeo* 'you were not considering', 332, and *éorgas* 'you have done', 347, all uttered by Achilles); personal pronouns, sometimes followed by the particle *ge* stressing the 'you'-piece of information (*toi* lit. 'to you', 335, by Achilles; *toi* lit. 'to you', 341 and 358, by Hector; *sé*, 335 and *s'(e)*, 351 both 'you' in accusative, uttered by Achilles; *s'(e)*, 356 and *sé*, 359, both 'you' in accusative, uttered by Hector; *sês ge* 'you' in genitive plus the particle *ge*, 348, and *sé ge* 'you' in accusative plus the particle *ge*, 352, uttered by Achilles; *soí ge* 'you' in dative plus the particle *ge*, 357, uttered by Hector; the possessive adjective *són* 'your' [parents], 338, by Hector). Column B represents the pragmatic counterpart of column A, as it selects 'I'-markers. Beside a few first-person pronouns, the following verb forms are found: *líssom'(ai)*, 'I beseech you', 338, central explicit performative verb linked to the act of kneeling (see column D); *protióssomai* 'I look upon you', 356 and *génōmai* '[that] I may become', 358, all uttered by Hector. In addition, Hector thematizes himself as already dead at 342 by saying *sôma . . . emón* 'my corpse'. The resonance singled out in column C is of a different kind, as it concerns an argumentative thread. Particles play an important role in the resonance as well as in the argument. In 335–336, Achilles juxtaposes the different destinies of Hector (*se mén* 'as for you'), who is going to be devoured by dogs and vultures, and

158 *Anna Bonifazi*

of Patroclus (*tòn dé* 'as for him' [=Patroclus]), who is going to be buried by his people. In 340–342, Hector replies by replacing previous content about 'you' and another corpse (see the particle *allá* overarching the two items *sù mén . . . sõma dé*) with a proposal: Achilles may accept compensatory gifts, and Hector's own corpse may be given to his own people for burial. Achilles, however, re-replaces Hector's content by means of another *allá* reintroducing the theme of mutilation by dogs and vultures (*allà | kúnes te kaì oiõnoí*, 354).

Column D puts together semantically related terms that actually relate to different notions; once again, sound-selection is crucial. At 335, the idiomatic expression *goúnat' élusa* 'I have loosened your knees' by Achilles metonymically conveys the idea of defeating; however, in 338 by Hector and 345 by Achilles, the genitive plural noun *goúnōn* 'knees' relates to something else, namely the (ritual) act of supplication by kneeling, which corresponds to the verb *gounázomai* ('implore/entreat by kneeling') used in 345 by Achilles (*gounázeo*). Column E and column H are all devoted to the theme of mutilation (see column C), of paramount importance in the there-and-then culture. As for E, the expression *kúnes ēd' oiõnoí* and *kúnes te kaì oiõnoí*, two different ways of saying 'dogs and vultures', are both uttered by Achilles in 335 and 354, respectively. Hector retrieves *kúnas* 'dogs' in 339, and in turn Achilles retrieves the same word in 348. Interestingly, Achilles echoes the same lexeme by insultingly calling Hector 'dog' in 345 (*kúon*). Column H completes this topic by highlighting the imminent action of mutilation and the devouring of Hector's corpse: Achilles utters *helkẽsous'* '[they] will tear apart' in 336, *édmenai* 'to eat up' in 347, and *katà . . . dásontai* '[they] will divide among themselves' in 354, while Hector utters *katadápsai* 'to devour' in 339. The dialogue also thematizes events projected in the future beyond the idea of mutilation, as column I shows, by means of the following verbs in indicative future tense: *helkẽsous'* '[they] will tear apart' and *kterioûs'* '[they] will bury', both in 336 by Achilles; *dōsousi* '[they] will give', 341, by Hector; *goẽsetai* '[she] will mourn', 353; and *katà . . . dásontai* '[they] will divide among [themselves]' in 354 by Achilles.

In column F, I identify resonance between Achilles' and Hector's parents: after evoking *sõn tokẽōn* '[of] your parents', 338, Hector associates with his own parents the gold that they may give Achilles to ransom his own corpse (*chrusón . . . patèr kaí pótnia mḗtēr* 'gold . . . father and mother', 340–341). Quite symmetrically, Achilles retrieves the word *tokẽōn* 'parents', 345, in the same genitive case, and echoes the connection between Hector's parents and gold: *chrusôi . . . Dardanídēs Príamos . . . pótnia mḗtēr . . . téken* lit. 'with gold . . . Priam son of Dardanos . . . the lady [your] mother . . . [who] bore [you]', 351–353. Column G collects a series of negative particles plus 'even if' (*eí kén*) and 'when' (*hóte*), stressing the negative evaluation of the outcome of the conversation by both heroes: Hector will not be buried, and Achilles is not persuaded. Finally, column G shows the most important category-selection of themes, which has an important sound counterpart: each turn includes a reference to death, and actually ends with such a reference. Achilles mentions the negated burial (*kterioûs'*, 'they will bury', 336), and visualizes (hypothetically) Hector's mother laying the son's corpse on

Dialogic Syntax in Ancient Greek 159

the deathbed (*entheménē lechéessi*, 353); Hector mentions himself dead (*thanónta*, 343), and foresees the moment of Achilles' death, when Paris and Apollo may let him perish (*olésōsin*, 360).

These hexametric lines offer rich evidence of metrical and sound resonance. The name of the Greek people 'the Achaeans' concludes verse 336 (*Akhaioí* uttered by Achilles), and 339 (*Akhaiôn* uttered by Hector); likewise, 'parents' (in genitive) *tokéōn* conclude verse 338 (by Hector) and 345 (by Achilles), and 'lady mother' *pótnia mḗtēr* occupies the last two dactyls in 341 (uttered by Hector) and in 352 (uttered by Achilles). The particle *allá* starts verse 340 (by Hector), and 453 (by Achilles). Various negations are found at the beginning of verses (339, 345, 348, 349, 351), after the bucolic diaeresis (345, 356), or after internal caesuras (352, 358). Finally, in the second hexameter of the third and the fourth turns (by Achilles and Hector respectively), the word *thumós* occurs (both in nominative case).

3.6. Comedy: Aristophanes (5th century BCE), Knights 80–117

The final passage under consideration is a relatively long sequence (19 turns) taken from a hilarious conversation between two slaves in the play *Knights*. Both humour and the socially low status of characters are distinctive features of comedy (as a genre) and of comic register. The two slaves in question are left anonymous in the text (they are called 'Slave 1' and 'Slave 2'); however, several hints in their exchanges traditionally have been taken as alluding to two prominent military and political personalities of Aristophanes' time, that is, Demosthenes and Nicias. The two slaves complain about their master, Demos ('the people') because he mistreats them. Demos recently has acquired a new slave, 'the Paphlagonian' (a nickname ridiculing the mode of speaking, from the verb *paphlázein* 'to foam'; in this case, the allusion is to the demagogue Cleon) who behaves in a quite despotic way with all his fellowservants, including Slave 1 and Slave 2. Early in the piece (lines 71–80), the two slaves consider how they could put an end to the very uncomfortable situation. Since escaping does not sound feasible to them, they decide to die—by getting overdrunk.[13]

Text 3.6 (Greek edition: Coulon and van Daele, 1923; translation: Henderson, 1998):

OI. B′	κράτιστον οὖν νῷν ἀποθανεῖν.	(80)
OI. A′	ἀλλὰ σκόπει,	(80bis)
	ὅπως ἂν ἀποθάνοιμεν **ἀνδρικώτατα**.	
OI. B′	πῶς δῆτα, πῶς γένοιτ᾿ ἂν **ἀνδρικώτατα**;	
	βέλτιστον ἡμῖν αἷμα ταύρειον πιεῖν·	
	ὁ Θεμιστοκλέους γὰρ θάνατος αἱρετώτερος.	
OI. A′	μὰ Δί᾿, ἀλλ᾿ ἄκρατον οἶ**νον ἀγαθοῦ δαίμονος**.	(85)
	ἴσως γὰρ ἂν χρησ**τόν** τι βουλευσαίμεθα.	

160 *Anna Bonifazi*

ΟΙ. Β′	ἰδού γ᾽ ἄκρατον. Περὶ ποτοῦ γοῦν ἐστί σοι.
	πῶς δ᾽ ἂν μεθύων χρηστόν τι βουλεύσαιτ᾽ ἀνήρ;
ΟΙ. Α′	ἄληθες, οὗτος; κρουνοχυτρολήραιον εἶ.

οἶνον σὺ τολμᾷς εἰς ἐπίνοιαν λοιδορεῖν;   (90)
οἴνου γὰρ εὕροις ἄν τι πρακτικώτερον;
ὁρᾷς, ὅταν πίνωσιν ἄνθρωποι, τότε
πλουτοῦσι, διαπράττουσι, νικῶσιν δίκας,
εὐδαιμονοῦσιν, ὠφελοῦσι τοὺς φίλους.
ἀλλ᾽ ἐξένεγκέ μοι ταχέως οἴνου χοᾶ,   (95)
τὸν νοῦν ἵν᾽ ἄρδω καὶ λέγω τι δεξιόν.

ΟΙ. Β′	οἴμοι, τί ποθ᾽ ἡμᾶς ἐργάσει τῷ σῷ ποτῷ;
ΟΙ. Α′	ἀγάθ᾽· ἀλλ᾽ ἔνεγκ᾽· ἐγὼ δὲ κατακλινήσομαι.

ἢν γὰρ μεθυσθῶ, πάντα ταυτὶ καταπάσω
βουλευματίων καὶ γνωμιδίων καὶ νοιδίων.   (100)

ΟΙ. Β′	ὡς εὐτυχῶς ὅτι οὐκ ἐλήφθην ἔνδοθεν	
	κλέπτων τὸν οἶνον.	(102)
ΟΙ. Α′	εἰπέ μοι, Παφλαγὼν τί δρᾷ;	(102bis)
ΟΙ. Β′	ἐπίπαστα λείξας δημιόπραθ᾽ ὁ βάσκανος	
	ῥέγκει μεθύων ἐν ταῖσι βύρσαις ὕπτιος.	
ΟΙ. Α′	ἴθι νυν, ἄκρατον ἐγκάναξόν μοι πολὺν	(105)
	σπονδήν.	
ΟΙ. Β′	λαβὲ δὴ καὶ σπεῖσον ἀγαθοῦ δαίμονος.	(106)
ΟΙ. Α′	ἕλχ᾽, ἕλκε τὴν τοῦ δαίμονος τοῦ Πραμνίου.	
	ὦ δαῖμον ἀγαθέ, σὸν τὸ βούλευμ᾽, οὐκ ἐμόν.	
ΟΙ. Β′	εἴπ᾽, ἀντιβολῶ, τί ἐστι;	(109)
ΟΙ. Α′	τοὺς χρησμοὺς ταχὺ	(109bis)
	κλέψας ἔνεγκε τοῦ Παφλαγόνος ἔνδοθεν,	(110)
	ἕως καθεύδει.	(111)
ΟΙ. Β′	ταῦτ᾽. Ἀτὰρ τοῦ δαίμονος	(111bis)
	δέδοιχ᾽ ὅπως μὴ τεύξομαι κακοδαίμονος.	
ΟΙ. Α′	φέρε νυν, ἐγὼ ᾽μαυτῷ προσαγάγω τὸν χοᾶ,	
	τὸν νοῦν ἵν᾽ ἄρδω καὶ λέγω τι δεξιόν.	
ΟΙ. Β′	ὡς μεγάλ᾽ ὁ Παφλαγὼν πέρδεται καὶ ῥέγκεται,	(115)
	ὥστ᾽ ἔλαθον αὐτὸν τὸν ἱερὸν χρησμὸν λαβών,	
	ὅνπερ μάλιστ᾽ ἐφύλαττεν. (. . .),	

[80] *Second Slave*: Then our best option is death.

First Slave: Well, figure out what would be the most manly death for us.

Second Slave: Let's see then, what would be the most manly? Our best course is to drink bull's blood: we should choose the death Themistocles chose.

[85] *First Slave*: God no, we should toast the Good Genie with neat wine instead! Maybe that way we might think up a good plan.

Second Slave: Listen to him, neat wine! You're always looking for an excuse to drink. But how could a tipsy person think up a good plan?

Dialogic Syntax in Ancient Greek 161

First Slave: Oh, is that right? You babbling bucket of birch water! [90] How dare you cast aspersions on the creative power of wine? Can you come up with anything more effective? Don't you see, it's when people drink that they get rich, they're successful, they win lawsuits, they're happy, they can help their friends. [95] So quick, go in and fetch me a jug of wine; I want to water my wit and come up with something smart.

Second Slave: Oh dear, what are you and your drink going to get us into?

First Slave: A good spot! Now go in and get it. (first Slave goes inside) I'm going to stretch out on the ground, because if I get drunk I'm going to sprinkle [100] everything with bits of plans, thoughts, and ideas.

Second Slave: (returning with a jug, a cup, and a garland) It's a lucky thing I wasn't caught swiping the wine from in there!

First Slave: Say, what's Paphlagon doing?

Second Slave: That devil's been licking the sauce off confiscated goodies, and now he's belly-up drunk on his hides, snoring away.

[105] *First Slave*: Come on then, slosh me the wine neat, a double libation.

Second Slave: Here you are; now pour one for the Good Genie.

First Slave: Down the hatch, down goes the libation for the Pramnian Genie! Ah, Good Genie, that idea's yours, not mine!

Second Slave: Tell me, please, what idea?

First Slave: Quick, [110] go steal Paphlagon's oracles and bring them out here while he's still asleep.

Second Slave: (going inside) OK, but I'm afraid I may transform our Genie from Good to Bad.

First Slave: Well then, I'll just pass myself the jug, to water my wit and come up with something smart.

[115] *Second Slave*: (returning with a scroll) Paphlagon's snoring and farting so loud, he didn't notice when I grabbed his holy oracle, the one he most closely guarded.

By considering the corresponding diagraph (3.6) in the Appendix, the words in column A contribute to the thematization of death representing a highest, or anyway a preferable, achievement. *krátiston . . . apothaneîn* 'the best [lit. the strongest] . . . to die', 80, by Slave 2, is answered by *apothánōmen andrikôtata* '[how] we would die in the most heroic way', 81, by Slave 1. The superlative neuter form *andrikôtata* 'in the most heroic way', 82 is retrieved by Slave 2, together with another superlative form, *béltiston*, 'the greatest thing', 82, and by a comparative verbal adjective, *hairetôteros* lit. 'better to be chosen', 84, related to 'death' (*thánatos*), 84. The category-triggering based on superlative or comparative forms expressing evaluations can be connected to the verbalization of a series of possibilities and potential deliberations by the two slaves, emerging from column B. Beside a further comparative adjective in *heúrois àn ti praktikôteron* 'could you find anything more effective?', 91, by Slave 1, we find *àn khrēstón ti bouleusaímetha* 'we may deliberate something useful', 86, again by Slave 1, echoed by *àn*

162   *Anna Bonifazi*

khrēstón ti bouleúsait', '[how] could [a drunken man] deliberate something useful?', 88, by Slave 2. The common category-triggering feature in these cases is the use of verbs in the optative or subjunctive mood with the modal particles *án/ én*. At the onset of the excerpt, we find two further such verbs in questions (one indirect, and one direct): *àn apothánōmen* '[how] we would die [in the most heroic way]', 81, by Slave 1 (mentioned earlier because of the thematization of death), and *génoit' án* '[what] could be [the most heroic way]?', 82, by Slave 2. Later, Slave 1 utters *hótan pínōsin* lit. 'whenever they would drink', 92, and in 99 he reasons about the possibly positive effects of getting drunk: *èn . . . methusthô* 'if I would get drunk', 99.

Column C encompasses the multiple references to wine and to drinking wine, which provide thematic coherence throughout the passage. The lexical and semantic range of these further category-triggers is quite wide. The term 'wine' (*oínos*) occurs in 85, 90, and 102 in the accusative case, and in 90, 91, and 95 in the genitive case. A series of etymologically related terms point to 'drink' in different, but resonating, ways: the noun *potoû* ('drink' in the genitive case), 87, and *tô sô potô* in the dative case 'to your drink', 97, resonate with the verb 'drink' in the subjunctive present *pínōsin* '[whenever they] would drink', 92. A further semantically related term is *khoâ* 'pitcher/jug', stemming from the verb *khéō* 'to pour', uttered twice: *oínou khoâ* 'a jug of wine', 95, and *tòn khoâ* 'the jug', 113. Furthermore, multiple occurrences of the same adjective *ákraton* 'neat' (lit. 'non-mixed', typically said of wine), 85, 87,[14] and 105, produce resonance within resonance, and establish a crucial metaphorical link: neat wine asked for by Slave 1 in 85, and echoed in 87 by Slave 2, is later connoted as neat libation (*ákraton enkánaxón moi polùn / spondḗn* '[come on,] pour for me neat abundant . . . libation', 105–106, by Slave 1);[15] in other words, the wine that the two want to steal from their master to get drunk becomes the liquid (or liquid combination) that people would pour in sacred or ritual or solemn circumstances. In line 106, the imperative aorist form *speîson* 'do the libation' (for 'pour the wine'), 106, by Slave 2, confirms their mutual understanding of this layered meaning. The verbatim repetition of the purpose clause *tòn noûn hín' árdō* by Slave 1 in 96 and in 114—lit. 'with the purpose that I give water to the mind'—further elaborates on the metaphorical extension of the powers of wine: the verb *árdein* means 'to water, to give drink' and also 'to foster, to cherish' in serious contexts. The first-person future verb *katapásō* 'I will besprinkle [everything with bits of plans, thoughts, and ideas]', 99, continues the metaphor of fostering ideas by reviving things with drops of wine. Non-metaphorical and quite down-to-earth are, conversely, the three mentions of the verb *methúō* 'to be drunken', once in a passive subjunctive form (*methusthô*, 99), and twice as participle (*methúōn*, 88, and *methúōn*, 104, the latter with reference to Paphlagon).

Column D presents a few pivotal semantic twists in connection to the action of drinking wine, all of them relying on the use of the expression *agathós daímōn* 'Good Genius', a semi-divine entity (daemon) to whom people would toast while drinking after dinner. In line 85, Slave 1 (the leading fellow of the

Dialogic Syntax in Ancient Greek 163

two) proposes to substitute the idea of drinking a bull's blood with the idea of drinking wine in honour of the Good Genius (*agathoû daímonos*). Later, when Slave 2 encourages Slave 1 to pour wine as a libation to the Good Genius (*agathoû daímonos*, 106), Slave 1 replies by twisting the sense of 'daemon' in a joke: 'Down goes the libation for the Pramnian Genius' (*toû daímonos toû Pramníou* lit. 'of the Genius, the Pramnian one', 107). The wine from Pramnius was known to be particularly good. Slave 1, then, takes the wine as the Genius of the situation; consistently, right afterwards he addresses the wine itself by using (irreverently) the vocative *ô daîmon agathé* 'Oh Good Genius!', 108. Slave 2 effects the second twist by turning the metaphorical meaning of the good genius from 'wine' to 'good destiny/good luck' a few lines later: as he enters the room to steal the oracles from Paphlagon, he comments: 'but I'm afraid I may transform our Genie from Good to Bad' (*daímonos* 'Genius', 111, *kakodaímonos* 'Bad-genius', 112).

The resonance concerning ideas, thoughts, and deliberations is exemplified in column E: beside the reference to 'the mind' (*tòn noûn* at 96 and 114) and to the power of thoughts (or inventiveness) (*epínoian*, 90), the two slaves thematize their pondering of what to do through the verbs *bouleusaímetha* 'we could opt for', 86, and *bouleúsait'* '[a generic drunken man] could devise', 88, and the lexically related noun *tò boúleum'* 'the resolution', 108. The climatic point of these usages comes in line 100, where Slave 1 envisions his own ability to besprinkle, by drinking, 'bits of plans, thoughts, and ideas' (in the translator's words; lit. '[of] little decisions as well as little opinions as well as little thoughts', *bouleumatíōn kaì gnōmidíōn kaì noidíōn*).

In this dialogue, the references to Paphlagon are confined to few utterances connecting (as in a single cognitive frame) his name, some 'inside' place, and the action of 'taking' or 'stealing' (column F): in lines 101–102, Slave 2 notes: 'It's a lucky thing I wasn't caught (*ouk eléphthēn*) swiping (*kléptōn*) the wine from in there! (*éndothen*)'. Immediately afterwards, Slave 1 associates the presence of Paphlagon to 'in there', and asks: 'Tell me: what is Paphlagon (*Paphlagṓn*) doing?' (102). Later, Slave 1 suggests that Slave 2 steals Paphlagon's oracles: 'Quick, go [inside; *éndothen*] steal (participle *klépsas*) Paphlagon's (*Paphlágonos*) oracles and bring (*énenke*) them out here while he's still asleep' (109–111). Dialogic syntax in this set of utterances lets entire 'packages' of information resonate with each other (notably, the first 'package' is split across speakers). This suggests that linguistic affinities may by triggered on the basis of cognitive frames, where the access to one element of the frame gives immediate access to all the other elements of the same frame.[16]

The final set of affinities (column G) concerns questions, both addressed to the interlocutor as well as self-answered. The passage overall encompasses five questions (90 and 91 work also as statements): four by Slave 2 and one by Slave 1. However, while Slave 2, through his questions, just wonders about the suggestions made by Slave 1 (twice by means of 'how'-questions, at 82 and 88, and twice by means of 'what'-questions, at 97 and 109), Slave 1 proactively uses his question to justify or even to directly prompt the following course of

164 *Anna Bonifazi*

action (at 102, 'what is Paphlagon doing?' prompts the idea of stealing wine from him).[17]

Internal dialogic syntax (that is, within the same turn of speaking) abounds. Here I will just mention the recurrence of *allá* plus imperatives (see 95 and 98, by Slave 1), and two highly similar lines, again by Slave 1: *all'exénenké moi takhéōs oínou khoâ / tòn noûn hín' árdō kaì légō ti dexión* 'So quick, go in and fetch me a jug of wine; I want to water my wit and come up with something smart', and *phére nun egō 'mautô prosagágō tòn khoâ / tòn noûn hín' árdō kaì légō ti dexión* 'Well then, I'll just pass myself the jug, to water my wit and come up with something smart' (95–96 ~ 113–114).

As for metrical resonance, the unity of the cognitive package split across speakers at 101–102 is actually confirmed by meter as well, as line 102 features *antilabe*, a stylistic device of Classical drama whereby two or even three different characters perform different parts of the same verse. The effect is a tighter relevance of the different contributions, by analogy, continuation, or contrast/juxtaposition—I would say an extreme form of dialogic syntax within the same metrical line. A further *antilabe* at line 106 shows very similar syllables on the first and second thesis (- *dén* ⁓ *dé*) across speakers, even if the syllables belong to different lexical items. A few words occur in the same metrical position: *andrikṓtata* (81 and 82); *agathoû daímonos* (85 and 106). Moreover, several lines start with an '*o*' sound (either in a syllable with long '*o*' or a diphthong, or in a syllable with short '*o*' made long by metrical position): see 81, 82, 84, 88, 90, 91, 92, 96, 97, 101, 106, 108, and 114. Finally, and more importantly, a metrically internal *homoteleuton* '*on*' in thesis positions in line 116 (*hṓst' élathon autòn tòn hieròn khrēsmòn labṓn* 'so that he didn't notice when I grabbed his holy oracle'), seem to confirm a remarkable convergence: throughout the passage, the syllable '*on*' is quite recurrent, especially at the end of words such as *ákraton* 'neat', *oínon* 'wine', *daîmon* 'Genius', and *khrēsmón* 'oracle', which ultimately represent what the whole passage is about. Dialogic syntax in this case is strengthened by the match between sound-triggering and topic management.

4. Conclusion

The six diagraphs and the corresponding analyses carried out in Section 3 confirm that dialogic syntax in Ancient Greek conversation is pervasively present independently of the discourse type. What constitutes dialogic syntax in the selected passages covers, to use Du Bois' terms, 'the horizon of shared prior texts' (2014, p. 364). Sound-selections and a great variety of category-selections (at the morphological, semantic, syntactic, and pragmatic level) are interwoven, and demonstrate that while reading or listening to dialogues, we integrate the meanings prompted on all these levels. Furthermore, the dynamicity, and ultimately dialogicality, of these meanings emerges only through sequences of combined phrases and clauses.[18] The 'clothing of sentence structure' (Jefferson, 1996, p. 5; see section 1) could really obscure the phenomena pointed out. In the examined set of passages, dialogic syntax's 'consequences for meaning' (Du

Dialogic Syntax in Ancient Greek 165

Bois, 2014, p. 366) regard the following: the use of the same lexical items to add nuances (e.g., negations in Plato to connect the sense of unease—'I am not strong at all'—to the dissuasion from drinking too much—'nobody is eager [to drink a lot]'), or to suggest semantic shifts (e.g., 'Good Genius' becoming 'good wine' in Aristophanes); the use of semantically related concepts to develop an argument in desired directions (e.g., numerous kinship terms to orient the terms of the request and counterproposal in Pindar) or to stress the ultimate point under discussion (e.g., death-related utterances at the end of each turn in the Homeric passage); the use of resemblance between linguistic forms and meanings (iconicity, in fact) to produce alignment (e.g., 'Are you alive?' 'I am alive' in Chariton's mutual recognition scene), or to strengthen crucial ideas (e.g., the use of passive forms in Thucydides to stress the concept of subjugation). When the resonance emerging from the diagraphs is not much (as, for instance, in the Pindaric passage), metrical resonance adds to the point. Dialogic syntax works as a linguistic engine enabling and facilitating inferences and understanding in general. It does so through natural-language conversations, just as in re-created or made-up literary dialogues, to the extent that the latter must resemble, and to be recognized as, natural dialogues.[19]

Works Cited

Allen, T.W. (1931). *Homeri Ilias* (Volumes 2–3). Oxford: Clarendon Press, 2:1–356; 3:1–370. Retrieved from: http://stephanus.tlg.uci.edu/Iris/Cite?0012:001:783013

Arminen, I. (2005). *Institutional Interaction: Studies of Talk at Work*. Surrey: Ashgate.

Blake, W.E. (1938). *Charitonis Aphrodisiensis de Chaerea et Callirhoe amatoriarum narrationum libri octo*. Oxford: Clarendon Press, pp. 1–127. Retrieved from: http://stephanus.tlg.uci.edu/Iris/Cite?0554:001:0

Bonifazi, A. (2001). *Mescolare un cratere di canti: pragmatica della poesia epinicia in Pindaro*. Alessandria: Edizioni dell'Orso.

Bosworth, B. (2006). The humanitarian aspect of the Melian Dialogue. In J.S. Rusten (Ed.), *Oxford Readings in Classical Studies: Thucydides*. Oxford: Oxford University Press, pp. 312–337.

Bowra, C. (1933). Metrical correspondence in Pindar I. *The Classical Quarterly*, 27, 81–87.

Burnet, J. (1901). *Platonis Opera* (Volume 2). Oxford: Clarendon Press (repr. 1967). Retrieved from: http://stephanus.tlg.uci.edu/Iris/Cite?0059:011:11725

Chafe, W.L. (1988). Punctuation and the prosody of written language. *Written Communication*, 5, 395–426.

Coulon, V., and van Daele, M. (1923). *Aristophane* (Volume 1). Paris: Les Belles Lettres (repr. 1967 (1st edn. corr.)). Retrieved from: http://stephanus.tlg.uci.edu/Iris/Cite?0019:002:4158

Dancygier, B., and Sweetser, E. (2014). *Figurative Language*. Cambridge: Cambridge University Press.

Drummen, A. (2016). Reusing others' words: resonance. III.3. In A. Bonifazi, A. Drummen, and M. de Kreij (Eds.), *Particles in Ancient Greek Discourse. Exploring Particle Use Across Genres*. Washington, DC: Center for Hellenic Studies. (http://nrs.harvard.edu/

166 *Anna Bonifazi*

urn-3:hul.ebook:CHS_BonifaziA_DrummenA_deKreijM.Particles_in_Ancient_ Greek_Discourse.2016).

Du Bois, J.W. (2014). Towards a dialogic syntax. *Cognitive Linguistics*, 25, 359–410.

Du Bois, J.W., and Campbell, E.W. (forthcoming). Dialogic syntax and language documentation: description, theory, and interaction. *Language Documentation & Conservation*.

Fowler, H.N. (1925). *Plato* (Plato in twelve volumes, Volume 9). Cambridge, MA: Harvard University Press; London: William Heinemann Ltd.

Goold, C.P. (1995). *Chariton. Callirhoe*. Cambridge, MA and London: Harvard University Press.

Hammond, M. (2009). *Thucydides. The Peloponnesian War*. M. Hammond (Trans.) with an Introduction and Notes by P.J. Rhodes. Oxford: Oxford University Press.

Harris, Z.S. (1952). Discourse analysis. *Language*, 28, 1–30.

Henderson, J. (1998). *Aristophanes. Acharnians. Knights*. Jeffrey Henderson (Ed. and Trans.). Cambridge, MA: Harvard University Press.

Hof, S. (2020). Resonance in the prologue of Sophocles' *Ajax*. In G. Martin, F. Iurescia, S. Hof, and G. Sorrentino (Eds.), *Pragmatic Approaches to Drama*. Studies in Communication on the Ancient Stage. Leiden and Boston: Brill, pp. 121–139.

Hummel, P.C. (1993). *La syntaxe de Pindare*. Louvain and Paris: Peeters.

Jefferson, G. (1996). On the poetics of ordinary talk. *Text and Performance Quarterly*, 16, 1–61.

Jones, H.S., and Powell, J.E. (1942). *Thucydidis Historiae* (2 Volumes). Oxford: Clarendon Press 1:1942 (1st edn. rev.); 2:1942 (2nd edn. rev.) (repr. 1:1970; 2:1967). Retrieved from: http://stephanus.tlg.uci.edu/Iris/Cite?0003:001:768068

Jong, I.J.F. de (2001). *A Narratological Commentary on the Odyssey*. Cambridge: Cambridge University Press.

Jong, I.J.F. de (2012). *Homer. Iliad, Book XXII*. Cambridge: Cambridge University Press.

Lattimore, R. (1951). *The Iliad of Homer*. Chicago and London: The University of Chicago Press.

Maehler, H. (1971) (post B. Snell). *Pindari carmina cum fragmentis* (pt. 1, 5th edition). Leipzig: Teubner. Retrieved from: http://stephanus.tlg.uci.edu/Iris/Cite?0033:003:40162

McCabe, M.M. (2019). Plato's ways of writing. In G. Fine (Ed.), *The Oxford Handbook of Plato*. Oxford: Oxford University Press, pp. 93–118. www.oxfordhandbooks.com/ view/10.1093/oxfordhb/9780190639730.001.0001/oxfordhb-9780190639730-e-10

Person, R.F. Jr. (2016). *From Conversation to Oral Tradition: A Simplest Systematics for Oral Traditions*. London: Routledge.

Piedrabuena, S. (2020). *Indirect Echo-questions in Classical Greek*. Invited Talk, University of Cologne.

Race, W. H. (1997). *Pindar: Victory Odes and Fragments* (2 volumes). Cambridge, MA: Loeb.

Romilly, J. de. (1963) [1947]. The unity of Athenian imperialism (II): the Melian Dialogue. In J. de Romilly (Ed.), *Thucydides and Athenian Imperialism*. P. Thody (Trans.). Oxford: Blackwell, pp. 272–310.

Sacks, H. (1992). *Lectures on Conversation* (2 volumes). G. Jefferson (Ed.). Oxford and Cambridge, MA: Blackwell.

Sommerstein, A.H. (1980). Notes on aristophanes' knights. *The Classical Quarterly*, 30, 46–56.

Stinton, T.C.W. (1977). Pause and period in the lyrics of Greek tragedy. *The Classical Quarterly*, 27, 27–66.

Sweetser, E. (2006). Whose rhyme is whose reason? Sound and sense in Cyrano de Bergerac. *Language and Literature*, 15, 29–54.

Woods, W.L. (1938). Language study in schizophrenia. *Journal of Nervous and Mental Disease*, 87, 289–316.

Diagraph 3.2 Plato, *Symposium* 176a–176d

	A	B	C	D	E	F	G	H	I	J	K
Pa. 176a	*egṓ* I · *légō* I say · *ékhō* I have · *déomai* I have/need to · *oîmai* I think	*piómetha* we shall drink · *pínoimen* we could drink		*ándres* men [voc.] · *humîn* to you [pl.] · *humôn* of you [pl.] · *paréste* you [pl.] were present · *skopeîsthe* you [pl.] may look	*tína trópon hrâista piómetha* in which way shall we drink conveniently? · *tíni trópōi àn hōs hrâista pínoimen* in which way we could drink most conveniently	*piómetha* we shall drink · *pótou* of (the) drink · *pínoimen* we could drink	*khthés* yesterday · *khthés* yesterday		*khalepôs ékhō* I feel bad		
Ar. 176b	*autós eimi* I myself am		*eû légeis, ô Pausania* you speak well, Pausania [voc.]		*tô pantì trópōi paraskeuásasthai hrâistṓnēn tinà tês póseōs* to provide by all means some recovery from the drinking	*póseōs bebaptisménōn* baptized in drink	*khthés* yesterday				
Er. 176b	*déomai* I have/need to	*hēmîn* to us	*Agáthōn* Agathon [voc.]	*kalôs légete* you [pl.] are speaking in a good way	*pôs ékhei pros tò errôsthai pínein* how he feels about resisting to drink	*pínein* to drink					

(Continued)

Diagraph 3.2 (Continued)

	A	B	C	D	E	F	G	H	I	J	K
Ag. 176b	*oud'autòs* *érrōmai* I am myself not in good health either							*oud'autòs* *érrōmai* I am myself not in good health either			
Er. 176c, d	*emoí* to me *exairô* I take out *moi* to me *egṓ* I *emoí* to me *oîmai* I think *ethelḗsaimi* I could want *sumbouleúsaimi* I could recommend	*hemeîs* we *poiômen* we could do		*humôn* of you [pl.] *humeîs* you [pl.] *apeirḗkate* you [pl.] give up		*pínein* to drink *pínein* to drink *methúskesthai* to be drunken *méthē* drunkenness *pieîn* to drink [fut.] *kraipalônta* to be intoxicated	*tês proteraías* the day before	*apeirḗkate* you give up *oudeís . . .* *prothúmōs* *ékhein* nobody is eager *khalepón* harmful	*iatrikês* of medicine	*àn* *sumbouleúsaimi* I could recommend	*állōs te kaí* and especially
Ph. 176d	*égōge* I *ge* *eiōtha* I am used to . . .		*soi* to you *légēs* you would say						*iatrikês* of medicine	*àn eû* *bouleúōntai* if they would be well recommended	*állōs te kaí* and especially

Dialogic Syntax in Ancient Greek 169

Diagraph 3.3 Thucydides, *Histories* 5.91–97

	A	B	C	D	E	F	G	H	I	J
Ath. 91.1	*hēmeîs* we *hēmetéras* our *athumoûmen* we are afraid *hēmîn* to us		*tês arkhês* of sovereignty *hoi árkhontes* the rulers *tôn arxántōn* those who had ruled	*toîs nikētheîsin* the defeated ones	*én* if *én* if	*ouk* not *ou* not *ou* not	*hôsper kai* like, for example	*hoi* *hupékooi* the subjects		
91.2	*hēmîn* to us *páresmen* we are present *hēmetéras* our *eroûmen* we love *dēlṓsomen* we will clarify	*humetéras* your [pl.] *humôn* of you [pl.] *humâs* you [pl. acc]	*tês arkhês* of sovereignty *árxai* to rule	*apheísthō* be it left [imper.] *sōthênai* to be saved					*khrēsímōs* ... *sōthênai* conveniently ... you are being saved	
Mel. 92	*hēmîn* to us	*humîn* to you [pl.]	*árxai* to rule		*án* [mod. ptc]		*hôsper kai* like, for example		*khrēsimon* ... *douleûsai* being convenient ... to become slaves	

(Continued)

	A	B	C	D	E	F	G	H	I	J
Ath. 93	*hēmeîs* we *kerdaínoimen* we might gain	*humîn* to you [pl.] *humâs* you [pl. acc]			*án* [mod. ptc] *án* [mod. ptc]	*mḗ* not		*hupakoûsai* to obey		
Mel. 94	*hēmâs* we [acc.]	*déxaisthe* you [pl.] could accept			*án* [mod. ptc]	*mēdetérōn* of neither of the two groups *ouk* not	*hôste* so that			*phílous* . . . *polemíōn* friends . . . of enemies
Ath. 95	*hēmâs* we [acc.]	*humôn* of you [pl.]		*dēloúmenon* made clear		*ou* not				*philía* friendship *ékhthra* enmity *mîsos* hate
Mel. 96		*humôn* of you [pl.]		*kekheírōntai* have been subdued		*mḗ* not	*hôste* so that	*hoi* *hupḗkooi* the subjects *ápoikoi* settlers		
Ath. 97	*hēmâs* we [acc.] *hēmîn* to us	*paráskhoite* you [pl.] may provide *perigénoisthe* you [pl.] could survive		*katastraphênai* to be subjected	*án* [mod. ptc] *ei* if	*oudetérous* neither of the two groups *ouk* not *mḗ* not	*hôste* so that			

Dialogic Syntax in Ancient Greek   171

Diagraph 3.4 Pindar, *Nemean* 10.76–88

	A	B	C	D	E	F	G
Pollux (76–78)	*páter Kroníōn,* 76 father son of Chronus [voc.]	*páter,* 76 father [voc.] *epíteilon, ánax,* 77 accomplish [imp.], Lord [voc.]	*emoí,* 77 to me	*epíteilon,* 77 accomplish [imp.]	*sùn tôd',* 77 with this one here	*thánaton,* 77 death [acc.]	*éssetai,* 77 it will be
Zeus (80–88)	*huiós,* 80 son [nom.]	*essí,* 80 you are *teaí,* 81 to your [f.] *toi,* 82 to you *théleis,* 84 you want *soi,* 85 to you *márnasai,* 86 you struggle *noeîs,* 86 you think *pnéois,* 87 you could breathe	*moi,* 80 to me *pardídōm',* 83 I grant {*emoi*}, 84 {to me}	*pardídōm',* 83 I grant	*tónde,* 80 this one here [acc.] *tônde,* 82 of these things	*thánaton,* 83 death [acc.]	*essí,* 80 you are *ésti,* 85 there is

Diagraph 3.5 Homeric poetry, *Iliad* 22.331–360

	A	B	C	D	E	F	G	H	I	J
Ach. 331–336	*Héktor*, 331 Hector [voc.] *éphēs*, 331 you said *opízeo*, 332 you were not thinking *nḗpie*, 333 fool [voc.] *toi*, 335 to you *sè*, 335 you [acc.]	*emé*, 332 me *egṓ*, 334 I	*se mén ... tòn dé*, 335–336 you on the one hand, ... him on the other hand	*goúnat' élusa*, 335 I have loosened your knees	*kúnes ēd' oiōnoi*, 335 dogs and vultures		*oudén*, 332 nothing	*helkḗsous'*, 336 they will tear apart	*helkḗsous'*, 336 they will tear apart *kterioûsin* 336 they will bury	*kterioûsin*, 336 they will bury
Hec. 338–343	*són*, 338 of your *éa*, 339 allow [imp.] *sú*, 340 you *dédexo*, 340 accept [imp.] *toi*, 341 to you *dómenai*, 342 do [inf. for imp.]	*lissom'(ai)*, 338 I beg *me*, 339 me *sôma ... emòn*, 342 my corpse *me*, 342 me	*allà sù mén ... sôma dé*, 340–342 but: you on the one hand, ... the corpse on the other hand	*goúnōn*, 338 of knees	*kúnas*, 339 dogs [acc.]	*sōn ... tokéōn*, 338 of your parents *chrusón ... patḕr kai pótnia mḗtēr*, 340–341 gold ... father and lady mother	*mḗ*, 339 not	*katadápsai*, 339 to devour	*dṓsousi*, 341 they will give	*thanónta*, 343 (me) dead

Diagraph 3.5 (Continued)

	A	B	C	D	E	F	G	H	I	J
Ach. 345–354	kúon, 345 dog [voc.] gounázeo, 345 kneel [imp.] éorgas, 347 you have done sês ge, 348 of your ge s'(e), 351 you [acc.] sé ge, 352 you [acc.] ge	me, 345 me me, 346 me	allà kúnes te kai oiōnoí, 354 but dogs and vultures	goúnōn, 345 of knees gounázeo, 345 kneel [imp.]	kúon, 345 dog [voc.] kúnas, 348 dogs [acc.] kúnes te kai oiōnoí, 354 dogs and vultures	tokéōn, 345 of parents chrusôi... Dardanidēs... Príamos... téken, 351–353 in gold... Priam son of Dardanos... lady mother... bore pótnia mḗtēr	mḗ, 345 not mḗ, 345 not ouk, 348 not oud' ei kén, 349 not if oud' ei kén, 351 not if oud', 352 and not	édmenai, 347 to eat up katà... dásont-ai, 354 they will divide up	goḗsetai, 353 she will lament katà... dásont-ai, 354 they will divide up	enthemḗnē lechéessi, 353 she having laid on the death-bed
Hec. 356–360	s'(e), 356 you [acc.] soí ge, 357 to you ge phrázeo, 358 be careful toí, 358 to you se, 359 you [acc.]	protióssomai, 356 I look upon you genōmai, 358 I would become					oud', 356 and not mḗ... hóte kén, 359–360 not... when			olésōsin, 360 they will let perish

Diagraph 3.6 Aristophanes, *Knights* 80–117

	A	B	C	D	E	F	G
Sl. 2 80	*krátiston . . .* *apothaneín*, 80 the best . . . to die						
Sl. 1 80–81	*àn apothánōmen* *andrikṓtata*, 81 we would die in the most heroic way	*àn apothánōmen,* 81 we would die					
Sl. 2 82–84	*andrikṓtata*, 82 the most heroic way *béltiston*, 82 the best *thánatos* *hairetṓteros*, 84 death better to be chosen	*génoit' àn*, 82 could be					*pôs dêta pôs* *génoit' àn* *andr-ikṓtata?*, 82 how then? how could there be a most heroic way?
Sl. 1 85–86		*àn khrēstón ti* *bouleusaímetha*, 86 we could deliberate something useful	*ákraton oînon*, 85 neat wine	*agathoû* *daímonos*, 85 Good Genius	*bouleusaímetha,* 86 we could deliberate		
Sl. 2 87–88		*àn . . . khrēstón ti* *bouleúsait'*, 88 could he deliberate something useful?	*(g') ákraton*, 87 ge neat *potoû*, 87 of the drink *methíōn*, 88 being drunken		*bouleúsait'*, 88 he could deliberate		*pôs d' àn* *methíōn* *khrēstón ti* *bouleúsait'* anḗr?, 88 how could a drunken man deliberate something useful?

Diagraph 3.6 (Continued)

	A	B	C	D	E	F	G
Sl. 1 89–96		*heúrois àn ti praktikṓteron*, 91 could you find anything more effective? *hótan pínōsin*, 92 whenever they would drink	*oînon*, 90 wine [acc.] *oínou*, 91 of wine *pínōsin*, 92 they would drink *oínou khoâ*, 95 jug of wine *tòn noûn hín'*, *árdō*, 96 with the purpose that I give water to the mind		*epínoian*, 90 inventiveness *tòn noûn*, 96 the mind		*ti poth' hēmâs ergásei tō̂ sō̂ potō̂?*, 97 What will you do with your drink?
Sl. 2 97			*tō̂ sō̂ potō̂*, 97 to your drink				
Sl. 1 98–100		*èn . . . methusthô*, 99 if I would get drunk	*methusthô*, 99 I would be drunken *katapásō*, 99 I will besprinkle		*bouleumatiōn kai gnōmidiōn kai noidiōn*, 100 of little decisions and little opinions and little thoughts		
Sl. 2 101–102			*tòn oînon*, 102 wine [acc.]			*hōs eutukhōs hóti ouk eléphthēn éndothen / kléptōn tòn oînon*, 101–102 It's a lucky thing I wasn't caught swiping the wine from in there!	

(Continued)

Diagraph 3.6 (Continued)

	A	B	C	D	E	F	G
Sl. 1 102						*eipé moi, Paphlagôn ti drâi?*, 102 tell me: what is Paphlagon doing?	*eipé . . . ti drâi?*, 102 tell . . . what is he doing?
Sl. 2 103–104			*methúōn*, 104 being drunken				
Sl. 1 105–106			*ákraton enkánaxon . . . spondēn* 105–106 pour neat . . . libation				
Sl. 2 106			*speîson*, 106 do the libation	*agathoû daímonos*, 85 of the Good Genius			
Sl.1 107–108				*toû daímonos toû Pramníou*, 107 of the Genius, the Pramnian (one) *ô daîmon agathé*, 108 o Good Genius	*tò boúleum'*, 107 the resolution		
Sl. 2 109							*eíp' . . . ti estí?*, 109 tell . . . what is it?

Dialogic Syntax in Ancient Greek   177

Diagraph 3.6 (Continued)

	A	B	C	D	E	F	G
	Sl. 1 109–111					*toùs khrēsmoùs takhù /* *klépsas énenke* *toû Paphlágonos* *éndothen / héōs* *katheúdei,* 109–111 quick, go inside; steal Paphlagon's oracles and bring them out here while he's still asleep	
	Sl. 2 111–112			*daímonos,* 111 of the Genius *kakodaímonos,* 112 Bad-genius			
	Sl. 1 113–114			*tòn khoâ,* 113 the jug *tòn noûn hín' árdō,* 114 with the purpose that I give water to the mind	*tòn noûn,* 114 the mind		
	Sl. 2 115–117					*hōs megál' ho* *Paphlagòn pérdetai* *kai hrēketai / hóst'* *élathon autòn tòn* *hieròn khrēsmòn labṓn,* 115–116 Paphlagon is snoring and farting so loud that he didn't notice when I grabbed his holy oracle	

178 *Anna Bonifazi*

Notes

1. Transcription by Du Bois. Here is a brief legend of the special signs in the transcription (from Du Bois, 2014, p. 361): ^ = primary accent; (H) = in-breath; @ = laugh; ¿ = appeal onset. In Du Bois' model, italics in diagraphs is reserved for words that are not claimed to show resonance with other words.
2. Further work in progress in Ancient Greek looks relevant to dialogic syntax, even if at this stage Du Bois' framework is not used: Rodríguez-Piedrabuena (presentation, 2020) focuses on echo questions in Classical drama and in Plato's dialogues. Echo questions are questions repeated by the respondent before the reply to a question posed by someone else. Sometimes echo questions are not explicitly uttered, but implicitly meant or meant to be inferred through the use of particles or other words. 'Echo' somewhat relates to resonance, and the conversational organization of questions and answers plays a central role in Rodríguez-Piedrabuena's analysis.
3. See especially *Callirhoe* 5.9.4, where the female protagonist addresses her own eyes: "εἴδετε" φησὶ "Χαιρέαν ὑμεῖς ἀληθῶς; ἐκεῖνος ἦν Χαιρέας ὁ ἐμός, ἢ καὶ τοῦτο πεπλάνημαι;" 'Do you really see Chaereas? Was that one my Chaereas, or am I mistaken right away?'
4. Ancient Greek is known to be a pro-drop language: nominative and accusative pronouns may always be omitted.
5. In turn, this verbal phrase resonates with *errôsthai* 'to be eager', uttered by Eryximachus in 176b, and the further negations *oud'* 'and . . . not' again by Eryximachus in 176b, and *oúte . . . oúte* 'neither . . . nor' by Agathon in 176c (not reported in the diagraph).
6. There is further resonance at the level of construction between *khalepôs ékhō* (uttered by Pausanias in 176a) and *prothúmōs ékhein* (uttered by Eryximachus in 176c), both including the verb *ékhein* lit. 'to have' and an adverb; it is an idiomatic construction used to express mental or emotional states.
7. See Bowra (1933) for metrical responsion; see also Stinton (1977) and Hummel (1993, p. 449) about metrical pauses.
8. Roughly speaking, while the chorus would move in one direction during the singing of one stanza (*strophe*, lit. 'turn'), and in the opposite direction in the next (metrically parallel) stanza (*antistrophe* lit. 'turning back'), in the epode they would stand at the center of the stage to sing the third (and metrically different) stanza.
9. De Jong (2012, p. 140) mentions a structural parallel concerning death scenes: a dialogue between victor and victim takes place also when Patroclus dies (see *Iliad* 16.829–854; two turns).
10. For an overview of basic data (speaker, length, etc.) regarding direct speech data in the *Iliad*, see www.dsgep.ugent.be, where the University of Ghent hosts a digital appendix about all the tokens of direct speech in Greek epic poetry.
11. In the narratological glossary preceding her commentary on the *Odyssey*, the term 'catch-word technique' is defined as 'when a character echoes, often at the beginning of his speech, a word or expression from his interlocutor's speech, often with a different tone or meaning' (De Jong, 2001, p. xii).
12. Both terms are words of strong reproach in Homeric diction.
13. Slaves' fondness of wine in Aristophanes is commented upon by e.g., Sommerstein (1980, p. 46) where he cites *Wasps* 9–10, *Lysistrata* 426–427, and *Ekklesiazousae* 1112–1124 as parallels.
14. In the diagraph I am reporting the particle *g'* (*ge*) preceding *ákraton* at 87, to record that *ge* contributes to resonance by signaling the retrieval and the stress on a particular piece of information. This point is made and elaborated by Drummen (2016, III.3 §§76–79, §100).
15. I am adding the suspension dots to render a possible joke: 'abundant libation' occurs across subsequent lines; therefore, a little performative pause before 'libation' at the onset of line 106 does not sound implausible.

Dialogic Syntax in Ancient Greek   179

16. See Dancygier and Sweetser (2014, pp. 101–102).
17. Explicitly CA-oriented input about lines 120–122 can be found in Drummen (2016, III.4§15).
18. I prefer to avoid the term 'sentence' taken as punctuation unit, because until early print editions, ancient Greek texts did not include full stops.
19. I warmly thank the editors of this volume for their perceptive feedback and for accommodating a particularly long piece. Most of all, I thank them for the invitation to contribute to the volume; it gave me the opportunity to read and listen to known dialogues with new eyes and new ears—irreversibly.

7 Repetition, Parallelism, and Non-Repetition

From Ordinary Talk to Ritual Poetry and Back Again

Frog

Introduction

Non-repetition is a distinct and widespread principle that is easily taken for granted. It occasionally comes into focus, for instance in writing style guides that valorize lexical variation and chide against an apparently natural tendency to reuse the same phraseology when talking about a particular topic. In traditions of verbal art with so-called *canonical parallelism*—i.e., where parallelism is a regular principle for organizing language into units (Jakobson, 1981 [1966], p. 98)—non-repetition is systematic, which makes such traditions of great interest for exploring the operation of non-repetition as a phenomenon. To my knowledge, non-repetition has not previously received focused attention as a fundamental feature of parallelism. The present chapter brings non-repetition in parallelism into the spotlight. Although parallelism is commonly recognized as being characterized by juxtaposing features of sameness and difference, the non-repetition of one or more constituents tends to be taken for granted. Nevertheless, where parallelism is expected, a lapse of non-repetition appears as non-ideal, if not a violation. Synonymic and analogical parallelism, in focus here, are based on equivalencies and commonly rely on lexical and phraseological alternatives for expressing 'the same thing' or things otherwise handled as equivalent, while a non-repetition constraint operates as a determinant on choices between these alternatives in the progression of a parallel group. Gail Jefferson's (1996) concept *category-triggering* offers a lens for considering the activation of lexical and phrasal alternatives.

Category-triggering describes vocabulary summoned through associations of sense in language production. Jefferson's focus is on empirically observable cases in conversation. In repairs, for example, someone says 'brother' and corrects it to 'sister' or says 'getting' and corrects it to 'giving' (Jefferson, 1996, p. 10), where errors reflect summoning the wrong word from a semantic category; *categorial flurries* are when a concentration of words or their homonyms belonging to a category like body parts are used, for instance in coproduced conversation (Jefferson, 1996, pp. 34–36). That homonyms and metaphorical usage occur in such flurries reflects the complexity of triggering as operating at

DOI: 10.4324/9780429328930-10

Repetition, Parallelism, Non-Repetition 181

the level of semantic categories, lexical sets associated with those categories, and signifiers of those lexical sets even when used with meanings identified with other categories. Triggering at the level of signifiers links category-triggering to *sound-triggering*, whereby words are summoned by associations of sound rather than sense. Although Jefferson's emphasis was on cases that bring the phenomenon into focus, her concept of triggering points to ways language is accessed in the brain, and can be assumed to operate even in the invisible selection between semantically equivalent alternatives when formulating a sentence. Non-repetition is interesting in this light because, as a constraint, it situates Jefferson's category-triggering as an unconscious process in relation to memory. As Nigel Fabb observes:

> If we assume that parallelism is psychologically real, such that parallelism is assigned to a text by some psychological process, then memory is crucial, because while composing or listening to the second line, the first line must be remembered: it is the relationship between the first and second line that constitutes the text as parallelistic.
>
> (Fabb, 2017, p. 355)

Non-repetition is here approached as at an intersection of category-triggering and remembering, which can then also be considered in relation to additional factors, such as conventions of phrasal use that may also drive choices in lexical selection, with the potential that conventions and constraints may be competing. In the analysis of ordinary talk, repetition is often treated as a blanket category, in which full repetition, partial repetition, near-repetition, and so forth are included, usually without much concern for distinguishing them or for distinguishing repetition from parallelism. Here, examples of the sorts of things that fall under the aegis of 'repetition' in research on ordinary talk are briefly outlined. Parallelism is then introduced as a distinct phenomenon and illustrated through a variety of oral traditions. These include Rotenese ritual discourse, where parallelism is systematic and units are structured based on semantics without a periodic meter or rhythm; Khanty and Finno-Karelian kalevalaic poetry, where parallelism is systematic and lines have a periodic meter; and in Old Norse eddic poetry, where parallelism is not systematic, but lines have a periodic meter. These four main traditions include research based on current and recent fieldwork, large corpora—or 'big data'—collected during the nineteenth and twentieth centuries, and oral-derived texts found in medieval manuscripts. Additional traditions are also discussed based on earlier research where these introduce relevant aspects of parallelism. The perspective gained from these cases are brought into comparison with evidence of ordinary talk and the types of everyday interactions on which Jefferson's ground-breaking work was based. It is hoped that the perspectives offered here will stimulate attention to non-repetition as a potentially significant and, in certain contexts, rule-governed feature in conversational discourse.

182 *Frog*

Repetition in Ordinary Talk (as Widely Addressed)

'Matching' verbal and intonational patterns of an interlocutor is found to be a basic feature of conversational interaction, both within and between utterances. Its forms and functions are legion, ranging from the production of cohesion to mimicry (Tannen, 1987; Couper-Kuhlen, 1996; Du Bois, 2014). Repetition is common in false starts, like the following repetition of 'you', which seems similar to nonlexical fillers like 'uh':

```
(Robinson and Kevoe-Feldman, 2010, p. 246)
TOM Oh. you- you talking about me, or: thuh deaf person.
```

Peter French and John Local (1986, pp. 173–177) found similar repetition to be a characteristic feature of interruptions in their English conversation data. In the following example, the repetition seems to both emphasize the immediacy of the speaker's desire to interject something, and also to prolong the beginning of what N intends to say until the other speaker has concluded his/her turn:

```
(French and Local, 1986, p.174)
V [...] still remains at some [point an agreement's got to be ^reached]
N                             [that- that's not- that's not the- ^that's not]
    the one we're worried about though
```

Deborah Tannen identifies a number of forms of repetition as 'automatic, rather than generative, language capacities' (1987, p. 592). She relates the automaticity in such repetition to efficiency in language production and interpretation: 'Its meaning does not have to be worked out anew on subsequent reference, but is carried over ready-made' (1987, p. 595). The reuse of lexical material and structures from preceding utterances has been widely discussed (see, e.g., Pickering and Garrod, 2004, pp. 171–175) and interpreted as facilitating response planning in conversation (Corps, Gambi, and Pickering, 2018, p. 235). In other words, repetition lightens the cognitive load by providing pre-processed units of utterance, as Tannen illustrates with the repetition of 'to recreate that image' with 'to recreate the image' in the following example:

```
(Tannen, 1987, p. 595)
N        When you speak,
         you use words to … to recreate that image.
         in the other person's mind.
C        Right.
N        And in sign language,
         you use ^signs to recreate the image.
```

Such repetitions are comparable to formulaic sequences. Formulaic sequences are complex, prefabricated linguistic units that are stored as wholes in the mental

Repetition, Parallelism, Non-Repetition 183

lexicon, allowing them to be produced and interpreted without the cognitive work of fabricating or analyzing the sequence through the lexicon and grammar (Wray, 2008, pp. 11–12; see also Frog and Lamb, 2021). The difference is that formulaic sequences become established in long-term memory, whereas 'automatic' repetitions are linked to the immediate situation of utterance; they seem to operate in working memory.

An interlocutor may repeat what is being said with only a slight delay, a phenomenon that Tannen (1987, pp. 592–598) calls *shadowing*, which she focuses on as a clear form of 'automatic' language production (square brackets indicate overlap of speech):

```
(Tannen, 1987, p. 593)
N          I don't know what … uh … port tastes like.
S          Port is very s[weet. Port is very rich.
C                       [Port is very sweet. Very rich.
S          Syrupy red wine.
C          And brandy's very alcoholic.
```

Shadowing can reflect that the listener is actively engaged, understands or is processing what is being said; it can reflect agreement with what is said or signal the interlocutor's desire for a turn in conversation. Conversation Analysis (CA) has brought attention to how participants manage epistemic issues in such sequences of talk, like establishing, as in the preceding example, equal authority to make evaluations and assessments (Heritage, 2014).

Repetitions are also commonly used in repairs. Repairs initiated within a turn of conversation may simply follow a non-ideal word or phrase with a replacement without repetition:

```
(Jefferson, 1996, p. 10)
LARRY Hi, I'm Carol's sister- uh brother
```

In some languages or speech communities, word-searches in such repairs may be marked by features like 'uh' here, but in other languages this is not necessary (Wouk, 2005). This type of repair reflects a little-discussed dimension of syntax according to which two or sometimes more syntactic elements within a clause or phrase are interpreted as doubles, between which the second offers a correction, specification, intensification, or may be intended for any number of additional situation-specific aims (Kitzinger, 2013, pp. 242–243). Such repairs may include repetitions of additional words. In the following example, the repair of 'five' is delayed and all intermediate words ('years that I've') are repeated for the continuation of the clause:

```
(Kitzinger, 2013, p. 241)
ANI        Meanwhile for the last five years that I've- (0.4) six-
           seven years that I've been in New Jerse:y […]
```

184 *Frog*

In the repair, repetition has a syntactic function of making salient the relationship of the correction to what has just been said. The repetition could be considered syntactically motivated, since '*for the last five years that I've- six-seven been in New Jersey' would probably not be intelligible, owing to the lack of indications of how 'six- seven' should be related to other elements in the clause. In contrast, an immediate juxtaposition of the repair with the error is readily interpretable: '*for the last five- six- seven years that I've been in New Jersey'. Such repetition may not always be essential, but it facilitates the analysis of the juxtaposition by creating a frame in relation to which the new word or words can be interpreted as alternatives filling the same slot ('X years that I've').

In the following, 'Nonny's arriving' is juxtaposed with 'my granddaughter's arriving', where the repair is for clarification:

(Kitzinger, 2013, p. 235)
ILENE   [...] Nonny's arriving my granddaughter's arriving from: uh hh uh:
        Caracas.

At least in principle, the speaker could have organized this as a delayed apposition '*Nonny's arriving, my granddaughter . . .'. However, my own, native-like intuition is that interpreting the latter phrase would require recourse to a grammatical analysis to relate 'my granddaughter' to the preceding phrase. The repetition of 'arriving' produces a frame that makes the relation between 'Nonny's' and 'my granddaughter's' salient, whereas a delayed apposition, though it might be fine grammatically, would require more cognitive work in the flow of conversational speech.

A repetition in repair might also have other motivations. In the following Indonesian example, *bukan ana[k]* ['not a child'] is juxtaposed with *bukan dokter* ['not a doctor']. This might be seen as merely a repair of the phrasal unit, but it may have been motivated to avoid ambiguity. The repetition of *bukan* ['not'] produces a frame through which the juxtaposition is interpreted as a repair, whereas **bukan anak dokter* can be interpreted through the grammar as 'not a child of a doctor':

(Wouk, 2005, p. 246)
tapi buka:n ana-, bukan dokter dia
But he's not a chil- not a doctor

Repairs initiated by an interlocutor very often involve repetition, for instance repeating part of the preceding utterance as a question when this is not understood, as in the following example where *Duck Man* is the name of a television program:

(Robinson and Kevoe-Feldman, 2010, p. 246)
DEE   Hey do you get duck ma:n?
MEGAN   Duck ma:n?
DEE: Duck man=it's a sho:w.

Repetition, Parallelism, Non-Repetition 185

The repetition points to the unit that the speaker considers to require a repair. The unit repeated may also be the full unit of a conversational turn (Robinson and Kevoe-Feldman, 2010). In the following example, the question 'Do you read?' marks a new topic that the interlocutor seems to have difficulty contextualizing:

```
(Robinson and Kevoe-Feldman, 2010, pp. 204-241)
DEBBIE       Do you re::ad?
PETER        Do I re:ad?
DEBBIE       D' you read things just for fun?
PETER        Y:e:ah.
```

Some questions may also be answered by repeating the word of the question as an affirmation:

```
(Schegloff, 2007, p. 115)
ANNE     Because it's better that way when we're driving, okay?
NAOMI    Oka(h)ay. [...]
```

In English, both positive and negative answers are often formed from questions built with the verb *to be* or an auxiliary verb. A common feature of such answers is ellipsis of the main verb and/or remainder of the clause, like answering a question *Did we X?* with *We did.*:

```
(Schegloff, 2007, p. 143)
DEB      I don't think I ever sent Marcia a birth- a present for
         her baby did I?=or did we buy something t'gether.
         (0.3)
DEB      Mo:m,
ANN      Yeah I think we dⱶ:d.
```

In situations that commonly recur, repetition may develop a ritualized quality, as in openings and endings of dialogic interaction. For example, many common greeting exchanges in European languages are organized on a principle of repetition. In the following opening of a telephone conversation, 'Hello?' initiates a summons-answer sequence (Schegloff, 1968, pp. 1080–1081), answered by the greeting 'Hi', and the same greeting is then repeated back to the speaker:

```
(Schegloff, 2007, p. 22)
         [ring]
AVA      H'llo?
BEE      hHi:,
AVA      Hi:?
BEE      hHowuh you:?
```

Corresponding structures are common in leave-taking, as well as in affirmations, as in the following conclusion of a phone conversation. In this example, a

186 *Frog*

repetition of affirmation is followed by the leave-taking formula 'bye', spoken by both participants simultaneously:

```
(Schegloff, 2007, p. 254)
REBECCA       Okay I'll talk to you later
ARTHUR        Okay
REBECCA       Okay=[bye
ARTHUR             [Bye
              [hang up]
```

The simultaneity of 'bye' here reflects both participants anticipating the same ritualized leave-taking exchange, and the participants seem to accept this as concluding the dialogue even though their speech is not sequentially organized.

Amid the myriad forms of repetition in ordinary talk, focus has generally been on features of verbal sameness, with features of difference mainly coming into focus in individual cases, as a feature of repairs, or when verbal sameness is considered complete and accompanied by difference in prosody (e.g., French and Local, 1986; Robinson and Kevoe-Feldman, 2010).

A Brief Introduction to Parallelism

It is not particularly surprising that research on ordinary talk often discusses repetition as a broad category without differentiating parallelism. Parallelism, as currently understood, is a modern concept that was established for the discussion of poetics. It was never brought into focus in classical rhetoric as a unified concept; instead, a number of different types of figures involving lexical repetition or combining sameness with difference were distinguished. The concept of parallelism took shape centrally through Robert Lowth's lectures on the poetry of the Hebrews (1753), where he described the phenomenon as *parallelismus membrorum* ['parallelism of members'], from which today's term *parallelism* derives. Lowth outlined three varieties of parallelism: *parallelismus synonymus* ['synonymous parallelism'], *parallelismus antitheticus* ['antithetical parallelism'], and *parallelismus syntheticus* ['synthetic parallelism']. Synonymous parallelism concerns parallelism of equivalence. Antithetical parallelism is contrastive. Synthetic parallelism was less clearly articulated, but Lowth later described it in English as *constructive parallelism* (Lowth, 1778, p. xvii), where it appears to equate to today's grammatical or syntactic parallelism.

The discussion and theorization of parallelism mainly developed across the twentieth century. Wolfgang Steinitz's (1934) detailed study of parallelism in kalevalaic poetry was an early milestone contribution, which included differentiating between semantic and analogous equivalence in parallelism, although the distinction is not always clear. Advances in theorizing parallelism in current scholarship are linked to the seminal work of Roman Jakobson (e.g. 1981 [1966]; see also Fox, 1977), which also seems to have stimulated interest in

Repetition, Parallelism, Non-Repetition 187

the topic and innovations in how it is understood (e.g., Urban, 1986; Fox, 1988). In recent years, parallelism has received new attention from a number of perspectives (e.g., Wagner, 2007; Du Bois, 2014; Fox, 2014; 2016; Frog, 2014; Fabb, 2015, ch. 6; Frog and Tarkka, 2017). Most research on parallelism in oral poetry has focused on parallelism at the level of a poetic line or its equivalent. Parallelism across longer stretches of text has also begun receiving attention, distinguished as *macro-parallelism* (Urban, 1986), leading to interest in how parallelism may operate on multiple levels in tandem (Frog, 2017a). Although Jakobson's work on poetics has been engaged in approaches to the poetics of ordinary talk (e.g., Tannen, 1987), parallelism was not the point of interest. Michael Silverstein (1984) stressed the significance of parallelism in structuring co-produced conversation. However, he handled the concept rather loosely: when lifted from poetic discourse with lines as formally regular units, Silverstein untethered the concept from formal conditions, with the consequence that all forms of deixis became included in his usage. John W. Du Bois (2014) has made considerable contributions, showing that parallelism is a basic structuring device of co-produced conversation, distinguishable from both repetition and resonance, but this work has appeared embedded in his research on stance (2007) and under a label of 'Dialogic Syntax' rather than a title that would point to parallelism or poetics (2014; see also Anna Bonifazi's chapter in this volume).

I define parallelism as follows:

> Parallelism is a perceivable quality of text in which a repetition of sameness is saliently juxtaposed with difference in commensurate units so that the units become interpretable as parts of a parallel group, more closely linked to one another than to preceding and/or following text.

As Du Bois (2014, pp. 397–400) emphasizes, parallelism is a phenomenon of syntax in the sense that it concerns the formal relation of signs to one another and thereby shapes the interpretation of the respective signs.

Parallelism and Non-Repetition in Oral Verbal Art

Discussions of parallelism in verbal art customarily remain focused on so-called *verse parallelism*, or parallelism at the level of individual poetic lines and couplets. However, the formal principles even of verse parallelism vary considerably by tradition. The ways of looking at juxtapositions of sameness and difference forming parallelisms have extended beyond the lexical and syntactic makeup of lines to melody, rhythm, and additional features (Turpin, 2017). Parallelism of linguistic text and non-linguistic signs has also received theoretical attention (Frog, 2017b).

In the examples that follow, synonymous and analogical parallelism are in focus, although some of the traditions in which parallelism is systematic allow other forms of parallelism in that function. Non-repetition is also present in antithetical

188   *Frog*

or contrastive parallelism and grammatical parallelism. However, non-repetition is more transparently visible as a principle where parallel members 'say the same thing' rather than where they say different things, where difference in wording may be interpreted as driven by the difference in meaning. The aim here is to illustrate rather than to survey non-repetition exhaustively.

Canonical Parallelism in Unmetered Discourse

In many forms of oral poetry, canonical parallelism regularly structures language into pairs of lines where each semantically significant element of the first line is matched in the second. In Rotenese ritual discourse of eastern Indonesia, for example, the idiom is constituted of conventionally paired words, most of which are exclusive, but words may also be parts of multiple conventional pairs linked to different meanings (Fox, 2014). For example, *bafi* ['pig'] is used in two central dyadic pairs as well as participating in others (Fox, 2016, p. 212–213). The pair *bafi//kapa* ['pig'//'water buffalo'] concerns wealth and thus *bafi* is linked to domestic livestock. The pair *bafi//kode* ['pig'//'monkey'] concerns destructive, undomesticated forces, in which *bafi* is instead understood as 'wild pig'. Although the pairs may be used in different contexts, they also get combined with other pairs like *ketu//na'a* ['pluck'//'eat'] and *betek//pelak* ['millet'//'maize'], building up into line-length formulae:

Kode ketu betek	The monkey plucks the millet
Ma bafi na'a pelak	And the pig eats the maize
	(Fox, 2016, p. 124)

In this poetry, all semantically significant elements should be reproduced in both parallel members, ideally with non-repetition of the lexemes. However, Rotenese parallelism prefers syndetic coordination, linking paired units with a conjunction like *ma* ['and'] here or *do* ['or'] in the following example. The coordinating conjunction is not treated as a component of the parallel units and thus needs no counterpart in the first member of a pair. Non-repetition is not as significant for semantically light elements like *esa* ['one'] in the following example:

Faik esa manunin	On one particular day
Do ledok esa mate'e-na	Or one certain time [literally: 'sun']
	(Source: Pono, *Suti solo* audio, lines 1–2)

It is customary to layout Rotenese ritual discourse with a regular line structure according to semantic units. Although parallelism usually follows a simple dyadic structure, variations in the structuring of parallelism are part of the aesthetics of performance and the dynamics of how the poetry varies. In the following, indentation has been added to draw attention to the parallelism between

Repetition, Parallelism, Non-Repetition 189

longer units laid out as couplets and the additional parallelism following the fourth of these lines:

Te bafi ka'a neni pelak	But if the pig chews the maize
Au dede'ak o se	With whom will I speak
Ma kode ketu neni betek	And if monkey plucks the millet
Au kokolak o se	With whom will I talk
Do se'ek o se	Or with whom be noisy
Ma oku-boluk o se	And with whom shout
Sama leo Lua Bafa	[With someone] just like Lua Bafa
Ma deta leo Lole Holu?	And exactly like Lole Holu?'

(Source: Fox, 2016, p. 63, word-order
adjusted in the translation of lines 5–6)

Parallel linguistic units do not have a uniform relation to rhythm and melodic contours in performance, producing additional variations. The following example is from the audio recording of a performance by Esau Pono in 2008. In it, there are three units that together form a complex parallelism. The first unit opens with the pronoun *ana* ['she'] and the verb *nggao na* ['takes up']. The second unit elides the pronoun and, as is customary, introduces the parallel expression with a conjunction, in this case *ma* ['and'], yet the verb is repeated rather than varied. In performance, these are rhythmically the same, drawing out *na*, followed by a rapid articulation of the following couplet so that each opening is of roughly equal duration to the subsequent pair. The couplet following the verb is here laid out on a single line because these parallel units repeat the term for 'net' and the dyadic pairing *seko// ndai* ['scoop-net'//'fishing net'] is between these couplets:

An' nggao na:::	
seko meti-na	fo seko matei besin
Ma nggao na:::	
ndai tasi-na	fo ndai mahamu lilo-na

She takes up	
her tidal scoop-net	the scoop-net with iron-weighed insides
And takes up	
her sea fishing net	the fishing net with gold-weighed belly

(Source: Pono, *Suti solo* audio, lines 5–8; translation
based on Jams J. Fox's of Esau's transcription of the performance)

In K'iche' Mayan ritual discourse, parallelism is also a central organizing principle, but it often only involves repetition of a portion of the complete unit of utterance. The structuring principle of parallelism also differs from that in Rotenese both in that it is asyndetic—i.e., not using conjunctions to link members of parallel groups—and, as William M. Norman (1980, p. 393) puts it, '[c]ouplets that differ in their lexical composition at more than one point are ill-formed'. The recurrent

190 *Frog*

phraseology of such parallel verses is described as a *frame*, corresponding to a partially-filled frame in construction grammar, while the varying elements that fill the slot in a frame can be called the *focus* (Cruz, 2014). In order to make parallelism visually salient, lines are laid out using Du Bois' technique of *diagraph analysis*, whereby parallel stretches of text are laid out on a grid, aligning parallel elements for comparison:

> Dyoos kuuk'a7n   sin aanimaa alaq
>   loq'chajin   sin aanimaa alaq

> God   he-has-with-him   EMP. your-souls
>   he reverently-guards   EMP. your-souls
>   (Source: Norman, 1980, p. 388)

> karaj ne7   (x)saqirik
> karaj ne7   xpakataj   jun saantalaj uwach uleew

> perhaps   it-got-light
> perhaps   it-dawned   a holy world

(Source: Norman, 1980, p. 388)

The structuring of parallelism is not simply a question of the scope of parallel units; it also exhibits hierarchies of organizing features. For example, Norman observes that Mayan parallelism is similar to Hebrew poetry in that parallelism is required at the level of words, but there may be variation in the specific syntax, in contrast to traditions of Chinese parallelism, where syntactic correspondence is a primary principle (1980, p. 391).

Canonical Parallelism in Metered Discourse

Canonical parallelism is also integrated into traditions of metered oral poetry, as found prominently in some Uralic languages. In Khanty, parallelism is commonly formed by varying only a single word, as in K'iche', yet the verse form requires the rest of the line to be completed:

> nēs tēləm taŋkw -śaxl ūsent
> nēs tēləm tunrä -śaxl ūsent

> in the algae -hilled forts which have arisen of themselves
> in the tundra -hilled forts which have arisen of themselves

(Source: Austerlitz, 1958, p. 53)

Even though varying a single word is most common, Khanty does not restrict parallelism to only a single word, so line frames may have multiple slots:

> punəŋa sēmpə ūnt tū.ŋx pox
> punəŋa sēmpə wur mē.ɲx pox

Repetition, Parallelism, Non-Repetition 191

the hairy-eyed forest-   tūꞐx's   son
the hairy-eyed mountain- mēꞐx's   son

(Source: Austerlitz, 1958, p. 54)

Whereas linguistic units such as phrases or parallel word-pairs that express a regular unit of meaning can be described as formulae (Wray, 2008; Frog and Lamb, 2021), Khanty poetry exhibits formal constructions for producing parallel lines that may vary lexically without being linked to specific meanings. That these are conventional constructions rather than simply recurrent patterns or a tendency for variable slots to occur in certain positions in a line is reflected in the potential for additional features to be integrated into the construction. The following example illustrates a fairly common line construction with three slots, in which the first two slots are customarily completed with a *figura etymologica* (Austerlitz, 1958, p. 55)—i.e., by words which are etymologically related:

ājəꞐ woj ājəlpa xoti wērtal
kēləꞐ woj kēləlpa xoti puštal

the speech   of   a speaking   animal how does he produce
acquaintance with an acquainted animal how does he make

(Source: Austerlitz, 1958, p. 55)

Although Khanty parallelism may be organized with more varying words than in K'iche' Mayan, lines remain characterized by a frame of lexical repetition with one or more slots for the focus or foci.

Finnic languages are another branch of the Uralic family with systematic parallelism (Steinitz, 1934; Kuusi, 1952; Saarinen, 2017; Sarv, 2017). In Finnish and Karelian kalevalaic poetry, the form of parallelism is at the opposite end of the spectrum in terms of variation. Non-repetition in parallelism appears to be historically driven by the poetic form (cf. Frog, 2019a). The meter is a trochaic tetrameter with conventions governing the placement of long and short stressed syllables, although with flexibility in the first foot. Thus, each line normally has eight syllables, which in these languages means lines are usually comprised of only 2–4 words. The poetry is characterized by systematic line-internal alliteration—i.e., beginning two or more words with the same sound. The systematic character of alliteration links it to sound-triggering. As Elias Lönnrot has described it:

Alliteration only comes to beautify a song when the song rises from within, as it does with the natural poets; in this way, they employ it in their songs without even knowing what alliteration really is, and can give no better explanation for it than that the words draw one another up that way.

(Lonnröt, 1845, p. 36, trans. Frog and Stepanova, 2011, p. 198)

192 *Frog*

For performers naturalized to the register of discourse, alliteration-based sound-triggering holds an integrated role in summoning vocabulary and making lexical choices *in situ*. In practice, much of this poetry was not improvisational or of a composition-in-performance type like that described by Albert Lord in his *Singer of Tales* (1960). Although some genres were quite flexible, kalevalaic epic is a short form, usually around 75–300 lines in length, and these tended to be remembered as fairly regular texts (see Frog, 2016). With only usually 2–4 words per line, sound-triggering would begin as a mnemonic for remembering phrases, which would then advance to formulaic sequences recalled as prefabricated wholes. In such formulae, alliteration could act like a constraint making them resistant to variation, for instance through category-triggering of semantically equivalent words that could fill the same metrical slot but that would eliminate alliteration.

In kalevalaic poetry, alliteration is not linked to metrical positions and operates on a spectrum. The ideal was repetition of the consonant and vowel of stressed (i.e., initial) syllables. The onset sound was, however, the priority[1] and, if the following vowel could not be matched exactly, vowels were on a hierarchy of preference by the similarity of their features (Krikmann, 2015). The alliteration of stressed syllables is not always possible in, for instance, a line of only two words, and alternative strategies could then be used to link a line into the acoustic texture of ongoing performance (Frog, 2019b). Lack of alliteration was not a violation, but parallel lines have been considered to have a greater tendency to be formed with alliteration, supporting the phonic texture even if a main line is phonically less-than-ideal (Sarv, 1999; 2018). When a line often only has 2–4 words, alliteration drives lexical variation in parallel lines. Alliteration can thus be seen as a major factor in developing the convention of non-repetition in parallelism, so that every word varies, for example (all translations of kalevalaic poetry are my own):

| Sormin | sortu | vetehen | with his fingers | collapsed | into the water |
| Käsin | käänty | lainehisen | with his hands | turned | into the waves |

(Source: *SKVR* I₁ 79.15–16)

Finnic languages are heavily inflected, and word-order in verse has a principle of 'right justification', whereby longer words are placed at the end of the line so long as this does not conflict with syllabic quantity rules—i.e., word-length determines word-order over syntax. This determinant can interfere with grammatical parallelism where lines should be semantically or analogically parallel. In the following parallel couplet, the longer word is at the beginning of the second line because of the syllabic quantity rules, which also results in inverting the order of the noun phrase and verb. This is presented here without reordering phrases to align them in the diagram so that the transposition is salient:

| Nousi | purjepuun nenähä | rose | | to the mast's top |
| Kasisliekaha | kavahti | to where ropes are fastened | jumped |

(Source: *SKVR* I₁ 54.311–312)

Repetition, Parallelism, Non-Repetition   193

Parallelism is systematic in that it permeates a poetic text, although it is not required for every line. Certain types of lines often lack parallelism, such as formulae for naming mythic heroes or introductions to direct speech, while parallel groups may be of three or more lines. In this tradition, every syntactic element in a parallel verse must have a correspondent in the preceding verse. Metrical form is primary, and variation in word-length is accommodated by allowing ellipsis of the elements that appear in the preceding verse, such as the preposition in the following couplet:

| Kulki | kuusissa | hakona | drifted | as a spruce | log |
| | Petäjäisä | pölkyn päänä | | as a pine | block's end |

(Source: *SKVR* I₁ 54.42–43)

Parallelism is between syntactic rather than semantic elements, allowing a further dimension of flexibility. A noun may match a noun phrase, like *länkiluun liha* ['collarbone's flesh'] and *oikie olkapää* ['right shoulder'], *purjepuun nenä* ['top of the mast (sail-tree)'] and *kasislieas* ['fastening-place'] in the previous example, or *hirvisellä* ['on a moose-like (horse)'] and both *kala-hauvin karvasella* ['on (a horse with) fur of a fish-pike'] and *lohem mussam muotosella* ['on (a horse with) the form of a black salmon'] in the following example:

Hevoisella hirvisellä
    Kala-hauvin karvasella
    Lohem mussam muotosella

on a horse, [on one] moose-like
    [on one with] a fish-pike's fur
    [on one with] a black salmon's form

(Source: *SKVR* I₁ 492.18–20)

Non-repetition of words is customary where verses are semantically equivalent, as well as where sequential verses are analogical with complementary information, as in the following couplet:

| Šat' | om mieštä | siipien | alla | a hundred | men | her wings | under |
| Tuhat | | hännän | tutkalmiśśa | a thousand | | in the tail's | tips |

(Source: *SKVR* I₁ 62.164–165)

Lexical repetition is used, but it is primarily associated with distinct rhetorical figures and, for example, analogical couplet parallelism, as in the following ordinal series:

Ampu	kerran	nuolellasa	Niin	meni	kovin alatschi
Ampu	toisen	nuolellasa	Niin	meni	kovin ylitsche
Koki	kerran kolmannengin		Siitä viimen	käypi	kohten

(Source: *SKVR* I₁ 79.8–13)

194 *Frog*

shot	once	with his arrow	so		it went	far too low
shot	a second time	with his arrow	so		it went	far too high
tried	still a third time			then finally	it went	straight

Diagraph analysis makes visible the role of lexical repetition in linking the failed attempts described in the first two couplets, while contrasting these with the success in the third.

Parallelism as an Added Form in Metered Discourse

In other forms of verbal art, parallelism appears as a type of added form that only structures particular passages of text. In Old Norse eddic poetry, each long line was constituted of two short lines linked by alliteration, which would sometimes be organized in parallel groups, as in the following example. The metrical form of this passage is a regular sequence of long lines, each constituted of two short lines linked across a caesura by alliteration. To make the metrical form more visible, the passage is presented by visually showing the caesura as a gap between short lines rather than using the diagraph layout:

Brestanda boga	brennanda loga	A stretching bow	a burning flame
gínanda úlfi	galandi kráku	a yawning wolf	a cawing crow
rýtanda svíni	rótlausum viði	a squealing swine	a rootless tree
vaxanda vági	vellanda katli	a rising billow	a boiling kettle

(Hávamál, st.85)

Such runs of parallelism are characterized by non-repetition. Old Norse eddic poetry is preserved almost exclusively in medieval manuscripts and the corpus is quite limited, but the poem *Alvíssmál* is particularly illustrative of non-repetition in parallelism. This poem is a dialogue in which a dwarf answers questions about how different things are called 'in all the worlds', and each of his thirteen answers is a stanza of six parallel formulaic phrases that are systematically selected according to alliteration (Acker, 1998; Frog, 2021b). Here, the point of interest is that non-repetition operates at the level of the lexicon rather than of semantic categories; in the following examples, 'gods' are mentioned twice. Metrically, the poetic form of these stanzas is two long lines of alliterating short lines each followed by a distinct line type with internal alliteration and no caesura (all translations of eddic poetry are my own; varying elements in formula slots are underlined):

Sól heitir með mǫnnum   enn sunna með goðum
    kalla dvergar Dvalins leika
eygló jǫtnar   álfar fagrahvél
    alskír ása synir

(Alvíssmál, st.16)

Sun$_1$ it is called among men   and sun$_2$ among gods$_1$
   the dwarves call [it] <u>Dvalinn's toy</u>
<u>ever-glow</u> [call it] the giants   elves <u>beautiful wheel</u>
   <u>all-pure</u> the gods$_2$'s sons [= gods]

In each response by the dwarf, category-triggering makes available to the presenter the open-slot formulae or their conventional completed forms relevant to the respective question. The complete version of *Alvíssmál* that is preserved exhibits systematic formula use in relation to alliteration. The choice of slot-filler in the first short line determines alliteration, and sound-triggering determines which formula follows in the second from among possible alternatives, while the choice slot-filler and formula are directly linked in the other line type. Independent quotations from the poem in a prose source show that some presenters used the formulae less systematically. Category-triggering and sound-triggering operate together in producing these passages, although in practice the lines may have crystallized in performers' memories through repeated performances, and should not be considered freely improvised. Nevertheless, these and similarly structured stanzas are interesting because non-repetition becomes a determinant on lexical choices by eliminating possible words that may be used in the progression through each passage, demanding that the performer remember which choices have been eliminated or hold a planned organization in memory.

Parallelism without Verbal Difference?

In some poetries, exclusive focus on the lexicon may leave additional dynamics of parallelism invisible. In her analysis of parallelism in Australian Aboriginal Arandic song-poetry, Myfany Turpin (2017) points out that verbal repetition can be turned into parallelism in this poetry through the systematic addition of sounds. In the following example, the four lines are repeated in cycles forming the complete song. The added sounds make otherwise identical lines different from one another, while also forming rhymes with their counterparts (i.e., $A_2 : B_1$ and $B_2 : A_1$):

A$_1$	larrinya	rrinya rriny	-a
A$_2$	larrinya	rrinya rriny	-ay
B$_1$	lerlangki	rrinya rrern	-ay
B$_2$	lerlangki	rrinya rrern	-a

   (Source: Turpin, 2017, p. 540)

Turpin further finds that principles of parallelism in verbal art may extend beyond lexical material, so that melody and rhythm might be considered features of difference juxtaposed with sameness in parallel utterances. For example, the following couplet is considered as parallel in spite of the lexical identity of its members because these features of sameness are contrasted through rhythmic difference. In many traditions, language is but one component of embodied activity. In this case,

196 *Frog*

difference is made more pronounced because it is also enacted in the movements of the performers toward and away from a ceremonial pole in conjunction with each rhythm:

tyarawi tyarerla tnenheka	tyawanta murrarla
tyarawi tyarerla tnenheka	tyawanta murrarla
In the distance they stood	The ones from Tyaw were the best
In the distance they stood	The ones from Tyaw were the best

(Source: Turpin, 2017, p. 540)

The study of parallelism began with a focus on linguistic texts, and this remains the emphasis in research today (e.g., Fabb, 2015), but that emphasis has been changing in recent years (Frog and Tarkka, 2017). Research has tended to focus on words, phrases, and formal units, taking for granted how these relate to what is being expressed or referred to, and only recently begun to theorize the more complex relations between parallelism, para-linguistic expression, and knowledge (Frog, 2017b). This is matched by research in linguistics, recognizing that parallelism operates above the level of language grammar (Carlson, 2002, p. 178; see also Du Bois, 2014, pp. 397–400). Although forming parallelism in a juxtaposition of sameness and difference is here centrally concerned with the level of linguistic signs, it is important to acknowledge its potential to operate at the level of combinations of linguistic signs with melody, rhythm, gesture, and so on.

Considering Oral Variation

Off-Target and Delayed Triggering within a Performance

In the performance of traditional oral poetry, a difference from conversational speech is that, if it is a composition-in-performance type (cf. Lord, 1960), the performer normally already knows the tradition and its prefabricated phraseology; if it is a textually more regular tradition like a kalevalaic epic, the performer 'remembers' lines and verbal systems for forming line sequences (Frog, 2016); and many traditions are somewhere in between. With parallelism, category-triggering presumably occurs in the process of summoning parallel verses. Where these vary by only a single word, whichever word is used first determines which word will be used in the following line. In an *ordered pair*, the sequence is established by convention. For instance, the Khanty pair *tōrəm//jeləm* ['God'//'sky'] will never be used with *jeləm* before *tōrəm* (Schulze, 1988, p. 69), but ordering is on a spectrum by convention, so the pair *wās//lunt* ['duck'//'goose'] is ordered but allows variation with *lunt* before *wās*, whereas *ān//put* ['bowl'//'kettle'] is an *unordered pair* that may vary freely (Schulze, 1988, p. 69). Consequently, category-triggering no doubt occurs in connection with lines with the *tōrəm//jeləm* pair, and convention determines which will be used first, whereas a line like the following can be viewed as an *in situ* variation in which the

Repetition, Parallelism, Non-Repetition 197

performer choses one member of the triggered pair, which then determines which is used in the second:

```
pāri -ān    siwal kātna mānl
pāri -put   siwal kātna mānl
the sacrificial  bowl's    steam goes in two [directions]
the sacrificial  kettle's  steam goes in two [directions]
```

(Source: Schulze, 1988, p. 69)

This type of variation is also found in Rotenese, where multiple words in lines might vary between performances. In the following example, the first couplet was recorded in 2008 and the second from the same performer in 2009, where *ndai* ['fish'] and *seko* ['scoop'] alternate in order:

```
De  ala  ndai  basa  namo-la    They        fish    in all the harbours
Ma        seko  basa  lek-ala          And  scoop   in all the waterholes
```

(Source: Fox, 2016, p. 178)

```
Tehu  ala  seko  basa  lifu la    But  they  scoop  in all the pools
Ma    ala  ndai  basa  lek ala    And  they  fish   in all the waterholes
```

(Source: Fox, 2016, p. 178)

Raymond Person (2021) has highlighted that such juxtapositions are also made by scribes when copying parallel expressions in an idiom that has been internalized, like Biblical Hebrew:

להקים את שבטי יעקב ונצירי ישראל
to raise up the tribes of Jacob and the survivors of Israel

(Masoretic Text, Isaiah 49:6; source: Person, 2021)

להקים את שבטי ישראל ונצירי יעקב
to raise up the tribes of Israel and the survivors of Jacob

(The first Isaiah scroll found in cave 1 of
Qumran, Isaiah 49:6; source: Person, 2021)

Thus, the reproduction of text in writing was not simply copying out words and lines, but triggered categories linked to parallel vocabulary, allowing the scribe to write out a different word first, while non-repetition determines the word written second.

Such variations may also be produced in the transcription of orally delivered text. For example, in his work with James J. Fox and Lintje Pellu, Esau Pono

198 *Frog*

always transcribed recordings of his performances himself (Fox, personal communication). In what is 126 lines in transcription, Pono appears to have 'improved' upon what was less than ideal by transposing parallel pairs of words in five cases, as well as rephrasing things in a few places and making some elisions. The revisions also include replacing the repetition of *nggao* ['takes'] in the previous lines with *tenga* ['picks'], indicating that the repetition was less than ideal (< indicates word-order changed for the diagraph):

Ana		nggao	na			
				seko	meti-na	
			fo	seko	matei besin	
	Ma	tenga	na	ndai	tasi-na	
			fo	ndai	mahamu lilo-na	

She		takes	up			
				her	scoop-net	< tidal
				the	scoop-net	with iron-weighed insides
	And	picks	up			
				her	fishing net	< sea
				the	fishing net	with gold-weighed belly

(Source: Pono, *Suti solo* transcript, lines 5–8, translation James J. Fox)

It was pointed out previously that the repetition of the word 'net' in each embedded parallelism points to these as being parts of the larger units between which the terms vary. In the transcription, this structure is also found in the following lines where the pair *lifa//lek* ['pool'//'waterhole'] is repeated within each couplet and varied between them:

Te lala lifu dua na
   Suti nala lifu dua
Ma lala lek telu
   Na Bina nala lek telu

But when they look in two pools
   Suti is in the two pools
And when they look in three waterholes
   Bina is in the three waterholes
(Pono, *Suti solo* transcript, lines 17–20, translation James J. Fox)

In the performance, however, Esau had alternated these:

Te lala lifu 'a na
Suti nal' lek dua

Repetition, Parallelism, Non-Repetition   199

Ma lala a lifu telu na
Bina nal' lek telu

But when they look in two pools
Suti is in the two waterholes
And when they look in three pools
Bina is in the three waterholes
 (Pono, *Suti solo* audio, 17–20, translation adapted from Fox's previously)

In this case, the change seems to reflect a conscious stylistic choice. Thus, within the transcription of a single text, both conscious and unconscious variations may be introduced, but the variations seem generally to polish the text for ideals of non-repetition.

Examples of variation in the ordering of a canonical pair are widely found but do not give much room for variation, and a context is needed to interpret whether the variation is random, significant, or influenced by particular factors. However, category-triggering may also create glitches, as in the following example of the Rotenese *kode ketu betek // bafi na'a pelak* ['the monkey plucks the millet'/'the pig eats the maize'] formula. The ritual poet Mikael Pellondou's style is characterized by repetitions of couplets and passages within a poem (Fox, 2016, p. 113), and he uses the formula five times within this performance. On its first use, he follows *kode* ['monkey'] with *na'a pelak* ['eat the maize'] rather than *ketu betek* ['pluck the millet'], and then repeats *na'a pelak* in the parallel line:

| Fo | kode | boso na'a pelak | So | the monkey | does not eat the maize |
| Ma | bafi | boso na'a pelak | And | the pig | does not eat the maize |

(Fox, 2016, pp. 114, 124)

In this case, the operation of memory is not only in remembering the first line and ensuring variation in the second, but also in remembering the formulae of the couplet. Mikael uses the conventional verb and object with *kode* ['monkey'] through the rest of his performance, indicating that he recalled the more-ideal phrasing while or after presenting these lines. I have elsewhere discussed the same phenomenon in the dwarf's answers of *Alvíssmál*, where the first uses of multiple formulae exhibit variations and then receive a regular form thereafter (Frog, 2011; 2021b). This phenomenon is also observed in other eddic poems (Frog, 2021a) and in kalevalaic poetry (Frog, 2016). This can be described as *off-target triggering*, resulting in an accidental *blend* of formulae (Wray, 2008, pp. 27–28), followed by *delayed triggering* within the performance that enabled Mikael to produce the more-ideal phrase some lines thereafter.

Working from James J. Fox's (2016) published versions of a poem in which this formula is used, the *kode ketu betek // bafi na'a pelak* ['the monkey plucks the millet'/'the pig eats the maize'] formula looks like an ordered pair: *kode ketu*

200 *Frog*

betek is the first line, followed by *bafi na'a pelak*. Mikael's fourth use of the pair thus appears inverted:

| Bafi ta na'a pelak | The pig does not eat the maize |
| Ma kode ta ketu betek | And the monkey does not pluck the millet |

(Fox, 2014, p. 117)

Dyadic lexical pairs do not vary individually between formulae in this couplet, presumably for semantic reasons: pigs lack the fingers to 'pluck', and 'plucking' is appropriate for millet but perhaps not for maize. The *pelak//betek* ['millet'//'maize'] pair does not regularly follow this order in other contexts and thus does not seem to be an ordered pair in itself, so lack of variation in order here appears linked to semantic constraints on how it is combined with other pairs.

Post-Performance Triggering

In the corpus of kalevalaic poetry, in addition to examples of off-target and/ or delayed triggering of traditional phraseology that is corrected during a performance, there are also examples where off-target phraseology is seen to change across performances. This is possible because, although mainly documented during the nineteenth and early twentieth century, the corpus is very large, with around 150,000 items, of which more than 87,000 are digitized (www.skvr.fi).

The best-known performer from the region of Ingria, where the tradition was quite flexible, is Paraske Larin (1834–1904).[2] Paraske was both talented and worked closely with someone who enthusiastically transcribed her repertoire from both sung performances and dictation across a period of time. Not only does the material recorded constitute a respectable corpus in itself, but it contains, unusually for the time, multiple variants of individual poems, including three examples of the mythological epic *The Singing Competition*. This epic has a simple linear plot; it was often about 70–100 lines in performance and in some regions still shorter. The poem was rare and extremely short in the region where Paraske lived, and her variants are exceptionally short, at only nine, eleven, and eighteen lines. The epic tradition was in steep decline across the nineteenth century. Although practices varied considerably across different regions where epics had survived at all, they were for the most part not being performed regularly, and some informants reported not having tried to perform particular poems since their youths. The variant recorded in 1892 notes that Paraske reported learning the song in 1887, although she would have been fifty-four at the time and had quite possibly heard or learned it earlier. All three of her variants present the same six- or seven-line opening of the poem, although the shortest has the name *Kaukamoinen* where

Repetition, Parallelism, Non-Repetition 201

Joukamoinen is expected (*SKVR* V₃ 43.2) and follows the opening with only a single couplet of direct speech from the epic's concluding dialogue (*SKVR* V₃ 43.8–9). The eleven-line variant uses the expected name *Joukamoinen* and includes three lines that give a narrative context for the couplet of dialogue, varying its second line for a different alliteration (*SKVR* V₃ 45). The eighteen-line variant is short, but forms a complete narrative (*SKVR* V₃ 44). The shortest variant was recorded in 1891; the longest in 1892; the date of the eleven-line variant is unknown, but was probably recorded between the other two.

When considering category-triggering, variation in Paraske's description of the two sleighs colliding in a series of parallel lines is illustrative. In the two longer examples, the three lines are all conventional and the phrasing of each line is regular, except that the first two lines are in reversed order and the expletive particle *on* ['is'] appears in the first two lines. In the first variant, two of these lines are phrased differently and the parallel series continues with a fourth line formed with *langet* ['harness']:

käi aisa aisan päähän	aisa aisaan tapasi	käi on vemmel vempeleehe
käi vemmel vempeleehen	käi vemmel vempeleehen	aisa aisaa on tapasi
rahe rahkeehen tapasi	rahe rahkeen nennään	rahe rahkien nenänii
käivät länket länkilöihen		
(1891, *SKVR* V₃ 43.4–7)	(189?, *SKVR* V₃ 45.4–6)	(1892, *SKVR* V₃ 44.4–6)
went shaft to shaft's end	shaft to shaft met	went ⁽ⁱˢ⁾ shaft-bow to shaft-bow
went shaft-bow to shaft-bow	went shaft-bow to shaft-bow	shaft to shaft ⁽ⁱˢ⁾ met
trace to trace met	trace to trace's end	trace to trace's end
went harness to little harness		

Langet ['harness'] is found only very rarely in this parallel series in any region, suggesting that a relevant line was occasionally produced independently by different singers rather than reflecting an archaic feature of a collective tradition. The line seems to be an *in situ* formulation developed from category-triggering of two-syllable words for parts of a sleigh, a process that can be equally assumed as behind its few scattered appearances in other variants of this well-attested poem.

Paraske was a talented performer: the first variant appears to be her formulation of the passage that she could not recall well, and which she inadvertently elaborated. Interviews stimulate thinking and reflecting on the topic or traditions inquired about, with the consequence that the informant may remember more in subsequent interviews (Sykäri, 2013). This can also be inferred in various examples in the kalevalaic corpus, although nineteenth-century collectors were not conscious of the phenomenon. For instance, when A. A. Borenius interviewed the singer Hökkä-Petri in 1871, he recorded a ninety-three-line variant of the epic *The Song of Lemminkäinen*, in what seems like a weak and confused performance (*SKVR* I₂ 789). When he interviewed him again in 1877,

202   *Frog*

Borenius added another sixty-five lines interlineally to the earlier transcript (*SKVR* I₂ 789a) and a seventeen-line supplementary passage (*SKVR* I₂ 789b). In fieldwork with James J. Fox and Lintje Pellu, we recently encountered this with the Tetun *makoan*—i.e., a keeper and conveyer of traditional knowledge—Piet Tahun. When we met with Piet in 2019, he brought up an origin story that he had performed for us in 2017 and was enthusiastic to perform a fuller version of it, which turned out to be considerably longer. In the variant first presented by Paraske, the transposition of the name of one hero for another is an indicator of issues remembering, suggesting that the triggering of categories and ideal phrasing may be off-target elsewhere, a probability supported by the narrative's fragmentary quality. Nevertheless, the situation also creates circumstances in which category-triggering becomes a more significant component in producing *in situ* formulations in traditions that are more reliant on memory, like kalevalaic poetry. In forming parallel groups, category-triggering guides the performer to relevant vocabulary for the production of new members, while non-repetition is a determinant on which vocabulary can be used as the parallel group is extended.

Competition and Interference

Parallelism in kalevalaic poetry does not normally exhibit the transposition of dyadic elements like Khanty *ān//put* ['bowl'//'kettle'] or Rotenese *ndai//seko* > ['scoop-net'//'fishing net'] because the syllabic structuring of lines and line-internal alliteration usually inhibit it. Something similar is nevertheless seen in a couplet widely found at the beginning of *The Song of Lemminkäinen*. More than a hundred variations of the couplet can be found connected with variants of the epic (see Frog, 2010, pp. 373–376), as well as being found occasionally outside of it (Kallio and Mäkelä, 2019, pp. 32–33):

| pieńi | ois | šovan | šavukši | small | [it] would be | for the smoke | of war |
| šuuri | | paimośen | palokši | great | | for the blaze | of a shepherd |

(SKVR I₂ 771.3–4)

The couplet exhibits a number of variations, some of which are regional, such as use of a synonym *tuli* ['fire'] for *palo* ['blaze'], which can disrupt line-internal alliteration (e.g., *SKVR* I₂ 743.2). However, several examples of the transposition of *pieni* ['small'] and *suuri* ['great'] are found:

| Suuri | on | sovan | savuksi | great | [it] is | for the smoke | of war |
| Pieńi | | paimozen | paloksi | small | | for the blaze of | a shepherd |

(SKVR I₂ 709.3–4)

This variation appears in examples scattered across different regions (*SKVR* I₂ 709.3–4, I₂ 710.3–4, I₂ 712.3–4, I₂ 724.3–4, I₂ 741.3–4, I₂ 834.3–4, II 223.4–5; see

Repetition, Parallelism, Non-Repetition 203

also *SKVR* II 207.4–5). Although a group of these may reflect its establishment in a local dialect, others can be considered a slip of transposition made by different singers independently. The slip is connected to alliteration as a systematic feature of the poetic form, which integrates sound-triggering into use of the register. Sound-triggering leads singers to link *suuri* ['great'] with *sovan savuksi* ['for the smoke of war'] and *pieni* ['small'] with *paimosen paloksi* ['for the blaze of a shepherd'] rather than vice versa. This effect of the poetic organizing principle for poetic lines on lexical choice can be described as *interference*, which in this case leads the sound-triggering of words with alliteration to supersede semantics. This type of example is interesting because it both points to category-triggering of the lexical pair and, when this slip occurs, the singers invariably uphold the principle of non-repetition: there is no example of *suuri* or *pieni* being repeated in both lines.

Conventional lexical pairs used in parallelism can themselves cause interference. The Old Norse corpus has very few oral-derived variants of particular poems and poetic passages, and such variants are usually only short quotations in prose that can be considered against a single full variant of the poem. Nevertheless, non-ideal expression can be observed in repetitions within a poem. In *Alvíssmál*, for example, a well-attested alliterating collocation is *æsir*//*álfar* ['gods'//'elves'], which normally carried a meaning 'the whole divine community', leads to a mix-up the first time the formula with *æsir* is used. The second short line in the dwarf's answers systematically mention 'gods', alternating between a formula with *goð* ['gods$_1$'] and another with *æsir* ['gods$_2$'], respectively triggered by alliteration. In the dwarf's first answer, *álfar* ['elves'] appears where *æsir* is expected, and *álfar* thereby appears twice in the same passage. This is the only such lexical repetition in the dwarf's thirteen answers, so editors consistently emend the first use to *æsir*:

> Jǫrð heitir með mǫnnum enn með álfum fold
>   kalla vega vanir
> ígron jǫtnar álfar gróandi
>   kalla aur upregin
>
>   (*Alvíssmál*, st.10)
>
> Earth it is called among men and among elves field
>   the *vanir* call [it] ways
> evergreen [call it] the giants the elves growing
>   the gods$_3$ call [it] clay

The use of *álfar* ['elves'] rather than *æsir* ['gods'] seems to result from category-triggering of the collocation. When the collocation was triggered, its conventional usage would have been as well: the *æsir*//*álfar* collocation is an ordered pair, in which *æsir* appears in the first short line and *álfar* either follows it in the same short line or in the second short line, but only *álfar*, never *æsir*, appears in the second long line in the collocation.[3] In *Alvíssmál*, triggering the

204   *Frog*

collocation appears to have led the presenter to use *álfar* rather than *æsir* in the second short line because the collocation's use was bound up with conventions of only using *álfar* but not *æsir* in the second short line. Cases like these highlight that an oral-poetic idiom is constituted of more than a simple lexicon that refers to 'things'; it is constituted of complex units like formulae and collocations that may have conventions of order and placement that are also triggered with the lexicon.

Parallelism in Ordinary Talk

From the perspective of CA, the gap between verse parallelism and parallelism in ordinary talk might seem insurmountable, especially if 'poetry' is imagined through modern literary poetry or in terms of a periodic meter with a fixed number of syllables in each line. However, the gap has been broken down in the ethnography of speaking (Hymes, 1981) and ethnopoetics (Tedlock, 1983), and Du Bois has brought into focus the prominence of parallelism in co-produced conversation. There are many poetries in the world of which semantic parallelism is the primary organizing principle without a periodic meter or even a periodic rhythm, as in Rotenese or Mayan language traditions discussed previously. A useful tool for analysis is Silverstein's (1984, p. 183) concept of *metered frame*, whereby each unit of utterance can be considered to present a formal frame in relation to which co-occurring utterances can be perceived. In order to make parallelism saliently visible, Du Bois' diagraph analysis will be used, laying out parallel stretches on a grid, as in the following example, although this subordinates the type of layout customary for CA:

```
(Tannen, 1987, p. 589; reformatted for diagraph)
L[ibby]      I       do      n't drink wine.
N            She     does    n't drink wine.
S            Libby   does    n't drink wine.
```

Tannen (1987, p. 589) describes this as *allo-repetition* because the three statements all express the same thing about the same person, varying only by the word referring to the person and the respective verb morphology. Allo-repetition is easily taken for granted in conversation because it is intuitive that deictic terms will vary across turns of conversation in relation to speaker position. In this case, however, N shifts from Libby's remark by using the third person rather than the second, objectifying her or reiterating her utterance to a third party, although she is still present. S then appears to reiterate N's utterance, exchanging the third-person pronoun for a proper name, or S reiterates Libby's utterance and responds to N's utterance by avoiding the pronoun and thereby producing a parallel utterance. In either case, the difference is salient because of variation between words that are semantically central for interpretation, and S's variation suggests a conscious or intuitive decision to avoid a full repetition of N's utterance.

Repetition, Parallelism, Non-Repetition   205

Parallelism is a fundamental feature of language use, creating tensions and reinforcements between reiteration and variation in communication. Grade-school teachers, for example, often use a lot of lexical repetition, but the repetitions are formally structured in relation to units of utterance. Each unit of utterance produces a metered frame in relation to which subsequent units can be compared, as diagraph analysis makes visible in the following example:

```
(Arminen, 2005, p. 114; reformatted for diagraph)
         Brownian motion.
What is Brownian motion?
                       If       you still       remember.
                       Anybody, who        can remember?
```

Correspondences across metered frames lead formal relations to become perceivable as parallelism. The role of formal commensurability at the level of metered frames distinguishes parallelism from other forms of deixis or mere density of lexical repetition without formal regularity. Since the first utterance establishes the metered frame for the second, 'What is Brownian motion?' here appears as parallelism because the additional words create a difference from the preceding utterance, whereas 'Brownian motion.' would be perceived as a partial repetition if it were the second member of the pair.

Not all variation in phrasing is necessarily salient in repetition. In the example presented earlier, where 'to recreate that image' is repeated as 'to recreate the image' (Tannen, 1987, p. 595), the variation may be linked to deixis: 'that' refers to a hypothetical image just introduced, whereas 'the' refers to the same image. It is not clear that the variation 'that' > 'the' is motivated or even noticed by the speaker or the listener. Both phrases could use the same word, and the article is semantically light in communicating the message. Diagraph analysis nevertheless reveals a much higher degree of complexity in the parallelism than the single phrase (both utterances are spoken by the same person, with the interlocutor's affirmation 'Right.' between them):

```
(Tannen, 1987, p. 595; reformatted for diagraph)
When you speak,       you use words to … to recreate that image.
                                      in the other person's mind.
And in sign language, you use ^signs       to recreate the image.
```

Parallelism here brings words and the signs of sign language into focus as equivalent by situating them in lexically and structurally similar utterances. The first element in each utterance is grammatically different, and the final prepositional phrase is subject to ellipsis in the second. Nevertheless, the parallelism of 'words'//'signs' to refer to linguistic signs in different systems is made salient as the focus within the frame *you use X to recreate that/the image.

It was noted previously that the reuse of phraseology in this example is comparable to use of formulaic language to lighten the cognitive load (see also

206 *Frog*

Pickering and Garrod, 2004, pp. 171–175; Corps, Gambi, and Pickering, 2018, pp. 235). The parallelism between these units can be viewed in the same light. Both phraseological and grammatical parallelism are widely recognized as easing the processing of conjoined phrases, although non-matching conjuncts can reduce or interfere with this (Carlson, 2002, pp. 4–6 and works there cited). In this case, repeated phraseology and the broader parallelism are complementary and integrated.

Research on the processing of parallelism has focused on continuous text,[4] to which the preceding example can be considered equivalent despite the other speaker's interjection of 'Right'. Du Bois brought into focus parallelism's role in dialogue, where it also operates in the processing of ellipsis (curly brackets indicate omitted elements):

```
(Du Bois, 2007, p. 166, ex.53)
SAM         I₁ don't like      those        .
ANGELA      I₂ don't {like}    {those} either.
```

Correspondences between utterances facilitate the interpretation of ellipses and help guide interpretation, and also operates in constructing contrasts:

```
(Du Bois, 2014, p.386, ex.26)
DAN         I    'm    not ^smart ?
JENNIFER    you  're       ^stupid.
```

In the following dialogue, parallelism does not emerge prominently in Jeff's laconic response to Jill's first utterance, but Jill then builds a rich parallel series linked to the two initial turns in her response to Jeff:

```
(Du Bois, 2014, p. 371, ex.5-7)
JILL  You   ^missed like                all the ^drama     here .
      (H)
JEFF                                ^No      drama        .
JILL  ^Yeah,              there was ^such   ^drama        .
                          There was         ^drama        ,
            and           there was         ^suspense     .
      (H)   And    then   there was         ^relief       ,
      (H)   and    then   there was         ^ecstasy      .
```

In this case, Jeff's repetition of 'drama' forms a contrastive parallelism with its use in the preceding noun phrase: 'all the drama'//'no drama'. The parallelism is less salient because it is both confined to the noun phrase without including the final word of Jill's utterance or equivalent deictic, and also because the utterance itself is so short. The contrastive parallelism of 'all the drama'//'no drama' operates as a repair. Although repairs were introduced in terms of repetition, they are characterized by variations that require them

Repetition, Parallelism, Non-Repetition 207

to be viewed here as parallelism, as becomes more salient through diagraph analysis:

```
(Jefferson, 1996, p. 10; reformatted for diagraph)
Hi. I'm Carol's sister-
                brother

(Kitzinger, 2013, p. 241; reformatted for diagraph)
Meanwhile for the last five  years that I've-
                            six-
                            seven years that I've  been in New Jersey […]

(Kitzinger, 2013, p. 235; reformatted for diagraph)
[…] because Nonny's              arriving
            my granddaughter's arriving from Caracas.

(Wouk, 2005, p. 246; reformatted for diagraph)
tapi bukan ana-
      bukan dokter dia

But he's not a chil-
        not a doctor
```

Repairs are syntactically interesting in a few respects. The juxtaposition as seen in these cases is of commensurate units that leads them to be interpreted as parallelism. Whereas most utterances become perceived as metered frames in relation to which subsequent utterances may be interpreted, the repeated verbal sequence of a repair produces such a frame that becomes mapped against the preceding utterance. This is similar to forms of parallelism in Mayan languages, where a parallelism may be formed with only the final words of a preceding utterance (see also Hull, 2017). These repairs appear marked by interrupting the rhythms of speech rather than being organized through them.[5] The formal structure of parallelism combines with the interpretation of the focus—the varying element in the frame—as contrastive. Where these are perceived as semantically irreconcilable alternatives, like 'five'//'six'//'seven', the unit is interpreted as a repair of replacement. The juxtaposition of semantically reconcilable elements may instead be interpreted as a repair of specification, like:

```
(Meyer, 1992, p. 105; reformatted for diagraph)
We don't have any          lectures,
            department lectures, in the morning.
```

In oral poetry performance, parallelism is not interpreted as a repair unless it either disrupts the rhythm of a line or it is built into a dialogue represented in narration. However, the type of construction found in repairs follows the normal syntax of apposition, so in some cases it may simply be a parallelism of equivalence for rhetorical emphasis or prolongation:

```
(Meyer, 1992, p. 105; reformatted for diagraph)
Of course, 1600 Pennsylvania,
          the White House , is the most famous address of the free world.
```

208   *Frog*

In the previous dialogue between Jill and Jeff, contrastive parallelism can be viewed as a series of counter-moves, in which Jeff contests Jill's claim with a repair, to which Jill contests Jeff's repair with her own: 'all the drama'//'no drama'//'such drama'. Jill then makes a near-repetition of her rebuttal, followed by a series of three parallel expressions in which the focus is a series of emotional states that she correlates with 'drama': 'drama'//'suspense'//'relief'//'ecstasy'. Although these may be described as specifications concerning the 'drama', the elaboration is a rebuttal through a rhetorical assertion by reiteration and prolongation rather than argumentation.

How parallelism works in conversation depends on the language. For example, Jerrold M. Sadock and Arnold M. Zwicky (1985, pp. 189–191) find that languages generally exhibit three basic systems for short answers to yes/no questions. Whereas English has a dominant 'yes/no system', in which positive and negative answers are formed by the respective lexeme, Japanese exhibits an 'agree/disagree system', in which the question is marked by an interrogative particle (indicated with 'Q') and the response begins with the positive or negative lexeme with a repetition of the phrase of the question, as in the following example:

```
(Muhammad, Roslina, and Hazlina, 2016, p. 191; reformatted for diagraph)
A          Benkyouwa            shite masu-ka ?
B                          Hai, shite  masu    .

A          Study       doing-Q              [Do you study?]
B                  Yes, doing               [Yes, I do.]
```

Sadock and Zwicky describe the third as an 'echo system', in which simple positive and negative responses are formed by repeating the verb of the question (with or without additional material varying by language). For instance, although Finnish has words for an affirmative answer like *joo* ['yes'], Marja-Leena Sorjonen (2001, p. 37) found in her study that the repetition of the verb was more than twice as frequent as *joo* in responses to yes/no questions. Although the verb is reused in the answer, the question is formed with an interrogative particle (*-ko/-kö*), so the answer invariably produces a parallelism rather than a full repetition, even in a basic pairing like *On-ko?//On.* ['Is it?'//'It is.']. The structure of a Finnish echo response tends to omit the pronoun, although this is marked in the verb inflection, as here:

```
(Sorjonen, 2001, pp. 41-42; reformatted for diagraph)
M    Ai niin sul on se, os- tilasi -t-ko kenkät.
L    No                     ti:lasi-n      [...]

M    Oh right you have that, bou[ght]- ordered-[you]-Q the shoes.
L    Well                             ordered-[I]          [...]
```

Repetition, Parallelism, Non-Repetition   209

Verb repetition in English answers is more commonly emphatic or reproduces only the auxiliary verb. This forms a parallelism that exceeds changes in pronoun and verb inflection or word-order motivated by the change in speaker and syntax of a question:

```
(Schegloff, 2007, p. 131; reformatted for diagraph)
DEB        [...]             did we        buy something together?
ANN        Yeah I think     we did
```

My native intuition anticipated that emphatic answers to *Is it ADJ?* questions would commonly follow the same type of parallelism: *Yes, it is.* or *No, it's not.* However, such examples seem relatively infrequent, whereas examples of repetition with variation seem much more common, such as:

```
(Pomerantz, 1984, p. 59)
JIM     T's- tsuh beautiful day out isn't it?
LEN     Yeh it's jus' gorgeous ...
```

This can be laid out on a diagraph with < indicating an element is out of order, and treating the adverb of emphasis 'just' as forming a single syntactic element with 'gorgeous' in parallelism with 'beautiful day':

```
(Pomerantz, 1984, p. 59; reformatted for diagraph)
JIM         T's- ts      uh beautiful   day out
            it<is    n't?
LEN   Yeh it's             jus' gorgeous              ...
```

This impression is consistent with the data presented by Anita Pomerantz (1984) in her study on agreeing and disagreeing with assessments, where the role of parallelism in such assessments seems a common response to evaluative statements rather than mainly occurring in answers. Pomerantz distinguishes three classes of agreements as *upgrades, same* evaluations, and *downgrades* (1984, pp. 68–77). Pomerantz's (1984, p. 65) classes concern the evaluations of the object, as in 'beautiful'>'gorgeous'. This is not to be confused with upgrades and downgrades of epistemic evaluations, as in the downgrading tag question 'isn't it' followed by the upgrading confirmation + agreement token ($EVALUATION_1$, 'isn't it?'>'Yeah', $EVALUATION_2$) (Heritage and Raymond, 2005, pp. 17, 23–24). If the evaluative term is weaker, the second evaluation is considered a downgrade in both respects, even if the response structure is the same, for example:

```
(Pomerantz, 1984, p. 60; Heritage and Raymond, 2005, p. 29; reformatted
for diagraph)
E      e-that Pa:t        isn'  she a do::ll?
L                    ↓Y eh isn't she pretty   ,
```

210 *Frog*

If Pomerantz's examples can be considered generally representative for English, same evaluations with reused phraseology customarily combine this with difference, whether lexically marking its position in a series with 'too':

```
(Pomerantz, 1984, p. 67; reformatted for diagraph)
C   She was a nice lady - I liked her
G                          I liked her too
```

Or through elision:

```
(Pomerantz, 1984, p. 67; reformatted for diagraph)
K       He 's terrific !
J       He is          .
```

Pomerantz's same evaluations seem less frequent than upgrades and downgrades. She stresses that same evaluations are also used to preface downgrades, as in the following example about a film seen by E's daughter (J and L are husband and wife who shadow each other's utterances; overlapping speech is indicated by square brackets within the diagraph; < indicates reordering of 'terribly depressing'):

```
(Pomerantz, 1984, p. 67; reformatted for diagraph)
E       ... 'n she said she f-        depressed   her terribly
J       Oh                     it's [depressing   <  terribly .]
L       [Oh                    it's  depressing              .]
E       Very
L                          But it's  a  fantastic [film    .]
J                              [It's a] beautiful  movie
```

The data suggests that full repetition is non-ideal or marked in some way, or that full repetition does different work.

Pomeranz's study is considered to show (e.g., Keel, 2016, p. 123) that evaluative upgrading illustrates agreement to the interlocutor, while same agreements get treated as ambivalent and 'disagreement implicative' (Pomerantz, 1975, p. 82), even if they do not preface a disagreement. Simple agreements are thus not necessarily considered convincing (Clark, Drew, and Pinch, 2003, pp. 9–10). The parallelism 'fantastic film'//'beautiful movie' does not exhibit upgrading, but J is not expressing agreement to L; rather, J is shadowing L and addressing E, which seems not to motivate upgrading. The evidence suggests that, in agreement responses structured by parallelism, the speaker draws on the initial utterance and category-triggering provides lexical and phrasal alternatives for the evaluative assessment. A driving concern in lexical choice appears to be an avoidance of an interpretation as ambivalent or downgrading. The impetus that makes upgrading commonplace appears to be to unambiguously communicate what is called *affiliation* in CA or *alignment* of stancetaking in other fields.[6] Consequently, semantic differences in phrasing appear

Repetition, Parallelism, Non-Repetition 211

rhetorically driven as a way to 'say the same thing', communicating that the second speaker takes the same stance to the referent. This does not necessarily require upgrading in all cases. It is absent from 'I liked her too', whereas interpreting 'beautiful'>'gorgeous' as an evaluative upgrade may link to expectation. Inverting the evaluations would give the same impression in the move from abstract to concrete: 'It's just gorgeous out, isn't it?'//'Yeah, it's a beautiful day'. In either case, memory of preceding utterances is in dialectic with category-triggering as the speaker prepares a response.

In assessments, the regularity of some degree of non-repetition may relate to assessments as implicitly claiming independent knowledge of the referent. Considered within a frame of 'systematic social competition' (Heritage and Raymond, 2005, p. 34), *Oh*-prefacing + confirmation is a construction that 'convey[s] superior knowledge of, and/or rights to assess, the matter under discussion' (Heritage and Raymond, 2005, p. 26). J uses this *Oh*-prefacing in the previous example, shadowed by L, where E has only second-hand knowledge of the referent. However, epistemic stancetaking may also be motivated by non-epistemic concerns. The frequency of same evaluations prefacing disagreement seems socially motivated by politeness or as a rhetorical strategy for softening a disaffiliation, while evidence that simple agreement is not regularly considered convincing (Clark, Drew, and Pinch, 2003) suggests that upgrades are also rhetorically motivated to unambiguously communicate agreement in some contexts. Also, epistemic upgrading is built into the conventional sequence EVALUATION$_1$ + *ISN'T IT*? *(OH / CONFIRMATION TOKEN) EVALUATION$_2$*, where it is commonly complemented by evaluative upgrading and supports the communication of affiliation. Devices like *Oh*-prefacing may potentially also combine with emphatic upgrading to stress affiliation and the construction or maintenance of rapport, leaving it unclear whether the following exchange about a neighbourhood dog reflects affiliative or competitive epistemic concerns ('Isn't he cute' reorganized):

```
(Pomerantz, 1984, p. 60; reformatted for diagraph)
B          he <  Is n't    cute        ?
A     O::h he::   s         a::DORable  .
```

Evaluative and epistemic moves can operate as complementary resources. Detailed work is needed with statistical assessments on ways these are combined and their usage of non-repetition. Sensitivity is needed to potential for variation between different Englishes, such as the 'isn't it?' tag appearing commonplace in British but not American English (Heritage and Raymond, 2005, p. 25, n.8), and to variation between registers, such as the evaluative upgrading common between adults not seeming customary for parents' talk with children (Keel, 2016, p. 57).

Several forms of simple dialogic interaction develop conventions of repetition like 'Hi.'//'Hi.' Tannen (1987) observes that, in these and similar uses of repetition, speakers may vary the pattern of intonation, with the result that lexically

212   *Frog*

identical phrases become formally different. This type of combination of sameness and difference is comparable to what Turpin (2017) discusses in Arandic song-poetry. In this light, lexical reproduction like 'A triangle?'//'a triangle' in the following example may also be viewed in terms of parallelism based on intonational differences that formulate them as a dyadic pair QUESTION//ANSWER, if 'Good' is a discreet utterance evaluating the student's success rather than a confirmation token like *Yes*:

```
(Arminen, 2005, p. 126; reformatted for diagraph)
ROBYN              A triangle ?
TEACHER     Good, a triangle .
```

Here, intonational difference is not simply a formal feature varied in performance; it has a signifying function, which creates a difference in signs between the two utterances. Jeffrey D. Robinson and Heidi Kevoe-Feldman (2010) found that repairs involving full repetition of an utterance on the lexical level were consistently marked by intonational difference, even in a case like the following, where a question is matched by a question:

```
(Robinson and Kevoe-Feldman, 2010, p. 252; reformatted for diagraph)
CARLA What abo:ut uh:m what- what vitamin makes your teeth whi:te ?
RICH                        What vitamin makes your teeth white ?
```

Although the questions are lexically identical, intonation introduces meaningful difference, which can be viewed as shifting repetition into parallelism.

Conclusion

Non-repetition is an essential—if easily overlooked—feature of parallelism at whatever level parallelism functions. As a condition of parallelism, non-repetition creates a constraint that interacts with category-triggering by progressively eliminating possible alternatives as they have been used in the emergence of a parallel group. Exploring variations and non-ideal formulations highlights the role of memory in off-target and delayed triggering, as well as the potential for interference from multiple triggering. The sort of blending observed in oral poetry is also common in ordinary talk; the density of complex linguistic units of phraseology often simply seems greater in oral poetry, and complicated by the practice of reproducing 'the same' texts. However, even simple exchanges reflect complex choices, for example the parallelism 'beautiful'//'gorgeous' is used in parallel constructions of *just X {out} // X day {out}*, with the selections in the *X, isn't it?* formula prompting alternatives in the *Yeah, X.* agreement response. Parallelism occurs at an intersection of: (a) remembering what has been said, (b) category-triggering, (c) interpretation or planning, and (d) communicative aims. The central difference between examples in ordinary talk and those previously discussed for oral poetry is that

Repetition, Parallelism, Non-Repetition   213

the forms of poetry considered have much more regularly structured idioms and formal conventions as well as practices for reproducing texts conceived as being 'the same'. Bringing the combinations of repetition and variation in ordinary talk into focus against the backdrop of parallelism in oral poetry leads to new questions about principles governing responses in conversation, and the degree to which formulating utterances as members of parallel groups may level lexical semantics or subordinate semantics to communicative aims under a condition or ideal of non-repetition.

Notes

1. Historically, Finnic languages did not allow consonant clusters at the beginnings of words.
2. There is a longstanding convention of writing her name 'Larin Paraske', but this causes confusion since Larin is her family name.
3. There is one exception (*Skírnismál*, st.17.1–2, repeated st.18.1–2), which is driven by the formula used in the second short line as in *Alvíssmál*, but with *álfar* in the preceding short line, yet at least one scribe also felt that this was a non-ideal inversion and 'corrected' their order.
4. Outside of poetry, see Carlson (2002); in poetry, see Fabb (2017).
5. The juxtaposition of syntactically equivalent words like *sister//brother* can also be viewed as producing a metered frame, although its scope is only a single word.
6. In conversation analysis, *affiliation/disaffiliation* concerns collaborative behaviour with compatible affect and is not limited to stance, while *alignment/disalignment* concerns collaborations at the structural level of conversational discourse. In discussions of stancetaking, *alignment/disalignment* refers to calibrating the relation specifically between stances.

Sources

Eddic poems. Eddic poems are cited from the edition of G. Neckel and H. Kuhn (Eds.) (1963). *Edda: Die Lieder des Codex Regius nebst vewandten Denkmälern i: Text* (4th edition). Heidelberg: Winter Universitätsverlag.

Pono, E. *Suti solo* 2008 audio recording. Unpublished audio recording made by James J. Fox and Lintje Pellu in collaboration with Esau Pono, 2008.

Pono, E. *Suti solo* 2008 transcript. Unpublished transcription by Esau Pono and English translation by James J. Fox, 2008.

SKVR = Suomen kansan vanhat runot, I–XV. Retrieved from: www.skvr.fi.

Works Cited

Acker, P. (1998). *Revising Oral Theory: Formulaic Composition in Old English and Old Icelandic Verse*. New York: Garland.

Arminen, I. (2005). *Institutional Interaction: Studies of Talk at Work*. Hants: Ashgate.

Austerlitz, R. (1958). *Ob-Ugric Metrics*. Helsinki: Academia Scientiarum Fennica.

Carlson, K. (2002). *Parallelism and Prosody in the Processing of Ellipsis Sentences*. London: Routledge.

214   *Frog*

Clark, C., Drew, P., and Pinch, T. (2003). Managing prospect affiliation and rapport in real-life sales encounters. *Discourse Studies*, 5(1), 5–31.

Corps, R.E., Gambi, C., and Pickering, M.J. (2018). Coordinating utterances during turn-taking: the role of prediction, response preparation, and articulation. *Discourse Processes*, 55(2), 230–240.

Couper-Kuhlen, E. (1996). The prosody of repetition: on quoting and mimicry. In E. Couper-Kuhlen and M. Selting (Eds.), *Prosody in Conversation: Interactional Studies*. Cambridge: Cambridge University Press.

Cruz, H. (2014). *Linguistic Poetics and Rhetoric of Eastern Chatino of San Juan Quiahije*. Unpublished PhD dissertation. Austin: University of Texas, pp. 366–405.

Du Bois, J.W. (2007). The stance triangle. In R. Engelbretson (Ed.), *Stancetaking in Discourse: Subjectivity, Evaluation, Interaction*. Amsterdam: John Benjamins, pp. 139–182.

Du Bois, J.W. (2014). Towards a dialogic syntax. *Cognitive Linguistics*, 25(3), 359–410.

Fabb, N. (2015). *What is Poetry? Language and Memory in the Poems of the World*. Cambridge: Cambridge University Press.

Fabb, N. (2017). Poetic parallelism and working memory. *Oral Tradition*, 31(2), 355–372.

Fox, J.J. (1977). Roman Jakobson and the comparative study of parallelism. In D. Armstrong and C.H. van Schooneveld (Eds.), *Roman Jakobson: Echoes of His Scholarship*. Lisse: Peter de Ridder Press, pp. 59–90.

Fox, J.J. (Ed.) (1988). *To Speak in Pairs: Essays on the Ritual Languages of Eastern Indonesia*. Cambridge: Cambridge University Press.

Fox, J.J. (2014). *Explorations in Semantic Parallelism*. Canberra: Australian National University Press.

Fox, J.J. (2016). *Master Poets, Ritual Masters: The Art of Oral Composition Among the Rotenese of Eastern Indonesia*. Canberra: Australian National University Press.

French, P., and Local, J. (1986). Prosodic features and the management of interruptions. In C. Johns-Lewis (Ed.), *Intonation in Discourse*. San Diego: College-Hill, pp. 157–180.

Frog. (2010). *Baldr and Lemminkäinen: Approaching the Evolution of Mythological Narrative through the Activating Power of Expression: A Case Study in Germanic and Finno-Karelian Cultural Contact and Exchange*. PhD dissertation. UCL Eprints. London: University College London.

Frog. (2011). Alvíssmál and orality I: formula, alliteration and categories of mythic being. *Arkiv för Nordisk Filologi*, 126, 17–71.

Frog (Ed.) (2014). *Parallelism in Verbal Art and Performance: Pre-print Papers of the Seminar-Workshop, 26th–27th May 2014*. Helsinki: Folklore Studies, University of Helsinki.

Frog. (2016). Linguistic multiforms in kalevalaic epic: toward a typology. *RMN Newsletter*, 11, 61–98.

Frog. (2017a). Parallelism and orders of signification (parallelism dynamics I). *Oral Tradition*, 31(2), 425–484.

Frog. (2017b). Multimedial parallelism in ritual performance (parallelism dynamics II). *Oral Tradition*, 31(2), 583–620.

Frog. (2019a). The Finnic tetrameter—a creolization of poetic form? *Studia Metrica et Poetica*, 6(1), 20–78.

Repetition, Parallelism, Non-Repetition 215

Frog. (2019b). Poetic principles on a hierarchy of scope: isolated metrical entanglement. *NordMetrik News*, 3, 9–20.

Frog. (2021a). Preserving blunders in eddic poems: formula variation in numbered inventories of Vafþrúðnismál and Grímnismál. *Scripta Islandica*, 73, 43–91.

Frog. (2021b). Text ideology and formulaic language in eddic mythological poems. *Saga-Book*, 45.

Frog and Lamb, W. (Eds.) (2021). *Weathered Words: Formulaic Language and Verbal Art.* Cambridge, MA: Harvard University Press.

Frog and Stepanova, E. (2011). Alliteration in (Balto-)Finnic languages. In J. Roper (Ed.), *Alliteration in Culture*. Houndmills: Palgrave MacMillan, pp. 195–218.

Frog and Tarkka, L. (Eds.). (2017). Parallelism in verbal art and performance. Special issue of *Oral Tradition*, 31(2).

Heritage, J. (2014). Epistemics in conversation. In J. Sidnell and T. Stivers (Eds.), *The Handbook of Conversation Analysis*. Oxford: Wiley Blackwell, 2014, pp. 370–394.

Heritage, J., and Raymond, G. (2005). The terms of agreement: indexing epistemic authority and subordination in talk-in-interaction. *Social Psychology Quarterly*, 68(1), 15–38.

Hull, K. (2017). 'The language of gods': the pragmatics of bilingual parallelism in ritual Ch'orti' Maya discourse. *Oral Tradition*, 31(2), 293–312.

Hymes, D. (1981). *'In Vain I Tried to Tell You': Essays in Native American Ethnopoetics*. Philadelphia: University of Pennsylvania Press.

Jakobson, R. (1981) [1966]. Grammatical parallelism and its Russian facet. In R. Jakobson (Ed.), *Selected Writings III: Poetry of Grammar and Grammar of Poetry*. S. Rudy (Ed.). The Hague: Mouton, pp. 98–135.

Jefferson, G. (1996). On the poetics of ordinary talk. *Text and Performance Quarterly*, 16(1), 1–61.

Kallio, K., and Mäkelä, E. (2019). Suullisen runon sähköisestä lukemisesta. *Elore*, 26(2), 25–41.

Keel, S. (2016). *Socialization: Parent-Child Interaction in Everyday Life*. London: Routledge.

Kitzinger, C. (2013). Repair. In J. Sidnell and T. Stivers (Eds.), *The Handbook of Conversation Analysis*. Oxford: Wiley Blackwell, 2014, pp. 229–256.

Krikmann, A. (2015). On the vowel euphony in Finnic alliterative folksongs. *FF Network*, 46, 12–17.

Kuusi, M. (1952). Kalevalaisen säkeen, säeryhmän ja runon painavoituvuudesta. *Virittäjä*, 56(4), 241–261, 351–352.

Lonnröt, E. (1845). Kokeita suomalaisessa laulannossa. *Suomi*, 1(5), 10–53.

Lord, A.B. (1960). *The Singer of Tales*. Cambridge, MA: Harvard University Press.

Lowth, R. (1753). *De sacra poesi Hebræorum: praelectiones academiae Oxonii habitae*. Oxonius: Clarendonia.

Lowth, R. (1834) [1778]. *Isaiah: A New Translation; With a Preliminary Dissertation, and Notes, Critical, Philological, and Explanatory*. Boston: Hilliard.

Meyer, C.F. (1992): *Apposition in Contemporary English*. Cambridge: Cambridge University Press.

Muhammad, H.S., Roslina, M., and Hazlina, A.H. (2016). An analysis of Japanese conversation in interview context. *Journal of Language and Communication*, 3(2), 181–194.

216 *Frog*

Norman, W.M. (1980). Grammatical parallelism in Quiche ritual language. In *Proceedings of the Sixth Annual Meeting of the Berkeley Linguistics Society*. Berkeley: Berkeley Linguistics Society, pp. 387–399.

Person, R.F., Jr. (2021). Formulas and scribal memory: a case study of text-critical variants as examples of category-triggering. In Frog and W. Lamb (Eds.), *Weathered Words: Formulaic Language and Verbal Art*. Cambridge, MA: Harvard University Press, pp. 147–172.

Pickering, M.J., and Garrod, S. (2004). Toward a mechanistic psychology of dialogue. *Behavioral and Brain Sciences*, 27(2), 169–226.

Pomerantz, A.M. (1975). *Second Assessments: A Study of Some Features of Agreements/ Disagreements*. PhD dissertation, University of California, Irvine.

Pomerantz, A.M. (1984). Agreeing and disagreeing with assessments: some features of preferred/dispreferred turn-shapes. In J.M. Atkinson and J. Heritage (Eds.), *Structures of Social Action: Studies in Conversation Analysis*. Cambridge: Cambridge University Press, pp. 79–112.

Robinson, J.D., and Kevoe-Feldman, H. (2010). Using full repeats to initiate repair on others' questions. *Research on Language and Social Interaction*, 43(3), 232–259.

Saarinen, J. (2017). 'Said a word, uttered thus': structures and functions of parallelism in Arhippa Perttunen's poems. *Oral Tradition*, 31(2), 407–424.

Sadock, J.M., and Zwicky, A.M. (1985). Speech act distinctions in syntax. In T. Shopen (Ed.), *Language Typology and Syntactic Description, I: Clause Structure*. Cambridge: Cambridge University Press, pp. 155–196.

Sarv, M. (1999). Regilaul: clearing the alliterative haze. *Folklore: Electronic Journal of Folklore*, 10, 126–140.

Sarv, M. (2017). Towards a typology of parallelism in Estonian poetic folklore. *Folklore: Electronic Journal of Folklore*, 67, 65–92.

Schegloff, E.A. (1968). Sequencing in conversational openings. *American Anthropologist*, 70(6), 1075–1095.

Schegloff, E.A. (2007). *Sequence Organization in Interaction: A Primer in Conversation Analysis*. Cambridge: Cambridge University Press.

Schulze, B. (1988). *Der Wortparallelismus als ein Stilmittel der (nord-) ostjakischen Volksdichtung*. Szeged: Universitas Szegediensis de Attila Josef Nominata.

Silverstein, M. (1984). On the pragmatic 'poetry' of prose. In D. Schiffrin (Ed.), *Meaning, Form and Use in Context*. Washington, DC: Georgetown University Press, pp. 181–199.

Sorjonen, M.-L. (2001): *Responding in Conversation: A Study of Response Particles in Finnish*. Amsterdam: John Benjamins.

Steinitz, W. (1934). *Der Parallelismus in der finnisch-karelischen Volksdichtung untersucht an den Liedern des karelischen Sangers Arhippa Perttunen*. Helsinki: Academia Scientiarum Fennica.

Sykäri, V. (2013). Dialogic methodology and the dialogic space created after an interview. In Frog and P. Latvala with H.F. Leslie (Eds.), *Approaching Methodology* (2nd edition). Helsinki: Academia Scientiarum Fennica, pp. 171–183.

Tannen, D. (1987). Repetition in conversation: toward a poetics of talk. *Language*, 63(3), 574–605.

Tedlock, D. (1983). *The Spoken Word and the Work of Interpretation*. Philadelphia: University of Pennsylvania Press.

Turpin, M. (2017). Parallelism in Arandic song-poetry. *Oral Tradition*, 31(2), 535–560.

Urban, G. (1986). The semiotic functions of macro-parallelism in the Sholkeng origin myth. In J. Sherzer and G. Urban (Eds.), *Native South American Discourse*. Berlin: Mouton de Gruyter, pp. 15–57.

Wagner, A. (Ed.) (2007). *Parallelismus Membrorum*. Fribourg: Academic Press.

Wouk, F. (2005). The syntax of repair in Indonesian. *Discourse Studies*, 7(2), 237–258.

Wray, A. (2008). *Formulaic Language: Pushing the Boundaries*. Oxford: Oxford University Press.

8 Poetics and List-Construction

A Study of Text-Critical Variants in
Lists Found in the New Testament,
Homer, and the Hebrew Bible[1]

Raymond F. Person, Jr.

Introduction

Some of the earliest literature includes lists—for example, the *Assyrian King List* (Yamada, 1994). These ancient literatures were produced in societies that had a low level of literacy; therefore, they are often interpreted in relationship to living oral traditions, in which lists are also common. The study of oral traditions includes various insights about lists.[2] For example, Yelena Helgadóttir (forthcoming) demonstrated how lists consisting of formulas could migrate from one tradition to another across related languages. Karl Reichl (forthcoming) showed that in some cases lists are not only made up of similar items, but may include sound-patterns. John Miles Foley noted that within the Serbian Muslim oral epics, 'lists of items and responses are common, but equally common is the omission of one or more items in the repetition' (1983, p. 196). This variation leads scholars to question what the function of these lists was, since, for example, if the primary concern is 'historical', then why did the *Assyrian King List* undergo editorial revisions over its thousand-year history of written transmission?

One approach to answering these types of questions is scribal performance. Since oral poets perform in ways that allow for creative flexibility as they compose-in-performance, then maybe scribes should be understood in analogous ways to oral performers, in that scribes seem to allow some creative flexibility in how they copy an existing manuscript before them as they create a new manuscript of the same literary text. The argument of scribes as performers coalesced in the work of Alger Doane (1994), which has been influential in the study of other literary traditions. The most thorough discussion of scribal performance is Jonathan Ready's monograph, *Orality, Textuality and Homeric Epic*. He concluded, 'A scribe never stops performing; he never disclaims responsibility. He performs both when he sticks to his exemplar and when he departs from it' (2019, p. 213). Thus, he stated, 'I find it preferable not to restrict the use of the term "(re)performance" to a particular kind of scribal act' (2019, p. 214). Although this study discusses 'a particular kind of scribal act', I nevertheless agree with Ready that scribal performance should be understood as active in all scribal acts.

DOI: 10.4324/9780429328930-11

Poetics and List-Construction 219

Scribal performance assumes scribal memory. 'Scribal memory' refers to the knowledge of traditional texts (oral and/or written) held in the collective memory of scribes. Thus, scribal memory is what underlies the scribal performance of those texts, including during the copying of physically present manuscripts that imperfectly represent the literature as it exists in the collective memory of individual scribes. Concerning the transmission of the Gospels, Alan Kirk wrote that 'scribal memory was the interfacial zone where writing and oral-traditional practices converged and interacted' (2008, p. 219). Drawing from the Dead Sea Scrolls, Shem Miller concluded that 'scribal memory included the written text of compositions, traditional interpretations (both oral and written) surrounding compositions, and past performances of compositions' (2019, p. 275–276). Thus, the idea of 'scribal memory' is helpful for understanding the interfaces between memory, orality, and writing in antiquity and the impact of these interfaces on the manuscript tradition, including the creation of text-critical variants during scribal performance.

In two previous studies, I have shown how category-triggering helps us understand the role of scribal memory in the composition/transmission process of ancient literature. In 'Formulas and Scribal Memory' (Person, forthcoming-a), I demonstrated how text-critical variants labeled 'synonymous readings' (Talmon, 2010, pp. 171–216) or 'memory variants' (Carr, 2011, pp. 13–36) as found in biblical texts and Homeric epic function within scribal memory in that one synonymous reading can be substituted for another in ways that are analogous to category-triggering. That is, the scribe's reading in the manuscript before him triggers a category of formulas from which the scribe may select when producing the new manuscript with the substituted synonymous reading. In 'Harmonization in the Pentateuch and Synoptic Gospels' (Person, 2021), I demonstrated how text-critical variants labeled 'harmonization' function within scribal memory in that, when a scribe is copying a passage in one biblical book, the wording in that passage that is similar to the wording in its parallel passage may trigger scribal memory in ways that the wording of the other passage may influence how the scribe copies the manuscript before him as he produces a new manuscript. For example, when copying the Ten Commandments from a manuscript of Exodus, a scribe may remember the wording of the Ten Commandments in the version in Deuteronomy, and may harmonize the text by bringing the wording of the two different passages into closer verbal agreement. That is, the similar wording between the two versions of the Ten Commandments caused category-triggering of the same commandment(s), so that in some cases, the scribe was influenced not only by the manuscript before him, but also his memory of the other text.

In this chapter, I build upon these two studies by showing how category-triggering works within list-construction, so that we can better understand that not only are lists common in oral traditions and literature with roots in oral traditions, but, in Foley's words, 'equally common is the omission of one or more items' or, to be more precise, the addition, omission, transposition, or substitution of one or more items. That is, a list in conversation, in oral

220   *Raymond F. Person, Jr.*

traditions, or in literature establishes a category, so that the 'same' list can serve the same function by establishing the same category, *even when* the list includes 'different' specific items. Therefore, although lists can serve various functions within their literary contexts, the 'same'-yet-'different' lists can function similarly in its specific literary context, even within what, from our perspective, may appear to be a high degree of textual fluidity. In the following section, I will begin with a discussion of category-triggering in ordinary talk and list-construction. I will then examine selected text-critical variants in three examples: Paul's list of vices in Galatians 5:19–21, Homer's Catalogue of Ships in *Iliad* Book 2, lines 494–877, and the lists of the 'seven nations' in selected passages in the Hebrew Bible. Note that I will generally ignore text-critical variants in these lists that do not pertain to the items in the lists—for example, orthographic variants. The analysis of these three examples within their text-critical variety will illustrate well how lists in literature function in analogous ways to conversational lists within the role that scribal memory plays in scribal performance. That is, a scribe can faithfully copy a list from the manuscript before him into a new manuscript that both may or may not have the exact same items, and the same items may or may not be in the same order, and yet a 'same'-yet-'different' list allows the readers/hearers of the list to access the same category so that the list may continue to serve the same function in its literary context, especially in ancient traditions in which textual fluidity is characteristic.

Category-Triggering and List-Construction in Conversation

'On the Poetics of Ordinary Talk' (Jefferson, 1996) is not the first publication in which Jefferson discussed 'the "poetics" of natural talk' (1990, pp. 68–73), because poetics was an important part of her discussion of list-construction. The 1996 article is based on a 1977 conference presentation that she published at the insistence of Robert Hopper. However, the fact that poetics was a significant aspect of her discussion of list-construction suggests that Jefferson herself took the observations about poetics more seriously than some of her dismissive hedges in the poetics article may suggest. In the following, I will often use terms from her poetics article that she did not use in her list-construction article. For example, although in her lecture she referred generally to 'mechanisms' (transcript lines 1385, 1386, 1407, 1427), she does not use more precise word phrases such as 'sound-productional mechanisms' (1996, p. 8), 'gross selection-mechanism' (1996, p. 9), or 'triggering mechanisms' (1996, p. 39) until its publication. In fact, these terms do not show up in her 1990 article on lists, where she simply refers to 'acoustic consonance and punlike relationships' (1990, p. 71). However, these relationships are obvious to the careful reader, so I will tend to use her more developed terms from the 1996 article, even when I am summarizing her 1990 list-construction article. My discussion is also influenced by other studies (especially Lerner, 1994).

Furthermore, the following summary of list-construction is selective—that is, I am emphasizing parts of the argument that most directly apply to my discussion of the literary examples, so that some of their important observations I am mostly overlooking. For example, I do not adequately discuss the role that list-construction plays in the turn-taking system in conversation, since turn-taking is (mostly) irrelevant to the transmission process of scribes copying manuscripts.

Jefferson gave a loose definition of 'category' as 'objects that very strongly belong together; sometimes as contrasts, sometimes as co-members, very often as pairs' (1996, p. 9). In this chapter, I am only concerned with category-triggering that includes co-members, since only this type is an important aspect of list-construction.

Jefferson identified the 'list-constructional principle of adequate representivity' (1990, p. 78). Even one item may suggest a category from which additional co-class items may be drawn in the formation of a list, but this suggestion may not be precise enough to represent the category accurately. Participants in a conversation need enough clues to adequately identify the category that the list-in-progress represents and, since 'a list can be constructed by more than one speaker' (1990, p. 81), exactly what category is being represented can be negotiated between the participants, so that it is possible that the list-in-progress may be produced at the end of the list-construction process in a way that might not have been projected at its beginning (see further in the following section).

An important practice that helps participants solve this potential problem of adequate representivity is a preference for 'three-part lists'. Jefferson observed that 'many lists occur in three parts' (1990, p. 63) and that 'three-partedness appears to have "programmatic relevance" for the construction of lists' (1990, p. 66). In Lerner's words, 'Lists require no more than three parts to establish that a class of items is being invoked' (1994, p. 24). One piece of evidence for three-partedness is that speakers who are constructing lists-in-progress can be observed to search for the final third item, or they may use what Jefferson labeled a 'generalized list completer'. Example (1) illustrates a word search for the third item. Note that Jefferson placed brackets around the list.

Example (1) (Jefferson, 1990, p. 67)
```
Mr. B:  It's not in the same league with [adultery, and murder,
        and—and—thievery,]
```

The first two items in this list ('adultery' and 'murder') suggest a category of serious moral wrongs or vices, and the delay in producing the third item ('thievery') suggests that Mr. B is searching for the right final co-class item in his list. Sometimes the third item in the list is occupied by a generalized list completer, thereby producing what Jefferson described as belonging to '[l]ess-than-three-*item* three-part *lists*' (1990, p. 66). In Example (2), Jefferson used

222 *Raymond F. Person, Jr.*

brackets to indicate repeating sounds, including in the list itself ('cakes and candy and crap'):

Example (2) (Jefferson, 1996, p. 13; see also 1990, p. 69)
Nora: there's only one on the Ways'n Means [C]ommittee. And I [c]annot
        serve on two: be[c]ause ˙hhhh all these [c]a[k]es and [c]a:ndy
        and [c]rap…

Jefferson identified 'and crap' as a generalized list completer 'selected from among such candidates as "and stuff," "and junk," "and things," etc.' (1990, p. 69). That is, this format (2 items + generalized list completer) makes explicit that the list represents a broader category—'not only do the named items not exhaust the possible array of nameables, but a third item would not do such work' (1990, p. 68). I chose this example from the many Jefferson provided—and copied it from her poetics article rather than the lists article—to illustrate that sound-triggering may also occur in list-construction, even though I generally avoid such discussion in this chapter. In this case, 'and crap' is selected from a range of possible generalized list completers, because it 'is acoustically consonant with a series of prior words, including the two just-prior list items' (1990, p. 69)—that is, the repeated k-sound that she marked with brackets.

Lists are context-sensitive in that they are constructed in ways that are consistent with the topic of the conversation, and as such, they can be the locus of both collaborative social action and disputes. Because the first two items of a list project a category and therefore a range of possible third (or otherwise final) items in a list, a list begun by one speaker can be completed by another participant in the talk. If the first two (or more) items have produced an adequate representivity, another speaker can produce a final co-class item in the list-in-progress that is readily accepted by the participant who began the list. However, it is also possible (although less common) that the other speaker produces an item as a way of moving the category in another direction in an uncollaborative manner, so that the participant who began the list rejects the proposed third item. In the following paragraphs are some examples that illustrate these possibilities. In Example (3), Louise begins a list about bad weather that Ken cooperatively completes with an appropriate third item.

Example (3) (Lerner, 1994, p. 24)
Louise: first of all they hit rain.
Ken: Mm hm
Louise: then they hit hail.
Ken: and then they hit snow.

Thus, Louise and Ken collaboratively create a list of bad weather—'rain,' 'hail', and 'snow'. In Example (4), Sally completes the list begun by Sheila with the use

Poetics and List-Construction   223

of a generalized list completer; however, Lerner noted that sometimes the generalized list completer does not only complete the list, but also identifies the category that is represented by the list as in this example:

```
Example  (4)  (Lerner,  1994,  p.  24)
Sheila:       then  I  turn  on  the  tee  vee:,  (0.2)
              an'  I  wanna  watch  (.)  Cheers
Sally:        mm  hm
Sheila:       or  (0.7)  Bill  Cosby=or
              (0.2)
Sally:        some  show  thatcha  wanna  watch
```

Lerner observed that such a use of generalized list completers can occur in a list produced by one speaker, but this example shows how recipients also can orient to this practice and can collaboratively complete the three-part list with a generalized list completer that demonstrates to the speaker that began the list that the other participant understood the first two items to have adequate representivity. 'The first two items are needed to establish the dimensions or range of class membership, and the generalized list completer transforms the list from being merely a collection of items to a reference to the class' (Lerner, 1994, p. 24). That is, the 'range of class membership' is the category of co-class items (in this case, TV shows that Sheila enjoys watching regularly). Example (5) is taken from a conversation in which Jessie has reported the death of a mutual friend to Goldie, who had no recent contact with the deceased prior to her death. Jefferson suggested that Jessie had entitled speakership as the bearer of the news, but this excerpt from the conversation can be seen as somewhat argumentative in that there is a lot of overlapping talk, so that Jessie and Goldie appear to be competing with each other for the turns at talk, and maybe even for who knows the friend best. Goldie interrupts Jessie. Then Jessie interrupts Goldie, takes Goldie's utterance, and uses it to begin a list by supplying another two items and a generalized list completer:

```
Example (5) (Jefferson,  1990,  p.  85)
Jessie:       I,  I-I  jis  couldn'  take  the  constant  repetition  of
              [uh:::[::::
Goldie:       [of-  [of  the  same  story.  Oh  don'  I  kno:w=
Jessie:       =or  how  enla:rged  it  was  or  why  huhr  artery  wz:  five
              times  larger  or  this  that,=
Goldie:       =en  [e v r y b o d y o]wes  me  a  livi[ng  'n,]
Jessie:            [the  othuh  thing,  ]              [`hhhhh]hhhhhh  k-
Jessie:       Well  uh-  (.)  uhhhh  this  is  something  that  uh::  yihknow
              uh  evrybody  owes  huhr.
```

Jessie turns Goldie's first utterance ('the same story') into the beginning of a list of things about the deceased friend that he 'couldn't take' anymore, claiming his

224　*Raymond F. Person, Jr.*

entitled speakership, by producing what could have been by itself a complete list with two items plus a generalized list completer ('or how enla:rged it was or why huhr artery wz: five times larger or this that, the othuh thing'). However, Goldie challenges Jessie's speakership again by interrupting and adding another item to the list ('en evrybody owes me a living'). The excerpt ends with Jessie producing the final item of the list by repeating, after some delay, what Goldie had proposed as the final item ('evrybody owes huhr'), thereby co-producing the final item in the list with Goldie.

With these examples, we can see how recipients of a list-in-progress can produce a range of items that can be understood as a '(co)-listing' or a 'counterposed response' and, in Jessie's repetition of Goldie's final item, how 'a potentially "counterposed response" can be reformulated as an "equivalent list co-member"' (Jefferson, 1990, pp. 87, 90). Participants in conversation actively interpret the list items in order to achieve adequate representivity—that is, in order to identify the category represented by the co-class members in the list.

Lists and Text-Critical Variants in Ancient Literature

In previous publications, I have applied CA to literature, assuming that we cannot fully understand literary discourse as a form of institutional talk without a careful comparison of literary discourse with practices in face-to-face talk-in-interaction. As with other forms of institutional talk, we must understand how the institutional setting adapts everyday practices, including how a change in modality from spoken to written discourse requires certain adaptations. Although I have concluded that in modern English all of the modalities of talk-in-interaction can be represented in literary discourse—for example, nonlexical items, body movement, and prosody—this representation nevertheless requires a translation into the written medium by various means—for example, prosody represented by adverbs ('mockingly') and punctuation (? or !) (Person, 1999). For our present purpose, we should note that some such modern adaptations were generally lacking in ancient literature—for example, some manuscripts were written without spaces between words, without punctuation, and without things like capitalization marking the beginning of sentences. Therefore, the representation of all the modalities of face-to-face interaction were much more limited in ancient literature than in modern English literature. Because of this important difference, I need to be explicit about what limitations I perceive in my application of list-construction to the selected lists I will analyze in the next passage.

First, this is in no way a comprehensive study of lists in literature. Therefore, for example, I can make no informed comments about the preference for three-partedness in these ancient languages. Although I am aware of three-part lists in these literary works, I am also aware that some lists are much longer, including many more items than the vast majority of lists in conversation. I argued in *From Conversation to Oral Tradition* (Person, 2016) that the poetic aesthetics in Homeric epic, *Beowulf,* and the Bible are exaggerations of poetics found in everyday conversation. Since the economy of literary discourse is drastically different from that of face-to-face talk—for example, oral bards and literary authors do not need to negotiate a complex turn-taking system—this economic change frees up cognitive resources that can be put to other purposes, such as aesthetics. To quote Jefferson, 'It's pretty much figured that all these wonderful mixtures of sounds and meanings are the provenance of poets who make it their business to work out, to seek, to really endeavor to find just the right word. . . . That's the poet's job. The *arrangement* of sounds and categories' (1996, p. 4). Therefore, I strongly suspect that the longer lists found in ancient literature are also stylized exaggerations of the practices of list-construction within literary traditions created by generations of poets/writers.

Before turning to my examples, I want to emphasize some of the implications from the previous section concerning list-construction in conversation. Lists function by establishing categories of co-class members in the social interaction between participants. Because of this function, the same category can be represented by other lists containing different co-class members and, therefore, the actual items in a list can be replaced with other co-class members and the list could continue to serve the same purpose—that is, representing the same category of co-class members. Once adequate representivity of the category of co-class members has been reached—often after the first two items—the participants other than the one who initiated the list can contribute to the list-construction in a collaborative way. In contrast, sometimes the responsive co-production of lists in conversation occurs in what appear to be competitive disputes, so that it is possible that the list-in-progress as projected by the speaker who initiated the list-construction can be hijacked in another direction. However, since this study concerns text-critical variants in lists that may have entered the transmission process when a scribe was copying a manuscript of traditional literature in front of him and was influenced by scribal memory, I strongly suspect that the ideological manipulation of the lengthy lists I am examining was extremely difficult to achieve, *even if* a scribe was inclined to do so (which I seriously doubt). Therefore, I suspect that the scribal 'variants' should be understood as collaborative list-construction—that is, the scribes are engaged cooperatively in an interaction with the manuscript they are copying as well as with other tradents and manuscripts held in their scribal memory, so that the addition, omission, or substitution of co-class members in the same category does not significantly change the function of the list in its literary context.

I also should express my serious doubts against what remains a common scholarly assumption concerning text-critical variants in general as well as those specific examples I will analyze in the following section—that is, that there was an *original* text that is somehow the literary ancestor of all of the existing manuscripts of each ancient literary work (Person, 2015). Although many text critics have given up the traditional goal as establishing the original text in a critical edition, many nevertheless hold on to the idea that there was an original text. They simply acknowledge that we do not have sufficient data and/or the

226   *Raymond F. Person, Jr.*

methodological tools to discover what it was. However, a growing number of text critics have abandoned the very idea of an original text, because of the textual plurality in which ancient and medieval texts often exist, and the textual fluidity implied by that textual plurality.[3] Nevertheless, in this chapter I will continue the practice of favoring the 'received' text, the 'vulgate' text, or a reconstructed critical edition in the presentation of the text and its variants out of convenience. *However*, since I assert that we need to reevaluate the presumed validity of what have been general principles in text criticism for a long time—for example, *lectio brevior potior* (the shorter reading is preferred)—the arrangement of the following texts should not be interpreted as my agreement with the scholarly consensus of what is and is not 'original' or even 'earlier'. Rather, I have abandoned the pursuit of the 'original text' (an anachronistic notion) altogether, and at this point remain agnostic concerning how we might methodologically determine with some accuracy what is earlier or later.[4] At least for the time being, I am comfortable simply describing the variety of evidence in the extant manuscripts for the vast majority of cases as I strive to better understand the cognitive-linguistic processes at work in scribal memory. Since the kind of methodological reevaluation for which I am advocating is far beyond the limits of this chapter, I will continue to structure my presentation of the material based on the scholarly consensus for practical purposes.

Now I turn to my three examples in order to understand better how category-triggering and list-construction may have influenced scribal memory in the copying of these literary works. Following an introduction for each example, I will give the standard text in the original language, followed by an English translation. I will then provide the significant text-critical variants that are relevant to list-construction (mostly variants in the list items) in the original language followed by an English translation. The list of the text-critical variants will begin by repeating the reading in the standard text followed by the other reading(s). Within the English translations of the list of variants, I will use **bold** to denote a plus reading (not in the standard text) and *italics* to denote a different word order from the standard text. All English translations are my own unless otherwise noted. I will close each section with a discussion of the example, referring to secondary literature. For those readers who are unfamiliar with text criticism, I will provide in footnotes the standard abbreviations that specialists in these areas use, and will point to secondary sources in which they can find further discussion; however, in general, readers simply need to be aware that different manuscripts have different readings, and sometimes different readings are preserved in discussions of the literature by ancient commentators, even when we have no direct manuscript evidence.

Paul's List of Vices in Gal 5:19–21

Paul's letters include numerous lists of virtues and vices, which have been discussed often (Schweizer, 1979; Borgen, 1988; Zaas, 1988). The fact that Paul's lists of vices vary from one letter to another—even within the same letter—has

Poetics and List-Construction 227

led scholars to conclude that Paul obviously used no one standard list of vices. For example,

> Although individual vices from Paul's catalogues can be located in older lists, the overlap between any one of Paul's lists and any other list is minimal. Likewise, the lack of overlap between any two of *Paul's* vice catalogues suggests that while the form may be traditional the content is not.
>
> (Zaas, 1988, p. 623)

Here, Peter Zaas noted that Paul's lists differ from vice lists in other Hellenistic literature as well as from each other; therefore, he suggests that Paul's lists may be a combination of his quoting traditional material from the broader culture, and his selection for the particular purpose of his writing that letter to a specific congregation and its circumstances. In the words of Eduard Schweizer, 'Details are picked up sometimes at random, sometimes according to a specific situation' (1979, p. 207). In what follows, I will discuss two sets of variants, one in verse 19 and one in verse 20; in both cases, I provide the reading in the critical edition (including the indication of which manuscripts that reading is based on) and alternative readings found in the critical apparatus (including the relevant manuscripts).[5]

Example (6): Gal 5:19–21:

Nestle[28]
[19]φανερὰ δέ ἐστιν τὰ ἔργα τῆς σαρκός, ἅτινά ἐστιν πορνεία, ἀκαθαρσία, ἀσέλγεια, [20]εἰδωλολατρία, φαρμακεία, ἔχθραι, ἔρις, ζῆλος, θυμοί, ἐριθεῖαι, διχοστασίαι, αἱρέσεις, [21]φθόνοι, μέθαι, κῶμοι καὶ τὰ ὅμοια τούτοις, ἃ προλέγω ὑμῖν, καθὼς προεῖπον ὅτι οἱ τὰ τοιαῦτα πράσσοντες βασιλείαν θεοῦ οὐ κληρονομήσουσιν.

NRSV
[19]Now the works of the flesh are obvious: fornication, impurity, licentiousness, [20]idolatry, sorcery, enmities, strife, jealousy, anger, quarrels, dissensions, factions, [21]envy, drunkenness, carousing, and things like these. I am warning you, as I warned you before: those who do such things will not inherit the kingdom of God.

א* A B C
[19] ... [ἅτινά ἐστιν] πορνεία, ...
[19] ... [which are] fornication ...

א² D
[19]... [ἅτινά ἐστιν] μοιχεία, πορνεία, ...
[19]... [which are] **adultery**, fornication ...

א B P[46]
[20]... αἱρέσεις, [21]φθόνοι, μέθαι, ...
[20] ... factions, [21]envy, drunkenness, ...

A C D F G
[20] ... αἱρέσεις, [21]φθόνοι, φόνοι μέθαι, ...
[20] ... factions, [21]envy, **murder**, drunkenness, ...

629
[20] ... [21]φθόνοι, αἱρέσεις, φόνοι μέθαι, ...
[20] ... [21]*envy, factions*, **murder**, drunkenness, ...

228 *Raymond F. Person, Jr.*

Before looking at the variations, we should note that the list in all of the extant manuscripts clearly represents the category 'the works of the flesh' and consists of a lengthy list of items plus a generalized list completer ('and things like these'), which denotes that 'there are "many more" relevant nameables which will not, and need not, be specified' (Jefferson, 1990, p. 68). That is, Paul's list of vices is explicitly not an exhaustive list for the category of 'the works of the flesh' (see also deSilva, 2018, pp. 460, 463). Therefore, it should be of no surprise that, when this list was copied in the early church, the number of items in the list could contract or expand and still adequately represent the category, especially since the list exceeds the minimum three items and therefore has more-than-adequate representivity. Thus, when we compare the list in various manuscripts, some manuscripts have a list of as few as 15 items + a generalized list completer (for example, B) and some as many as 17 + a generalized list completer (for example, D). Furthermore, one manuscript (629) has a different word-order for 'envy, factions' than the others. It would certainly be a ridiculous mistake to conclude, for example, that manuscripts A B C represent some faction in the early church that did not think that 'adultery' should be included among the 'works of the flesh', and that manuscript D and the second 'corrector' of manuscript א (א²) represent a different faction that is argumentatively correcting that of A B C. That is, we can agree with Peter Borgen that 'various catalogues were used by him [Paul], and not only one form' (1988, p. 133), but add that this same idea of variability within Paul's list-construction continued in the work of the earliest scribes that transmitted Paul's list in Galatians 5 and that the scribal performance of copying a manuscript was influenced by scribal memory that understood that the category of 'the works of the flesh' included other vices even from the very first moment of Paul's dictation of the letter. Therefore, in a real sense these pluses ('adultery' and 'murder') are not at all 'additions' (even if we could definitively determine that they are additions), because they belonged within the category from the very beginning and the list itself (in whatever form) triggered in scribal memory those items that were not explicitly included in the written list. In fact, the 'addition' of 'murder' (φόνοι) to the list, according to Hans Dieter Betz, may be based on a 'word-play φθόνοι φόνοι . . . which is known since Euripides *Tro[ades]* 766ff. and which is often quoted in antiquity' (1979, p. 284 n. 119). Translating Betz's observation into Jefferson's poetics, this well-known wordplay/ co-class pun, which also includes sound-triggering, may have influenced the list-construction within scribal memory as well, so that during the copying process this item (φόνοι) was 'added' immediately following φθόνοι, both of which belong to the same category.[6]

Homer's Catalogue of Ships in Iliad *Book 2, Lines 494–877*

Lists are understood as an important literary genre in classical Greek literature— for example, the catalogue of Nereids in Hesiod's *Theogony* (233–264) (see Faraone, 2013). In fact, a specialized list genre called a 'catalogue' is widely discussed in the literature. The following distinction between 'list' and 'catalogue' made by

Poetics and List-Construction 229

Elizabeth Minchin (2001, pp. 74–75) is representative of how these two terms are often understood:

> the term 'list' will refer to those passages . . . where the poet presents a sequence of four or more place names, personal names, or items, all modified by little or no descriptive material. . . . A catalogue, on the other hand, is equally a list, but one in which some items are supplemented with enlivening description or comment, often rendered through narrative.

In his study of the 'poetics' of catalogues, Christopher Faraone identified a specific type of catalogue, 'the catalogue with a superlative cap' (2013, p. 298) as follows: 'a traditional form of genealogical catalogue begins with three or four individuals to a verse, and gradually decreases the number until it arrives at a single and final individual, who is usually described as superlative and accorded, uniquely for the list, one or more extra verses of description or narrative' (2013, p. 312).

Discussions of Homeric lists are well informed by the larger context in Greek literature and the Catalogue of Ships (*Iliad* 2.494–877) is often viewed as the catalogue *par excellence*. For example, Minchin (2001, p. 97) wrote:

> The Catalogue of Ships, by virtue of its comprehensiveness and its duration, clearly presages events on a grand scale. It is designed, that is, not only to make a statement about the mass of troops assembled, nor simply to gratify the pride of his listeners or to provide an entertaining interlude in the evening's performance. This catalogue and the Trojan catalogue together, through their scope and their elaboration, point to the scale and significance of all events and outcomes in the *Iliad*: they are designed to arouse in the audience expectations of a great story.

The Catalogue of Ships consists of the Greek catalogue (2.494–760) and the Trojan catalogue (2.761–877), both of which have introductions and lists of, respectively, the Achaian and Trojan forces (with their allies) and heroes.[7] The Catalogue of Ships fits within its narrative context well.[8] Before the catalogue, Nestor gave Agamemnon the following advice: 'Separate the men by tribes (φῦλα), by clans (φρῆτραι), Agamemnon, so that clan may aid clan and tribe tribe' (*Iliad* 2.362–363; Wyatt trans.) (Allen, 1921, p. 33). The Greek catalogue is then 'an orderly description of the Achaian force, contingent by contingent' (Minchin, 2001, p. 84), and the Trojan catalogue serves a similar purpose for their opponents. Faraone described the Catalogue of Ships and the following narrative of the epic as follows: 'we seem to have a kind of superlative cap to a long catalogue that eventually singles out Achilles and his chariot-horses as the greatest and most powerful, followed (eventually) by a long narrative that will illustrate their greatness and power' (2013, p. 320). That is, the Greek catalogue identifies Achilles as the greatest of the Greek heroes, which will become evident in the remaining narrative of the *Iliad* as the heroes from both catalogues confront each other in battle.

230   *Raymond F. Person, Jr.*

Most previous studies have not taken seriously the text-critical evidence, and have assumed that the vulgate represents Homer's original text. For example, Allen wrote: 'The later versions had no effect upon the Homeric text, no new State made its entry into Homer' (1921, p. 31). Even recent scholars who clearly embrace the Parry-Lord school's oral-formulaic approach to Homer often assume that the genre of list limits variation. For example, Minchin wrote that 'a traditional list does not permit alteration' and that '[t]here is more emphasis in a list-song on memorization and near word for word reproduction and less scope (than in other oral genres) for innovation' (2001, p. 79). However, text critics of Homer have recognized that 'the Catalogue has been interpolated elsewhere to make it as complete as possible' (West, 1967, p. 50). These 'interpolations' have generally been dismissed, again assuming the authenticity of the vulgate. George Bolling concluded that 'the bulk of all interpolations are the work of the copyists' (1925, p. 15), thereby dismissing most of the text-critical variants.

The text-critical approach I am taking is much more consistent with the recent positions of Graeme Bird (2010) and Ready (2019)—that is, the very idea of an 'original text' is problematic, given the oral-traditional context from which the Homeric epics emerged. Bird concluded: 'The variation in our surviving manuscripts of Homer . . . is inconsistent with a single archetype, but rather points back to a multiplicity of archetypes, a situation which arises from the oral nature of the transmission of Homeric epic' (2010, p. 32). Furthermore, Bird (2010, p. viii) described the variants in the Ptolemaic papyri, the earliest manuscript evidence of Homer, as follows:

> The nature of the variation is 'organic'—lines have not been 'dropped' into place arbitrarily; rather, they give the appearance of having 'grown' in their current locations, in the process modifying their surroundings and resulting in a coherent 'version' of an episode that is no less 'Homeric.'

In other words, the Ptolemaic pluses preserve the poetic structures of Homeric epic—that is, the hexameter poetic line and related formulaic system—and they are incorporated into the thematic structures in ways that are consistent with the Homeric tradition. Similarly, Ready has argued that literary texts that come 'from a process of dictation should be understood as cocreations of the poet, scribe, and collector' (2019, p. 104). That is, scribes must be considered as a potential part of the creative processes that have led to some ancient and medieval literature, whether the scribes were producing a dictation of an orally composed epic for the very first time or were copying an existing manuscript. Thus, like Bird, Ready can characterize multiple variants as authentic or 'original' in that they belong within what Albert Lord called the 'special grammar' of the tradition (1960, p. 35–36).

In the following, I examine four variants in the Catalogue of Ships (*Iliad* 2.494–877). Although I give the 'vulgate' text first, I do not assume that this text is the 'original' text from which variations occur. Rather, I understand that the Catalogue

Poetics and List-Construction 231

of Ships, a list with embedded lists, was not understood to be comprehensive and exhaustive. In fact, the so-called 'additions' or 'interpolations' necessarily suggest that the ancient scribes also did not understand the list to be complete. We will see that the plus-verses draw from the adequate representivity of the various lists within the Catalogue of Ships, so that in some sense they only make explicit what was already implicit, not only in the rest of the *Iliad*, but even in the Catalogue of Ships.[9]

Example (7): Homer, *Iliad*, Book 2, 848–850 (Allen, 1921, p. 16; Bolling, 1925, p. 77; West, 1967, p. 61; Erbse, 1969, p. 345; Erbse, 1977, p. 154; van Thiel, 2010, p. 46)

vulgate   848 αὐτὰρ Πυραίχμης ἄγε Παίονας ἀγκυλοτόξους,
849 τηλόθεν ἐξ Ἀμυδῶνος, ἀπ᾽ Ἀξίου εὐρυρέοντος,
850 Ἀξίου, οὗ κάλλιστον ὕδωρ ἐπικίδναται αἶαν.

Wyatt   848 But Pyraechmes led the Paonians, with curved bows,
849 from afar out of Amydon from wide-flowing Axius—
850 Axius whose water flows the fairest over the face of the earth.

schol. T 21:140[10]

~~848 αὐτὰρ Πυραίχμης ἄγε Παίονας ἀγκυλοτόξους,~~
848a Πηλεγόνος θ᾽ υἱὸς περιδέξιος Ἀστεροπαῖος,
~~849 τηλόθεν ἐξ Ἀμυδῶνος, ἀπ᾽ Ἀξίου εὐρυρέοντος,~~
~~850 Ἀξίου, οὗ κάλλιστον ὕδωρ ἐπικίδναται αἶαν.~~

~~848 But Pyraechmes led the Paonians, with curved bows,~~
848a and son of Pelegon, ambidextrous Asteropaios,
~~849 from afar out of Amydon from wide-flowing Axius~~
~~850 Axius whose water flows the fairest over the face of the earth.~~

This plus-reading comes from the scholia in discussions of the character Asteropaios in Book 21 of the *Iliad*. Both scholion T and POxy 221 quote from the catalogue, using 848a (Allen, 1921, p. 16; Bolling, 1925, p. 77; West, 1967, p. 61; Erbse, 1969, p. 345; Erbse, 1977, p. 154). According to POxy 221, vi, 16ff. this reading was in Euripides' text of the *Iliad*. The reading is also found in a glossary from the Ptolemaic papyri (P Hamburg 137 vv 6–7; West, 1967, pp. 60–61). Although there have been those who accepted this plus as 'original', the majority of scholars have understood this line as a later addition, 'an interpolation—a belated effort to make the *Catalogue* correspond exactly to the poem' (Bolling, 1925, p. 77). That is, this plus is generally understood as an addition that 'corrects' the catalogue, so that it now includes Asteropaios, who is mentioned as a Paonian hero in *Il.* 21:139–143 (West, 1967, pp. 50,61; van Thiel, 2010, p. 46).

I suggest that this variant is the result of scribal memory. That is, *if* it is an addition, scribal memory of the acts of Asteropaios in Book 21 influenced his inclusion

232   *Raymond F. Person, Jr.*

in the Catalogue of Ships. However, since lists are not necessarily exhaustive, such an 'addition' to the text would not be considered an addition to the list, especially since Asteropaios plays a role in the events in Book 21. *If* it is an omission in the text, it would not necessarily be considered an omission of Asteropaios, since he appears in Book 21. According to either interpretation, the catalogue is not understood to be exhaustive, so that Asteropaios can be considered present in the category of Greek (specifically Paonian) heroes, even if he is not included in the list. The catalogue is not exhaustive, but representative.

> **Example (8): Homer, *Iliad*, Book 2, 855–856 (Allen, 1921, p. 16; Bolling, 1925, p. 77; West, 1967, p. 42; Erbse, 1969, p. 347; Erbse, 1977, p. 57; Ready, 2019, p. 258)**

vulgate	855 Κρῶμνάν τ' Αἰγιαλόν τε καὶ ὑψηλοὺς Ἐρυθίνους. 856 Αὐτὰρ Ἁλιζώνων Ὀδίος καὶ Ἐπίστροφος ἦρχον
Wyatt	855 and Croman and Aegiales and lofty Erythini. 856 But of the Halizones Odius and Epistrophus were leaders
P40	855 ... **855a [Κ]αύκω[νασ δ'αῦτ' ἦγε Πολυκλέοσ υἱὸσ Ἄμειβοσ, 855b [οἱ] περὶ Πα[ρθένιον ποταμὸν κλυτὰ δώματ'ἔναιον.** 856 ...
Ready	855 ... **855a and in turn Ameibos the son of Polykles led the Kaukones, 855b who had famous homes by the Parthenios river.** 856 ...

These two plus lines occur in one of the Ptolemaic papyri (P40) but must be earlier. Strabo (*Geography* 12.3.5) rejected these lines as original, stating that they are interpolations of the fourth-century BCE historian Callisthenes (Bolling, 1925, p. 77; West, 1967, pp. 49–50; Ready, 2019, p. 258). Some scholars have argued that these lines may have predated Callisthenes (West, 1967, p. 50; see similarly Ready, 2019, p. 227). These plus-lines are also quoted in scholion T at 3.329 (Bolling, 1925, p. 77; West, 1967, p. 49).

Despite the antiquity of these lines, they are often understood as interpolations, as harmonizations with references to the Kaukones in *Il.* 10.429 and 20.329 (Bolling, 1925, p. 77; West, 1967, p. 50; Ready, 2019, p. 258). Since the catalogue makes no mention of the Kaukones (in the vulgate, presumed to be the original), these plus-verses 'intruded to repair this omission' (Bolling, 1925, p. 77). In fact, West went so far as to describe any text that contained lines 853–855 followed by 855a,b as a 'monstrosity' that would have been 'intolerable' (West, 1967, p. 50).

As argued previously for Example (7), the addition or omission of a hero, or in this case an ethnic group of heroes, to the catalogue is possible within scribal memory. The list provides access to a larger category—in this case, of the Trojans and their allies. Including the Kaukones does not really change the function of the catalogue, just as excluding them does not, especially since the Kaukones are mentioned elsewhere. Furthermore, the fact that '[n]either Polycles nor his son is

Poetics and List-Construction 233

mentioned elsewhere' (West, 1967, p. 50) is insignificant. Even though Ameibos is not mentioned by name among the Kaukones in Books 10 and 20, this does not mean that the vulgate text necessarily assumes that he was not present in the battle. That is, both the catalogue and the following narrative about the battle are understood as incomplete lists and narrative reports of what happened in the epic past.

Example (9): Homer, *Iliad*, Book 2, 603–614 (Allen, 1921, p. 7; Bolling, 1925, p. 74; West, 1967, p. 50; Erbse, 1969, p. 313; Erbse, 1977, p. 105)

Here I do not provide the Greek text, because the variant text is not available. Stentor, the character who is mentioned only in *Il.* 5.785, is lacking in the extant versions of the catalogue. However, according to scholia AT (at 5.785), Stentor is mentioned in some (no longer extant) versions. 'Some say that Stentor is Arcadian and that in the Catalogue they assemble in ranks around him' (τινὲς δὲ Ἀρκάδα φασὶν εἶναι τὸν Στέντορα καὶ ἐν τῷ καταλόγῳ πλάττουσι περὶ αὐτοῦ στίχους; Bolling, 1925, p. 74; West, 1967, p. 50; Erbse, 1969, p. 313; Erbse, 1977, p. 105; my translation). That is, rather than quoting the Greek text as is sometimes the case, here a plus reading is simply referred to in the scholia. Thus, presumably, someone knew of a version that had a variant reading of the section of the Trojan catalogue concerning the Arcadians (2.603–614) that did include Stentor in the list of Arcadian heroes. Note that Aristarchus and scholion T have provided textual evidence for the plus-lines discussed above in Examples (7)–(8), so that we can conclude that Aristarchus had access to a version of the *Iliad* that included various plus-verses in the Catalogue of Ships, so that, even though the extant text-critical evidence of different versions of the catalogue may be fairly minimal (as in this case), we nevertheless have evidence that points to more text-critical variation in the catalogue than present in the extant manuscript evidence.

Example (10): Homer, *Iliad*, Book 2, 536–537 (Allen, 1921, p. 3; Bolling, 1925, p. 72; West, 1967, p. 42)

vulgate	536 Οἵ δ'Εὔβοιαν ἔχον μένεα πνείοντες Ἄβαντες,
	537 Χαλκίδα τ'Εἰρέτριάν τε πολυστάφυλόν θ' Ἱστίαιαν.
Wyatt	536 And the Abantes, breathing fury, who held Euboea
	537 and Chalcis and Ereteria and Histiaea, rich in vines
Strabo 40.453	536–537 Οἵ δ'Εὔβοιαν ἔχον καὶ Χαλκίδα τ'Εἰρέτριάν τε
	536–537 And those who held Euboea and Chalcis and Ereteria.

Both readings in their larger literary context identify the Abantes and the land that they hold. Bolling dismissed the reading in Strabo, because he 'is probably quoting only as much as is useful for his argument' (1925, p. 72). Nevertheless, the addition/omission of Histiaea to the list of the land of the Abantes does not significantly affect the identification of the Abantes within the catalogue, even if

234 *Raymond F. Person, Jr.*

it might complicate modern attempts to derive geographical information from it. That is, the list of their territory may not be exhaustive, but the list in either reading is sufficient for the purpose of identifying the Abantes, especially since Eretria, Chalcis, and Histiaea are all cities probably located on the Greek island of Euboea (see Allen, 1921).

When we look at Examples (7)–(10) together, we observe that the Catalogue of Ships could expand or contract in its transmission. When the scant text-critical evidence is compared to the vulgate text, we have pluses for two Trojan heroes (Asteropaios in 2.848a in Example (7) and Ameibos in 2.855b in Example (8)) and one Greek hero (Stentor somewhere in 2.603–614 in Example (9)), a plus-reading for the Kaukones who fought with the Trojan forces (2.855 a,b; 10.429; 20.329 in Example (8)), and a minus-reading of Histiaea from the list of cities on Euboea from which the Abantes came (2.536–537 in Example (10)).

Working only with the vulgate, Benjamin Sammons discussed what has often been seen as evidence that either Homer was using a traditional catalogue or that the Catalogue of Ships was a later interpolation. Concerning the Greek catalogue, he (2010, p. 158) noted the following:

> Of the forty-four leaders named in the catalogue, ten appear nowhere else in the *Iliad*. . . . Two appear again only in other catalogues. . . . Eight appear again only to be killed. . . . Two others appear only in other catalogues before being killed in battle. . . . In all, the above represent twenty-two of the forty-four leaders named in the catalogue.

Sammons is pointing to an oddity—that is, fifty percent of the named leaders in the Greek catalogue are minor. He then concluded 'that the poet found it useful to have a store of such dispensable figures, and could make use of them for dramatic effect' (2010, p. 159). He also noted that Iasos is not included in the catalogue, even though he is killed in battle (15.332). Sammons was approaching the insights revealed in this study; however, he focused too exclusively on the 'composition' of the *Iliad* and assumed that the vulgate was Homer's original text. That is, not only did the poet 'have a store of dispensible figures', but the broader tradition of which the poet is but one player had those that Sammons identified and others held within scribal memory (including Ameibos, who is found in the plus in 2.855b, but not elsewhere in the *Iliad*). Thus, the catalogue as list provided audiences with more-than-adequate representivity of the Greek and Trojan forces, but was not considered to be exhaustive. Rather, it opened up the category of Greek heroes and Trojan heroes and, even though it provided a much more thorough list of heroes than might be typical in everyday conversation, the list itself represents the categories, which contain other minor figures not explicitly listed. This observation suggests that we need to reject the much too common notions in Homer scholarship that 'a traditional list does not permit alteration' (Minchin, 2001, p. 79) and 'the catalogue form's methodical presentation of data, its claim to precision and completeness under a specified rubric, seems to promise that the information it presents is neither distorted, diminished, nor exaggerated' (Sammons, 2010,

Poetics and List-Construction 235

p. 165). Although I would not describe the kind of textual fluidity found in scribal performance as 'distorted, diminished, [or] exaggerated', I also do not think that the ancient scribes would have understood written lists as 'precise' or 'complete' in modern conceptions, because such completeness resides within scribal memory, not individual manuscripts.

The List of the 'Seven Nations' in Selected Passages in the Hebrew Bible

The Hebrew Bible contains many lists of different types of items. In *Theme and Context in Biblical Lists*, Benjamin Scolnic provided a 'Master List of Lists Proper' that contains 101 different lists (1995, pp. 15–17). Many studies begin with an assumption that, although common, is unfounded—that is, lists tend to be fixed, written genres independent of the literary context. Scolnic wrote, 'To understand the importance of lists in the development of written forms, we must first recognize that lists had to be written down; inventories were a necessary precaution against theft' (1995, p. 5). Similarly, Zecharia Kallai (2003, p. 95) concluded as follows:

> The fundamental characteristic observed is the preeminent position of established formalized records that have attained normative status. Any variations due to changes of territorial or habitational circumstances are formulated on the basis of these underlying records, introducing modifications only. To this end certain segments are exchanged, added or eliminated, all within the basic structure that is otherwise maintained in its primary form.

That is, many biblical scholars assume that authors accurately copied 'established formalized records' as sources in the composition of their literary works 'in order to convey completeness, comprehensiveness' and 'to give a text the impression of factuality' (Scolnic, 1995, p. 12). Based on this assumption, many biblical scholars further assume that these 'records' can be used for accurate historical reconstructions. Of course, they often recognize that there are discrepancies between the 'same' list, whether in different passages within the same manuscript (for example, the Benjaminite genealogies in Gen 46:21; Num 26:38–40; 1 Chr 7:6–12; 1 Chr 8:1–40 in MT; Levin, 2004) or differences among manuscripts for the same passage (for example, the difference between MT and LXX of the list of Jerusalem's residents in Neh 11:3–19; see Knoppers, 2000); however, as illustrated by the previous quote from Kallai, many still assume that the 'basic structure' of the 'established formalized records' remains, so that with the application of standard historical-critical principles (such as *lectio brevior potior*, the shorter reading is preferred) the 'records' can be recovered. However, a few biblical scholars have questioned this assumption. Yigal Levin argued that the genealogies in 1 Chronicles 1–9 reveal 'a large degree of *fluidity*', so that '[t]he resemblance to oral genealogies is unmistakable' (2003, p. 235). James Watts wrote the following: 'Lists, by their nature, invite readers and listeners to choose items relevant to themselves and ignore the rest' (2016, p. 1143). If we translate this into Jefferson's terminology, we

236   *Raymond F. Person, Jr.*

get the following: due to the principle of adequate representivity, lists give readers and listeners access to the category of co-class items from which they may choose the most relevant ones.

Here I will focus on one set of lists in the Hebrew Bible, the list of the 'seven nations'—that is, the foreign nations that Israel must avoid contact with at all costs, including commandments of genocide towards them.[11] These lists occur in various biblical passages and exhibit some variation in the text-critical evidence as well. The starting point for my research was the thorough work done by Kevin O'Connell (1984). With one exception, I have selected those examples in his study for which we have text-critical variants in Hebrew manuscripts, thereby reducing the number of passages to analyze from 28 to 10. This should be understood in no way as to deny the credibility of the Greek evidence of the Septuagint (LXX) to the question; rather, it is simply a way of reducing the number of examples. However, since all of the Hebrew evidence that differs from the Masoretic Text [MT] comes from the Samaritan Pentateuch [SP], I will include one example from LXX outside of the Pentateuch (Josh 11:3) to point to the additional complexity that would occur if I had included all of his examples. Also, some of the evidence from the Dead Sea Scrolls was unavailable to O'Connell, so I have updated his work in relationship to new text-critical evidence. Despite this reduction in number, the examples I have chosen illustrate well the textual fluidity of this list; therefore, I think my limited selection will sufficiently serve my current purposes. Although previously I discussed each example in turn, here I will simply provide Examples (11)–(20) in their canonical order and then discuss them as a collective.[12]

Example (11): Gen 15:19–21

MT

אֶת־הַקֵּינִי֙ וְאֶת־הַקְּנִזִּ֔י וְאֵ֖ת הַקַּדְמֹנִֽי׃
וְאֶת־הַחִתִּ֥י וְאֶת־הַפְּרִזִּ֖י וְאֶת־הָרְפָאִֽים׃
וְאֶת־הָֽאֱמֹרִי֙ וְאֶת־הַֽכְּנַעֲנִ֔י וְאֶת־הַגִּרְגָּשִׁ֖י וְאֶת־הַיְבוּסִֽי׃

the Kenites, the Kenizzites, the Kadmonites, the Hittites, the Perizzites, the Rephaim, the Amorites, the Canaanites, the Girgashites, and the Jebusites.

SP

אֶת־הַקֵּינִי֙ וְאֶת־הַקְּנִזִּ֔י וְאֵ֖ת הקדמוני׃
וְאֶת־הַחִתִּ֥י וְאֶת־הַפְּרִזִּ֖י וְאֶת־הָרְפָאִֽים׃
וְאֶת־הָֽאֱמֹרִי֙ וְאֶת־הַֽכְּנַעֲנִ֔י וְאֶת־הַגִּרְגָּשִׁ֖י ואת החוי וְאֶת־הַיְבוּסִֽי׃

the Kenites, the Kenizzites, the Kadmonites, the Hittites, the Perizzites, the Rephaim, the Amorites, the Canaanites, the Girgashites, **the Hivites,** and the Jebusites.

Example (12): Exod 3:8

MT

ו יֵּֽגְעֲנַכְהֶ֤ךְ יֹמֵֽאֱהֶ֙ן יִתְּחֶ֔ה וְהַפִּדִּ֖י וְהַֽחִוִּ֥י וְהַיְבוּסִֽי

the Canaanites, the Hittites, the Amorites, the Perizzites, the Hivites, and the Jebusites.

Poetics and List-Construction 237

SP הַכְּנַעֲנִי הַחִתִּי וְהָאֱמֹרִי וְהַפְּרִזִּי והגרגשי וְהַחִוִּי וְהַיְבוּסִי
the Canaanites, the Hittites, *the Amorites, the Perizzites,* **the Girgashites***, the Hivites,* and the Jebusites.

4QGen-Exod[a] הכ]נעני והחתי והפ[ר]זי והאמרי החוי הגרגשי והיבוסי
the Canaanites, the Hittites, *the Perizzites, the Amorites, the Hivites,* **the Girgashites***,* and the Jebusites.

Example (13): Exod 3:17

MT וְהַחִתִּי הַכְּנַעֲנִי וְהָאֱמֹרִי וְהַפְּרִזִּי וְהַחִוִּי וְהַיְבוּסִי
the Canaanites, the Hittites, the Amorites, the Perizzites, the Hivites, and the Jebusites

SP הַכְּנַעֲנִי וְהַחִתִּי וְהָאֱמֹרִי וְהַפְּרִזִּי וְהַחִוִּיוהגרגשי וְהַיְבוּסִי
the Canaanites, the Hittites, the Amorites, the Perizzites, **the Girgashites**, the Hivites, and the Jebusites

Example (14): Exod 23:23

MT הָאֱמֹרִי וְהַחִתִּי וְהַפְּרִזִּי וְהַכְּנַעֲנִי הַחִוִּי וְהַיְבוּסִי
the Amorites, the Hittites, the Perizzites, the Canaanites, the Hivites, and the Jebusites

SP הכנעני וְהָאֱמֹר והגרגשיוְהַחִתִּי וְהַפְּרִזִּי הַחִוִּי וְהַיְבוּסִי
the Canaanites, the Amorites, the Hittites, **the Girgashites**, the Perizzites, the Hivites, and the Jebusites

Example (15): Exod 23:28

MT אֶת־הַחִוִּי אֶת־הַכְּנַעֲנִי וְאֶת־הַחִתִּי
the Hivites, the Canaanites, and the Hittites

SP את הכנעני ואת האמרי ואת החתי
ואת הגרגשי ואת הפרזי ואת החוי ואת היבוסי
the Canaanites, **the Amorites***,* *the Hittites,* **the Girgashites, the Perizzites***, the Hivites, and* **the Jebusites**

SP mss את הכנעני ואת האמרי ואת החתי
ואת הגרגשי ואת החוי ואת היבוסי
the Canaanites, **the Amorites***, the Hittites,* **the Girgashites***, the Hivites, and* **the Jebusites**

Example (16): Exod 33:2

MT אֶת־הַכְּנַעֲנִי הָאֱמֹרִי וְהַחִתִּי וְהַפְּרִזִּי הַחִוִּי וְהַיְבוּסִי
the Canaanites, the Amorites, the Hittites, the Perizzites, the Hivites, and the Jebusites

SP אֶת־הַכְּנַעֲנִי וְהָאֱמֹרִי וְהַחִתִּי והגרגשי וְהַפְּרִזִּי הַחִוִּי וְהַיְבוּסִי
the Canaanites, the Amorites, the Hittites, **the Girgashites**, the Perizzites, the Hivites, and the Jebusites

238   *Raymond F. Person, Jr.*

Example (17): Exod 34:11

MT   אֶת־הָאֱמֹרִי֙ וְהַכְּנַעֲנִי֙ וְהַחִתִּי֙ וְהַפְּרִזִּי֙ וְהַחִוִּי וְהַיְבוּסִי
     the Amorites, the Canaanites, the Hittites, the Perizzites, the Hivites,
     and the Jebusites

SP   אֶת־הַכְּנַעֲנִי֙ וְהָאֱמֹרִי֙ וְהַחִתִּי֙ והגרגשי וְהַפְּרִזִּי֙ וְהַחִוִּי וְהַיְבוּסִי
     the Canaanites, the Amorites, the Hittites, **the Girgashites**, the
     Perizzites, the Hivites, and the Jebusites

Example (18): Num 13:29

MT   וְהַחִתִּי וְהַיְבוּסִי וְהָאֱמֹרִי֙ יוֹשֵׁב בָּהָר וְהַכְּנַעֲנִי֙
     יֹשֵׁב עַל־הַיָּם וְעַל יַד הַיַּרְדֵּן
     the Hittites, the Jebusites, and the Amorites, who live in the hill
     country; and the Canaanites, who live by the sea and along the
     Jordan

SP   וְהַחִתִּי וחהוי וְהַיְבוּסִי וְהָאֱמֹרִי֙ יוֹשֵׁב בָּהָר וְהַכְּנַעֲנִי֙
     יֹשֵׁב עַל־הַיָּם וְעַל יַד הַיַּרְדֵּן
the Hittites, **the Hivites**, the Jebusites, and the Amorites, who live in the
hill country; and the Canaanites, who live by the sea and along the
Jordan

Example (19): Deut 20:17

MT   הַחִתִּי וְהָאֱמֹרִי֙ הַכְּנַעֲנִי וְהַפְּרִזִּי֙ הַחִוִּי וְהַיְבוּסִי
     the Hittites and the Amorites, the Canaanites and the Perizzites, the
     Hivites and the Jebusites

SP   הכנעני והאמרי והחתי והגרגשי וְהַפְּרִזִּי֙ וְהַחִוִּי וְהַיְבוּסִי
     the Canaanites, the Amorites, *the Hittites*, **the Girgashites**, the
     Perizzites, the Hivites, and the Jebusites

Example (20): Josh 11:3

MT   הַכְּנַעֲנִי֙ מִמִּזְרָח וּמִיָּם וְהָאֱמֹרִי וְהַחִתִּי וְהַפְּרִזִּי וְהַיְבוּסִי בָּהָר
     וְהַחִוִּי֙ תַּחַת חֶרְמוֹן בְּאֶרֶץ הַמִּצְפָּה
     to the Canaanites in the east and in the west, the Amorites, the Hit-
     tites, the Perizzites, and the Jebusites who are in the hill country, and
     the Hivites who are under Hermon in the land of Mizpah.

LXX^B   καὶ εἰς τοὺς παραλίους Χαναναίους ἀπὸ ἀνατολῶν καὶ εἰς τοὺς
     παραλίους Αμορραίους καὶ Ευαίους καὶ Ιεβουσαίους καὶ
     Φερεζαίους τοὺς ἐν τῷ ὄρει καὶ τοὺς Χετταίους τοὺς ὑπὸ τὴν
     ἔρηπον εἰς τὴν Μασευμαν
     to the coastal Canaanites in the east, the coastal Amorites,
     the Hivites, the Jebusites, the Perizzites who are in the hill
     country, and *the Hittites* who are under the wilderness of
     Maseuman.

Poetics and List-Construction   239

LXX[s]   καὶ εἰς τοὺς παραλίους Χορραίους καὶ Αμορραίους καὶ τοὺς Χετταίους καὶ Φερεζαίους καὶ Ιεβουσαίους τοὺς ἐν τῷ ὄρει καὶ τοὺς Ευαίους τοὺς ὑπὸ τὴν ἔρημον εἰς τὴν Μασεμμαθ

to the coastal **Horites** in the east, Amorites, the Hittites, the Perizzites, the Jebusites who are in the hill country, and the Hivites who are under the wilderness in the land of Masemmath.

LXX[pt]   καὶ εἰς τοὺς παραλίους Χαναναίους ἀπὸ ἀνατολῶν καὶ εἰς τοὺς παραλίους Χορραίους καὶ εἰς τοὺς παραλίους Αμορραίους καὶ τοὺς Χετταίους τοὺς ὑπὸ τὴν ἔρημον εἰς τὴν μασφου καὶ Φερεζαίους τοὺς ἐν τῷ ὄρει καὶ Ιεβουσαίους τοὺς ἐν τῷ ὄρει καὶ τοὺς Ευαίους τοὺς ὑπὸ τὴν αερμων εἰς τὴν Μασσηφαθ

to the coastal Canaanites in the east, the coastal **Horites**, the coastal Amorites, the Hittites who in the wilderness of Mizpah, the Perizzites who are in the hill country, the Jebusites who are in the hill country, and the Hivites who are under Hermon in the land of Massephath.

All of these lists clearly refer to the foreign peoples who were imagined to have lived in the area of the promised land, most generally referred to as Canaan. Although according to tradition there are 'seven nations' (based on Deut 7:1), the number of peoples mentioned in these lists spans from three (MT-Exod 23:28) to 11 (SP-Gen 15:19–21). We see variation within the same manuscript tradition (for example, three peoples in MT-Exod 23:28 to 10 in MT-Gen 15:19–21) as well as between different manuscripts of the same passage (for example, three peoples in MT-Exod 23:28 to seven in SP-Exod 23:28). When we look only at those Hebrew manuscripts that have the traditional number of seven, we find that, although they contain the same set of seven, there are nevertheless four different orders: (1) 'the Canaanites, the Hittites, the Amorites, the Perizzites, the Girgashites, the Hivites, and the Jebusites' (SP-Exod 3:8; 3:17), (2) 'the Canaanites, the Amorites, the Hittites, the Girgashites, the Perizzites, the Hivites, and the Jebusites' (SP-Exod 23:23; 23:28; 33:2; 34:11; Deut 20:17), (3) 'the Canaanites, the Hittites, the Perizzites, the Amorites, the Hivites, the Girgashites, and the Jebusites' (4QGen-Exod[a]-Exod 3:8), and (4) 'the Hittites, the Girgashites, the Amorites, the Canaanites, the Perizzites, the Hivites, and the Jebusites, seven nations' (MT-Deut 7:1). Moreover, we should note that LXX[pt]-Josh 11:3 also has seven nations, but, in comparison to the Hebrew manuscripts, it differs in that, instead of the Girgashites, it has the Horites. When all of these observations are combined, I find it difficult to imagine that this tremendous variety began with one list from which modifications were made sparingly in the composition/transmission process.

Despite this tremendous diversity, O'Connell still assumed that he could reconstruct the original 'seven nations' (those in Deut 7:1), even though he could not determine the original order with certainty. He concluded that the 'MT has all seven names only three times' (1984, p. 224), due to its tendency toward haplography, especially the omission of 'the Girgashites' from the list (1984, p. 226).

240 *Raymond F. Person, Jr.*

Nevertheless, he described the list behind the literature as having a 'closed formulaic character of the original seven-name list' that 'was already fixed formula and symbol' before the earliest written source of the Pentateuch (his 'Yahwist'), reflecting 'experiences of the settlement (or at least of the pre-monarchical period)' (1984, p. 227). In these quotes, we can clearly see his desire for lists to be able to take us back to the earliest period of ancient Israel, before the written texts of the canonical books, in order to recover 'historical' data for the reconstruction of ancient Israelite history.

I began this section by noting how unfounded the assumptions made by biblical scholars often are concerning the fixity and historicity of lists, but I also included the following insightful quote: 'Lists, by their nature, invite readers and listeners to choose items relevant to themselves and ignore the rest' (Watts, 2016, p. 1143). It seems to me that the list of foreign peoples fits Watts' observation well. It does not matter how many foreign peoples are on the list, because the list itself refers to the category of foreign peoples who are to be avoided in the text's xenophobic attitude towards the ethnic/religious other. Therefore, scribal memory could influence the 'copying' of the list by allowing it to contract or expand as the scribe produced a new piece of literature (as 'author') or copied an existing piece of literature (as 'copyist'). The list in scribal memory gave the scribes access to the category of co-class members (in this case, foreign peoples), so that, even in their copying of the list from a manuscript in front of them into a new manuscript, the scribes were not constrained to copy the list verbatim. Even a list with a different number of items (typically three or more) in whatever order could nevertheless adequately represent the category of co-class members—in this case, foreign peoples to be feared and annihilated.

Conclusion

Previous studies of lists in literature tend to share the following unfounded assumptions: (1) There was an 'original' form of the list that as a source had some independent integrity prior to its incorporation into its current literary context; (2) although there may have been some adaptation of the 'original' list by the author when the list was incorporated into its literary context, the variations tended to be so insignificant that the 'original' list can be recovered with some degree of confidence; (3) the 'standard', 'received', or 'vulgate' text remains so close to the 'original' text and the extant text-critical variants come from the later transmission of the text as a result of scribal error or deliberate, ideologically motivated changes (mostly in the form of 'additions' or 'interpolations'); and (4) therefore, the study of literary lists (in the 'standard', 'received', and 'vulgate' texts) can provide valuable data for the reconstruction of historical information behind the text. This certainly applies to the three examples discussed previously. New Testament scholars generally assume that Paul selected specific items for each list of vices, depending on the situation in the church to which he is writing. Homerists generally assume that the 'poet' drew from traditional lists of heroes and geography that reflected the political-geographical reality of an earlier time as he composed his Catalogue

Poetics and List-Construction   241

of Ships. Scholars of the Hebrew Bible generally assume that the 'original' list of 'seven nations' reflected a particular historical period of time during which the authors were composing their works, so that any variation in the lists may reflect a later historical period.

This study undermines all of these assumptions. Drawing from recent text-critical studies, I argued that the textual plurality in which most ancient literature exists strongly suggests a high degree of textual fluidity, especially in the earliest periods of the composition/transmission process for which we lack text-critical evidence. That is, the earlier we go back in the text-critical record, the more we find 'wild' variants that nevertheless seem to fit well organically into their literary traditions; therefore, rather than simply giving up on our ability to reconstruct the 'original' text (an anachronistic idea, in my opinion), we should accept the textual plurality in which ancient literary works often existed.

One of the best explanations for this textual plurality is the idea of scribal performance—that is, much like oral performers, ancient scribes performed their texts, even in the highly literate activity of copying physical manuscripts before them as a way of transmitting and preserving these living literary texts for their communities. Much like oral performers, the composition/transmission process allows for what may appear to be 'differences' from our modern perspective but can be understood as the 'same' from their perspective, especially within scribal memory. No individual manuscript can contain the breadth of the tradition, which is stored in scribal memory, the collective memory of scribes whose knowledge of written and oral texts preserves the literature within the tradition. Therefore, even when copying a manuscript, scribal memory allows what we perceive as additions, omissions, transpositions, and substitutions in the new manuscript, but what in a traditional sense are not variants, because they already existed within the tradition, within scribal memory.

Although some previous studies have discussed scribal performance and scribal memory, the identification of the cognitive-linguistic processes that illuminate how the composition/transmission process can allow such textual fluidity has been lacking. This study's main contribution comes from its application of how category-triggering works in word-selection in talk-in-interaction, especially in list-construction, to text-critical variants in literary lists. Within conversation, list-construction consists of selecting from co-class members of a category so that there is adequate representivity of that category. Therefore, a list in conversation provides participants with common access to that same category. As noted by Foley, in living oral traditions (such as South Slavic), oral poets often produce lists in which 'the omission, or substitution, of one or more items' is common (1983, p. 196). That is, lists composed in oral performance have similar functions to lists in conversation, in that the lists open up a category of co-class members to the poet and the traditional audience, and this continues to happen even when the items in the list may differ from one performance to another, because the list nevertheless has adequate representivity.

In literature, we could translate some earlier conclusions as follows: during the composition process, authors produce lists that serve similar functions

242   *Raymond F. Person, Jr.*

between them and their audience—that is, the list opens up a category of co-class members, making it available to readers. The problem with such a translation would be that the 'author's original text' is based on an anachronistic assumption. Rather, we have seen that the lists discussed previously exist in textual plurality, so that list-construction, including what items may or may not be included, does not occur only in 'composition', but throughout the entire composition/ transmission process. In other words, because of the adequate representivity of literary lists first composed by 'authors', their 'readers' understand those lists in ways that are analogous to lists in conversation and oral traditions, so that even the 'copyists' of those lists (themselves 'readers') can create 'variants' within the lists, but the lists continue to have the same function of providing more-than-adequate representivity of the same category. Or stated even better, scribes (whether 'authors' or 'copyists') perform their texts in ways that help their audiences (whether 'readers' or 'hearers') to understand the category of co-class members represented by the list. Therefore, in Albert Lord's words, 'we cannot correctly speak of a "variant," since there is no "original" to be varied' (1960, p. 101). All of the 'versions' of these lists point to the same category with more-than-adequate representivity that includes more co-class items than the extant lists can possibly represent fully.

Notes

1. I want to thank John P. Rae and Robin Wooffitt for comments on an earlier draft.
2. For a good introduction to the early history of the comparative study of oral traditions, see Foley (1988). For a more recent survey, see the special volumes in the journal *Oral Tradition* 18 (2003): 'Synopses of Oral Traditions (1)' and 'Synopses of Oral Traditions (2)'.
3. Brooke (2005); Epp (2005); Bird (2010); Martin (2010); Talmon (2010); Delnero (2012); Gurd (2012). The 'new philology' school also dismisses the idea of an original text—for example, Cerquiglini (1999); Lundhaug and Lied (2017).
4. For my most critical assessment of the current methodology, see Person and Rezetko (2016).
5. I provide the Greek text as published in the standard critical edition (the 28th edition of the text published by the German Bible Society and edited first by Nestle) and a widely used English translation (the New Revised Standard Version). For a widely accepted introduction, see Aland and Aland (1987).
6. In Person (forthcoming-b) I devote an entire chapter to text-critical variants based on sound-triggering, including multiple examples concerning word-play.
7. There are some variations in the secondary literature concerning the beginning and ending of the Catalogue of Ships. For example, some scholars use the term to refer only to the Greek catalogue. I have chosen to follow Allen (1921). However, even if others disagree with this choice, my discussion of the Homeric catalogue(s) should remain generally valid.
8. These comments are based on the vulgate. Note, however, that some manuscripts omit the Catalogue of Ships and some have it after Book 24. For the text-critical evidence, see the critical apparatus in Allen (1921, p. 1); van Thiel (2010, p. 36).
9. I take the Greek text of the 'vulgate' and the English translation from the Loeb Classical Library volume (Murray, 1965) and provide variants from either the manuscript evidence or the scholia (medieval copies of ancient commentary on the

Poetics and List-Construction 243

Homeric epics). Unless otherwise noted, the English translations of the variants are my own.

10. Note that the scholion only has 848a, but it is widely understood that it reflects the broader text that I have provided with cancellation lines—that is, the cancellation lines denote that these lines are not quoted in this scholion, but are provided to give my readers the broader literary context as generally understood for this plus line.

11. For my discussion of the theme of the annihilation of everything related to the 'seven nations' in Deuteronomy, see Person (2014, pp. 45–55, 93–98). This theme is certainly one of the most problematic in the Bible, and unfortunately continues to influence xenophobia in today's society.

12. 'Masoretic Text' (MT) refers to medieval Hebrew manuscripts that are used in Jewish worship and are the basis of most translations. 'Samaritan Pentateuch' (SP) refers to Hebrew manuscripts used by Samaritans in their worship, both historically and today. 'Septuagint' (LXX) refers to manuscripts of the ancient Greek translation of the Hebrew Bible, first used in Jewish communities but then mostly by Christians. 'Dead Sea Scrolls' refers to manuscripts found in caves near Khirbet Qumran and the surrounding area. The individual manuscripts are identified by the cave in which they were found, the literary text of the manuscript, and for those texts in which multiple copies are found in the same cave a letter denoting which manuscript. Therefore, '4QGen-Exod^a' denotes the first scroll containing Genesis and Exodus found in cave 4 near Qumran. Sometimes even within these textual traditions there are differences between some manuscripts (in one case, in both SP and LXX). All reconstructions of the purported Hebrew or Aramaic text behind the Greek translation are my own, unless otherwise noted.

For the most widely accepted introduction, see Tov (2012). The following abbreviations refer to the following published volumes: MT = *Biblia Hebraica Stuttgartensia*; SP = Tal and Florentin (2010); 4QGen-Exod^a = Ulrich (2010); and LXX for Joshua = Brooke and McLean (1917).

Works Cited

Aland, K., and Aland, B. (1987). *The Text of the New Testament: An Introduction to the Critical Editions and to the Theory and Practice of Modern Textual Criticism*. Grand Rapids: W.B. Eerdmans.

Allen, T.W. (Ed.) (1921). *The Homeric Catalogue of Ships*. Oxford: Clarendon Press.

Betz, H.D. (1979). *Galatians: A Commentary on Paul's Letter to the Churches in Galatia*. Philadelphia: Fortress.

Bird, G.D. (2010). *Multitextuality in the Homeric Iliad: The Witness of the Ptolemaic Papyri*. Washington.

Bolling, G.M. (1925). *The External Evidence for Interpolation in Homer*. Oxford: Clarendon Press.

Borgen, P. (1988). Catalogues of vices, the apostolic decree, and the Jerusalem meeting. In J. Neusner et al. (Eds.), *The Social World of Formative Christianity and Judaism: Essays in Tribute to Howard Clark Kee*. Philadelphia: Fortress Press, pp. 126–141.

Brooke, A.E., and McLean, N. (Eds.) (1917). *The Old Testament in Greek according to the text of Codex Vaticanus, supplemented from other uncial manuscripts, with a critical apparatus containing the variants of the chief ancient authorities for the text of the Septuagint*. London: Cambridge University Press.

Brooke, G.J. (2005). The Qumran scrolls and the demise of the distinction between higher and lower criticism. In J.G. Campbell, W.J. Lyons, and L.K. Pietersen (Eds.), *New Directions in Qumran Studies: Proceedings of the Bristol Colloquium on the Dead Sea Scrolls, 8–10 September 2003*. London: T&T Clark, pp. 26–42.

244 *Raymond F. Person, Jr.*

Carr, D.M. (2011). *The Formation of the Hebrew Bible: A New Reconstruction*. Oxford: Oxford University Press.

Cerquiglini, B. (1999). *In Praise of the Variant: A Critical History of Philology*. B. Wing (Trans.). Baltimore: Johns Hopkins University Press.

Delnero, P. (2012). Memorization and the transmission of Sumerian literary compositions. *Journal of Near Eastern Studies*, 71, 189–208.

deSilva, D.A. (2018). *The Letter to the Galatians*. Grand Rapids: W.B. Eerdmans.

Doane, A.N. (1994). The ethnography of scribal writing and Anglo-Saxon poetry: scribe as performer. *Oral Tradition*, 9, 420–439.

Epp, E.J. (2005). The multivariance of the term "original text" in New Testament textual criticism. In *Perspectives on New Testament Criticism: Collected Essays, 1962–2004*. Leiden: Brill, pp. 551–593.

Erbse, H. (Ed.) (1969). *Scholia Graeca in Homeri Iliadem (scholia vetera)* (Volume 1). Berlin: Walter de Gruyter.

Erbse, H. (Ed.) (1977). *Scholia Graeca in Homeri Iliadem (scholia vetera)* (Volume 5). Berlin: Walter de Gruyter.

Faraone, C.A. (2013). The poetics of the catalogue in the Hesiodic Theogony. *Transactions of the American Philological Association*, 143, 293–323.

Foley, J.M. (1983). Literary art and oral tradition in Old English and Serbian poetry. *Anglo-Saxon England*, 12:183–214.

Foley, J.M. (1988). *The Theory of Oral Composition: History and Methodology*. Bloomington: Indiana University Press.

Foley, J.M. (Ed.) (2003). Synopses of oral traditions. Special issue of *Oral Tradition*, 18.

Gurd, S.A. (2012). *Work in Progress: Literary Revision as Social Performance in Ancient Rome*. Oxford: Oxford University Press.

Helgadóttir, Y.S. (Forthcoming). Poetic formulae in Icelandic post-medieval þulur: Transatlantic migration. In Frog and W. Lamb (Eds.), *Weathered Words: Formulaic Language and Verbal Art*. Washington, DC: Center for Hellenic Studies.

Jefferson, G. (1990). List-construction as a task and resource. In G. Psathas (Ed.), *Interaction Competence*. Washington, DC: University Press of America, pp. 63–92.

Jefferson, G. (1996). On the poetics of ordinary talk. *Text and Performance Quarterly*, 16, 11–61.

Kallai, Z. (2003). Simeon's town list. scribal rules and geographical patterns. *Vetus Testamentum*, 53, 81–96.

Kirk, A. (2008). Manuscript tradition as a tertium quid: orality and memory in scribal practices. In T. Thatcher (Ed.), *Jesus, the Voice, and the Text: Beyond the Oral and the Written Gospel*. Waco, TX: Baylor University Press, pp. 215–234.

Knoppers, G.N. (2000). Sources, revisions, and ditions: the lists of Jerusalem's residents in MT and LXX Nehemiah 11 and 1 Chronicles 9. *Textus*, 20, 141–168.

Lerner, G.H. (1994). Responsive list constructions: a conversational resource for accomplishing multifaceted social action. *Journal of Language and Social Psychology*, 13, 20–33.

Levin, Y. (2004). From lists to history: chronological aspects of the Chronicler's genealogies. *Journal of Biblical Literature*, 123, 601–636.

Lord, A.B. (1960). *The Singer of Tales*. Cambridge, MA: Harvard University Press.

Lundhaug, H., and Lied, L.I. (2017). Studying snapshots: on manuscript culture, textual fluidity, and new philology. In L.I. Lied and H. Lundhaug (Eds.), *Snapshots of Evolving Traditions: Jewish and Christian Manuscript Culture, Textual Fluidity, and New Philology*. Berlin: De Gruyter, pp. 1–19.

Martin, G.D. (2010). *Multiple Originals: New Approaches to Hebrew Bible Textual Criticism*. Atlanta: Society of Biblical Literature.

Miller, S. (2019). *Dead Sea Media: Orality, Textuality and Memory in the Scrolls from the Judean Desert*. Leiden: Brill.

Minchin, E. (2001). *Homer and the Resources of Memory: Some Application of Cognitive Theory to the Iliad and the Odyssey*. Oxford: Oxford University Press.

Murray, A.T. (Ed.) (1965). *Homer, The Iliad*. Cambridge, MA: Harvard University Press.

O'Connell, K.G. (1984). The list of seven peoples in Canaan: a fresh analysis. In H.O. Thompson (Ed.), *The Answers Lie Below: Essays in Honor of Lawrence Edmund Toombs*. Lanham: University Press of America, pp. 221–241.

Person, R.F., Jr. (1999). *Structure and Meaning in Conversation and Literature*. Lanham: University Press of America.

Person, R.F., Jr. (2014). *Deuteronomy and Environmental Amnesia*. Sheffield: Sheffield Phoenix Press.

Person, R.F., Jr. (2015). Text criticism as a lens for understanding the transmission of ancient texts in their oral environments. In B. Schmidt (Ed.), *Contextualizing Israel's Sacred Writings: Ancient Literacy, Orality, and Literary Production*. Atlanta: SBL Press, pp. 197–215.

Person, R.F., Jr. (2016). *From Conversation to Oral Tradition: A Simplest Systematics for Oral Traditions*. London: Routledge.

Person, R.F., Jr. (2021). Harmonization in the Pentateuch and Synoptic Gospels: repetition and category-triggering within scribal memory. In D. Beck (Ed.), *Repetition, Communication, and Meaning in the Ancient World*. Leiden: Brill, pp. 318–357.

Person, R.F., Jr. (Forthcoming-a). Formulas and scribal memory: a case study of text-critical variants as examples of category-triggering. In Frog and W. Lamb (Eds.), *Weathered Words: Formulaic Language and Verbal Art*. Washington, DC: Center for Hellenic Studies.

Person, R.F., Jr. (Forthcoming-b). *Scribal Memory and Word Selection: A Cognitive-Linguistic Approach to the Text Criticism of the Hebrew Bible*. Atlanta: SBL Press.

Person, R.F., Jr., and Rezetko, R. (2016). The importance of empirical models to assess the efficacy of source and redaction criticism. In R.F. Person, Jr. and R. Rezetko (Eds.), *Empirical Models Challenging Biblical Criticism*. Atlanta, GA: SBL Press, pp. 1–35.

Ready, J. (2019). *Orality, Textuality, and the Homeric Epics: An Interdisciplinary Study of Oral Texts, Dictated Texts, and Wild Texts*. Oxford: Oxford University Press.

Reichl, K. (Forthcoming). Formulas in oral epics: the dynamics of metre, memory and meaning. In Frog and W. Lamb (Eds.), *Weathered Words: Formulaic Language and Verbal Art*. Washington, DC: Center for Hellenic Studies.

Sammons, B. (2010). *The Art and Rhetoric of the Homeric Catalogue*. Oxford: Oxford University Press.

Schweizer, E. (1979). Traditional ethical patterns in the Pauline and post-Pauline letters and their development (lists of vices and house-tables). In E. Best and R.McL. Wilson (Eds.), *Text and Interpretation: Studies in the New Testament Presented to Matthew Black*. Cambridge: Cambridge University Press, pp. 195–209.

Scolnic, B.E. (1995). *Theme and Context in Biblical Lists*. Atlanta: Scholars Press, 1995.

Tal, A., and Florentin, M. (Eds.) (2010). *The Pentateuch—The Samaritan Version and the Masoretic Version*. Tel Aviv: Tel Aviv University Press.

Talmon, S. (2010). *Text and Canon of the Hebrew Bible: Collected Essays*. Winona Lake: Eisenbrauns.

246   *Raymond F. Person, Jr.*

Tov, E. (2012). *Textual Criticism of the Hebrew Bible*. Minneapolis: Fortress Press.

Ulrich, E. (2010). *The Biblical Qumran Scrolls: Transcriptions and Textual Variants*. Leiden: Brill.

van Thiel, H. (Ed.) (2010). *Homeri Ilias*. Hildesheim: Georg Olms Verlag.

Watts, J.W. (2016). Narratives, lists, rhetoric, ritual, and the Pentateuch as a scripture. In J.C. Gertz, B.M. Levinson, D. Rom-Shiloni, and K. Schmid (Eds.), *The Formation of the Pentateuch: Bridging the Academic Cultures of Europe, Israel, and North America*. Tübingen: Mohr Siebeck, pp. 1135–1145.

West, S. (Ed.) (1967). *The Ptolemaic Papyri of Homer*. Köln: Westdeutscher Verlag.

Yamada, S. (1994). The editorial history of the Assyrian King List. *Zeitschrift für Assyriologie*, 84, 11–37.

Zaas, P.S. (1988). Catalogues and context: 1 Corinthians 5 and 6. *New Testament Studies*, 34, 622–629.

Author Index

Abbott, A. 98, 114
Acker, P. 194, 213
Aland, B. 242n5, 243
Aland, K. 242n5, 243
Allen, T.W. 155, 165, 229–234, 242nn7–8, 243
Andrews, M. 122, 124, 138
Anwar, M. S. 94n8, 94
Arminen, I. 140, 165, 205, 212, 213
Aronsson, K. 16, 26
Ashby, J. 138
Atkinson, J.M. 16, 25, 50, 78, 107, 114, 216
Austerlitz, R. 190–191, 213

Beach, W.A. 14–15, 25, 98, 114
Bergen, B.K. 94n12, 94, 135, 138
Berger, I. 79, 94
Bergmann, J. 26, 32, 33, 50, 102, 108, 115
Betz, H.D. 228, 243
Bilmes, J. 93n5, 94
Bird, G.D. 230, 242n3, 243
Blackledge, A. 110, 114
Blake, W.E. 145, 165
Blommaert, J. 110, 114
Blum-Kulka, S. 16, 26
Bolling, G.M. 230–233, 243
Bonifazi, A. 21, 23, 140, 152, 165–166, 187
Boomer, D.S. 85, 94
Borgen, P. 226, 228, 243
Bosworth, B. 149, 165
Bowles, H. 17, 21, 23, 25–26, 93, 94n11, 119, 134, 138
Bowra, C. 165, 178n7
Brooke, A.E. 243n12, 243
Brooke, G.J. 242n3, 243
Broth, M. 91, 94
Brown, G.D. 85, 95

Brown, R.H. 98, 114
Buchstaller, I. 35, 50
Burnet, J. 146, 165
Butler, C.W. 16, 26
Butterworth, B. 85, 94
Button, G. 50, 51, 67, 77

Campbell, E.W. 142, 166
Campbell, J.G. 243
Campbell, R. 16, 28
Carlson, K. 196, 206, 213n4, 213
Carr, D.M. 219, 244
Cartmill, J. A. 79, 94
Cekaite, A. 16, 26
Chafe, W.L. 144, 165
Chapman, R. 120, 122, 137n1, 138
Clark, C. 210, 211, 214
Clift, R. 14, 26, 35, 50
Clifton, C. 138
Collins, P. 134, 138
Collins, P.J. 124, 138
Cooper, W.E. 94, 95
Corps, R.E. 182, 206, 214
Coulmas, F. 27, 35, 50
Coulon, V. 159, 165
Couper-Kuhlen, E. 5, 26, 34, 51, 182, 214
Creese, A. 110, 114
Cruz, H. 190, 214
Cutler, A. 79, 85, 94, 95

Dancygier, B. 165, 179n16
D'Arcy, A. 46, 51
Davidson, D. 79, 95
Dell, G.S. 86, 95
Delnero, P. 242n3, 244
deSilva, D.A. 228, 244
Dickens, C. 21, 23, 119–138
Dickens, M. 134, 138
Doane, A.N. 218, 244

248 *Author Index*

Dressler, W.U. 84, 95
Drew, P. 26, 32, 33, 36, 50, 57, 62, 63, 77, 80, 95, 102, 108, 114, 115, 210, 211, 214
Drummen, A. 143, 165–166, 178n14, 178n17
Du Bois, J.W. 21, 22, 141–143, 155, 164, 165, 166, 178nn1–2, 182, 187, 190, 196, 204, 206, 214

Edmonds, P. 80, 93, 95
Edwards, D. 16, 26
Ellis, A.W. 84, 95
Epp, E.J. 242n3, 244
Erbse, H. 231–233, 244

Fabb, N. 181, 187, 196, 213n4, 214
Faraone, C.A. 228, 229, 244
Fasulo, A. 16, 27
Fay, D. 79, 95
Fernyhough, C. 134–135, 138
Florentin, M. 243, 245
Fludernik, M. 17, 26, 120, 138
Foley, J.M. 17–18, 26, 218, 219, 241, 242n2, 244
Fowler, H.N. 146, 166
Fowler, R. 17
Fox, B.A. 96
Fox, J.J. 187–189, 197–200, 202, 213, 214
French, P. 182, 186, 214
Freud, S. 5, 83, 84, 95
Frog 22, 23, 104, 180, 183, 187, 191, 192, 194, 196, 199, 202, 214–215, 216, 244, 245
Fromkin, V.A. 85, 94, 95
Fuentes-Calle, A. 16, 28

Gambi, C. 182, 206, 214
Garnham, A. 85, 95
Garrod, S. 80, 93, 96, 182, 206, 216
Glenn, P. 27, 66, 76n2, 77, 96
Goffman, E. 34, 35, 50
Golato, A. 46, 50
Golding, R. 122, 138
Goodwin, M. H. 16, 26
Goold, C.P. 145, 166
Greatbatch, D. 107, 114
Grøver, V. 16, 26
Günthner, S. 34, 50
Gurd, S.A. 242n3, 244

Hammond, M. 149, 166
Harris, Z.S. 141, 166

Hazlina, A.H. 208, 215
Helgadóttir, Y.S. 218, 244
Henderson, J. 159, 166
Heritage, J. 25, 50, 77, 107, 114, 183, 209, 211, 215, 216
Herman, V. 119, 138
Hirst, G. 80, 93, 95
Hof, S. 143, 166
Holt, E. 19–20, 23, 34, 35, 38, 50, 52, 55, 57–58, 60–75, 77, 94n14, 97
Holt, N. 16, 28, 94n12, 96, 98, 114n5, 116
Hopper, R. 14, 21, 26, 27, 41, 50, 87, 94n11, 95, 97–98, 112, 113, 114, 135, 137n5, 138, 220
House, M. 132, 138
Hu, R. 110, 114
Hull, K. 207, 215
Hummel, P.C. 166, 178n7
Hutchby, I. 14, 19, 23, 26, 31, 35–36, 50, 98, 114
Hymes, D. 18, 98, 110, 113, 114–115, 204, 215

Ivanova, O. 34, 50

Jakobson, R. 115, 180, 186, 187, 215
Jefferson, G. 1, 3–27, 31–34, 39, 41, 42, 49, 50–51, 52–55, 58–60, 66, 70–73, 75–77, 80–88, 90–91, 93–96, 97–115, 119–120, 124, 125, 127–130, 135–138, 140–143, 148, 164, 166, 180–181, 183, 207, 215, 220–225, 228, 235, 244
Jones, H.S. 149, 166
Jong, I.J.F. de 155, 166, 178n9, 178n11

Kallai, Z. 235, 244
Kallio, K. 202, 215
Keel, S. 210, 211, 215
Keevallik, L. 91, 94
Kempler, D. 124, 138
Kendrick, K.H. 93, 95
Kevoe-Feldman, H. 182, 184–186, 212, 216
Keyser, S.J. 129, 138
Kirk, A. 219, 244
Kitzinger, C. 16, 28, 183–184, 207, 215
Klewitz, G. 34, 51
Knoppers, G.N. 235, 244
Krikmann, A. 192, 215
Kuusi, M. 191, 215

Lamb, W. 191, 215, 216, 244, 245
Lambert, M. 120–121, 138

Author Index 249

Lattimore, R. 155, 166
Laver, J.D.M. 85, 94
Leech, G. 120–121, 138
Lerner, G.H. 220, 222–223, 244
Levelt, W.J.M. 80, 93, 95
Levin, Y. 235, 244
Lewes, G.H. 133, 138
Lied, L.I. 242n3, 242
Local, J. 182, 186, 214
Lonnröt, E. 191, 215
Lord, A.B. 17, 26, 192, 196, 215, 230, 244
Lowth, R. 186, 215

Maehler, H. 152, 166
Mahl, G.F. 94n10, 95
Mäkelä, E. 202, 215
Markee, N. 14, 26
Martin, G. 166
Martin, G.D. 242n3, 245
Mayer, K. 84, 93n4, 95
Maynard, D.W. 98, 115
McCabe, M.M. 146, 166
McLean, N. 243n12, 243
McQuarrie, E.F. 107, 115
Melville, H. 91, 95
Meredith, J. 17, 26
Meringer, R. 83, 84, 93n4, 95
Meyer, A.S. 80, 93, 95
Meyer, C.F. 207, 215
Mick, D.G. 107, 115
Mill, A.I. 85, 95
Miller, S. 219, 245
Minchin, E. 229, 230, 234, 245
Molder, H. 16, 26, 28, 94n12, 96
Mondada, L. 92, 95
Muhammad, H.S. 208, 215
Mulkay, M. 26

Nevile, M. 1, 26, 85, 90, 96, 113n1, 115
Niemelae, M. 34, 51
Norman, W.M. 189–190, 216
Norrick, N.R. 17, 26, 98, 115

O'Connell, K.G. 236, 239, 245
Ong, W. 136, 138
Oppenheim, G.M. 85, 95

Page, N. 120, 138
Peebles, J.M. 134, 136, 138
Person, R.F., Jr. 1, 5, 17–18, 23, 25, 25n1, 27, 92, 93n1, 96, 98, 102, 113, 114n6, 115, 141, 166, 197, 216, 218–219, 224–225, 242n4, 242n6, 243n11, 245

Pickering, M.J. 80, 93, 96, 182, 206, 214, 216
Piedrabuena, S. 166, 178n2
Pinch, T. 210, 211, 214
Poe, E.A. 129, 138
Pollatsek, A. 138
Pomerantz, A.M. 209–211, 216
Pono, E. 188–189, 197–199, 213
Pontecorvo, C. 16, 27
Potter, J.E. 16, 26, 28, 94n12, 96
Powell, J.E. 149, 166

Race, W.H. 152, 166
Rae, J.P. 1, 20, 23, 25, 79, 91, 96, 113, 113n2, 242n1
Raymond, J. 209–211, 215
Rayner, K. 134, 138
Ready, J. 218, 230, 232, 245
Reichl, K. 219, 245
Rendle-Short, J. 17, 27
Rezetko, R. 242n4, 245
Robinson, J.D. 182, 184–185, 186, 212, 216
Roelofs, A. 80, 93, 95
Romilly, J. de. 149, 166
Roslina, M. 208, 215
Ross, J.R. 95
Rostand, E. 152

Saarinen, J. 191, 216
Sacks, H. 1–4, 8, 10–11, 20, 24, 27, 31–33, 41, 48, 51, 52–55, 59–60, 63, 66, 75, 76, 77, 78, 81–82, 96, 98, 99, 102, 104–105, 115, 128, 136, 138, 141, 166
Sadock, J.M. 208, 216
Sammons, B. 234, 245
Sarv, M. 191, 192, 216
Saussure, F.D. 52–53, 77
Schegloff, E.A. 8, 16, 27, 31–33, 37, 40–41, 48, 51, 52–53, 60–61, 75, 77–78, 80, 83, 85, 96, 106, 115, 185–186, 209, 216
Schenkein, J. 113, 115
Schulze, B. 196–197, 216
Schweizer, E. 226–227, 245
Scolnic, B.E. 235, 245
Selting, M. 5, 26, 214
Semino, M. 120, 138
Sheridan, R.B. 79, 96
Shillcock, R.C. 85, 95
Short, M. 17, 27, 119–121, 138–139
Sidnell, J. 14, 27, 60, 78, 115, 215
Silverstein, M. 187, 216
Sommerstein, A. H. 166, 178n13

250 *Author Index*

Sorjonen, M.-L. 208, 216
Soulaimani, D. 34, 51
Staats, S.K. 110, 115
Steinitz, W. 191, 216
Stepanova, E. 191, 215
Stevenson, N. 98, 115
Stinton, T.C.W. 166, 178n7
Stivers, T. 14, 27, 107, 115, 215
Stokoe, E. 14, 17, 26, 27
Storey, G. 132, 138
Stringer, J.L. 14, 27
Sweetser, E. 152, 165, 166, 179n16
Swingewood, A. 98, 115
Sykäri, V. 201, 216
Szczepek-Reed, B. 109, 115

Tagliamonte, S. 46, 51
Tal, A. 243n12, 245
Talmon, S. 219, 242n3, 245
Tannen, D. 25n2, 27–28, 51, 98, 115–116, 132, 139, 182–183, 187, 204, 205, 211, 216
Tarkka, L. 187, 196, 215
Tedlock, D. 18, 204, 216
te Molder, H.E. 16, 26, 28, 94n12, 96
Ten Have, P. 28
Teubal, E. 16, 26
Thiel, H. van 231, 242n8, 246

Thomas, B. 119, 139
Tillotson, K. 132, 138
Toolan, M. 17, 28
Tov, E. 243n12, 246
Turpin, M. 187, 195–196, 212, 216

Ulrich, E. 243n12, 246
Unnsteinsson, E. 79, 96
Urban, G. 187, 217

van Alphen, I. 35, 50
van Daele, M. 159, 165
Vitevitch, M.S. 79, 96

Wagner, A. 187, 217
Wales, K. 129, 137n2, 139
Watts, J.W. 235, 240, 246
West, S. 230–233, 246
Wilkinson, S. 16, 28
Woods, W.L. 4–5, 12, 20, 28, 91, 96, 101–102, 105–107, 110, 140, 166
Wooffitt, R. 1, 14, 16, 20–21, 23–25, 26, 28, 93n1, 94n12, 96, 98, 107–108, 114n5, 114, 116, 242n1
Wray, A. 183, 191, 199, 217

Zaas, P.S. 226–227, 246
Zwicky, A.M. 208, 216

Subject Index

alliteration 17–18, 102, 120, 127–128, 132, 141, 191–192, 194–195, 201–203
assonance 128
audience 21, 34, 43–49, 85, 108–113, 144, 229, 241–242

blank verse 21, 130–133, 136

category-triggering/category-selection 6, 192, 219, 221, 226
collocation 74, 128–129, 203–204

delicacy 31, 35, 43, 45, 74, 77n3
direct speech 34, 37, 43, 44, 46–48, 120–124, 137, 144, 145, 152, 178n10, 193, 201; *see also* reported speech/ representation of speech

ethnopoetics 98, 110, 204

footing 8, 35, 44–45
formula/formulaic 18, 67, 182–183, 186, 188, 191–195, 199–200, 203–204, 205, 212, 213n3, 218–219, 230, 240
Freudian slip 12, 14, 83–84, 87–88

gist-preserving error 127–128
gross selection-mechanism 11, 13, 220

idiom 3, 6, 58, 64, 87, 127–128, 133, 140, 188, 197, 204
indirect speech 34, 37, 43, 120–121; *see also* reported speech/representation of speech
inner speech 21, 134–135

laughter 32, 34, 40, 42, 47, 64, 73, 110
list 22, 41–42, 102, 107–109, 132, 218–243

near-synonym 20, 23, 79–94
nonlexical 39, 182, 224
non-natural speech 34, 37, 40, 43, 49

onomatopoeia 39–40, 48, 49

parallel 178n8, 180, 180–213, 219
parallelism 22, 104, 127, 132, 141–142, 155, 180–213
para-verbal phenomena 35, 43, 45, 47
parody 40, 47
performance 18, 22, 35, 37, 48, 144, 152, 188–189, 192, 196, 198–201, 208, 212, 218–219, 220, 228–229, 235, 241
prosody 5, 17, 19, 34, 37, 40, 46, 186, 224
pun 2–3, 6, 7, 8, 10–11, 19–20, 22–24, 33, 52, 55, 57–59, 65, 76n1, 79, 82, 86–87, 90, 93, 94n15, 220, 228

recipient alignment 35, 38, 41–42, 149, 165, 210, 213n6
repair 5, 31, 32, 36, 70–71, 74, 100–102, 109, 128, 180, 183–186, 206–208, 212, 232
reported speech/representation of speech 8, 17, 34–35, 37, 43, 44, 46–48, 52, 120, 122, 125, 137, 224; *see also* direct speech; indirect speech
rhythm 110, 127, 130–133, 144, 181, 187, 189, 195–196, 204, 207

self-correction 87, 114
sequence organization 18, 140
sound-patterns/sound-row/sound-run 3, 6, 7, 12, 19–21, 55, 71, 99–102, 120, 126–127, 128–130, 218

252   *Subject Index*

sound-productional mechanisms 11–12, 84–85, 220

sound-triggering 17, 21–22, 76, 125–130, 133, 135, 140, 142, 164, 181, 191–192, 195, 203, 222, 228, 243n6

spreading activation 21, 85–86, *86*, 94n11, 135, 137

stance-taking 14, 34–36, 46, 87, 187, 210–211, 213n6

storytelling 33, 123

synonym 20, 22, 79, 81, 83, 90, 92, 93n6, 202

triggering mechanisms 11, 72, 135, 220

turn-taking 3, 8, 10, 17–18, 32, 221, 225

variant 3, 22, 103, 200–203, 218–243

vocalization 21, 134–136

wild side of CA 1, 4, 8, 25, 25n1, 31, 33, 49, 53–54, 93n1, 98

word-search 128, 183

word-selection 1–2, 5, 14, 18, 21, 23–24, 34, 49, 80, 83, 85, 92–93, 101–102, 105–106, 110, 113, 125, 130, 135, 241

Milton Keynes UK
Ingram Content Group UK Ltd.
UKHW031502071224
451979UK00020B/225